THE FIELD OF PHILOSOPHY

THE FIELD OF PHILOSOPHY

AN INTRODUCTION TO THE STUDY OF PHILOSOPHY

by

JOSEPH A. LEIGHTON, PH.D., LL.D.

DEFINITIVE EDITION

GYAN

Published by

Gyan Publishing House
5, Ansari Road
Daryaganj, New Delhi-110002
Phone: 011-47034999, 9811692060
E-mail: books@gyanbooks.com

Distribution Network
gyanbooks.com
India, USA, Canada, UK, Australia, France

ISBN : 978-81-212-6186-9 (PB)
First Published, 1923

2nd Impression 2021

Printed at: Gyan Press, Delhi.

The field of Philosophy
Author: Joseph A. Leighton

THE FIELD OF PHILOSOPHY

AN INTRODUCTION TO THE STUDY OF PHILOSOPHY

BY

JOSEPH A. LEIGHTON, Ph.D., LL.D.

PROFESSOR OF PHILOSOPHY IN THE OHIO STATE UNIVERSITY,
AUTHOR OF "MAN AND THE COSMOS," ETC.

DEFINITIVE EDITION

: :　　　: :

PREFACE

Many years experience in teaching introductory courses in philosophy led me to conclude, some years ago, that the best method is a combination of the historical and the topical or systematic methods. A beginning course which attempts to cover, in detail, the entire History of European and American Philosophy is beyond the grasp of most beginners. They are bewildered by the constant succession of theories not easily distinguishable, and become confused as to the fundamental issues and standpoints. They fail to get the connections between philosophy and the general culture of a period.

On the other hand, a purely topical and systematic introduction does not bring the student into contact with the most significant historical developments of philosophy. He does not, in this way, begin to see what rôle philosophy has played in the life of civilization.

The increasing lack of a common cultural perspective, on the part of students, makes it imperative to supply something in the way of a historical background. I am of the opinion that a sketch of the historical growth of Greek philosophy best meets this need, because of the simplicity and logical symmetry and completeness with which it unfolds. On the other hand, when the student comes to the beginning of modern thought he immediately meets problems, concepts and theories that still function largely in our intellectual life. I have, therefore, in the present outline presented: first, a rapid historical sketch of the development of occidental philosophy from its beginnings up to the opening of modern thought; and have followed this with a more systematic and critical survey of the chief modern problems and standpoints, laying stress on the most recent forms of thought. The third part of the book presents, in outline, a survey of the present status of systematic philosophy, as I understand its problems and their interrelationships.

The teacher might, if time be lacking to cover the whole work, omit either a large portion of Part I, or he might omit Part III. The work is so framed that, either the historical development or the present day problems and theories, can be stressed. There is some advantage either way.

I first began the preparation of this book in the winter of 1917-18, at the suggestion of my then assistant, Dr. R. D. Williams. Through his aid and that of Dr. W. S. Gamertsfelder I was able to have a large part of it printed in outline, for the use of our own classes, in the summer of 1918. A number of other institutions adopted it. It became necessary to have a much larger edition printed in the summer of 1919. I took the opportunity then to revise and enlarge it.

In preparing the present definitive edition for the press, I have thoroughly revised the entire work. I have rewritten several parts. I have added the following chapters: The Introduction—"Philosophy and the Crisis in Civilization," "Recent Realism," "Temporalism," "Instrumentalism," and "Ethics and Social Philosophy." I have omitted the chapter on the "Fundamental Concepts of Metaphysics," since the treatment was too condensed for the beginner and the subject is fully treated in my book, *Man and the Cosmos.* I have also omitted the Appendix, since the matters therein treated are much more fully discussed in the new chapters. The other changes and additions are too numerous to specify here. Dr. A. E. Avey's *Readings in Philosophy* has been prepared as a companion source book.

I may add that, before preparing this work for the press I sent a questionnaire to more than a score of experienced teachers, who had used the work in its earlier forms. The consensus of opinion was that it would be unwise to depart radically from the general plan of the work. I thank my correspondents for the pains they took. I am indebted especially to Professors W. K. Wright, A. R. Chandler and A. E. Avey for suggestions.

JOSEPH ALEXANDER LEIGHTON

CONTENTS

PART I

THE CHIEF PROBLEMS AND STANDPOINTS OF GREEK AND MEDIEVAL PHILOSOPHY

PART II

THE CHIEF PROBLEMS AND STANDPOINTS OF MODERN PHILOSOPHY

PART III

AN OUTLINE OF THE CHIEF PROBLEMS OF CONSTRUCTIVE PHILOSOPHY

THE FIELD OF PHILOSOPHY

THE FIELD OF PHILOSOPHY

INTRODUCTION

PHILOSOPHY AND THE CRISIS IN CIVILIZATION

Civilization to-day seems to be passing through one of its periodic crises. Resemblances may be found between the present transitional era of culture and previous ones. Common to all such eras are: the dissolution of traditional systems of social custom and belief; the breakdown of inherited sanctions in religion, morality, and law; and the consequent confusion in regard to social ethics, the principles of government, and the values and ends of social culture.

The culture of the fourteenth, fifteenth, and sixteenth centuries in Western Europe exhibited a transitional character—the movement away from social unity and the authority of traditional forms, and towards a particularistic conception of social life and the supremacy of abstract reason; that is, towards the a priori construction of principles and ideals of social order, regardless of the historical development of social structures. This movement reached its culmination in the eighteenth century, to give way, in the nineteenth century, to the historical and evolutionary standpoint.

Another great transitional era was the long period during

which the culture of the pagan Roman Empire disintegrated and its place was taken by the Catholic Christian system of the Middle Ages. This period occupied about one thousand years. Catholic Christian culture reached its apogee in the thirteenth century, and began to decline in the fourteenth century. A still earlier example was the transitional era of Greek culture, extending from the early philosophers to the flourishing of the Stoics. The Platonic and, later, the Epicurean and Stoic philosophies took the place of tradition and custom, and furnished guiding principles for the conduct of life. The Stoic philosophy also furnished inspiration and guidance for social administrators in the Roman Empire up to the time of Marcus Aurelius. It was an ethics and a religion. Its influence passed into Christianity through St. Paul.

One might draw many engaging parallels between previous transitional eras and the present one. But one must beware of assuming that history repeats itself without important variations. Cultural history seems to move chiefly in irregular spiral lines. At times it moves in zigzag fashion. The present critical phase of civilization covers a much vaster area than any previous one. Indeed, the ancient cultures of India and China are being sucked into the maelstrom. The present crisis likewise goes deeper than any before. Probably the most revolutionary occurrence in human history, since the discovery of fire making and working in metals, was the "Industrial Revolution," which began early in the eighteenth century, but did not reach full tide until late in the nineteenth century. The revolution in the methods of producing and distributing material goods, the rise and spread of social democracy, and the triumphant march of natural science until the entire life of man has been made subject to its methods and principles, are the chief causes of the present crisis in society. The methods and results of natural science have undermined the foundations of traditional religion, and have seemed to destroy the motives and sanctions of social morality supplied by religious tradition. The rise and spread of a mechanically industrialized society, in which the only final touchstones of distinction are money and the power which comes from the backing of numbers, have tended to make the crowd-mind the arbiter of social standards in education, art, manners, and morals, no less than in things economic.

The tremendous development of large-scale machine production has put a great and unwonted strain on the human soul, which does not derive any lasting satisfaction from the rapid and monotonous repetition of simple mechanical processes. It has also put a great strain on family life. It has greatly modified social intercourse. It has resulted in an attitude of nervous haste inimical to thoughtful reflection. It has lined up, in battle array, the groups of organized "capital" on one side and organized "labor" on the other side, with the noncombatants between to suffer most of the damage from their intermittent warfare. The comparative poverty of the worker is not the sole, perhaps not even the chief, cause of the persistent social unrest. I think the latter comes largely as a blind protest of the soul of man against a monotonous and mechanized existence—against a life in which he toils without full and active mental participation in his work, and in which his leisure is not spent in ways which satisfy the impulsions thwarted or repressed during his hours of bread winning labor.

The comparative study of human institutions, customs, and beliefs, in the light of evolution, has revealed their apparent and complete relativity to circumstances; so that none have more authority than belong to convenient makeshifts. Indeed, the "newest" psychologies, the Freudian and mechanistic behaviorism, teach us that human ideals, aims, and reasons are but conventional make-believes in which are disguised, for public and social intercourse, by a more or less unconscious hypocrisy, the real driving forces of human nature which are the biological mechanisms of the sexual impulse, hunger, gregariousness, the lust for power, the possessive impulse, et cetera.

A stable social order is ruled chiefly by customs and social habits. A society in flux is one in which the inherited customs are challenged. To-day there is no inherited social pattern which escapes challenge. From the ethics of industry, property, and sex, to the ethics of political and international relations—everywhere we meet the note of interrogation. Even the political institutions of representative democracy seem unable to cope with the economic class-conflicts and the complex problems of social administration. Radicals in social theory (the Bolshevists), propose the scrapping of all our inherited social institutions and the dictatorship of the class-conscious minority of the proletariat.

In this critical pass the greatest danger lies in the substitution, for the waning social patterns of belief and conduct, of uncriticized mass-impulses, crowd-emotions, class-passions and resentments. Our civilization has grown so enormously complex, so hurried and noisy, the individual is at once so remote from the sources of accurate information and so jostled by the crowd that he is apt to fall an easy prey to the first suggestion or wave of feeling that impinges upon him. The individual withers and the crowd is more and more. In particular we depend chiefly upon newspapers for our information and guidance, and what we get is mostly either hastily put together and sensational scraps of misinformation, or deliberately colored partisan reports and arguments. The need was never greater for a cool, dispassionate, and critical or "reflective" attitude, on the part of the citizenry than it is to-day. If people in general, who are the arbiters of social destiny, will not or cannot, either think hard and critically on social problems, or follow leaders who do think things out honestly, democracy will not last long.

Reason is the power of critically analyzing data, putting them together and drawing conclusions from them. There never was so much need of reasoning in regard to the problems of social life as there is to-day. But many tendencies in our social life have conspired to make reasoning difficult, to belittle its social value, and even to deny to it any large usefulness. Irrationalism is now much in evidence in art, letters, and criticism, as well as in social philosophy and practical politics.

In plastic art there is the striving for the bizarre, the fantastic, the unintelligible. In painting, the cubists and futurists have gone the pace towards a complete irrationalism; and, significantly enough, they call it a return to the primitive. There is the literature of a disillusioned hedonism, a cynical realism, which depicts man, and especially woman, as the mere creature of sexual desire. Freudian psychoanalysis is assumed to be the sole key to unlock the secrets of human nature and to reveal man's essential impulses. Most of the current literary criticism is without any objective standards of value, without any philosophy of life. It is written in a jaunty cocksure vein by persons devoid of solid information or proportioned perspective in regard to the development of culture.

As more or less blind reactions of the soul from the pressure of mechanism and materialism, one notes the rise of all sorts of unscientific mysticisms and occultisms, from "new thought" and "spiritualism" to Christian science and theosophy. These things are expressions of the soul's thirst for communion with a spiritual reality; attempts to satisfy man's metaphysical hunger. For man, as Hegel truly said, is the metaphysical animal. He *must* commune with some sort of higher reality, lest he perish. So recourse is had to that mysterious hybrid of body and soul, "the subliminal self," which is accounted the channel of man's communion with God and the source of all our deeper and wiser insights.

One notes a similar irrationalism in the revolt against the existing social institutions which finds its extreme expressions in syndicalism and the Industrial Workers of the World, whose aim seems to be to paralyze the present system by any and every means in order to give control to the "workers." How, after wrecking the present order, the "workers" (so-called) are to build up a better one, without expert managerial training or exceptional ability, does not appear. But the flames of revolt are fanned by those captains of industry who, ignoring the rise of democracy, would stamp out labor organizations and deny to the honest and intelligent workman any partnership in industry. This is a sure way to breed revolution.

There is a general blindness to the need of a public-minded expertness in the making of law and the administering of social affairs. The making, interpretation, and execution of law are treated too much in the spirit of class-interest. The fundamental rights and interests of the whole community are frequently ignored.

The critics of the present disorder argue that the real rulers in industrial and political life are the captains of finance and industry. It is true that large-scale production and distribution put enormous power into the hands of the few who control the finances and policies; and who may be concerned primarily rather to get profits than to give service. What is forgotten is that the power of big business is based on its success in catering to the public tastes. In the last analysis the dominance of the money power to-day is derived from its ability to satisfy the desires of the masses for food, clothes, and cheap amusements. No escape can be found from this vicious circle, except by an extension of the practice of thought, by more intelligent judgments of values and choices of ends on the part of the many. *The only sure way to improve our social life is to alter the scale of human valuations or preferences, to raise the standards of taste in consumption for living and the enjoyment of leisure.* Education is the one sure means to this end. And education is applied philosophy; it is philosophy in action.

But in education there is an increasing clamor that vocational training shall begin in the grade schools. Education must be made useful, that is, *gainful,* from the very outset. The age is a commercial one. Bread and butter studies are of paramount importance. Moreover, the doctrine that individuality should be given free play in education is pushed to the extreme. Let the pupil choose what he likes, what interests him most.[1] We are told that individuality is sacred and must be allowed to grow, but we are given few hints as to what constitutes true individuality. As a consequence, we are now in a state of educational anarchy. Engaged as we are in training a vast and heterogeneous democracy, without any well-defined educational philosophy, without a homogeneous cultural tradition, and with the material demands of the people constantly increasing, the cultural studies, especially the humanities, are threatened with extinction. This means increasing ignorance in regard to the historical continuity of civilization. The liberally educated man, in distinction from the specialist and technician, seems to be passing away. The "scholar and gentleman" is a vanishing type. The permanent value of cultural studies lies in the fact that they impart to each succeeding generation an intelligent consciousness of the historical continuity of civilization.

---

1 Often he chooses the easiest studies or those that come at the most convenient hours.

The chief causes of the present cultural and spiritual chaos are three—one springing from a scientific fallacy and the other two from the confusions of thought incident to great social and industrial changes.

The first is the fallacy of attempting to interpret the life of human culture in terms of conceptions carried over uncritically from biology into the study of man. In the animal world the ruling principle is struggle to adjust life to the given environment by a process of blind adaptation of spontaneous variations. In this brute struggle for existence, impulse and instinct are the ruling powers. The animal has not the capacity for reflection or rational interpretation and organization of its experience and, consequently, cannot recreate its environment. It must simply struggle blindly to adjust itself to the given situation. Generalization, prevision, "imaginative foreshadowings of a better world" are foreign to it. It blindly obeys the vital impulse. Does it follow that the animal lives more fully than the thinking man? To ask this question is to answer it. *Biology cannot give us a valid philosophy of human life.* We are not here to live by instinct and to be content with adjustment to the natural environment. Truly human behavior is more than a biological response to the impact of the physical surroundings. Our true vocation is to build up another environment by the divine power of creative vision. Our roots are in the soil of nature, but our topmost leaves should inhale the serene and clear atmosphere of intelligence and spirit. *Beware of these teachers whose philosophies would degrade the reason and thus reduce us to the level of the brutes! Beware of the impiety and ignorance which would destroy the hard won and precious achievements of our human culture in the name of progress!* If we are to build fairer mansions for the spirit of man, these must be erected on the foundations which our race has already laid, in ancient

Greece, and in the whole development of West-European and American culture. We need no violent break with the past of our own race.

The second principal cause of the revolt against thought and its objective values is the struggle of the democratic spirit against the plutocratic forces that have become so firmly entrenched in the economic control of society—the warfare of King Demos and King Plutus. The meaning of the democratic right of every individual to the development and enjoyment of his full humanity has been somewhat misinterpreted. Democracy properly implies the effective enjoyment, by all human beings, of the right to participate as fully as they are able in the natural and spiritual heritage of the race. Democracy is the means of bringing the average man nearer to the highest human level attained by the spiritual leaders of the race. But democracy is misconceived when it is taken to mean that all men, irrespective of their innate endowments, special training, or personal efforts, are equally fitted to judge of the relative values of things in philosophy, science, art, and letters, or even in social polity and law. Shall we submit our standards of æsthetic, scientific, educational, and philosophical values to a plebiscite? Shall we take a popular vote on Darwinism, the Kantian philosophy, or the Celtic movement in literature?[2] Is the voice of the people the voice of reason no matter what subject it may elect to utter itself on?

Equality of opportunity is a sound social ideal. It means that there should be the fullest possible *equalization of opportunity* for the development of the human life in all. But, taking it strictly, absolute equality is impossible in any form of social organization. For realized opportunity

[2] In this year of grace, 1922, the Kentucky State Legislature came within one vote of prohibiting the teaching of Evolution in State-supported institutions!

is a resultant of two variable components, which cannot be isolated—the social situation in which an individual finds himself and his reaction to the situation. The former component can never be given such a fixed and unvarying value that the latter will not introduce the element of inequality. Nor is it desirable that there should be complete equality. The greatest danger which besets democracy is a low mediocrity of taste and judgment, an indifference to refinement of life, an unthinking ignorance of what has been already achieved. The hardest problem of a democratic culture is, while extending to all the opportunity to participate freely in the finer things of life, to conserve and improve the highest values which have been wrought out in the race's cultural evolution. These values are always the creations of the relatively few who are highly dowered with the creative imagination.

The third cause of the confusion and lowering of the cultural values of civilization is the increasing rule of mechanical processes. Quantity production is cheapest and most profitable. Thus, in every department of life, from food and clothes to education, literature, and the theatre, what is happening now is the crowding to the wall of the thoroughly and artistically fashioned product, into which the maker has put his individuality, in favor of the cheap, machine-made product distributed by the million. Individuality and distinction tend to vanish. For reflection and selective choice are substituted gregarious imitation and suggestion. The crowd-mind rules. Even our mental life grows sheepish. Many even of our university graduates, from whom better things might be expected, exhibit only the crowd-mind. Imitation and suggestion, class and party slogans and catch-penny phrases, rule the public mind.

The cynical realism, the disillusionment and pessimism, which pervade so much of our current literature, especially that written by the younger ones, express the protest of hungry souls, starving for spiritual nutriment, against the emptiness, trivialness and lack of spiritual [3] unity and purpose in our social life. These things voice the nostalgia of the soul for a finer, more significant, and more harmonious experience. Our civilization is being built on a narrow specialization of productive functions. *The greatest danger to it is the loss of a vital sense of the organic wholeness, the living unity, of the spiritual or soul-life in the individual and in the social order.* No man can be happy in so far as he is not at unity with himself. No man can be satisfied to live by a disjointed collection of separate impulsions. And no man can be at unity with himself, no man can achieve inner harmony, if he lives in a society whose members lack a common understanding and a communal feeling. Our civilization is in danger of disintegration by the drifting apart, to the point of complete misunderstanding, of its constituent members. What we need most is a living and energizing sense of the mutual interdependence, and common interests in fundamental spiritual or humane values, on the part of the various functional bodies or "classes" which make up society. The integrity, the organic wholeness of society, is at once a condition and result of the integrity or spiritual wholeness of its individual members. Without it, society will fly apart into atoms and the individual spirit, too, will suffer distraction.

We must overcome the isolation, the loneliness, and lack of mutual understanding which have resulted from the mechanical overspecialization of social life which has brought, at once, a differentiation and an impoverishment of the individual's life. We must achieve a more vital and all-pervading sense of the human and spiritual unity of life

---

[3] I use the word "spiritual" in a broad sense to include all that appertains to the intellectual, æsthetic, and moral health of the human soul.

in the individual and the group. We need not despair of civilization. If there be any truth in history, civilization is most often in transition. The epochs of unified and stable culture are rare and brief. They are no sooner achieved than they begin to disintegrate. Glorious and short-lived was the blooming of Greek culture. Noble and transient was the Christian classical culture of the thirteenth century. The goddess of reason of the eighteenth century was soon dethroned. At the turn of the present century, great was our satisfaction and our faith in a providential evolution, carried on by applied science and machinery. Nothing could stay the inevitable march of progress. To-day we are learning anew that men cannot hold and use what goods they have, much less gain new goods, without unceasing individual effort. Belief in progress had become a callow superstition. Social progress, as an ideal, is a dangerous and empty illusion, unless it mean the *growth of individuals* in intelligence, self-mastery, self-determination, and fuller and more harmonious action and experience.

The crumbling of the sentimental and silly belief in the speedy perfection of human society is a salutary event, if it reminds us, however harshly, that to face the facts and meet the actual issues squarely is the only way in which human beings become strong and mature individuals. What civilization needs to pilot it through its present stormy and rock-infested waters, is more men and women whose dynamic and creative energies are illumined and guided by a liberal or humane insight into the problems and duties of the time.

Democracy, as an ideal of human progress towards perfection, as well as a form of political government, has probably come to stay for some time. But democracy cannot conserve what the race has already achieved, and progress towards the wider participation of men and women in the life of culture, it cannot furnish a favorable soil for the nurture of the creative spirit, unless it be guided and led by the intellectual and spiritual élite, recruited from men and women of exceptionally high native endowment, trained to be exponents of the reflective life, animated by the motive of service and dedicated to the creative vocation of conserving and adding to the spiritual wealth of civilization.

It is to the institutions for liberal education, which, in its essence, is identical with philosophy, that we must look chiefly for the conservation and enhancement of the culture-values of civilization. We need, more than ever before, centers where the contemplative life is nurtured, where young men and young women can gain an intelligent appreciation of the history of culture and of the chief part which the creative imagination has played in the uplift of the race; where by a free and earnest contemplation of the problems of humanity and nature, undisturbed by the clamor for action and quick returns, they may win the power of evaluating the current shibboleths in the light of objective standards.

Our nation urgently needs exemplars of the contemplative life—needs witnesses to the surpassing excellence of ideas—needs constructive thinkers to challenge and examine the popular nostrums in social polity, literature, education, and religion. It needs men and women to show forth in their lives the beauty, power and enduring quality of devotion to the principles of order, coherence, and harmony. Not mere existence but the rational life, not mere action but action based on the contemplation of worthful ends—in short to live and work under the guidance of a rational interpretation of the meanings and values of the spiritual order—such is the vocation of the thinker and scholar. For the true thinker is identical with the philosopher. He is one equipped with a vital insight into the essential achievements of man's cultural life, capable of open-minded and penetrating judgment in applying this insight to the problems of the present, and having a courageous and loving spirit dedicated to the service of the best.

There is no type of individuality which our democracy needs more than the exponent and example of the philosophic life. He is one who thinks constantly upon the *values* to be attained by action before he acts, one who persistently asks himself what is worth while, one who brings to bear a power of balanced judgment, that has been nourished by an appreciative knowledge of the best that has been thought and done, upon the problems, beliefs, and proposals of the present. The devotee of the philosophic life sees that much of the activity of the so-called practical man is but vanity, since much of what he strives for with might and main is worthless when attained. The truly practical man is he who strives for what is worth while in the long run. And this is a clear-sighted individuality, informed and inspired by an intelligent appreciation of the crowning achievements of the spirit in man, ennobled by sympathy with the race's moral heroes, refined through the joy of companionship with the truly beautiful products of the race's creative imagination, mastering and possessing as its own instrument the methods of science, working in sympathy with our common humanity for the uplift of the race, and calmed and steadied by faith in a Supreme Spiritual Order. Such a life can preserve its poise amidst the distractions and follies of the present and contribute something to the progress of individuals in reason, justice, love, and towards perfection.

No notion could be more erroneous than that which regards thought as separate from life and individuality. Thinking goes on only in individual minds. It is the most intense sort of living. The individual who thinks most persistently is the one who has the most individuality.

And Philosophy is simply the most penetrating, comprehensive, and consistent thinking. It is thinking upon the basic concerns of living—upon the meanings and values of life and its place in the universe. As Novalis said, "To philosophize is to dephlegmatize one's self; to philosophize is to vitalize one's self." As Aristotle put it, man is distinguished from all other animals by his capacity for thinking. The more he thinks the more human he is.

Therefore, every thinking individual must have a philosophy of some sort. He cannot take his philosophy at second hand from his fellows or tradition. For philosophy is not a garment to be put on, and off. *It is a life.* Thus, while the average intelligent person, or even the person of superior intelligence, cannot expect to be highly original in the sense of making a brand-new philosophy, he must be original in the sense of making philosophy his own living possession, of working it into the very marrow of his spiritual being. Otherwise it will be a meaningless encumbrance to him. Only he who lives the life of persistent thinking develops a philosophy. For, while it deals with the deepest and broadest interests of man, a philosophy is a man's own life-attitude. Therefore, it is the most intimate and personal quality of an individual life.

To argue in behalf of the value of philosophy to-day is simply to argue that the most thoughtful life is the best life. This position is by no means generally accepted. In our world at large, and even in our colleges, persistent thoughtfulness is more honored in the breach than in the observance. The major tendencies of our restless, nervous, motion-loving, machine-serving, sensation-mongering civilization seem inimical to that repose, detachment, and concentration of spirit, without which genuine reflection cannot go on. One must have the firmness of mind and resolution of purpose to separate himself from the clamorous but empty trivialities of the moment, in order to philosophize. In so doing he will learn to know himself, his fellow men, and the real world; and will become more of a real individual.

The greatest representatives of the reflective life in history have never claimed that thought was either the whole of life or a sufficient substitute for action and reality. The Greeks are still our exemplars here. Socrates, Plato, and Aristotle were no mere intellectualists. They held it to be the function of thought to illumine and organize the otherwise dumb and chaotic facts of sense-experience and thus to harmonize and direct impulse and emotion, and to interpret life in terms of order, measure, and proportion; in short, to transform human life into a well-ordered whole, a harmonious and balanced integrity in feeling, insight, and action. Sanity, proportion, moderation, harmony, attained through rational reflection—such is the Greek ideal. Such is the Christian conception in St. John, and Origen.

In this matter the greatest of the moderns—such men as Dante, Leonardo da Vinci, Michelangelo, Spinoza, Leibnitz, Kant, Goethe, Hegel, Locke, and Bishop Butler, to name only a few, are at one with the greatest of the ancients.

Reason or thought is the organizing power of the reflective life. Primitive impulse and emotion are, by themselves, chaotic and disintegrating. It is the function of thought to universalize the raw impulses of life, to establish systematic connections and objective standards of value in science, the social order, and the individual life. Reason and creative imagination are but two names for the same great function, twin aspects of the constructive power of thought. The philosopher, the scientist, and the poet see and depict, in differing fashion because of the differences in the materials they work in and the ends they seek, the bonds of unity that hold the universe together. The same vision of order and harmony amidst diversity guides a Sophocles, a Shakespeare, or a Goethe in his treatment of human life that guides a Newton, a Helmholtz, or a Darwin in his treatment of physical and biological facts; a Plato, a Spinoza, or a Hegel in his quest for a reflective unifying insight into reality as a whole; and an Isaiah, a St. Paul, or a St. John, in his spiritual vision of the relation of the human soul and the universe to the supreme source and ground of the spiritual life.

Nor is there anything irrational in genuine freedom and individuality. The very principle or standard of thought in the quest for truth is the standard of true individuality and freedom. To be a genuine individual is not to be a freak or oddity. It is to be a harmonious unity of life and reflective thought. Here, as elsewhere, the true is the harmonious whole. The integrity of a coherent character, with an organized system of purposes illuminated and guided by reflection, is the quality that makes a genuine individual. The thoughtful life is the coherent and harmonious life, in contrast with the random and disjointed life of blind feeling and impulse. The same standard of harmony or coherence is the standard of truth. The *true is the whole.* Self-consistency, harmony, organization into a coherent system—these are alike notes not only of the most true in science, but, as well, of the highest type of social order and individual life. The mainspring of religion and philosophy is the quest for a harmonious life, individual and social, and for a coherent insight into the meaning of life and the nature of things. Reality is more than thought. But the very progress of science and culture, brought about by the unceasing effort of reflection, is a witness to the truth that the same principle of harmony, which animates the human reason is embodied on the grand scale in the order of nature itself. The world is mind writ large. Mind is the world concentrating itself in centers of reflective consciousness and thereby winning new values. Harmony, organization, life in a well-ordered whole—such are the genuine ideals of religion and philosophy.

The same principles are exemplified in the whole history of human culture. The social structures of human life, the family, the community, the state, and the church, have their roots indeed in natural instinct and impulse—in the sexual instinct, parental feeling, gregariousness and sympathy, self-preservation and self-defence, the feeling of dependence on higher and mysterious powers. But the life of culture, as distinguished from savagery, has consisted in the emergence of thought as orderer and ruler of these primitive instincts. Stability and coherence in social structures and in standards of conduct are indispensable to the maintenance and further development of a high civilization. Life according to nature is for a man a chimera. The Stoic philosopher, the original preacher of life according to nature, meant by it life in harmony with reason. Man is, in part, a child of nature, but he is much more. The truly human part of him is the rational and spiritual power which has created morality, social order, science, art, and religion. Man's true vocation is not to adjust himself to his natural environment by instinct; but to create and maintain a cultural and spiritual environment. Human civilization consists in this social and spiritual atmosphere in which the individual can grow to the stature of rational manhood. It is man's vocation to fashion out of the materials supplied by nature, this objective rational order of social, moral, and spiritual institutions, through which alone he can attain and exercise true freedom and be a rational personality.

Freedom is not caprice or license. It does not consist in the rule of instinct, but in the rule of reason. Freedom is rational self-determination in the light of an ideal whole. All that distinguishes cultivated man from the brute is the result of the rational constructive activity, which gives him control over nature and control over himself; which teaches him not merely of the dust from which he is sprung, but more especially of the spiritual glory unto which he may attain; which shapes, by its creative power, ideal values and bodies these forth in institutions—in law and polity, in objective moral and intellectual standards; finally, in the vision of a Supreme Rational Spirit, the source and sustainer of man's own spiritual life, the conserver of his most cherished values. The human life begins in "the moment of contemplative insight when, rising above the animal life, we become conscious of the greater ends that redeem man from the life of the brutes." (Bertrand Russell).

The true philosopher cannot make common cause with either the social reactionary or the social radical. His attitude towards all social problems is that of the genuine liberal. His usual counsel is that we make haste slowly. On the one hand, he recognizes clearly the great amount of thoughtful endeavor that has gone into the fashioning and maintenance of our historic social institutions—family, civic institutions, industrial and economic order, law, the state, and the church. He sees that the continuance of social order and the growth of culture depends on the maintenance of these institutions. Without them man reverts to anarchic savagery. The presumption is in favor of any human institution that has long endured. The philosopher will be slow to advocate its radical alteration, and will usually oppose its abolition. On the other hand, in view of changing conditions, he will recognize the need of criticism and reconstruction in established institutions. As against blind revolt and blind reaction, he is the advocate of an experimental, gradual, and thought-directed improvement of human institutions, so that these may the better serve the development and enjoyment of human personality. For the philosopher measures and weighs all human institutions, customs, beliefs, and activities in terms of their contributions to human spiritual values.

There can be no intelligent and fruitful individual self-direction or social control without a clear-sighted and comprehensive doctrine of human values. The individual cannot order his own life aright, or participate usefully in the ordering of social effort, unless he have a well-thought-out scheme of values, interests, and ends. *He must have a vision of the meaning of life as a whole,* and of its place in the total order of reality. He must be able to relate the interests, the choices of values, the purposes, of his own life, with those of his fellow man. He must, furthermore, have some intelligent conviction as to the place of human values, human purposes, in the total scheme of things. This is what is meant when one says that philosophy seeks to comprehend the fundamental values of life as a whole; that it seeks a total and consistent view of life and its place in reality. Our partial and ephemeral acts and purposes need to be knitted up with the whole of reality. We need to get beyond a life of fragmentary and disjointed acts. We need to escape from living by this impulse and that habit, from a one-sided and maimed activity and existence, into a life in the open and full universes of human culture and physical nature. The personal quest for a rich and consistent doctrine of human values and purposes and for an understanding of the meaning of human life as a whole is the essence of philosophizing. This is what is meant when it is said that philosophy enables us to distinguish between the trivial and the essential, the passing and the permament, the show of life and its substance.

What Matthew Arnold said of poetry is true only of

philosophy, whether it be expressed through the medium of prose or poetry. Philosophy is the criticism of life; it is the application of ideas to life. It is the guide to civilization. For the philosophical thinker evaluates and orders in their places, both the ineradicable natural impulses of man and the changing customs which are the frameworks of his civilizations, in the light of the most penetrating, comprehensive, and consistent conception of human life and its values that can be formed by thought. Philosophy is not the system of any man or school. It is the individual mind animated by the spirit of open-minded and persistent endeavor to discover the whole truth in regard to life and reality. It is man thinking out the most ultimate, perplexing, and interesting problems of existence. The primary aim of the following work is to show how philosophy has served, serves now, and must continue to serve, as the interpreter of the essential spirit of human culture.

PART I

THE CHIEF PROBLEMS AND STANDPOINTS OF GREEK AND MEDIEVAL PHILOSOPHY

CHAPTER I

PHILOSOPHY, ITS MEANING AND SCOPE

I. Definition of Philosophy

The word "philosophy" is derived from the Greek words *philein,* meaning "to love," and *sophia,* meaning "wisdom." Hence the true philosopher is a lover of wisdom. The term "wisdom" means knowledge and insight directed towards the attainment of the best life possible and to the endurance of immedicable ills. In popular speech, to be philosophically minded is to endeavor, by the exercise of reason, to make the best of time and circumstance; it is to use one's intellect to achieve solid satisfactions and to bow gracefully to the inevitable. The philosophical life is a life in which practice is guided by theory, in contrast with the life guided merely by custom and imitation and with the life ruled by impulse. In order that one may guide one's life by reason, one must think out some sort of view of the meaning of the world and the place of human life in the world.

The philosopher strives, as Plato so finely puts it, to attain a synoptic vision of things, to see things as a whole or together, that is, to see all the main features of experience, life, and conduct in their interrelationships. The philosopher strives to be "the spectator of all time and existence." This does not mean that the philosopher must compass in minute detail all knowledge and all experience. It means rather that, in trying to reach a unified and consistent view of things, the philosopher will not neglect to consider the general significance of any of the main fields of human experience, knowledge, or conduct.

A complete philosophy includes a *world-view,* or reasoned conception of the whole cosmos, and a *life-view,* or doctrine of the values, meanings, and purposes of human life. Philosophy, like science, consists of theories or insights arrived at as a result of systematic reflection or reasoning in regard to the data of experience. It involves, therefore, the analysis of experience and the synthesis of conception. Philosophy seeks a totality and harmony of reasoned insight into the nature and meaning of all the principal aspects of reality.

Plato distinguished between Ignorance, Right Opinion, and Knowledge or Wisdom. Ignorance is not to know, nor to know why you do not know. Right opinion is a belief which corresponds to the facts but is devoid of reasoned insight into its own foundations. Knowledge is belief with reasons. If one knows wherein his own ignorance lies or the limitations of the possibilities of the subject, he may be rightly said to possess knowledge of the subject.

II. Relation of Philosophy to Science

Philosophy is more fundamental and comprehensive than science; otherwise they are identical in their aims. Philosophical knowledge has these three characteristics:

1. It is fundamental knowledge.
2. It is most comprehensive or generalized knowledge.
3. It is most unified and consistent knowledge.

The idea that philosophical knowledge is the most fundamental and comprehensive knowledge is embodied in such expressions as "the philosophy of life," "the philosophy of art," "the philosophy of politics," et cetera.

The "philosophy" of anything is the theory of its first and most fundamental principles.

The aim of philosophy is to discover the full meanings and relations of Truth, Beauty, and Goodness, and to determine their places in the universe of reality. Philosophy is an attempt to interpret reflectively human life in all its relations. The philosopher aims to "see life steadily and to see it whole." Plato says "the unexamined life is not a truly human life." Philosophy is rational reflection upon experience, belief, and conduct. It is closely related to science, conduct, and religion.

Science is a careful scrutiny of the grounds of our common sense beliefs. It analyzes and describes our common experiences. It is organized common sense. The special sciences are the children of philosophy, and can never replace philosophy. All the sciences give rise to philosophical problems and theories. Among the Greeks, philosophy included all science. In fact, Aristotle was the first to map out the field of knowledge into distinct sciences. In the course of intellectual history the various sciences have gradually been split off from philosophy in the following order: mathematics, astronomy, physics, chemistry, biology, psychology, and sociology. But this separation of the special sciences from philosophy does not mean that, with their complete differentiation, there are no longer any philosophical problems involved in the work of the special sciences. Indeed, there are three sets of problems of a philosophical character which have been rendered more acute by the development of modern science. These are as follows:

1. All sciences make assumptions. Philosophy examines these assumptions.

2. The mutual adjustment of the principles of the several sciences into a unified and coherent view of things is a philosophical task.

3. The adjustment of the principles of science and the principles and beliefs which underlie the practical conduct of life is a task of philosophy.

The data of the sciences are really *sense-data* or perceived facts. In reducing these data to orderly and compact bodies of conceptual description and explanation, science makes assumptions. These basic assumptions of the sciences, philosophy must critically examine; for example, the uniformity of the causal order—like causes produce like effects. Moreover, it is generally assumed in the practical affairs of the common social life that each individual is responsible for his own acts. But if we are machines, as the physiologist might assume, this is not true. Philosophy is thus a clearing house for the sciences, adjusting their several conclusions to one another and to practical life.

In so far as scientists, working in special fields, examine their own working assumptions, widest generalizations or "laws of nature," and the relations between the laws of their special scientific fields and other fields, they become philosophers. It is possible to carry on investigations in physics without inquiring into the ultimate nature of matter or energy; it is possible to study the phenomena of life without raising the questions as the ultimate relations of life, matter and energy; it is possible to carry on work in any of the special sciences without considering the ultimate meaning of the connection of Cause and Effect; but as soon as one raises any of these final questions, which lie at the roots of science, one enters the field of philosophy.

In brief, the assumptions and conclusions of the several sciences call for critical examination and coördination, and this is a principal part of the work of philosophy. For example, what are Matter, Life, Mind, Space, Time, Causality, Purpose? What are their interrelations? Is the living organism merely a machine, or, is it something more? What is the mind or soul, and what are its relations to life and matter? What are Space and Time? Is the world really boundless in space and endless in duration? What are the enduring realities? Or, does nothing really endure? What is the status of purpose in the universe? Does everything that happens, happen blindly and mechanically? Are our human beliefs in the permanent significance of the purposes and values achieved by the rational individual illusions? What may we hope for in regard to the realization and conservation of the highest human values? Such are the exceedingly difficult and important questions to which philosophy seeks reasoned answers.

Judgment should not be passed as to the meaning of human life and its status in the cosmos until all the evidence is in. The one fundamental faith or postulate in philosophy is that nobody can be too intelligent. Great evils have come in the past through lack of intelligence.

III. The Relation of Philosophy to Practical Life, Especially to Conduct and Religion

Natural science is impersonal and indifferent to human weal or woe. It is not concerned with the *values* of life; it is essentially nonhuman. Material progress does not necessarily mean improvement in human nature.

In short, the standpoint of natural science in regard to the ethical and other personal interests of human selves is *neutral. The business of natural science is to consider everything which occurs, whether in the physical world or in human nature, as an inevitable event in the endless march of physical causation. Its fundamental postulate, or working principle, is that of a thoroughgoing mathematical and physical determinism.* But there is, besides the physical realm, the human realm of psychical interests, purposes, ends; *in short, the realm of human values.*

Two chief kinds of human values may be distinguished, namely:

1. Instrumental values, which are of use as means to realize ends

2. Intrinsic values realized within the self, experiences valued in themselves or for their own sakes

The good life is the life which contains great intrinsic or satisfying values. Ethics deals with intrinsic values or goods for selves. Ethics is thus the philosophy of the intrinsic or immediate values which may be achieved and enjoyed through the voluntary acts of individuals as members of society. Æsthetics, dealing with the *beautiful*, is also a part of the philosophy of values. A third form of human value is *religious value*. In the religious relation or experience, men enjoy such values as: peace of heart, harmony of will, communion with God, Divine forgiveness, salvation, spiritual joy, and strength. For the religious man these are the highest and most inclusive values of life, and the best life is one controlled by such values.

Religion claims to answer the question: How do values endure? The life that is best is the only one that endures, on account of its harmony with the supreme purpose of the universe; such is the central tenet in religion. All religion is faith in the supremacy in the universe, and therefore, the permanence, of the best life, the life having the most worth. Religion is close to conduct because it attempts to give firm foundation for the intrinsic values of life.

The atheistic or materialistic view of the universe is that blind physical forces will finally overcome human existence and effort, and engulf all human values. Philosophy is interested in what nature is, but also in what are the values of life, and what is the status of the highest human life; that is, philosophy asks: What is the status of values in the real world?

What are the highest values of life, is the problem of

ethics, an important branch of philosophy. Religion affirms dogmatically that what a society or individual members thereof regard as the highest values are promoted and conserved by a Higher Power. Religion pictures the highest values of life as incorporated in the Supreme Reality or Perfect Power who rules the Cosmos.

IV. Methods of Religion and Philosophy

The procedure of philosophy is intellectual, finding reasons for our beliefs, and rejecting beliefs that are inconsistent with the facts or with well-grounded principles. Religion is not primarily intellectual. It is based chiefly upon tradition and feeling. Hence, religion is one of the most conservative and unchanging factors in human life. For the power of *Tradition* makes for social conservatism, for the maintenance, unchanged, of the social institutions inherited from the past; and *Feeling,* or the native and emotional reaction of the individual, is the most intimately personal and unvarying psychical factor in the self, since it strikes its roots deep down in the subsoil of man's inherited and unconscious primal appetites and needs, from which spring into conscious action all his aversions and strivings, loves and hates, hopes and fears, joys and sorrows. The emotional life early takes, in childhood and youth, a set or bent which the individual can never greatly alter in later life. He may gloss it over or deck it out in new garb, but he cannot uproot it or alter its direction. The future character of the individual is probably fully determined before he is much past twenty-one.

It may happen, especially in changing cultural conditions, that an individual, with pronounced native idiosyncrasy and sensitiveness to the currents of the cultural life, will revolt against the prevailing traditional forms of religion, because they are not in harmony with the ideas and emotions of his own soul. Thus arise prophets, recreators, reformers, innovators, and critics in the religious sphere. Thus an individual may, in company with a few like-minded persons, try to reform the actual religion of his social group; or he may reject it as hopeless, and either join another group or endeavor to form a new group. Religion is preëminently a group matter. It is only in highly sophisticated societies, and even then among the minority, that an individualistic type of religious attitude appears. (*Mysticism* is, we shall see, the most individualistic type of religious attitude.) Seldom does the individual break away from the religion of the group. Even in advanced civilizations, the influence of social traditions and group sentiments, intermingled in some measure with individual peculiarities of ideation and emotion, chiefly determine a man's religious attitude.

The method of philosophy is sustained rational inquiry. *Philosophy originates and flourishes in the rational activity of the individual mind. The group-mind is seldom guided by reason.* Moreover, the scope of philosophy is wider than that of religion. Philosophy must determine not only the nature and meaning of religion, but also its relation to the principles of the sciences and to other main interests of life, such as moral conduct, social order, art, and culture.

Philosophy has three main problems:

1. The interpretation of nature
2. The interpretation of human values
3. The determination of the place of human values in the order of nature

Why the frequent conflict between religion and philosophy? Religion is conservative and philosophy is not conservative, but radical, skeptical, and reconstructive. Since religion is based largely on social customs and personal feeling, it is not always very careful as to whether there is consistency in its beliefs or not. Philosophy seeks consistency above all things else.

Does philosophy make assumptions? No. But it has progressively realized that there is some kind of intelligibility in the world, that the world can, in part, be understood, and that we have experiences which, if properly interrogated, will yield answers to our questions.

V. Poetry and Philosophy

The more serious poetry of the race has a philosophical structure of thought. It contains beliefs and conceptions in regard to the nature of man and the universe, God and the soul, fate and providence, suffering, evil, and destiny. Great poetry always has, like the higher religion, a metaphysical content. It deals with the same august issues, experiences and conceptions as metaphysics or first philosophy. For example, the author of Job, Æschylus, Sophocles, Euripides, Pindar, Lucretius, Omar Khayyám, Dante, Milton, Shakespeare, Coleridge, Wordsworth, Matthew Arnold, Browning, Tennyson, Goethe, Schiller, Molière, are philosophical poets. Poetry is more concrete, vivid, and dramatic in its treatment of these high themes; it is more intuitive in its thought processes and expressions than philosophy; hence it makes a more direct appeal to the emotions than philosophy. A philosophical poet is a metaphysician who does not think in a predominately conceptional, ratiocinative manner. A metaphysician is a thinker who does not think in concrete pictures, or, if he does, is unable to express himself in rhythm, color, and swift movement of speech as does the poet, and, at the same time, has a genius for analysis and ratiocination. Sometimes, as in Plato, a genius is supreme in both orders of spiritual creativeness, and then we get the absolute best in the spiritual realm, the profoundest thought wedded to the noblest expression

REFERENCES

* AVEY, ALBERT E., *Readings in Philosophy,* Chapter I. (This work is a compilation of source-readings in philosophy designed as a companion to the present volume.)

CALKINS, MARY WHITON, *Persistent Problems of Philosophy,* Chapter I.

* *Encyclopædia Britannica,* 11th edition, Article "Philosophy."

FLETCHER, ORLIN O., *Introduction to Philosophy,* Chapter I.

FULLERTON, GEORGE S., *Introduction to Philosophy,* Chapter I, and *The World We Live In.*

* JAMES, WILLIAM, *Some Problems of Philosophy,* Chapter I.

JERUSALEM, WILHELM, *Introduction to Philosophy,* First Division.

* KULPE, OSWALD, *Introduction to Philosophy,* Chapters I and IV.

* PAULSEN, FRIEDRICH, *Introduction to Philosophy,* Introduction.

* PERRY, RALPH BARTON, *Approach to Philosophy,* Chapters I–V.

* PLATO, *Symposium* and *Phædo.*

* ROYCE, JOSIAH, *The Spirit of Modern Philosophy,* Introduction.

* RUSSELL, BERTRAND, *The Problems of Philosophy,* Chapter XV.

SELLARS, ROY WOOD, *Essentials of Philosophy,* Chapter I.

WATSON, JOHN, *Outline of Philosophy,* Chapter I.

Asterisks are prefixed to the references considered suitable for beginners.

CHAPTER II

PRIMITIVE THOUGHT

I. The Primitive World View

Although prehistoric man has left no records of his inner life, the earliest traditions and literature throw light on primitive views, and the facts entitle one to assume that savage belief and thought to-day are very like primitive belief and thought. This assumption is supported by the study of the earliest literature of civilized peoples, of savage lore, and of the theory of evolution.

We do not know what the cave man thought; but, since he has left some fine artistic records, it is fair to conclude that he had a good deal of intelligence, and that he thought as capably in regard to the world and himself as do so-called savages and the masses of unscientific minds in high civilizations to-day.[1] There are millions of people to-day, living in high cultures, whose beliefs are not one whit in advance of savage beliefs, in so far as rational belief depends on the individual thinking out for himself the grounds of his beliefs. I see no evidence that the rank and file of humanity has any greater innate capacity to think than primitive or so-called savage peoples. Wherein the masses in highly civilized lands are in more advantageous position, is in their accessibility to the heritage of the race's pioneers in thinking. The achievements of the pioneers are preserved in an ever increasing social inheritance, and facilities for

---

[1] On savage logic compare F. B. Jevons, *Introduction to the History of Religion*, pp. 28-35.

their distribution are improvable through a wise policy of education. How far the average person assimilates and makes his own the processes, as well as the results, of the work of the pioneers, is another question. Perhaps, the great majority of human beings are born without *the passion for understanding.* "Knowledge comes, but wisdom lingers." Possibly, this is due, in part, to the present conditions in the economic struggle for existence; and, in part, to inadequate and defective educational instruments. But, under the most favorable conditions, the thinkers would always be in the minority. It is doubtful whether our present system of popular education does not retard independent or self-thinking as much as it promotes it. *All genuine education is self-education.* It will incite the individual to think for himself, by rethinking what the race's great thinkers have already thought for him, thus enabling him to go ahead under his own mental steam.

Primitive man believed that everywhere in the world everything was alive; there was a universally diffused energy. The world was not orderly to him, it was only alive. Man had not yet arrived at the distinction between animate and inanimate things. Moreover, he had no conception of personality. Wherever anything was *done,* there was *energy* and *life.*

The simplest and therefore, probably, the earliest philosophy of nature is the belief in a widely and indefinitely diffused *power* or *influence* (Mana).[2] This power is believed to be operative wherever anything striking or unusual happens. It produces catastrophes, diseases, death; is present in conception and birth; it causes plants and animals and human beings to increase and multiply; it gives

---

[2] The word *Mana,* which has come into general use as a name for this power or influence, is the Melanesian name. (See Bishop Codrington, *The Melanesians.*) Among the North American Indians *wakanda, orenda,* and *manitou* are names for the same notion.

prowess to the great warrior and skill to the mighty hunter; it works in the medicine man, in the good canoe, and the deadly spear. The gods and the evil spirits wield it. It is liable to break out anywhere, especially in unusual occurrences. Mana is not evenly distributed and does not work in an orderly manner, since it is subject to the control of gods, heroes, and demons, although in its essence it is distinct from them. It is not soul or spirit but *power*. Therefore it is better to call this early philosophy of nature *Animatism* or *Pan-Vitalism* rather than *Animism,* since the latter term rather implies the notion of a soul differing in kind from the body. (I follow here R. R. Marett in his *Threshold of Religion* and other writings.) The doctrine of Mana or *Animatism* is the ancestor of our modern doctrine of a universal Energy. It recognizes no distinction between animate and inanimate beings. A rarefied form of the same doctrine is our modern *Panpsychism*—the theory that all activity is an expression of Soul or Conscious Life. The early Greek hylozoism (all matter is alive) seems a direct descendant of the Mana doctrine.

II. Primitive Idea of the Soul

Primitive men do not think of the soul as immaterial. The soul has no specific mass or weight. It is of much more tenuous material than the body. It is an active principle. But it is not different in kind from the physical objects with which it is associated. It differs only in degree. It is elusive. It can leave the body and enter other bodies. It hovers around after death; so food and drink are given for it. Many primitive peoples do not regard the soul as being generated with the body. The Australian savages, it is said (according to Spencer and Gillen, *Northern Tribes of Central Australia*), do not regard generation and birth as a result of the sex relation. They think the child is the result of a preëxisting soul—a reincarnation. Many consider the soul as a manikin, like an image or a shadow of the body. Mysterious powers are attributed to a person's shadow. Savages are often afraid to have their pictures taken because their souls might be harmed by exposure of the photograph. The soul is sometimes conceived as like a bird, also as air, for example, by the ancient Hebrews and Romans. The ancient Egyptians held that every person had a *Ka,* or guardian spirit, which enabled him at death to become a *Ba,* a bird-man or immortal soul. Mr. Crawley (*The Idea of the Soul,* Chapters IV and V) holds that the primitive idea of the soul is that of a mental duplicate of the living and bodily self. The soul is a miniature of the body, a little image thereof, and the idea of it is derived from memory-images of the living person, especially visual images. Thus it is a refined and more elusive and active body than the external body. It may be so perfect a replica of the latter that it reproduces in little all the malformations and mutilations of the external body. It may be small enough to be held in the hand or may even be no larger than the image of the body, seen in the pupil of the eye. On the other hand, it may assume colossal proportions. It may be colored—red, white, or black. It may be identified with the blood, or breath, or, more vaguely, with life, or with flesh and blood without bones. A man may have a plurality of souls. The Bavili, an African people, are said to credit each man with four souls. The Laos people of India credit him with thirty. The soul is separable from the body, leaves it at night, and, especially in dreams, is more rapid, elusive, and evanescent in its movements; "a light, fluttering, or gliding thing, quick to come and quick to go, hard to catch and hard to detain."[3] It is more real and permanent than

[3] E. Crawley, *The Idea of the Soul,* p. 211. Mr. Crawley's theory of the origin of the various ideas and images of the soul is the most

the body, because, says Mr. Crawley, the memory-image is more constant than the percept. Hence, since the naïve mind finds it hard to believe in absolute death and since, during the present life the soul is held to be able to leave the body at will, primitive thought easily forms the belief in the continued existence of the soul after bodily death. In sum, then, the primitive or early view, which persists in naïve thought to-day, even amongst highly civilized peoples, is that the soul is a finer, more active, more enduring, more elusive, and more vital replica of the bodily personality or self, and that it continues to live after the death of the bodily self.

The causes for making a distinction between, and a separation of, body and soul, were reflections upon the persistence and recurrence of memory-images of other selves both in waking hours and during sleep, in dreams and visions of terror and delight, the mysteriousness of death, disease, and misfortune, and the feeling of being environed by mysterious forces potent for good and evil.

The third conception is that of spirits. The great spirits were believed to be free from the hampering influence of ordinary physical events. A striking phenomenon will cause the supposition of spirits. Some spiritual agencies are beneficent and others are maleficent. The high spirits would be called the high gods. But, in early thought as in naïve thought to-day, there does not appear to be any clear distinction made between soul and spirit. The distinction, when it does appear, is rather one of degree than

---

plausible that I have seen. Because of the immense part which the idea of immortality played in their social, ethical, and religious beliefs and practices, the ideas of the ancient Egyptians are of peculiar interest in this connection. On the latter subject, see J. H. Breasted, *Development of Religion and Thought in Ancient Egypt.* Belief in the immortality of the soul is, of course, closely bound up with systems of ancestor worship. The classical instance of this worship is the religion of China. See especially the work of Professor J. J. M. de Groot, *Religion in China.*

of kind. In fact, even where thought has reached a considerable degree of refinement, as among the Hebrews, Greeks, and Romans, the same words may be used for both ideas; for example, Ruach, Psyche, Pneuma, Anima. Most savage tribes believe in a creator god, remote and inaccessible.

Primitive man draws no clear distinction between man and animals. Totemism considers some animals sacred. The totem is an animal having a mysterious connection with the origin and well-being of the clan or tribe. Members of a totem clan do not kill the animal of their totem except under special circumstances. They must marry out of their totem. Plants, too, are supposed to be controlled by the spirits. Moreover the spirit of ancestors may or may not be deified.[4]

III. Tabu

This is an important item in primitive beliefs. Anything which is tabu must not be touched. It is set apart —sacred. A prohibition of any kind of food is tabu, for example, with the Jews, pork, and with the Hindus, the cow. To violate tabu would bring injury to the clan. A woman after childbirth is tabu, also a dead body. At puberty, boys and girls are tabu. The person of the king, and even words, may be tabu.

Why are things tabu? Because there is believed to be some mysterious power resident in them, or associated with

---

[4] The distinction between soul and spirit is not sharply drawn in primitive thought. The distinction between body on the one hand, and mana, soul or spirit, on the other hand, is made in terms of *behavior*. Anything that behaves in an unusual or unexpected manner has mana, soul or spirit, in it. The arrow, fishing spear, or canoe that behaves queerly is possessed by mana or spirit. The body is that which behaves in the ordinary fashion. At the points where social groups behave or need to bel ave in an unusual way, the great spirits or gods are conceived and invoked.

them, in some way, which, if the tabu is violated, will work injury to the violator or his tribal associates.

IV. Magic

One of the most striking features of primitive conduct is the belief in and use of magic. Magic consists of various special devices and procedures through which control of the mysterious powers which surround man is obtained for the advantage of the group or the individual.

Out of the technic of primitive magic has arisen two very different types of technic. One is the technic of science which aims, by the use of delicate and standardized instruments of observation, measurement, and calculation, such as fine balances, micrometers, microscopes, microtomes, dividing engines, statistical tables, and algebraic formulas, at acquiring an accurate and economic intellectual control or shorthand formulation of the order of nature. The other is religious technic, which aims, by its symbols, rites, prayers, et cetera, at bringing into right relation with one another the human group and individual on the one hand, and the Supreme Power, who is the custodian and dispenser of the values on participation in which depend individual and social well-being, on the other hand. In brief, religious technic aims at vital, moral, and spiritual control. Both these technics have grown out of primitive magic which was primitive science and religion in one. Religion and magic became differentiated as religion came to embody more clearly and rationally the organization of human values into a coherent and socialized whole, and thus to furnish explicitly the motives and sanctions for a higher social-moral order; while magic, incapable of development into an agency of social moralization and rational spiritualization, remained merely a technic for the satisfaction of isolated interests and irrational passions. The Hebrew-Christian and the Greek lines of development are most instructive and significant in this regard.

Magic is the ancestor of technology, the ancestor of what we call applied science. Medicine springs from it. The individual medicine man or Big Medicine among the aboriginal inhabitants of this continent was a man who, by reason of special ability and training, was able to do things that the ordinary individual could not do in the way of controlling mysterious forces of nature. The word "medicine" was applied not merely to what we call medicine, but to rain making, cloud making, wind making, getting strength into the war party, harming their enemies, et cetera. When we want anything done in what we call the arts of technology, we go to a special individual, for example, physician, engineer, carpenter, plumber, who has a special training. The medicine man was a man technically trained and able to control mysterious forces. Of course, the ordinary member of the tribe as a hunter, fisher, et cetera, had his training, and he could do the ordinary things in the ordinary way. But if he wanted any special thing done, he went to the medicine man—the Shaman.

Two kinds of magic are found, that is, two kinds of magical control, namely:

1. Contagious
2. Homeopathic

The basis of the belief in contagious magic is that power is transmitted by contagion, by contact with some being in whom this power resides. That belief is the source of one of the most widespread and solemn ceremonies in religion, the partaking of the god in the sacred meal—the banquet with the gods.

Where totemism exists, we find that, whereas ordinarily the individual would not kill the animal, a certain part of that animal is eaten in the sacred meal and strength is derived therefrom. Cannibalism is partly due to this. The savages did not always eat the bodies of their enemies because they were hungry. Possibly they had plenty. But if the enemy were particularly strong, they would get some of the strength by eating their bodies. And similarly, if the individual or the tribe, not being able to get hold of the whole persons of their enemies, could get hold of some parts of them, they could do them deadly injury. If you have his hair, clothes, scalp lock, et cetera, you have the enemy in your power. The magical use of names of birds was due to the supposition that extraordinary power resided in the names.

There is a tendency to believe, and there are people who still believe, in the efficacy of the bones of the saints, even the very small bones and fragments of their garments, to cure diseases. Some people, especially the peasantry of Europe, have recourse to love charms and to injurious magic.

The other form of magic is homeopathic. Not only like cures like, but like causally affects like. The original dogma of homeopathy is found deeply imbedded in primitive thought. So, if you could not get hold of anything belonging to your enemy, you might make an effigy and vent your anger on it. This practice has come down to modern times. Primitive man believed that he was hurting the original by injuring the image. Rain making, wind making, cloud making, the dance, imitating the corn planting, imitating the activities of war and the chase—these procedures were means of tapping *mana,* the mysterious force pervading nature.

As a familiar instance of homeopathic magic, I would cite the story of the brazen serpent. The Israelites on the way through the wilderness were attacked by a plague of serpents, and the brazen serpent was the means of curing that plague by homeopathic magic.

In the course of the development of civilized society, a differentiation took place in the magic, between black and white magic. The rulers and the people of Israel were forbidden to have recourse to soothsayers. We find in the Middle Ages in Europe a belief in black art, black magic, evil eye, and various forms of witchcraft, a belief which is still in existence in the minds of a good many people who still live in the Dark Ages. Many students of that subject have argued that, from the first, there was a fundamental difference between magic and religion. I believe they have one origin—the belief that superhuman agencies may be employed for either human ill or weal. The differentiation into magic and religion takes place gradually. Those special and mysterious methods, through which the mysterious powers which environ man are controlled, are placed in some person or group of persons. Of course, whatever ceremony or deed is for the welfare of the group is good. But now the individuals who want to satisfy their desires, their loves and hates as individuals, will have recourse to magic to gratify a passion which may disturb the order of the group. An individual, for example, falls in love, and has recourse to a magician to get another person as a husband or wife, which may be bad for the social order. One has a grudge against an individual and tries to bring him to destruction by working a magical agency. There thus arises a difference between antisocial magic and religion. Magic in general is a specialized kind of method for obtaining control over these mysterious forces that surround and invade the life of man.

V. Mythology

Among all primitive peoples and in the early literature of civilized peoples we find a great variety of stories to account for the origin of the various things in the world and to account for how things took place. Man asks from the beginning, *why* and *how?* Why and how, are the questions which we try to answer by science and philosophy. Myth is the lineal ancestor of science and philosophy. Myths are stories invented to account for the world, for man, and for his various customs and beliefs; in short, to explain why and how. We have, for example, cosmogonic myths, stories to account for the origin of the world, and anthropogenic myths, to account for the origin of man. Then we have stories to account for the origin of culture. We have culture heroes.

Death is not regarded as a natural affair by primitive man. Death is believed to be due to the intervention of some malevolent or at least not well-disposed power. Normally it should not take place. So we have all through history crude explanations of death, as for example, the influence of the serpent, the devil, sin. Now the fact that many of the stories seem very childish should not blind us to their purpose. St. Paul said: "When I was a child, I spake as a child, I felt as a child, I thought as a child; now that I am become a man, I have put away childish things." At the time of the origin of these myths, mankind was in a state of intellectual childhood.

The savage gave free play to his imagination, and was not checked by any acquired body of scientific principles and of scientific methods of procedure. Nor was he checked by the evidence of the validity of these principles. Consequently he thinks in pictures, and just as he interprets the phenomena of nature in the way we have seen, so he must make use of his own crude, disjointed picture-thinking to account for the origin of things. For instance, to-day, if anybody asks a scientist how man came on this earth, the scientist will say that he descended from an apelike ancestor, who lived in trees and later developed language, invented fire and tools, and organized societies. That is the evolutionary explanation of the how of things. We say that the earth was formed through the condensation of a nebula, or through the aggregation of meteoric star dust on the little core of the planet. Development or evolution by natural processes extending through immense periods of time and proceeding from the simple to the more complex—such is our evolutionary doctrine of the origins of the earth, animals, and man.

When we come to the higher types of myth as to the origin of things, we find two main kinds or types, though not all, perhaps, can be thus classified. One type of explanation of the origin of things is that they are due to a male and a female principle. It is very obvious why man would explain things in terms of his own experience, as due to male and female powers. Another type is the notion that from the beginning there were two opposing natures in things. The whole process of creation is due to the conflict of these principles. This notion embodies on a cosmical scale that conflict which is so universal a feature of common life. The Chinese, for example, have two principles, Yang and Yin—light and darkness. Sometimes they regard these principles as male and female. They are opposed principles, positive and negative. All things have sprung into being from them. The Universal Order or *Tao,* the whole system of heaven and earth, is due to them. The ancient Persians have two conflicting principles. Sometimes in Persian literature we find the view that these two principles sprang from the same original source; but on the whole the Persian thought is that two opposing principles were in actual conflict, namely, Ahura Mazda and Ahrimanes.

We find, among other peoples, various conceptions confusedly intermingled. For example, one myth is that the sky is the female principle and the earth the male principle, and from these all things came, from a primeval chaos. Without any consistency, the ancient Egyptians believed the separation of earth and sky was due to the sun. They forgot their own myths of the genesis of the sun by the earth and that the sun was formed from chaos. Another conception was that the sun god is the father of gods and men.

The Hebrew and Babylonian myths have a fundamental similarity. They both presuppose a primeval chaos. Tiamat is the primeval chaos. The Babylonians conceived it as water. And the origin of things was due to Marduk. In the book of Genesis it is stated that "in the beginning God created the heavens and the earth," the meaning being, not out of nothing, but out of chaos. And the word that occurs for this primeval chaos is Tehom—"the abyss." There is no question but that the story of genesis in the book of Genesis is an elevated form of the Babylonian story.

It is of special interest to note briefly the features of some of the main Greek cosmogonies because mankind emancipates itself first from this confusion we are dealing with, among the Greeks. Homer does not represent a very religious point of view. Some of the actions of the gods as depicted by Homer aroused the ire of Plato and other philosophers. Of course, we are not to take these seriously. The Homeric poems were compiled in the present shape in a very sophisticated civilization tinged with skepticism and irony. The original beings in Homer are Oceanus—heaven, and Tethys—earth. But behind both stands the goddess Night. The Orphic cosmogony is similar. First was Time; then came Ether and Chaos; out of these Time formed a silver egg, from which came Phanes, god of light, and first-born of the gods. Zeus swallowed Phanes and the world began anew. The special god of the Orphic religion, Dionysus, was the son of Zeus and Persephone.

Two other stories are worth noting. Hesiod says that all things sprang from chaos, which meant space. From space first came Gaia, the earthly mass and Eros—love or desire. Then sprang Erebus and Night, then Ether—day. Pherecydes brings in a trinity the first member of which is an eternal, spiritual principle. The first and mightiest is Zeus; then comes Chronos—time. From Chronos sprang fire, air, and water. The third principle is Chthonia, Earth-Spirit. These three seem to be alike eternal, although Zeus is the most powerful and, as Zeus-Eros, is the principal agent in creation. It would be interesting to compare, in some detail, the principal myths as to the origins of the world, of gods and men, among the chief culture-peoples. But I have not space for that. The general trend seems to have been from animatistic, through quasi personal, to rational and impersonal or superpersonal, principles of explanation.

References on the Primitive World View

* Avey, Albert E., *Readings in Philosophy,* Chapter II.

Brinton, Daniel G., *The Religions of Primitive Peoples.*

* Carpenter, J. Estlin, *Comparative Religion,* Chapters III and IV.

* Clodd, Edward, *Animism,* sections 1-9.

* Coe, George A., *The Psychology of Religion,* Chapters V, VIII, IX.

Crawley, Ernest, *The Idea of the Soul.*

Durkheim, Emile, *The Elementary Forms of the Religious Life.*

* *Encyclopædia Britannica,* 11th ed., Articles on "Animism Magic and Mythology."

* *Encyclopædia of Religion and Ethics,* Articles on "Cosmogony and Cosmology," "Mana and Magic."

* FRAZER, JAMES G., *The Golden Bough,* Vol. I, Chapters I–III.
* HADDON, A. C., *Magic and Fetishism.*
JEVONS, FRANK BYRON, *Introduction to the History of Religion.*
KINGSLEY, M. H., *West African Studies,* Chapters V-VIII.
MARETT, ROBERT R., *The Threshold of Religion.*
MOORE, G. F., *History of Religions.*
* REINACH, SALOMON, *Orpheus,* Chapters I-IV.
THOMAS, WILLIAM I., *Source Book for Social Organs,* pp. 651-735.
TOY, CRAWFORD H., *History of Religion.*
See also the series, *American Lectures on the History of Religions.*
TYLOR, E. B., *Primitive Culture.*

REFERENCES ON GREEK AND HEBREW RELIGION

ADAM, JAMES, *The Religious Teachers of Greece.*
* *Encyclopædia of Religion and Ethics,* Article "Israel" by Kennett.
CORNFORD, F. M., *From Religion to Philosophy,* pp. 73-122.
CUMONT, FRANZ, *Astrology and Religion among the Greeks and Romans.*
* *Encyclopædia Britannica,* 11th ed., Articles "Greek Religion and Hebrew Religion."
FOWLER, H. T., *History of Hebrew Religion.*
* GUNKEL, H., *Legends of Genesis.*
* KAUTSCH, E., "Religion of Israel," in Hastings' *Dictionary of the Bible.*
* MURRAY, GILBERT, *Four Stages of Greek Religion.*
ROBERTSON SMITH, W., *Religion of the Semites.*

CHAPTER III

THE DIFFERENTIATION OF PHILOSOPHY AND SCIENCE FROM RELIGION

I. The Rise of Philosophy to Independence

The first influence that made for independent intellectual inquiry into things was the breakdown of the primitive world view. In order that man may understand and control the forces operative in the world, it is necessary that he discover the sequences among phenomena. Now when man discovers that there is regularity of sequential relations among phenomena, that is a discovery of what we call the causal relation, that is to say, one thing is invariably dependent for its appearance on other things. The regular antecedent is cause, and the regular consequent is effect.

From the beginning man must have tried, in so far as he exercised his intelligence, to discover causal relations, and, as I have pointed out, the primitive world view is a theory of the causal dependencies, of the regular sequences of events. And from that theory there follow certain practices. Magic and religion aim at methods of control over the causes of things. Surrounded by mysterious forces that affected him, that operated on him for weal or woe, early man formulated a theory of the characters of these forces from his experience. He regarded things that affected him as expressions of forces, spirits, gods, as mysterious or supernatural operations, and devised means to control them. Science to-day is concerned with the same problem. But between our science and practice, and the beliefs and practices of primitive man lies the whole history of science and philosophy as independent enterprises.

There are three fallacies to which the primitive man was prone. There are many fallacies, but these are the three most prevalent and persistent. The modern man is still a prey to them. A training in scientific habits of investigation and of persistency in analyzing things into their elements, is to get rid of the influences of these fallacies.

They are:

1. "Post hoc ergo propter hoc"
2. The neglect of negative instances
3. Classification by means of superficial resemblances

The fallacy of "post hoc ergo propter hoc" in English means this: That because we once or twice observe one thing to follow another, therefore, that which follows, is the effect of that which it follows upon. Conversely, that which we have occasionally observed to immediately precede an event is the cause. Because of man's native propensity to jump to conclusions, a single instance of a sequence will be taken as evidence of a causal dependence, His primitive and persistent credulity makes such a belief, once formed, very difficult to dislodge. The superstitions that still prevail among human beings, especially feminine beings, are due to the persistence of primitive causal theories and beliefs that owe their rise to this fallacy. For example, that it is unlucky to take journeys on Friday; certain things bring bad luck; thirteen is an unlucky number, because disasters have occurred when something was done on the 13th, or thirteen were at the table—these are instances of primitive causal theories.

Now, suppose the members of a tribe were starting on a hunting expedition and something unusual happened, as, for example, there was a great clap of thunder, a brilliant flash of lightning, or strange birds flew across the sky. Anything strange arrested attention. To primitive man, anything that is mysterious has supernatural significance. They started out with that in their minds. They went on and were defeated, or did not get game, or the game turned on them and some of them were killed. Immediately the conclusion followed naturally, that there was a causal connection, that they should not have started, or that they should have propitiated the spirits who sent the birds or the lightning. We only are able to eliminate these fallacies by a thoroughly exact analysis which leads us to determine that there is some *constant* relation.

Now, as to the fallacy of making further observation suit one's already formed belief and neglecting the negative instances; having observed that once or twice A follows B, the conclusion that A *always* follows B is made, and men never look for the instances in which A occurs and there is no B; and they never try to analyze A and B to separate relevant from irrelevant factors. The tendency to neglect negative instances is a consequence of that primitive tendency to believe what one sees in the lump, without further inquiry.[1] Suppose, for example, you believe in the prophetic significance of dreams. Whenever a dream occurs that turns out to be even vaguely anticipatory of a later occurrence, you will chalk it down and other dreams will be overlooked. This is often the sole source of belief in the efficacy of certain therapeutic methods. You take some medicine and get well. The medicine may have had nothing to do with it. Nature cures ninety per cent of ills. So the doctor, no matter what the trouble is, has a tremendous advantage over the credulous patient, because when a person is in distress, physical or mental, and looks for some remedy, and is told by someone else that something is good, whether faith healing or medicine, immediately, if he gets well, the patient

[1] As Mr. Crawley well puts it, primitive thinking is done in terms of *totalities* or *wholes*.

concludes that it was the consequence of the advised remedy.

The following is a story from the ancient Greeks. A certain Greek was skeptical as to the power of Neptune —in Greek, Poseidon—to really control the waves. A friend took him into the temple and showed him a large number of votive offerings that had been put into the temple by sailors and fishermen, who had called upon Neptune and the sea had become calm. This proved the case to the pious believer. But the skeptic said, "Before I make up my mind I would like to hear from those who were drowned"; that is, to hear the negative instances of those who had called upon Neptune in vain. It is very hard for humankind not to make up its mind until it hears from the drowned. Most people tend to jump to conclusions.

The third persistent fallacy is classification by means of superficial resemblances. Identity of nature and operation is attributed to things that look alike in outline or behavior. A stick, a stone, or a cloud looks or moves as an animal or man might; therefore it is animated by similar motives. The trees in the forest or the wind at sundown or dawn make sounds like the voice of men or animals, therefore they are alive. Animatism has one of its most powerful supports in this mode of reasoning which is, of course, the primitive form of the *argument from analogy*. Resemblance or analogy furnishes one of the permanent modes of arranging facts in order, but we must *weigh* as well as count the points of likeness and balance them, as to both weight and number, against the differences. This precaution the primitive mind commonly fails to observe.

What leads to the breakdown of faith in the primitive world view? The development of civilization; the growth of social organization; the establishment of stable, well ordered states; the development in the arts of life, agriculture, and the industrial arts. When civilization develops so that it includes a large number of families with stable civil organization, and advance is made in agriculture, works of architecture, engineering, and the household arts, and especially when one people comes into contact with other peoples and observes differences in customs and arts, keen-minded individuals make discoveries. They discover that the primitive theory does not work; that good crops do not always follow on the propitiation of the gods; that success in war does not always follow upon the propitiation of the deities and supernatural powers. They discover that beliefs running back to immemorial antiquity are often a hindrance to the welfare and progress of the individual and the group. In other words, a question arises as to the validity of these beliefs, because they do not produce the results expected. In fact they may produce bad results.

By familiarity with the qualities of natural objects gained through manual work, men discovered that there is a regularity of sequence and a constancy of behavior in things, and that you can get certain results only by taking account of certain qualities. It is discovered that by rubbing amber you can get sparks, and if you do not rub, no incantation will bring forth the sparks.

The development of political life through the organization of strong and stable states leads to higher moral conceptions. Some of the old customs are seen to be hindrances to the proper conduct of business, industry, and to proper administration and the progress of social order. The development of social life in stability, the growth of justice, the definition of property rights, rights of contract, the growth of man's whole moral and social life as a member of society, bring to pass an increasing recognition of the significance of the personality of the individual. There is more leisure, more opportunity, more scope for exceptional individuals, for inventors and critics of the established beliefs and customs. The discoveries of new ways of thinking are always made by individuals. Masses of men never discover anything, never invent anything. It is always the exceptional individual who creates new ideas and values. The crowd is irrational, imitative, and subject to the influence of suggestion. Therefore, the type of society in which there is development, scope, and stimulation for the exceptional individual, is the type of society which progresses most rapidly in the arts and sciences, which progresses intellectually and spiritually.

Our intellectual culture is descended from the Græco-Roman culture system. Our culture is a continuation of the European culture, and what I have to say about the genesis of philosophy and science will have no reference to the history of India or China. Up to the present time, China has had no influence on the development of our culture, and India has had hardly any. So it is the development of European science and philosophy, of which we are the heirs, that I am concerned with.

The earliest important civilizations were along the rivers, in the fertile river valleys. Assyria and Egypt attained a high degree of development in written language, social organization, agriculture, and the mechanical arts. Some of their architectural achievements are still sources of wonder, and their social and religious ideas were the ancestors of some of the most fundamental ideas of the Hebrews and even of the Greeks.

The next period of civilization after the river period was the Mediterranean. The shores of the Mediterranean were naturally favorable environs for the development of civilization. It is not very large, the shores are near enough together to promote traffic, the climate is good, there are clear skies, varied rocky shores, fertile plains, and picturesque river valleys. Apparently in the island of Crete there developed a high degree of civilization, the Minoan civilization. Crete was one center of its advancement, but it was not confined to Crete. Asia Minor, the Hellespont, and other contiguous regions had their share in it. This civilization spread over the whole region and probably over a large part of the Mediterranean littoral.

There came down upon this early civilization and conquered the representatives of it, a people whom we call the Greeks, and who call themselves Hellenes. They were in many respects less highly civilized than the people they conquered. They were Aryans, the race which we belong to. The Greeks had certain common features in their physical build, the shape of the head, et cetera, which characterized them.[2] A great advance in civilization, I think, has always involved intimate contact of two peoples. An isolated people does not advance. And the contact of the Hellenes with the other peoples stimulated the Hellenes. It gave them material to work on, and they worked in a favorable environment. The geography of the eastern Mediterranean is favorable to the development of human culture. There were beautiful promontories, inland mountains and valleys, good climate and plenty of sunshine, which afford favorable conditions to stimulate humankind. The economic conditions were also good, material wants were easily provided for in a genial clime and with slave labor.

This is where we find the origins of science. Why were the Greeks so keen and creative? Originally, why did they possess such eager curiosity, such fertility of thought? They must have had them from the first, to some extent. Somehow, in their racial characteristics, there was a capacity for more advanced civilization. They intermarried with the aboriginal inhabitants. The most progressive races are always mixed races. The parents of science and philoso-

---

[2] Perhaps the invaders were of the same racial stock as the more civilized people whom they conquered. This is an unsettled question.

phy are the Greeks. Science and philosophy's first independent disciples appeared about 600 B. C.

The Greeks were traders, industrialists, travelers. One of the richest Greek cities of that time was Miletus, the birthplace of science and philosophy. Thales of Miletus, who flourished about 585 B. C., was the first philosopher and physicist. His school was called the Milesian School. Of his school were Anaximander, who flourished about 570 B. C., and Anaximenes, who flourished about 540 B. C. The general term applied to the Greek colonists on the coastland of Asia Minor and the adjacent islands is "Ionian." They were one of the main divisions of the Greek race. Thales is the father of Ionian philosophy.

II. The Development of Early Greek Philosophy

The two basic and interconnected problems that arise when man begins to reflect systematically upon the course of nature, are: 1. What is the *permanent stuff* or *substance* which endures through all the mutations of finite and transitory existences? Is this stuff one, or many, in kind? 2. What is the *cause,* or what are the *causes,* of the incessant origination, change, and decease of finite beings?

The perennial significance of the Ionian or first Greek philosophers, lies in the fact that they all attempted answers to the two fundamental questions of thought in regard to nature *by concepts that were formed by reflection upon the observed facts of nature.* They were all rationalists, in that they assumed that all the seemingly chaotic changes, all the diversified qualities in nature, are the results of an order that can be apprehended by human reason. By the exercise of observation and thought man can understand nature and his own place in it. They were naturalists in the sense that they held nature and man to be products of the same universal order or causation.

In their various essays to interpret the world in terms of reason, the Ionians hit upon the most basic questions of metaphysics: 1. What is the nature of the permanent or eternal Order of Being? 2. What are the causes or forces by which the permanent being is diversified ceaselessly into the multiform and ever changing procession of finite beings? What causes the incessant transformations of the permanent substance or substances of things? 3. What is the relation between Being and Becoming, Permanence and Change, Eternity and Time? 4. Is the enduring Being one, or are there many enduring beings and, if so, are they the same or different in kind? This is the problem of Singularism and Pluralism discussed in its modern forms in Chapter XXIV.

Thales said that the first principle of things, the substance or stuff of all things, was water. This does not seem like a very significant statement. The cosmogonies had already said that Oceanus was first. We have traditions that Thales did various things. He was a mathematician and astronomer, and foretold an eclipse. But for our purpose, the important point is, what is the significance of the theory that the substance of things is water? Thales held that every finite thing that comes into existence is a modification of water. He held the view that, by condensation and rarefaction of water, all things rise, and he actually attempted an evolutionary account of the genesis of man, and plants, and animals. Thales regarded the substance, water, as having in it life. None of these early thinkers recognized any distinction between living and nonliving, or mental and nonmental. They believed that every particle of the substance of things had the germ of life in it. They were all Hylozoists. In other words, for them *Reality is living matter*. They were all, in a broad sense, Evolutionists.

Anaximenes said air or the ether is the substance of

things. Anaximander said that the unlimited (to apeiron), a boundless, animated mass, is the substance of things.

Why does Thales' theory constitute the birth of independent philosophy and science? First, it is a *natural principle,* one natural substance, and not a multitude of mysterious spirits; an *empirical substance* is made the stuff and cause of all things. Second, Thales, I think, was undoubtedly led to his view by observation and reflection upon the mutations that water undergoes, its rarefaction and condensation. It solidifies into ice and rarefies into vapor. It enters into so many things, into rocks and breaks them. Things die without water, with enough water they flourish. Thales lived on an island in the Ægean Sea off the coast of Asia Minor, and his situation possibly suggested his hypothesis that water was the basic and all-inclusive substance of things.

Herein lay the significance of the first theories advanced by the Ionians, Thales and his disciples; these theories all have this in common, however otherwise they may conceive the one substance, that they consist in the notion that there is *one* natural substance, stuff, material, out of which all things are fashioned, and that the whole variety of particular things which exist, animals, plants, men, as well as rocks, air, ocean, the whole variety and the endless succession of actual beings, are fashioned out of the one natural substance, the primeval stuff which is not conceived as merely material. Its material characteristics are most obvious, but it is dynamic and living, and is distributed throughout the entire world, and all things arise from it through the operation of natural causes. So this one substance is living matter (Hylozoism).

Now, once a conception of this sort has been definitely formulated and shaped, there are several questions which logically arise. And the first question which arises is this: *What is permanent amidst or through all the ceaseless changes in particular beings? If the primeval stuff is constantly undergoing modification, then it never exists as such in the form in which it is conceived. What is it that is permanent?* That is the first question. The second question is: *What is the cause, or the causes, of the ceaseless flux, the endless modification of things, things arising, changing, passing away, and new ones arising?* The clearness and consistency with which the early Greek philosophers raised and answered these various questions, once they hit upon the trail, is a mark of their genius.

One of the greatest thinkers, Heraclitus (538-475 B. C.), of Ephesus, a city of Asia Minor, on the coast, answered the question by saying that nothing is permanent, all is change, ceaseless flux is the nature of things. There is no substance that retains the same characteristics and qualities. The world of nature is the theater of incessant mutation, "panta rei," πάντα ρεῖ, all things flow. But all change takes place in an orderly fashion, according to the eternally fixed law or decree—Logos, which in Greek means both word and reason, or thought, expressed. The Logos is the divine reason immanent in the cosmos.

This conception of Heraclitus is the ancestor of our doctrine of natural law. So far as the actual course of particular things is concerned, their unending fate is ceaselessly to arise and to pass away, but this fate is not the expression of the wills of animated beings or spirits, nor is it the result of chance. *It is the expression of rational order in the universe,* and that rational order Heraclitus identified with God—Zeus.

Now as to the *causes* of change, the doctrine of Logos or Reason or Universal Law means that there is no disorder. *There is nothing that happens without reason or cause.* As to the question, what is the ultimate cause, what in the last analysis is it that keeps things going, why this constant cyclical process of generation and decease,

Heraclitus says strife is the father of all things finite. Struggle or conflict is an inexpugnable feature of reality. This old Greek thinker anticipated by many centuries the Darwinian doctrine of the struggle for existence, as well as Hegel's doctrine of the development of reality through conflict. "War is the father and king of all things." The world is the theater of the ceaseless conflict, with ever varying results, of two opposing tendencies, the tendency toward discord, and the tendency toward harmony. But whichever may be in the ascendancy at a particular time in a particular region of the universe, whichever may have the upper hand, whether it be peace or war, all takes place according to law, according to reason, according to the eternal divine order.

As to the *stuff,* the *substance* of things, Heraclitus regarded fire as the best symbol, the nearest approximation that we have in experience. That may be conceived as the primary stuff. This is one radical solution of the problems of the relations of change and permanence, multiplicity and unity.

But another equally radical solution and way to get rid of the problem of the opposition between the ceaseless changes that the world shows and the permanence of the primary stuff, is to say that there is no such thing as change. And this is the way that Parmenides of Elea, who flourished about 475 B. C., solved the question. For him the substance of things is one and unchangeable. Consequently, all the changes which we see are illusory, and all the multiplicity that we see in things is illusion. There is no motion or change in reality, that too is an illusion of our senses. There is no growth and decay in reality, and there is no plurality of beings, there is one and only one substance—"hen kai pan," ἕν καὶ πᾶν, the One and All.

Parmenides was probably stimulated by Xenophanes, who was a religious poet. He was especially interested in the religious aspect of philosophy and insisted that there was but one supreme and divine being. He criticized the popular doctrine of the gods, saying that the Ethiopian's gods were Ethiopians in color and made in the image of the worshipper himself, and that an ox's god would be like an ox. He criticized the attribution of human qualities to the gods. Parmenides solves the problem of the contrast between permanence and change, unity and plurality, by saying that what we call change, growth and decay, birth and death, are illusions. What we apparently see through our senses, that there exist a multitude of beings, the things I see with my eyes and touch with my hands, all these perceptions are illusions. There is only one being. He conceived the One as like a material sphere, because the sphere was round and complete. And he defended his theory by arguments, showing the irrationality of belief in change and multiplicity. Zeno, his disciple, with great acuteness, developed a series of contradictions involved in the assumption that motion is real (the Achilles, the flying arrow); that there exists a plurality of beings (the infinite divisibility and the infinite extensibility paradoxes). These contradictions, he says, show the utter untrustworthiness of the senses.

Zeno had for his primary aim the task of refuting the assumption that reality is many and changing. Zeno shows that belief in the senses lands us in contradictions. If knowledge is reached by perception, then if a corn-measure full of corn be taken and the corn be dropped on the floor, a noise will be heard. Then, if we take one grain and drop it, it ought to make a noise, but it does not. Thus, in this instance, the senses deceive us. The senses declare that many things exist, but if the many things do exist, they must be made of indivisible units. These units can have no magnitude, but if the component units can have no magnitude, then the sum has no magnitude. If there are any two objects, then between the two there must be a third, and between these again there must be still another, and so on indefinitely, therefore being must have infinite magnitude. In regard to the phenomenon of motion, Zeno shows that those who hold that there is motion appeal to the senses. And in the discussion of this question, the well-known paradox of the flying arrow, and that of Achilles and the tortoise, are given. An arrow in order to pass from one point to another must pass through an infinite number of points in a finite time; moreover, if at one instant it be at one point and at the next instant at another point, it must have passed from the one to the other point in no time. If Achilles runs ten miles per hour and the tortoise one mile per hour, and if the tortoise be given one hour's start, Achilles can never catch the tortoise. For while he covers the first mile, the tortoise will cover one-tenth of a mile, and while Achilles covers the one tenth mile, the tortoise will cover one-hundredth of a mile, and so on forever. Since any finite distance is made up of an infinite number of positions, no finite space can be traversed by a moving object in a finite time. Motion is impossible. Zeno's arguments are all aimed at proving the utter untrustworthiness of sense-perception. His conclusion is that through reason alone have we knowledge of the one and unchanging Being or Reality.

Now, of course, Parmenides and Zeno did not have to solve the problem, what is the cause of change? There is no need to seek for a cause if there is no change or plurality to be accounted for. But they escaped that problem to face another, namely, what is the cause of the illusion that we are all under? What is the cause of the universal belief that there is change and multiplicity? They failed to explain this satisfactorily, and that failure is an immediate factor in developing a consciousness of a new problem, namely, that of knowledge and error. The very difficult and important question arises as to why we should err and how we can know anything, if our senses are wholly untrustworthy.

The Eleatics solved the problem of permanence and change by eliminating change. Heraclitus solved it by making change universal and by affirming that the only thing which is permanent is the law and order of change. Another series of thinkers tried in various ways to combine the two notions. Empedocles of Agrigentum (495-435 B. C.) advanced the theory that there are four elements. These are permanent: earth, air, fire, and water. He took these from the myth-makers, his predecessors. These are the permanent and original things. The succession of particular beings that constitute our world is due to the intermixture of these elements in various proportions. They are always being mixed and separated, combined, dissolved, and recombined. And he conceived every particular thing as a mechanical mixture of the four elements. As to the cause of this intermixture, he says there are two forces that exist through all time, they are eternal—Love and Hate. This is a more pictorial form of Heraclitus' doctrine of harmony and discord. Love and hate are always striving against one another. This is the reason why we have in nature the ceaseless succession of all sorts of things and events. It is worth noting that Heraclitus, Empedocles and others believed that the course of the universe runs in cycles.

Anaxagoras of Clazomenae (500-428 B. C.) was another early Greek thinker who formulated an original theory of permanence and change, or unity and multiplicity. Like Empedocles and Leucippus, his idea was that the substance of things consists of indestructible elements. His elements he calls seeds, spermata. Aristotle calls them homoiomeries

—like parts. Anaxagoras says that, when we analyze our perceptions, we find a very considerable variety of distinct qualities. We have, of course, to begin with, the qualities perceived through the senses; colors, shapes, sounds, tactual perceptions, temperature sensations, et cetera. Besides that, when we dissect a living being, we find different kinds of stuff or structure, bones, nerves, blood vessels, muscles. That is the starting point of the doctrine. Corresponding to every quality that we find, there is an indefinite number of minute parts or elements which have the same qualities. Bone is made up of bone parts, nerve of nerve parts, muscle of muscle parts, heat of heat parts.

We can smile at Anaxagoras because he did not have behind him the history of scientific analysis, of the minute analysis of things by use of the microscope, test tube, et cetera, which we have. But Anaxagoras' doctrine of the elements is the ancestor of the modern chemical doctrine. The chemist, as a chemist, does not say that he can reduce all the elements to the same kind of atoms. The physicist says that all the chemical substances may be composed of the same primary stuff, and if he is a metaphysical physicist, he is now apt to say that they are constellations of electrons. But the chemist simply reduces the physical world to things that cannot be further analyzed by chemical methods.

The elements of Anaxagoras represent the not further analyzable qualities of the world, and he regards these qualities as due to the presence of a large number of minute particles which have the same qualities. That is, the substance of things, and all the ceaseless variety of beings which exist in our world are due to the intermixture and separation of these elements.

As to the cause of these ceaseless processes of intermixture and separation, Anaxagoras is quite original. He says that these things cannot move of themselves. There must be something which moves them. He says we know that, when our bodies undergo a change, when we move our bodies, it is because there is a mind causing the body to move. As to the cause of movement, therefore, he argues that, just as you and I intentionally move our bodies, and through moving our bodies move other things to a limited extent, so there is a universal mind which is the cause of movement. He calls this *Nous—Universal Intelligence.* He does not conceive this mind in a strictly immaterial way, and he does not, so far as the preserved fragments of his teaching show, work out the difficulties and problems of how mind can act on matter. He does not even apply his theory of mind as the prime mover, except when he can find no other explanation. Mind imparts only the original rotatory movement to things.

You may ask for the difference between Anaxagoras' view and the primitive animistic view. We may say, on the one hand, that Anaxagoras has a clearly defined doctrine of material elements, and, on the other hand, he conceived the universe as a unity, with one universal mind as the first cause of all the motion in the world. Neither of these views, in a clearly defined form, were present in the primitive animistic view of the world.

References

* Avey, Albert E., *Readings in Philosophy,* Chapter III.

* Bakewell, Charles M., *Source-Book in Ancient Philosophy* (well-chosen selections from all ancient philosophers).

* Benn, Alfred W., *Early Greek Philosophy.*

* Burnet, John, *Early Greek Philosophy,* and *Greek Philosophy from Thales to Plato,* pp. 1-36 and 57-86.

Cornford, F. M., *From Religion to Philosophy.*

Gomperz, Th., *Greek Thinkers.*

Grote, G., *History of Greece,* Vol. VIII.

* ROGERS, ARTHUR K., *A Student's History of Philosophy*, pp. 8-48.
* SEDGWICK AND TYLER, *A Short History of Science*, pp. 35-68.
* THILLY, FRANK, *History of Philosophy*, pp. 7-50.
* WINDELBAND, WILHELM, *History of Ancient Philosophy*, pp. 16-151.
* ZELLER, EDWARD, *Outlines of Greek Philosophy*, pp. 35-101.
ZELLER, EDWARD, *The Pre-Socratics.*

CHAPTER IV

ATOMISTIC MATERIALISM

I. The Greek Atomists

Leucippus (dates unknown, reputed teacher of Democritus) is the originator of atomic materialism. It was Democritus (about 460-370 B. C.) who brought the theory to the completeness given it by the Greeks. The Epicurean School, one of the most important Schools after Aristotle, adopted or affixed atomic materialism to its theory of conduct. One of the chief causes of superstition has been the fear of the gods, but on the basis of this atomic theory, there is no place for the gods; and it was for this reason largely that atomism was taken up by Epicureans. The great Latin poet, Lucretius, in his philosophical poem, "On the Nature of Things," also expounds the philosophical system of atomism.

The influence of atomism then died out, and was revived again when adopted by Gassendi and Hobbes. And in modern experimental physical science it has played an important part. The electron theory is only the latest development of this atomic theory. The modern scientific atomist is not concerned about the substrata of the mind or the problems of value. In physical science the atomic theory is simply a working hypothesis that best seems to fit all the facts. It is the best scientific policy there is. To assume that matter is discrete and not continuous, enables the physicist and chemist to get forward in their investigations. In Democritus and Leucippus, atomism is a metaphysical doctrine. It is put forth as being adequate to explain the whole of reality. Leucippus, who was younger than Parmenides and older than Democritus, was a contemporary of Empedocles and Anaxagoras. Democritus was a contemporary of Socrates and in part, of Plato. We have only a very fragmentary account of Democritus. Of him we are told that he had the greatest acquaintance with natural science next to Aristotle.

Parmenides of Elea had taught that the one substance is unchanged, eternal, and homogeneous. Heraclitus, on the other hand, taught that all is change. The law of change alone is permanent. Leucippus combines the ideas of permanence and change in such a way as to admit both without making either illusory.

The way out of the opposition between permanence and change, as proposed by the atomists, is as follows: Reality consists of an infinite number of mass particles. These exist eternally. They are ungenerated. They exist and move in empty space. *Atoms* and the *void* are the original and indestructible data of reality. These atoms differ in size, and they differ to an infinite degree in their forms and shapes. Some of them have hooks, others have eyes, grooves, protuberances, et cetera. While moving in space, these atoms impinge upon one another and rebound. They incessantly move, and the falling together of the atoms produces a vortex movement, and it is this movement that gives rise to a world. There is an endless procession of worlds—our world is only one of an endless number of worlds that arise and pass away. This world of ours swings in empty space like a ball. On the outermost bounds of the world is a rind, as it were, of closely packed atoms. From the impact and rebound of atoms arise all things. The four elements, of which fire is the most important, also arise in this manner by the intermingling of atoms. Inasmuch as the atoms have only those qualities which we approximately call primary, that is, only spatial and mechanical properties, size, shape, weight, and motion, the question arises, how is it that we come to perceive all the other qualities in the bodies such as color, sound, and taste; and how do we know that these qualities exist only for the human organism? And also, how do we know that the other qualities exist in the objects? The reply to this question is given us in the atomistic theory of knowledge.

The soul consists of the motion—nothing but the motion—of fine, smooth, round, fiery atoms. Objects throw off eidola, images, and these images enter the sense organs and then give rise to the secondary qualities. These images are not good copies of the objects because they are due to the meeting of the motions of sense organs with the systems of motion in the form of the images thrown off from the objects. They are distorted, and therefore the senses do not acquaint us with the nature of reality. The external world has no sounds, no tastes, no odors, no colors, no harmony or discord, no warmth or music. There is simply everlasting motion of mass particles in space. The soul itself consists of the finest motion of the finest particles. Thus thought is also regarded as being the resultant of mass particles. It is through thought, urge the atomists, that the wise man knows that the world consists only of atoms moving in a void. Most men know only what is given them through the senses, but the wise man through intuition learns the truth.

As to the nature of the Good, Democritus assumes that happiness is to be attained only through the exercise of thought. Materialist though he is, he is one of the most extreme rationalists. Genuine knowledge of the real is attained through the exercise of thought and not through the senses. In this type of intuitive knowledge, there is a harmony of the soul, a calm, a gentle, harmonious reaction of the soul atoms. In sense knowledge, we have those passions, those hurricanes that lash the soul and make it impossible to desire true knowledge.

II. The Essence of Materialism

Materialism is one of the main types of world view or metaphysics. The essence of materialism lies in the following four doctrines:

1. All qualitative varieties and changes in the world of human experiences are reducible to quantitative terms and statement.

2. All perceptions, feelings, thoughts—the whole content and activity of mind, are reducible to the motions of mass particles in space.

3. Because of this, all so-called secondary qualities of objects are merely phenomena in the human organism—these secondary qualities do not exist in the objects themselves. It is only the primary qualities which really exist apart from the *human percipient* organism.

4. Every event which occurs, every happening in the endless process of things, is the result alone of blind mechanical motion. There is no purpose, no meaning, either in the sum of things or in the elements of things. What the man in the street calls purpose or providence, are illusions of his own provincial, self-centered point of view. What really goes on and really determines, with inexorable necessity, the sequence of events, is the eternal, unmeaning, unconscious dance, the collision and rebound, of mass particles in space. No one guides the process to an end, and no one controls it. Our desires, our intents, our purposes, have no more significance in the blind and insensate organization of the universe than has the dancing of a mote in the sunbeam.

We shall examine later, in Chapter XVI, the modern form of materialism, and the new arguments adduced for it. The reader is asked to bear in mind that every plausible form of materialism, including the latest theory that the human mind is a by-product of a certain configuration of electrons or electrified points, is a form of atomism. The Greek atomists originated one of the classic forms of philosophical thought.

III. Summary of Pre-Socratic Philosophy

To sum up the course of pre-Socratic philosophy, we may say that it all centers in two problems—what are the substances or elements of which things are made, and what are the causes of the making and unmaking of things, that is, of their origination and decay? In short, *Substance and Causality are the two fundamental concepts of early Greek philosophy.*

For Thales and his followers substance consists of a homogeneous stuff (water, air); Heraclitus has one stuff, too (fire); Empedocles has four (earth, air, fire, and water); Anaxagoras and the Atomists agree in assuming an infinite number of minute particles, but, whereas the particles of the latter differ only in form and mass, those of Anaxagoras differ qualitatively.

For Thales and his followers the primeval stuff is dynamic, that is, has the power of motion and life in itself. Heraclitus invokes two opposing principles—harmony and strife—to account for the mutations of things. Empedocles, likewise, has two principles of motion—love and hate. Anaxagoras separates the principle of motion from the stuff moved, making the original impetus of mind the cause of all motion. Finally, the atomic conception attempts a thoroughly mechanistic explanation of change.

All of these conflicting theories, in more elaborated forms, have engaged man's attention throughout the centuries, since the doctrines of one or more natural substances and causes are attempts to account for the mutation and multiplicity of things in various ways. We have the doctrine of the universal law according to which all changes take place. We have a doctrine of a multitude of elementary substances in place of the one homogeneous substance. We have various theories as to the causes of change: the love and hate of Empedocles, the harmony and strife of Heraclitus, and the elements and Nous of Anaxagoras. We have also the very radical doctrine that the whole world of sense perception is an illusion.

References

* Avey, Albert E., *Readings in Philosophy,* Chapter IV.
* Bakewell, Charles M., *Source Book in Ancient Philosophy,* pp. 57-66.
* Burnet, J., *Greek Philosophy,* Part I, pp. 94-101, 193-201.

CHAPTER V

SKEPTICISM AND SOPHISTRY

I. The Greek Enlightenment

The conflict of the various theories outlined in the two previous chapters brings into the foreground new problems of which man had not hitherto been conscious. The first is the *problem of knowledge.* The debate between the representatives of these theories begets the critical spirit, and man begins to ask himself, what is the relation between my thoughts and the things I think about, between my senses and the physical world, between my intelligence and the world? The development of the critical spirit means further that the spirit of inquiry does not stop with theoretical questions; more particularly, it takes hold of the questions of belief and conduct.

Critical reflection on the ancestral mores and religion of the Greeks resulted in the dissolution of the authority of the mores and traditional beliefs. So the problem of conduct becomes a central problem. The critical spirit directs the light of intelligence upon the inherited customs and beliefs in matters of conduct, statecraft, and religion. So we have the nature and authority of the good, the rules of conduct, and the rites and beliefs of religion, becoming problems of critical study. When man becomes conscious of the fact that there are problems of knowledge, conduct, and religion, and sets about to deal with these problems systematically, then he has become conscious of the central position which his own mind occupies in relation to things.

Out of these problems of knowledge, the good, and religion, arises the consciousness of the problem of spirit, of the meaning and nature of spirit or mind itself. All these problems come to a focus in Plato.

The work of Socrates and Plato was evoked by the critical and inquiring spirit of their time. In this they shared. Critical inquiry into the grounds of custom, usage, and traditional belief, the challenge that these things validate their authority before the bar of reflection, the demand for a rational foundation for law and morals—such was the spirit of the Greek Enlightenment, such is the ruling spirit of every age of enlightenment. The distinction was sharply drawn between practices and rules and beliefs which have the sanction of *convention alone* and those which, *being inherent in the nature of things,* have the sanction of *reason.* The critical spirit may be employed in a chiefly negative fashion and have mainly destructive results. *It may destroy the old beliefs and undermine the authority of the old customs, laws, and moral convictions, without putting any objectively determined, rationally established, principles of conduct and thought in their places. This is precisely what was happening in Athens in the days of Socrates and Plato.* The conflict of theories and the spread of the critical spirit was leading men to the view that there was no objective truth attainable, and that there were no objective or binding principles of social conduct—that self-interest is the primal and only law of human association. Men rejected *in toto* the authority of the traditional customs and established laws and rules of conduct of the city-state. They repudiated the immemorial usages, as well as beliefs, of the ancestral religion of the state, and, in so doing, *they denied the reality of any other principle or sanction for conduct than those of self-interest and power, basing their denial on the impossibility of finding any universally valid propositions.* The Sophists, who were the popular teachers of the time and who instructed their fellow-Greeks in speechmaking, legal argumentation, political debate and practice, as well as in the entire scientific and literary culture of the age, are represented by both Plato and Aristotle as having had, on the whole, an influence that made for frivolous skepticism, the pretense of knowledge without the reality, and the spread of license, venality, and demagoguery.

The doctrine of Heraclitus, *that all things flow and nothing is permanent,* was applied to the problem of knowledge and issued in the famous saying of Protagoras: "Man is the measure of all things; both of the being of things, that they are; and of the non-being of things, that they are not." This saying was interpreted to mean that whatever appears to the senses of the individual to be true or right is the only rule of truth or right for him. The source of all knowledge is held to be sense perception, and this is the result of the meeting of movements without and movements within the sense organ. Since everything is in perpetual flux and movement, the process of perception, in which the thing perceived and the process of perceiving are identical, is always changing; therefore there can be no stable and universally or objectively apprehensible objects of knowledge. It may be that Protagoras did not himself interpret his principle in the completely relativistic, individualistic, and subjectivistic fashion that involves the denial of the objective validity of any propositions in social ethics, law, religion, as well as in science; but it is evident that many of his disciples did so and with good reason.

An even more extreme and dogmatic skepticism was that of the sophist Gorgias, who is reputed to have said: (1) nothing is; for that which is cannot be thought, either as one or many, imperishable or perishable; (2) if anything were it could not be known, for knowing and the object known must be different, otherwise error were impossible, but if knowing and the object known be different the one cannot compass the other; (3) if anyone knew anything he could not communicate it, since communication requires signs, and the signs and the things signified are different.

It was on account of their pretensions to universal wisdom and capacity to instruct their fellows, coupled with intellectual frivolity, demagogical shallowness and inordinate greed for gain and renown, that Plato so mercilessly pilloried the sophists. He probably did some of them some injustice. Nevertheless, it seems evident that, at the time when Plato became the pupil of Socrates, there was rife among the Athenian intelligentsia a spirit of skepticism, smart, irreverent, flippant, superficial, and pretentious, which was made the cover for private license; and for chicanery, corruption, violent demagoguery, and partisanship, and ruthless pursuit of self-interest, in the body politic. No one can reflect on the fact that the conviction of Socrates was due to Athenian political intrigue, or on the evidence from Plato's dialogues, and avoid the conclusion that the moral and social skepticism fostered by the Sophists fell in with and reinforced the evil tendencies of the Athenian democracy. Both the extreme radicals and standpatters of the present hour would do well to ponder a bit on this historical situation. Socrates and Plato tried to save Athens. Both failed, and the political life of Greece soon became extinct. Since then she has enjoyed only the vicarious and spiritual immortality of her prophets, whom she rejected.

After the days of Plato and Aristotle skepticism was developed in more systematic form. We will now consider the arguments for it.

II. Skepticism

Skepticism literally means a thoughtful inquiry, the looking at a problem in a disinterested spirit, the surveying of a question from many sides. In this sense it is the very essence of philosophy and science. It has come to have, however, a new meaning, that is, it doubts the possibility of knowledge. Skepticism may be either partial or complete. Most of the great Greek philosophers, Plato among them, denied that the senses alone give us true knowledge. These great thinkers held that we could know reality through reason. Thus they were rationalists, not skeptics. In fact there is scarcely a great philosopher who was a thorough skeptic, save David Hume, and even Hume held that utter skepticism could not be maintained in practical life.

Under the head of complete skepticism we have what is called *dogmatic* skepticism, the denial of the possibility of knowledge. This is often identified with agnosticism. (This term was coined by Huxley, and he did not mean dogmatic skepticism but an attitude of ignorance in regard to ultimate problems.) *Critical* skepticism involves suspense of judgment on all problems. This form of skepticism was first formulated by Pyrrho, 365-275 B. C., and was further developed by Carneades, 215-130 B. C. Dogmatic skepticism is self-contradictory, for to say that it is impossible to know is to make a dogmatic statement which claims to be truth. It asserts so much as to the nature of mind and reality as to negate its own presuppositions. A skeptic of this kind is an arrant dogmatist. Pyrrhonic skepticism tries hard not to contradict itself. It is critical. Its standpoint is that we are not certain whether we know something or whether we can know nothing. Since we do not know whether we do know nothing or something, the only consistent attitude is that in which there is a suspension of all judgment. To be thoroughly consistent, the Pyrrhonic skeptic would have to hold that he was not certain whether we ought to suspend judgment. The skeptic, to be consistent in all respects, should add that he cannot know whether one ought to say that one ought to suspend judgment, and that one cannot know whether one cannot know whether one ought to say that one ought to suspend judgment and so on *ad infinitum.* Carneades argues that since certitude is impossible, (a dogmatic statement!) then probability is the guide of life, and he further holds that there are degrees of probability:

1. The first degree is plausibility.
2. A proposition may be not only plausible but also not contradicted by other sensations, and thus has added plausibility.
3. A proposition thoroughly consistent with other propositions is still more plausible.

At this point Carneades, in making consistency his basis or test of judgment, is inconsistent with his initial proposition.

Practically all the arguments of present skeptics were devised by the Greek skeptics. The first and chiefest argument is the argument against the trustworthiness of the senses. Skeptics for the most part presuppose a sensationalistic theory of knowledge, and then, noting the unreliability of the senses, they either doubt or deny the possibility of knowledge.

Zeno, the Eleatic, had already developed, with great acuteness, arguments against the trustworthiness of sense perception, based on their contradictory deliverances. But Zeno had complete faith in the power of reason to apprehend reality. This faith is lacking in the skeptics, who trust neither the senses nor reason. Hence, the arguments of the later skeptics are not of the same rationalistic character as those of Zeno and his School. The later arguments are of a more empirical nature.

The first and chief set of arguments for skepticism are empirical ones. They are drawn from considerations involved in the limitations and variations of sense perception. These arguments fall under four heads:

1. Variations are due to differences in the organization of animal forms. The various species have various degrees of sensitivity of sensation. Even human beings differ in their sensory reactions, some being duller in one sense and more active in some other sense. It is a notorious fact, says the skeptic, that there is no use in discussing tastes; "de gustibus non disputandum." "One man's meat is another man's poison."

2. The second body of items in support of skepticism is drawn from the variations of an object's appearance to the different sense organs. An orange is round and yellow to the eye, it is rough to the touch, sweet to the taste, and to the merchant it means a certain amount of cash.

3. The same individual's organism varies from time to time. If one has a bad cold in one's head, then the delicate flavor of food does not exist for him; and to one having either fever or chills, the temperature conditions are quite different from what they are to the same individual in a normal condition.

4. There are all sorts of differences in men's reactions to their surroundings which are due to moral customs, beliefs, traditions, prejudices. The effects of environment and early habits largely determine what we regard as right or wrong, true or false, beautiful or ugly. Our so-called judgments about these types of relations are largely, if not entirely, determined by education, habit, and environment. A study of the different peoples at different levels of social development also indicates this. These four types

of argument are all based on the relativity of the percipient organism.

There is still another group of differences which make valid knowledge impossible. Here fall cases of the relativity of the objects themselves. The object depends for its sensory qualities upon its relation to other objects. A distant object looks smaller than the same object near by; an object in bright light has a different color from the same object in twilight. This holds true also of sounds. Qualities differ also according to quantities. A man, for instance, may take a little wine and feel good; he may take more and feel bumptious; he takes still more and he gets roaring drunk. Arsenic in its behavior also shows pronounced differences in reaction in proportion to the quantity taken. Qualities all seem to vary with quantities.

All judgments are relative. Thought cannot give us the truth. Even in the special sciences, it is seen that demonstrations proceed from underlying assumptions, and these assumptions, which are the final grounds of knowledge, are without proof.

The Stoic philosophers maintained that true propositions are those which are clear and self-evident. But, says the skeptic, clearness and self-evidence is a matter that is wholly relative to the individual. What is clear and self-evident to one person, may be the opposite of what appears so to another person. The Stoics formulated a second criterion, namely, the "consensus gentium." This means the universal consent of mankind to a proposition. At this point again the skeptic replies, there is no such proposition.

The conclusion of the whole matter is this: The wise man will not be sure that he can be sure of anything. He will guide his life wholly by probability. Like Cratylus and others, he will not pass judgments; he will not even wag his thumb.

I shall now briefly indicate the nature of the reply to

skepticism. As to sense perception, it can be said that the very fact that mind recognizes the inconsistencies of different reactions of different individuals and species is due to the ability of thought to formulate standards of truth. Doubt means inquiry, a thoughtful turning over of things, and this in turn implies reference to a standard. I cannot doubt the deliverances of sense unless I already have a standard. In physics we have our standard thermometer and our standards of weight and measure. In all our experimental investigations care is taken to have the standard constant and to eliminate all disturbing conditions. In science the statistical method has for its chief function the reduction of error to a minimum. As to thought, it must be admitted that knowledge does ultimately rest on assumptions. We do assume the validity of certain basic principles. The three laws of thought are illustrative of this, and in our empirical investigations we assume the uniformity of nature. Having made these the most universal and most fundamental working hypotheses, we then proceed to learn to control nature.

The ultimate standard of truth is not a judgment of all mankind,—"tot homines, tot sententiæ," so many men, so many opinions. There are all kinds of human thinkers, good, poor, and indifferent. Truth in science is not determined by counting heads or noses. Many heads have very little in them. Even in social and political matters, the majority is not always right. But there is, however, a criterion or standard. True propositions are those that are consistent with one another and with the further interpretation of experience.

References

* Avey, Albert E., *Readings in Philosophy,* Chapter V.
* Burnet, J., *Greek Philosophy,* Part I, pp. 105-125.

* *Encyclopædia Britannica,* 11th ed., Articles *Sophists* and *Skeptics.*

* MacColl, H., *The Greek Skeptics.*

Patrick, Mary Mills, *Sextus Empiricus.*

* Rogers, Arthur K., *A Student's History of Philosophy,* pp. 37-39 and 160-165.

* Thilly, Frank, *History of Philosophy,* pp. 40-49 and 116-120.

* Windelband, W., *History of Ancient Philosophy,* pp. 100-123 and 329-336.

* Zeller, Edward, *Greek Philosophy,* pp. 268-273.

Zeller, Edward, *Stoics, Epicureans and Skeptics.*

CHAPTER VI

THE PERSONALITY, MISSION, AND INFLUENCE OF SOCRATES

I. The Personality of Socrates

It is impossible to separate the teaching of Socrates from that of Plato. Plato makes Socrates his mouthpiece. It is a difficult and perhaps insoluble problem as to where to draw the line of separation between their doctrines.

Xenophon, who wrote, in his Memorabilia of his revered master, an account of the personality and teaching of Socrates, was an upright soldier, but was incapable of conveying an adequate account of the philosophical teachings of Socrates. He conveys only the reverence of an honest soldier for the greatest man he ever knew. In Aristotle also, we have some condensed information as to Socrates. Here we are told that Socrates was the first philosopher to develop deduction and induction as a means of definition; and further, that he was the first to develop the process of division or classification of concepts.

Socrates was in 469 B. C., at a time when Athens was passing through the most brilliant period of her history. From 479 to 431 Athens was the most brilliant of all city states. Socrates died in 399 B. C. by drinking hemlock poison in fulfillment of the sentence of death imposed upon him by the Athenian jury.

Athens had entered upon the greatest period of her history, upon her age of supreme sacrifice and effort; and it was in just such an age that she developed her greatest glory. (The age of Shakespeare, and the present situation in America afford epochs that are quite similar to this.) Socrates' work was carried on (as he prophesied it would be) by Plato, the greatest of all prose writers. He in turn was followed by Aristotle, "the master of those who know."

The age of Socrates was one of enlightenment, criticism, an age of keen intellectual activity. This is evidenced by the great activity of the Sophists. This age of inquiry and criticism was succeeded by an age of creativeness. Athens was not only the center of Greek political life; it was also an intellectual center. This age in Athens was, in view of its brevity and the comparatively small size of the Athenian state, the greatest intellectual period in the history of the world.

The Sophists, or "wise men," sarcastically so-called by Plato who did not like them, are contrasted with the philosophers as lovers of wisdom, who do not pretend to be wise. The Sophists arose in response to a definite social situation. They were professional teachers in a time when there were no colleges and universities. Plato's Academy was founded and directed by Plato, and it is here that we first find the true features of a university, namely:

1. Research into all fields of knowledge
2. The training of men for public service

Plato carried on his work in the belief that the state could not prosper without using the best trained men that were available. This was the high standard of Plato's academy. As contrasted with this, in our state life, men of the highest training are often not wanted in public life.

The spirit of critical inquiry was rife in Athens as it was in France before the French Revolution, and as it is in America to-day. It was an inevitable consequence that, in such a situation, hoary customs and time-honored traditions and beliefs would be called into question. Students in the colleges and universities of America to-day, coming into touch with the sciences and philosophy, may be similarly disturbed in their views. But this questioning attitude must be aroused if there is to be personal development and progress. The same is true in the life of a state. Traditions and customs must be critically analyzed and subjected to rational treatment.

The Sophists made many claims, one being that they were able to make the worse cause appear the better. Some of them, notably Protagoras, held the view that man is the measure of all things. There are, indeed, two ways of taking this attitude of the Sophists: First, the individual with all his limitations, that is, the particular, changeable individual, may be taken as the measure of all things; second, human nature in general, that is, the immutable and necessary rational and moral element common to all mankind, may be taken as the measure of all things. If the first view be accepted, then there is nothing objective in our moral distinctions and rules for conduct, and it may even seem that there are no means by which objective truth and good can be ascertained. It was in this attitude that some of the Sophists pandered to the gilded youth of their day and taught them that whatever one may want to do is right. Conservatism took alarm at this teaching. The standpatters of the day maintained that Athens was going to ruin, and that all civic foundations were being undermined.[1] The solution offered by the standpatters of the day was that this procedure must be stamped out and that the customs of the city state must be blindly and unquestionably accepted and obeyed. "The old is the best," this is the constant attitude of the standpatter.

Socrates saw the danger that would result to the individual and to the state from both of these attitudes. He sought to use rhetoric and argumentation for other purposes than to justify the momentary whims and opinions of the

---

[1] See the plays of Aristophanes.

individual. While men were openly preaching that "might is right" and declaring that the only test of conduct is "does it pay in financial or political success," Socrates saw another way out of the dangers of the situation, namely, not by cessation of thought, not by a dumb and blind adherence to tradition, but through earnest and persistent thoughtfulness. The way of reason was the only way out for Socrates. The cure for the ills of the day as proposed by Socrates was not the suspension of reason, but the systematic, persistent exercise of reason.

Socrates felt that the Sophists were not in earnest and not intellectually equipped for the work to which they set themselves. He looked upon them as pretenders, fakers, (a goodly number of such Sophists are at large in our country to-day), men who said one thing to one crowd and something else to another crowd. Their own interest was their constant aim. The trouble with Athens, Socrates saw, was that the leaders had not made a deep inquiry into the principles of conduct and the social order. The way of salvation for the state and the individual, Socrates said, is to think out earnestly the problems of conduct. It was the problem of conduct, and not the problems of the early cosmologists, that engaged Socrates' attention. He cared only for social and ethical inquiries.

Socrates was a man of powerful frame and of great endurance. He was abstemious in his habits, but not ascetic, and was not given to eating or drinking to excess, even though his companions all did so. He was kindly and good-humored, but unflinching in his devotion to the right, noble and magnanimous in temper. He devoted himself whole-heartedly to his mission, and carefully avoided mixing in politics, believing that if he did his life would be shortened. Three times he had the deciding vote on public questions, and at these times he braved the clamor of the multitude and the voice of authority. He faced death without a tremor. His passions and his body were the complete servants of his rational will. He always regarded himself as entrusted with a mission from on high and as being always under divine guidance. He repeatedly spoke of his *dœmon* or spirit, the supernatural, inner voice, which gave him warning at all the crises of life.

Socrates was accused of the following three charges:

1. Corrupting the youth
2. Teaching atheism
3. Introducing false divinities

The real causes of the accusation, however were:

1. Desire for revenge on the part of the exposed humbugs of the day
2. The democratic reaction against the tyrants with some of whom Socrates had been closely associated, notably Alcibiades

Socrates, of all those in Athens interested in the problem of knowledge, knew that he was ignorant. The first step in the acquisition of true knowledge is the consciousness of ignorance.

II. The Method of Socrates

Socrates' method was directed towards elucidating or educing from the ordinary opinions of men in regard to virtue, the good, temperance, justice, et cetera, consistent and adequate conceptions. He believed that there is latent or implicit in moral common sense (in the opinion of the average decent citizen) sound conceptions in regard to conduct, but that these conceptions are implicit, that is, not yet thought about. The ordinary man dealt with particular cases as they arose and had not thought things out. Socrates refers to his art as that of an intellectual midwife. He helped men bring forth conceptions that were latent or implicit in their ordinary opinions.

The following will illustrate his method of procedure:

Suppose the question to be, "What is justice?" The ready answer came: "Justice is an eye for an eye, a tooth for a tooth, good for good, and evil for evil." Socrates would ask: "Is the man who returns good for evil an unjust man?" His answer was: "No; one sees that such a man is just in a much higher degree." Thus by questions and answers he sought to elucidate universal ideas, aiming to get definitions that were applicable to every concrete case.

Instead of the current sophistical view that the thing to do is simply to do what you feel like doing, Socrates maintained that we must reflect, think, and form rational notions of conduct. We must carry rational thinking through to the bitter end. In doing this Socrates took the definitions given off the bat, as it were, by those who knew (thought they knew), and showed that such definitions did not square with the moral common sense of man. Socrates took a definition, set it up as an hypothesis, and then examined it to see if it stood the test at the hands of particular cases. He reflected upon facts and the foundations of hypotheses, and sought to test them by concrete cases. Such was the nature of the Socratic method.

III. The Substance of Socrates' Teaching

The substance of Socrates' teaching may be expressed thus: "Virtue is knowledge; vice is ignorance. No man willingly does evil; every man seeks the good." This seems to be an extraordinary statement. Offhand we would say it is false. "I see and approve the better, but I do the worse"; this statement we would approve. There is a wide gap, we think, between knowing and doing. We ordinarily believe we know what is right. We often say, "where ignorance is bliss, 'tis folly to be wise." We often think that knowledge produces corruption, and that it is wrong to think upon certain sacred matters and other matters that are evil. Socrates held that there could be no permanently good and useful conduct that is not guided by sustained thoughtfulness and that knowledge earnestly sought and used would never lead to evil.

If Socrates were here to-day, he would doubtless say that much of what we call knowledge he would call degraded knowledge, or even not knowledge at all. Our handing out of cold storage pabulum to blindly accepting pupils is not the true way of imparting and acquiring knowledge. Knowledge for Socrates was personal insight which men acquire by their own persistent activity. No one has any genuine knowledge which he has not discovered for himself. We find no peptonized, predigested, after-breakfast knowledge-tablets in Socrates. Belief must cost the sweat of the intellectual brow, or it is not knowledge. It was knowing that had reference to conduct that chiefly interested Socrates. If one persistently endeavors to find out what is right or wrong, one will do so, for he has put his whole personality into the quest. Knowledge that has to do with conduct is only attainable through an active quest; it is the result of a voyage of self-discovery. This voyage of self-discovery must be made by each individual for himself. Only such knowledge is knowledge at all in Socrates' view.

In literature we have some magnificent presentations of persons like Milton's Satan, who knew the difference between good and evil and deliberately chose the evil. Satan says: "Evil, be thou my good." Such an attitude Socrates would regard as impossible. He would say that Satan must have mistakenly regarded *ruling at any cost* as the highest good. In short, Satan's choice Socrates would regard as based on a lack of true insight into the good. And indeed, the prevalent notion is that goodness requires little or no reflection. This is the very opposite of Socrates' view. This view is only the exaggeration of a great truth. Enduring good must be built on knowledge. There has been more evil wrought in this world by ignorant fanatics than by all the wise devils. This conception is strictly in line with Socrates' teaching. There is urgent necessity for the application of knowledge to the conduct of daily life, and it is the little attention that has been paid to the theoretical problems of conduct and social organization that is perhaps responsible for our present international situation. This generation needs to be reminded that Socrates has lived. We are puffed up with knowledge about everything, but we have gained but little knowledge about the social and political conditions of good conduct, and as a consequence of this we have been lately using knowledge in that most stupid business of blowing each other to pieces. By our industrial processes we have increased a thousandfold productivity in material things, but we have not learned how to distribute these goods equitably so as to increase the common weal.

Socrates' conception of goodness was this: Goodness consists in the health or harmony of the soul; it is the subordination and organization of the appetites and impulses under the guidance of reason and the good. This, said Socrates, is the truly useful. There is nothing of use that is comparable to the welfare of the soul.

There is a view current that philosophy is useless, since it does not tell us how to pile up riches, win law cases, achieve political preferment, and operate machines. Socrates would doubtless ask us to-day: "Of what use are your machines, your vast riches, your thousands of pairs of shoes made over a similar pattern, your fast trains, your telegraph lines, your telephones, and motors?" We might reply: "See how luxuriously we live, how sumptuously we fare, how fast we ride, and how readily we communicate with each other!" But Socrates would reply: "Does all this contribute to the health and harmony of the individual? Does it add to the poise and harmony of the people?" The health and harmony of the soul are the only ends that are supremely worth seeking, and thus the good alone is truly useful.

In matters of religion Socrates never spoke disrespectfully or lightly of the finer aspects of the traditional forms of Greek religious life. Evidently his own belief was that there is but one divine being or principle, the guardian of righteousness, the moral governor of the universe. The deepest article in his own faith was this, "No evil can happen to a good man either in this life or in any to come." A supreme righteous order rules in the universe, and ultimately no harm can happen to a good man. It is, indeed, far better to suffer than to do an injustice. To return evil for evil is to injure one's own self. Such were the moral intuitions of Socrates. Coupled with these he had also a strong hope of immortality.

References

ARISTOTLE, *Metaphysics* (I, 6; XIII, 4), translated by W. D. Ross.

* AVEY, ALBERT E., *Readings in Philosophy,* Chapter VI.

BENN, ALFRED W., *The Greek Philosophers.*

BURNET, JOHN, *Greek Philosophy,* Part I, pp. 126-192.

* CROSS, R. NICOL, *Socrates, The Man and His Mission.*

* *Encyclopædia Britannica,* 11th ed., Article "Socrates."

GOMPERZ, THEODOR, *Greek Thinkers,* Vol. I.

GROTE, GEORGE, *History of Greece,* Vol. VII.

* PLATO'S *Dialogues,* translation by Jowett; especially "Charmides," "Crito," "Euthyphro," "Gorgias," "Meno," "Protagoras," "Apology," "Phædo," "Symposium," "Phædrus."

* THILLY, FRANK, *History of Philosophy,* pp. 50-58.

* XENOPHON, *Memorabilia.*

* ZELLER, EDWARD, *Outlines of Greek Philosophy,* pp. 103-118.

ZELLER, EDWARD, *Socrates and the Socratic Schools.*

CHAPTER VII

PLATO (427–347 B. C.)

Plato extends the Socratic method of inquiry to other spheres, such as mathematics and the physical sciences. There were four great problems which Plato attempted to solve, namely:

1. The problem of truth and of knowledge (Logic and Epistemology).
2. The problem of the nature of ultimate reality (Metaphysics and Philosophy of Religion).
3. The problem of the soul. This is the problem of philosophical psychology.
4. The problem of values, that is, what is the good for men in society, and by what kind of conduct and social organization can the good be attained? (Ethics and Politics.)

I. The Problem of Truth and Knowledge (Logic)

In the skeptical theory of the Sophists, knowledge was derived from sense perception. Truth is therefore simply what you taste, touch, smell, feel, see. This theory Plato criticized. If this is the nature of truth, he argues, then there is no truth. The pig or dog-faced baboon is a measure of truth equally with the wisest man. Indeed "wisest" has then no meaning. This view denies that there is any test or standard of truth. Thus these skeptics, by saying that there are no standards of truth, refute themselves. If there is no truth this statement itself is not true.

Plato does not deny that sensation is a factor in our knowing. Sensations furnish the stimuli by which we are led to think. True knowledge, however, is the soul's conversation with itself. By this Plato meant that knowledge is arrived at through the activity of reason or of thought, and not through the senses alone. The senses furnish the stimuli and the material for knowledge, but this material must be reflected upon before we can have knowledge.

Plato insisted that knowledge is reminiscence. Inasmuch as we are unable to account for knowledge in terms of the senses and inasmuch as we have knowledge, the soul must have been born with an inherent capacity for it, and only gradually does the soul awaken to a consciousness of the knowledge that is implicit in its own being. Plato is here formulating the view that true thinking is not something derived from, but applied to, sense perception. True knowledge is not to be explained as the result of sensation or sense perception. We do not apprehend the contents of true knowledge through the senses alone; there must therefore be an inborn capacity in the soul which comes to consciousness through the stimulation of sense perception. Sense perception is merely the occasion for getting knowledge, but there is no possibility of deriving knowledge from the qualities of sense perception alone. This position of Plato is expressed in Wordsworth's "Ode on The Intimations of Immortality" when he says:

> The Soul that rises with us, our life's Star,
> Hath had elsewhere its setting,
> And cometh from afar:
> Not in entire forgetfulness,
> And not in utter nakedness,
> But trailing clouds of glory do we come
> From God, who is our home.

What Plato means by the doctrine that all true knowledge is recollection, is probably that genuine knowledge, which a man really gains and possesses, is the result always of his own intellectual self-activity. It is not put into the mind from without, but is evoked or educed by external stimulation, which stirs the mind to self-activity. Thus, knowledge is the result only of the sustained energy of the mind itself, which is incited or occasioned, but never produced, by the influence of a teacher or a sensory experience.

Consider some of the kinds of knowledge that Plato has in mind. Knowledge of relationships is one kind or type. Relationships are not proved through the senses. Suppose that we deal with the properties of a triangle. We say that the three interior angles are equal to 180 degrees. Draw as many triangles as one chooses; they all differ in size, shape, et cetera, and of them all we say that the three interior angles of any triangle equal 180 degrees. But it is not true of these particular triangles as we measure them, for we cannot measure them absolutely. All actually figured triangles are more or less than we define them to be. We cannot draw a line having no breadth. Thus all the way through the complete body of mathematical relations there is something absolute about these relations that is not perceived by the senses.

Note briefly the relations: equals, greater than, and less than. Suppose I say that John Smith equals in height John Brown. He may also be shorter than X and taller than Y. Therefore John Brown is at the same time equal to, shorter than, and taller than. Columbus is north of Circleville and south of Delaware. Columbus is also east of Dayton and west of Zanesville. Columbus is therefore both north, south, east, and west. We do not apprehend the relation of direction through perception alone. We do not perceive north and south. We cannot say where north begins and south ends. It is only by thought that these relations are apprehended.

In knowledge we further classify data. There is no knowledge without the systematic ordering of things we have knowledge about. We order things in groups, series, classes. I refer to Teddy, my dog. There are dogs and men with this name. What do I mean by dog, man, bear? By man I mean a specific type of being who belongs to a certain class distinct from dogs, and that this class is distinguished by certain characteristics. The empiricist claims that we perceive or "sense" those characteristics. Suppose that we had seen a bear that walked like a man; would it be necessary to interpret and to classify that bear as a man? There must be a body of typical ways of behavior present before we classify the object as a man. As every triangle is a particular case of triangularity, so every man is a particular case of humanity. He shares in the attributes of humanity which make him such. No single man, however, embodies absolutely the attributes of humanity. Each individual is only a partial embodiment of these attributes, and as this is the case we do not perceive the attributes of humanity by the senses. We perceive through the senses only the particular individuals, and no individual incorporates all the attributes of a class; no individual is the universal man. No man is humanity; no dog is caninity; no horse is equinity. One perceives this man, this dog, this horse, and that exhausts the range of perception.

Justice, injustice, temperance, and intemperance—what about these moral attributes? We never say of any particular act that it is *the* complete embodiment of self-control. We never think that any act embodies all of justice. Each act is *an* embodiment of some universal quality or qualities. Every one of our experiences implies that there is a universal, and the universal is thought, not perceived, apprehended by the reason, and not through the senses. Mathematical relations, logical relations, class terms or class concepts, such as humanity, caninity, ideas of value (good, evil, beautiful); these are universals known only through the intellect, and only through these is knowledge possible. Without reasoning there would be only a disconnected riot, no sequence of perceptions. That is what our experience would be without thought. But the fact that our experience is not such a riot, the fact that we order and classify and serialize all the facts of nature and the moral life, implies that the soul is born with the capacity to think universals.

The main types of these universals are:

1. Relationships
2. Class concepts
3. Values

What we grasp with our senses alone is without thought. Sense material is mutable, it ever fluctuates. Long since, Heraclitus said that the world is in constant flux. These universals, however, are not in the flux, they are changeless and eternal. The propositions of geometry are eternally true; they do not depend upon someone seeing or smelling them. And we indicate this fact by saying that truth is discovered and not made or invented. The same consideration is true in regard to all relationships. Relationships never fluctuate. Equality remains equality, no matter what the empirical condition of any particular object may be. The relationship "greater than" is always "greater than." *Particular things* become equal to, greater than, less than other particular things, but *universals* remain eternally the same. The fact that we judge acts as just and unjust means that there is a universal, unchanging justice. There is a universal of temperance or self-control. There is also a universal of beauty. Men may come and men may go but "humanity" remains forever the same. The type remains constant, and it is only on the basis of this permanence of type that all our forms of classifications are possible.

Suppose that some explorer discovered a new type of animal life in some distant country and that the scientists were not sure whether this newly discovered creature is an anthropoid ape or a man. How would this new specimen be classified? The scientist seeks to know whether it has tools, whether it speaks, whether it has society, art, et cetera, that is, the scientist applies the universal idea of humanity and only on this basis can the new instance be manipulated.

The means by which we acquire or develop knowledge is through the possession by the soul of this capacity for grasping universals. True knowledge comes only from the activity of the soul in the acts of ordering and classifying the particular data in terms of the universals.

II. The Platonic Theory of Reality (*Metaphysics*)

These universals through which we know, Plato calls *Ideas* (εἴδη, ἰδέαι) forms, kinds, types, universals. These words all mean the same in Plato.

In the Platonic theory there are two realms. The one is the realm of the *Ideas,* which is the realm of the eternal. The other is the realm of sense perception. This is the region of the mutable.

It is important to guard from the beginning against a confusion which prevails even in the camps of philosophers themselves as to the use of the Platonic term *idea.* The ordinary man takes ideas to be something in someone's mind. This is the psychological sense of the term idea, and this use we have inherited from Locke, Berkeley, and other British empiricists. These men declare that we know only what is in the mind, therefore we cannot know an objective physical world. Plato is not a subjective idealist. To damn a dog we need only call him a bad name—this has been done in the case of Plato, but the Platonic idea is never intended to be something *in our mind.* The Platonic idea is a form, a pattern, a universal type, and exists whether any human mind apprehends it or not. These ideas exist eternally in the realm of ideas. Thus we see that Plato does not mean what we usually mean by ideas —they are patterns, forms of which the things of sense are merely bad copies or imitations. Or again, a Platonic idea is an eternally existing type seeking embodiment in particular contents, and because of the obstructing character of the material, no single particular is an adequate embodiment of the idea.

This brings us to Plato's conception of matter. He called it nonbeing (τὸ μὴ ὄν). Matter in Plato is the primitive, formless stuff out of which individual specimens or beings are formed through the influence of ideas or universal types. He does not mean, however, that matter does not exist; he means to suggest that it is not a *specific* type of being. He means to imply that there is indefinite potentiality. Matter is nothing in itself, but it is that out of which all particular things are made.

What then is the Platonic conception of the mode of operation of universals on matter? At this point Plato has a variety of answers. Things of sense, and also our particular acts, get their specific characteristics by participation in or imitation of the ideas. Every just act shares in the idea of justice, every man shares in the idea of humanity. The realm of matter is the abstract possibility of both particular beings and particular acts. There are therefore three logically distinguishable factors or aspects of reality:

1. The Ideas, the perfect realities
2. Particular things and acts, which actually exist
3. Pure Matter or Nonbeing. This is an abstraction and does not exist *as such*

What exist are particular facts, which are due to the shaping influence of the Ideas working on matter.

The ideas are dynamic, they are causes. They effect the work of molding matter into the form of particular things that exist in the world of our experience. Our world is, therefore, the product of the causal action of ideas on matter. If the ideas are eternal and thus have causal efficacy, why do they not produce perfect particulars? Why does not the kingdom of God immediately emerge? Why does not perfection in our ethical experience manifest itself? Here in our world there are no perfect dogs, no perfect justice, no perfect wisdom. Why not? The source of all particular things is perfect. The reason why no particular instance is perfect is that matter offers obstruction. It is recalcitrant to the operation of the ideas. Matter is mulish. There is a brute, irrational necessity in matter that obstructs the realization of ideas in matter. The Platonic view, therefore, is a *teleological idealism* involving a *dualistic* element. It is teleological in that it interprets the world in terms of purpose or final cause. It is dualistic in its conception of the two kinds of existence, matter and ideas.

Aristotle holds that Plato severed the realm of ideas from the world of sense. Whether or not Aristotle's criticism be just, at any rate we are justified in saying that there is a dualistic tinge in Platonism. But whether Plato regarded the realm of Ideas as constituting *in itself*, an entirely *separate world*, one existing quite apart from the material embodiments of the Ideas, is a question in the interpretation of Plato into which there is not space to enter here. At least he meant that there are two clearly distinct orders of being:

1. Order of ideas
2. Order of perceptual existence

The order of ideas is *above,* but it enters into and shapes the order of matter into perceptual existence. The realm of ideas is thus both *transcendent* and *immanent.* The ideas of Plato are transcendent in that they go beyond actual experience, and are immanent in that they are indwelling and operative in experience. Plato's theory of reality is also pluralistic to this extent, namely, that there is an indefinitely large number of universals, each of which really exists. The essence of pluralism is that there are many existents, many beings that exist. But Platonic philosophy is not a chaotic pluralism. The ideas constitute a system, the copestone of which system is the supreme, unitary idea—The Good, the many in one or the one in many.

It is unlikely that Plato meant that the two logically distinct spheres, perceptual existence and the ideas, should be regarded as two wholly sundered worlds. The probability is that he regarded them simply as logically distinct *orders* of existence. It is not easy, however, to say what Plato's view was. He examines the difficulties in the way of his own theories and repeatedly revises them. His mind did not crystallize into an unyielding structure. In this respect Plato is the paragon of scholars. The constant prayer of the scholar should be this: "God deliver me from having a crystallized mind, from having a shut up mind." There is nothing so impenetrable as such a mind. It is more impenetrable than steel. There are minds into which no novel idea can penetrate.

The lowest factor of existence is that of brute matter —mere matter which, in itself, is nonbeing. The precise meaning of this concept in Plato's system is not clear. Some authorities say that by mere matter he meant space. At any rate it is the formless stuff about which nothing more could be said, because it is formless. The second factor is the realm of sense experience, and in this realm we can distinguish a number of stages. As an illustration, one may take a tree. The tree embodies more universals than its seed. Imagine this tree sawed into planks. The planks mean more than the log. These planks may be further utilized and elaborate pieces of furniture made out of them. The furniture embodies more universals than the planks. An amœba is not a very highly organized being, but man is highly organized, and thus he expresses more and higher universals. The scholar is much higher than the ditch digger because he also embodies a greater diversity of universals. You may take two volumes, both made out of wood pulp. Suppose that one of these is the latest best seller, and the other a volume of Plato or Bergson. The difference between these two is tremendous. The Plato or Bergson is vastly richer in *meanings,* that is, universals, than the best seller. The third factor is the realm of ideas or universals. Whether this is for Plato an entirely separate realm that exists by itself and communicates itself to the lower stages of existence is not clear. At any rate, this much is clear, that the Ideas or Universals are the formative and ordering principles or powers from which all finite beings derive their structures, their places, and worths in the order of existence. All meanings and values are derived from the realm of universals.

The particular thing participates in many ideas or universals. Plato does not mean that man participates in nothing but humanity, or that dog participates only in caninity. A particular is a meeting-point for many universals. If this were not the case one could never predicate any attribute of any subject. The only possibility would be to say, man is man and dog is dog, et cetera. But we say,

Socrates is { good, wise, older than, shorter than, et cetera.

Good, however, is not tall, or young, or old, Good is good. But unless the particular does participate in a multiplicity of universals, it would be contradictory to make any judgments. Only on this basis is predication possible. The empirical world, therefore, is seen to be a system, not a chaos. For the universals constitute the network that binds particulars together. Anything may have anything in common with something else. A bottle of ink on the table and the symbol, square root of two, on the blackboard, have the common character of being in the same spatial whole. It is a fact, therefore, that every individual is a meeting-point of ideas, and thus is the sense world constituted a system.

Particulars of sense perception never adequately embody universals, and it is for this reason that sense particulars are always imperfect. Inasmuch as particulars are a system through sharing in the universals, the universals themselves constitute a system. All the ideas, or forms (of which the particulars are the imperfect embodiments), constitute a system. The forms are all interrelated, and, though we may not see how *all* the universals are related, we can see how *some* are, as, ideas of justice and wisdom. We see that we cannot be truly brave without being just. We can see how moral qualities are interrelated. We can also see how certain metaphysical universals, as one and many, sameness and difference, are related. Sameness has no meaning apart from the idea of difference, and vice versa: If the world were a blank identity—as Hegel said, a dark night in which all cows are black—then our judgments involving predications of differences in all their forms would be impossible. It is the fundamental contention of Plato that universals are interrelated.

The supreme work of knowledge is to discover what are the true universals or Ideas and how they are related. The business of right conduct is to live by the light of the Ideas.

The *idea of the good* is the copestone of the Platonic system. This is the supreme idea. The *Idea of the good* is, for Plato, at once *the ultimate Source or Ground of all concrete existence, and the eternally real Ideal or Pattern of all excellence.* All earthly beauty is an imperfect reflection of the Eternal Beauty, all earthly truth a fragmentary apprehension of the Eternal Truth, and all earthly good a copy of the Eternal Good. The Eternal Good, the unitary principle of all Truth and Beauty, the changeless fulfillment of values is GOD. God, for Plato, is *the principle of absolute spiritual perfection,* everlastingly real, the source of all lesser perfections and the pole star of the spirit. The spirit in man is awakened first to the love of beautiful bodies; thence it passes to the love of souls; thence to love of the Ideas; its final love is for God. Plato's rationalism ends in a mystical vision of union with the Divine. All the order and intelligibility, all the meaningfulness in our world, is an expression of the divine and absolute reality. In so far as we understand and feel and act wisely, just so far we grow in character and intellect into the likeness of the absolute and divine reality.

The Final Cause of the world is the Idea of the Good. The world exists in order that the good may be expressed in a multitude of beings. Plato says that God, being animated by love and having no jealousy, desires that all things should be as like him as possible.

As to the details of creation, it is impossible to give any

exact scientific account. The doctrine of the ideas, however, Plato holds is scientific. It is not a myth, although he invents many myths, and many of these have entered deeply into the texture of Christian theology. Before creation there was this primeval potentiality of things (matter), and out of this God fashions the world. In doing this God first creates the Demiurge, the agency of creation intermediate between Him and the world to be created. This is the divine, creative principle in making the world. Its functions are like those of the Logos in the New Testament. This demiurge is the energy of God at work. The demiurge then fashioned a world soul, and then fashioned souls for each planet and star, after which he fashioned souls for human beings. Thus we have:

1. World soul
2. Planetary souls.
3. Human souls

All this process is effected that there may be as many souls as possible in the likeness of the divine.

III. Plato's Doctrine of the Soul (*Psychology*)

The soul means for Plato the principle of life and consciousness. We are here interested in his doctrine of the nature of the human soul. The human soul is tripartite:

1. Highest part (noetic part), νοῦς; its seat is in the head;
2. Next lower part (executive part), θυμός; its seat is in the thorax;
3. The lowest part (appetitive part), επιθυμία; its seat is in the abdomen.

In the human being, however, these parts form an interacting whole.

Plato compares the human soul to a chariot drawn by two steeds and driven by a charioteer. The two steeds are the spirited part and the part which consists of the animal desires. Desire wishes to turn aside and delay at the pleasant places of life while the spirited part is impetuous to rush on, and so it is the province of *nous* or reason to regulate the conduct of these two.

Nous is divine. The reason of man is the highest source of knowledge. It is through the reason that we apprehend universals. And it is this part of the soul that did not originate with the body. It is this rational part of the soul which shares *directly* in the nature of the ideas. The other parts thus share only so far as they are penetrated by reason. The origin and destiny of the νοῦς is independent of the body. True, it is now immersed in the body, but it is independent of the body. In the Phædo this is Plato's main argument for immortality.

IV. Plato's Theory of Human Good

(*Ethics and Social Philosophy*)

Plato does not separate ethics from social philosophy. His position as to the true nature of man is the same as that of Aristotle. Man realizes his nature only through a well-ordered society. The function of the state as the highest form of social organization is the realization of virtue on the part of its citizens. The state exists as an instrument of culture. The chief means whereby the state fulfills its function as such an instrument is education. The ends of education are the development of the *virtues* of the self. Plato is here everlastingly right. This is the only sound theory of the state's function. Plato insists that the state is to afford the means for the fullest development of its citizens, and that education is the chief means. This calls for a clear and consistent doctrine of conduct and character. Plato bases his whole social doctrine on his psychological analysis. The good is the harmonious functioning of the three parts of the soul:

1. The virtue of desire is self-control.
2. The virtue of the spirited part is courage.
3. The virtue of the rational part is philosophic insight.
4. The virtue of the whole system is justice and righteousness.

When one satisfies appetites under the consciousness of consequences, he exercises self-control. When one lets loose his vigor only under proper circumstances, then one exhibits courage. Courage is not the running amuck of rashness. Courage for Plato is the fixed resolve to go ahead and do the right with a clear consciousness of the dangers involved. Wisdom is philosophy, and philosophy is insight into the relations of life. It is love of the truest and the best. The exercise of wisdom is impossible to one who has a keen intellect but no enthusiasm, no love for knowledge and goodness. Wisdom is the fruit of the union of devotion to the best with rational insight.

As to the function of the state, Plato holds that it is to provide adequate means for the development of virtues. It is the cultivation of the individual as a member of society that the state is to effect; and the great truth in Plato is that he bases his social and educational theory on the psychological analysis of the individual. *The state is the individual writ large.*

As to the organization of the state in regard to its end and the mode of reaching it, Plato's idea is that the moral culture of its citizens is what is to be furthered by this organization. And this end will be best furthered if the state be ruled by an aristocracy of character and intellect. Etymologically the term "aristocracy" means the rule of the best and not the rule of those who have inherited wealth or special privilege. *We* mean by aristocracy, a class having special privileges. But this is not Plato's meaning. He invariably means those best trained for the service of the state. It is to make one fitted to play his part in the state that is the real task of life. When one is so fitted, he will have personal well-being. This, however, is not a picture of an actual state; it is the ideal of what a state might be, ought to be.

There are three classes in this ideal state, and they correspond respectively to the three divisions in the soul of the individual. A large number of individuals, Plato thinks, are born without capacity for achieving any high degree of intellectual insight—most people are not born to be philosophers. A good many also are not born to be defenders, guardians, of the state, because they lack that moral courage which is necessary to a guardian. They are to supply the material conditions of life; they are to be agriculturists, artisans, business men, bankers. We think to-day that the business man exercises a much greater amount of insight than Plato ever ascribed to men following this type of service. The virtue which stands out in this class is *self-control.* To be good traders, farmers, artisans, bankers, they must exercise self-control. In this class Plato will allow private property as a stimulus to their more effectually providing the physical conditions for all the social classes. The two upper classes, however, are to be supported at the expense of the state, but are not to be allowed private property. For Plato is of the opinion that the quest for riches would distort their sense of service, would interfere with their disinterestedness of spirit.

The men of strong will, of courage, are to be the guardians, the defenders of the state,—here as well as in the lowest class, Plato, of course, assumes that a modicum of wisdom is required.

The third class consists of philosophers for whom the consuming passion in life is knowledge and virtue. These are to be the kings or rulers in the ideal republic. Plato holds that only those born with the fairest and noblest souls, and trained from their youth up, are fitted to rule. Only the wisest and best should rule. The fundamental virtues of the lower classes are theirs as well as wisdom. Self-control and courage, crowned by the knowledge of the nature and vocation of human life, this is the life of the philosopher. Those born with the highest endowments are to be trained until about fifty years of age. Then they are ready to begin the work of ruling. There are to be no young rulers in the Platonic republic.

Education is the one instrument for realizing this ideal, and in the Republic he outlines his theory of education. The basis of education in early youth is bodily exercises. A sound physical foundation must be laid. There must also be moral instruction and this is to come through narration of myths and of stories, with a view to stimulation of the imagination in the direction of right conduct. There is to be a cultivation of the feelings and an inculcation of right ideals. Before teaching the youths the stories of the past, Plato would take the poets and their stories of early heroes, and, indeed, also the historians, and he would go through them with a blue pencil, he would strike out all unseemly stories of the gods, he would present no intellectual food to the plastic imagination of the child that is degrading or suggestive of evil. Thirdly, music is to be taught. By means of music the individual's feelings are stirred, refined and harmonized; and for all the Greeks the sense of harmony, of proportion, is indispensable to the good life. Plato rests the education of the child on a threefold foundation, namely, physical, moral, and æsthetic.

At the age of about twenty, a selection can be made of those fitted to go on further, and to those so selected, a thorough training is to be given in mathematics. Mathematics is *the* type of science for Plato. Then would come the study of the interrelations of the subjects already studied, the beginning of dialectic or philosophy. At the age of thirty, a still further selection of those excelling in mathematics is made. Those who show a capacity for leadership are now to take up the study of dialectic, this to continue for about five years, after which they are ready to serve the state in minor offices and military commands. Thus at the age of about fifty, having already served the state for approximately fifteen years, those who have acquitted themselves best are qualified to rule and to continue to do so until they retire, whereupon they are supported at the expense of the state, for they have "done their bit."

The idea of the science of eugenics is developed in Plato. We are beginning to-day to think that a child has a right to decent parentage; criminals, idiots, and confirmed drunkards ought not to be allowed to propagate their kind.

Plato was the first to advocate eugenics. He would place marriage under the control of the state. The state exists for the production of the highest type of virtue in the citizen, and for this the individual must be born with good capacities.

Lately we have been diligently and aggressively making the world safe for Democracy. It behooves us now to ask searchingly what Democracy is and what are its limitations? Let us be clear as to what Democracy is to mean and as to what are its possibilities and problems. Plato is everlastingly right in saying that no amount of demagogic oratory will alter the fact that individuals are not born with equal capacities. No romancing about Democracy will alter the fact that a state not run on the basis of merit will never realize the highest good. Any state policy which prevents the best from serving their state has something wrong in it. Even our own democracy has many defects, among which are a general lack of recognition of need of the highest training and best character for service of the state and society in public office and low educational, cultural, and administrative standards. We believe that democracy affords the best opportunity for the individual to develop his native powers, but actually, as a people, we show scant respect for individual distinction outside the fields of business and politics.

Hints to the Study of Socrates-Plato

The dialogues of Plato constitute the most fascinating extant collection of writings by a single philosopher. They all show profundity of intellectual and moral insight, marvellous keenness in analysis, skill in dialectic, and power of comprehensive synthesis. In addition, most of them have a wonderful charm of style and dramatic quality of movement. Nevertheless, their systematic study involves considerable difficulty. The chief sources of this difficulty are: 1. The method pursued is that of persistent *critical inquiry,* "following the argument wherever it leads." The primary aim of the dialogues is to set the reader *thinking* about the great concerns of human life. But the education of the reader has hitherto been, almost invariably, it is safe to say, *dogmatic.* He has been engaged in *learning* facts and theories. The teaching of science in our schools is often even more dogmatic than the teaching of literature and history. He who would profit by Plato must be ready to set out upon a voyage of critical inquiry, without being in a hurry to get into port, and must abandon all "get rich quick" educational aims.[1] 2. The very dramatic and living movement of the dialogues makes it often hard to keep in mind the thread of the argument, since it shifts from one subject to another. But there is always reason for the shift. 3. It is sometimes difficult to say which position taken in the discussion is Plato's own. Usually Socrates is the dramatic mouthpiece of Plato, but the reader must bear in mind that the dialogues are a series of *intellectual or spiritual quests,* proceeding, now inductively now deductively, but *always undogmatically.* Therefore, the arguments *con,* as well as *pro,* are given full consideration. Plato often deliberately aims to bring out the difficulties in his own position. 4. We have no means,

---

[1] Plato's *Dialectic* or Argumentation is both inductive and deductive in method.

except the internal character of the dialogues, for determining their order, and Platonic scholars differ very much on this question. It is clear, for instance, that the Laws are the work of Plato's old age, and that in the Phædo, Phædrus, Philebus, Sophist, Symposium and Republic, we have the expression of Plato's matured views at the zenith of his powers. But where are we to place the Parmenides, which contains a severe criticism of the Theory of Ideas? And are we to regard the Charmides and the Laches, the Protagoras, Meno, Gorgias, as well as the Apology and the Crito, in none of which is the Metaphysical Theory of Ideas fully developed, as earlier works devoted chiefly to perpetuating the Socratic personality and method, or are we to conclude that, since Socrates remains the central figure throughout the dialogues, Socrates was the real author of the Theory of Ideas and Plato only its literary expounder and amplifier? If all the chief dialogues represent the historical Socrates, then he was more than the originator of a method of inquiry which he applied chiefly to moral and political questions. Then he was a dialectician and a synthetic metaphysician or great speculative philosopher. It is beyond the scope of the present volume to discuss this question. I shall assume the prevalent view, which is that Socrates was primarily the author of a method of inquiry, which he applied chiefly to moral and social issues, but not the author of the Platonic Metaphysics or Theory of Ideas. This view is in harmony with the statements of Aristotle, who is usually a trustworthy source.[2]

From this standpoint the chief dialogues of Plato would fall roughly into the following groups: [3]

1. Socratic—Lysis, Laches, Charmides, Euthyphro. Application of Socratic method to the investigation of the meaning of virtue. Crito and Apology (biographical memorials of Socrates).

---

[2] It does not seem possible, in the present state of our knowledge, to draw any sharp dividing line between the work of Socrates and Plato. Nor is it essential to an understanding and appreciation of the Dialogues. One might, indeed, call the whole system the philosophy of "Platocrates."

[3] I am not here attempting to determine the chronological order of the Dialogues. I am not competent to this task. It is clear that certain of the dialogues are, preëminently, memorials of the personality of Socrates, that certain others are dedicated to the discussion of ethical questions in the spirit of Socrates, and that others are concerned with the building up of a systematic theory of knowledge and reality.

2. Refutation of the Relativistic and Skeptical theories of the Sophists and development of a constructive theory of Truth by the Socratic method. Protagoras, Euthydemus, Meno, Gorgias, Theætetus.

3. Full expression of the Platonic Theory of Ideas — Phædo, Phædrus, Symposium, Philebus, Sophist, Republic, especially sections 476 ff., Parmenides.

4. Application of the Theory of Politics and Cosmology respectively; Republic (in part) and Timæus.

5. The Laws.

The following hints may be of aid to the student in reading the dialogues selected. Unless otherwise stated all numbers refer to the sections of the text of Plato which are printed in the pages of the Greek text and the translations.

Protagoras

Notice the essential community of interest of Protagoras and Socrates: both are interested in the moral education of the young. Both hold that virtue can be taught, and that all men have it potentially. Their disagreement is on the *method* of teaching. Notice how Protagoras dictates his views in an authoritative manner (*cf.* the tale of Prometheus, and the discussion of the poets), while Socrates seeks by questions to draw out the ideas of the learner. Notice that Socrates, too, can make speeches, but does not set any value upon that method. Here is the typical opposition between the Socratic-Platonic theory of knowledge and the Sophistical theory. Notice how Socrates bases his conviction, that virtue is teachable, upon the position that virtue is the practical working out of an *idea* or *ideal,* and ideas are the things which above all others are teachable. (*Cf.* the classification of all particular virtues as cases of a single unitary conception.) And note finally that Socrates maintains that pleasure alone is not man's highest good, but the intelligent choice of pleasures.

Meno

Note 1. The general subject of discussion. 2. The line of thought represented by the several characters. 3. The subdivisions of the question. 4. The light thrown upon the following important questions: (a) The Socratic-Platonic theory of virtue, (b) the theory of knowledge, (c) the solution of the

Sophistical difficulty as to how one knows when he knows, (d) the potentiality of even a slave's mind. In the Meno the general subject of discussion is whether Virtue can be taught. The view is advanced that *Virtue,* and hence *Happiness,* depends on *Wisdom* or *Knowledge;* and the doctrine that Knowledge presupposes the latent presence of *Ideas* or *Universals* in the mind, in other words, the Platonic doctrine of *Recollection,* is, for the first time, perhaps, clearly set forth. The conclusion seems negative, but the statement "that virtue is neither natural nor acquired, but an instinct given by God to the virtuous" is really in harmony with the doctrine of Recollection.

Gorgias

The *Gorgias,* which is a fitting companion to the Republic, starts out with an inquiry into the nature of Rhetoric. After some debate, the conclusion is reached that Rhetoric is the art of persuasion about the just and the unjust (453). Then Socrates points out the difference between *belief,* which may be true or false, and *knowledge,* which can only be true. Rhetoric produces false beliefs and gives no instruction. Rhetoric is a form of flattery having to do with politics (463-467). This leads to the inquiry into the end of politics and government. What is power for? Socrates contends that power must be exercised for the sake of the good (468 ff.), and that doing injustice is the greatest of evils, greater even than suffering injustice. He contends too, that the unjust man is more miserable if *not* punished than if punished (473). Injustice, and, in general, the evil of the soul, is the most disgraceful and worst of all things (477). The true rhetoric, then, is of no use in enabling men to excuse injustice (480). The wrongdoer ought to accuse himself, in order to save his soul. At this point Callicles intervenes with the protest that all this philosophy is for youth and children, not for grown-ups, and that Socrates is making himself ridiculous. Callicles takes up the cudgels for politics, first as the rule of the many, then he shifts to the rule of the superior who are wise and courageous. He contends that pleasure is the good (492). Socrates argues that the good is not the same as the pleasant, but the pleasant is for the sake of the good (497 ff.). All seek the good (500), but the bad man does not know how to find it. The good is *order* and *harmony* (504), and the true rhetorician he who seeks to implant justice in the souls of men. There follows a severe indictment of the popular politician, who seeks power by flattery, and thereby makes men worse. Pericles and others are included in this class (509-521). Socrates contends that *he* is the only true politician of his time, since he seeks only *to improve the souls* of his fellow Athenians (522). The dialogue ends with a myth or story, embodying Socrates' belief that the fulfillment of justice requires a future life for the souls of men, in which judgment is meted out to them for the deeds done in the body. Punishment is of two kinds (a) corrective, to improve the souls of those punished, (b) exemplary, in the case of those incapable of being corrected, to warn others who have not yet gotten irreparably lost in wickedness. The Gorgias makes a very vigorous and dramatic contrast between the true life and the false one. It is, in spirit, a truly *Socratic* dialogue. In the ideal of the just man we have one of those *ultimate moral insights* which mankind owes to the prophetic vision of one or two members of its own race.

Theætetus

The dialogue is concerned with the definition of knowledge, and this involves a definition of error. Three conceptions of knowledge are discussed: 1. *Knowledge is perception* (151): 2. *It is true opinion* (187): 3. *It is true opinion, based on insight into the grounds or reasons for it* (201, 202). The first conception of knowledge is that of Protagoras, the Sophist. It is based on the doctrine of Universal Becoming, that is, of the "river-gods" (Heracliteans). If all is in flux, then the individual percipient is the measure of truth. But then a pig or a dog-faced baboon is the measure of all things (161). Then there is no distinction between truth and falsehood. On the universal-flux doctrine there can be no error. But mankind does distinguish true and false (170), and counting heads does not determine truth. Therefore he must be a *wise man* who is the measure of things. *Knowledge does not consist in impressions of sense, but in reasoning about them.* Thinking is systematic reflection, by which the soul contemplates *universals* in all things (185). Thus we do not see and learn *by* the eyes and ears, but *through* them. Note the reasons for rejecting the identification of knowledge with perception in sections 154, 158, 161, 163, 165, 170, 171, 178, 182, 184 f. Note the four proposed explanations of error in sections 189, 191, 192, 193.

Symposium and Phædrus

These two dialogues are best read in sequence, since the theme of the *Symposium* is continued in the first part of the *Phædrus*. The theme is *Love,* which is treated as being the supreme motive in human life and conduct. Love is intermediate between the mortal and the divine (Sym. 203, 204), between having and not having. Love is the desire for immortality, sought through birth in beauty. Love is the desire for the everlasting possession of the good (206 A). The lower love seeks immortality through birth in physical beauty and the procreation of children. The highest love seeks immortality through union with absolute beauty, which is one with the absolutely Good and True—in other words true immortality is attained through spiritual procreation, through the rebirth of the soul into eternity, by the reproduction in it of justice, temperance, wisdom (208). The final cause or goal of all our toils is a life consisting in the contemplation of "beauty absolute, separate, simple and everlasting, which without diminution and without increase, or any change, is imparted to the ever-growing and perishing beauties of all other things" (211). Thus life is an ascent, motivated by the ascent of love or desire, from union with the sensuous to union with the ideal and eternal realities of the spirit.

In the *Phædrus* the same theme is carried on up to Sec. 257. Love is the desire for the beautiful and good (237-241); for union with the divine, which is beauty, wisdom, goodness, and the like. Everyone chooses the object of his affections according to his character (252), and thus sees the beauty that he is able to see, sensuous or ideal. Here we find (245-251) Plato's psychology outlined. The soul is self-moving, therefore eternal, immortal (245); it consists of three parts symbolized as a pair of winged horses, one ignoble and the other noble, driven by a charioteer—the *mind* or *reason.* Mind or intelligent soul alone is able to behold the colorless and formless and intelligible essences of beauty, wisdom, goodness, and the like (247 ff.). Mind is able to do that in this present life, because it has preëxisted. Plato explicitly brings forward the doctrine of *reincarnation* (249 etc.), and of *recollection* or *anamnesis* (250-251), as the only plausible theory to account for the mind's possession and use of universals or abstract ideas. This is the form of *a priorism* or rationalism found in Plato. We shall find it repeated in a more abstruse form in Kant.[4] Truth is the recollection of, the awakening to, in this life, the visions of the eternal essences or ideas formerly seen while dwelling in other realms of being. The soul which attains any vision of truth, beauty and goodness, during its worldly peregrinations, is thereby preserved from harm. In the Symposium and Phædrus love is depicted as a kind of madness or enthusiasm. The lower love of the senses is not evil unless the soul is content to remain in it and does not use it as a ladder to mount to the spiritual love.

The second part of the Phædrus, beginning with S. 257, is a discussion of the nature of rhetoric, and would better be omitted on a first reading.

Phædo

The *Phædo, Republic, Philebus, and Sophist,* constitute a group of dialogues in which the Theory of Ideas, and its application to ethics, social philosophy, metaphysics and religion, are expounded in full and mature form. The *Parmenides* and the *Statesman* belong here, but the Parmenides is too difficult and puzzling a dialogue to be considered by the beginner. In fact, so puzzling is the problem of its relation to the other chief dialogues of the master, that many scholars reject its authenticity.

The *Phædo* is a discourse on the Immortality of the Soul, which develops into a statement of the *Theory of Ideas,* of *Preexistence* and *Recollection.* The immateriality of the intelligent soul, and the contrast between soul and body are strongly emphasized. Death is but the culmination of the constant aim of the lover of wisdom and truth—freedom from the thraldom of the senses (63, 64, 66-69). The soul attains truth, the vision of the abstract and absolute essences—justice, beauty, good (65), mathematical essences or universals such as likeness, unlikeness, equality (73, 74, 75)—not through the eye of the body but through the inward eye. (*Cf.* also 100.) All genuine knowledge is *recollection.* The soul must, therefore, have existed before the body which it now inhabits and will survive the body (73-78). The soul is invisible, since it knows the invisible realities; the body is its instrument (79). The soul is in the likeness of the divine, and immortal, and intelligible, and uniform, and un-

[4] *Cf.* Chapter XVII.

changeable; and the body is in the likeness of the opposites of these qualities (80). The purified soul will depart at death from hence to the invisible world (81). Impure souls will descend lower. Philosophy is the means for the purification of the soul and its consequent release from its bodily prison (82-84). In 85-95 the theory that the soul is the harmony of the body is examined critically and rejected on the ground that it makes the soul depend on the body. The culminating argument, in 101-106, from the nature of opposites, is that the soul is essentially Life and, since this is the opposite of Death, it must be eternal. The discussion ends with a myth or poetic fable in regard to the realms beyond this world and the fate of souls therein. The dominating doctrine of the Phædo is that the supreme reality is a system of *Unchangeable Essences,* the *Ideas.* These are identified with *Life* or *Soul.* By means of the Ideas the changing realm of the sensible order is known. The ruling law of Being is the Good, which is identical with order or Cosmos. Note that the Phædo is the most ascetic or dualistic in strain of Plato's dialogues. Nowhere else does he speak, with such repeated emphasis, of the body as a hindrance and clog to the soul. It is to distort Plato's life view and world view to isolate this single phase of so many-sided and comprehensive a philosophical mind as his and make it representative of the whole. Not only the Symposium and Phædrus, but the treatment of pleasure in the Philebus and elsewhere, and the consideration accorded bodily training in the Republic forbid our regarding Plato as an ascetic kill-joy. His prevailing doctrine is that the body, with its appetites and impulses, is the instrument of the rational soul. There is a bodily soul, the seat of desire and emotion, which is spiritualized through the *Nous* or intelligent soul.

The Republic, Philebus, and Sophist

The Republic is the widest in scope, and the richest in content, of all Plato's dialogues. It is too many-sided to be even briefly summarized here. But attention may be called to some of its most salient features, as an aid to the reader.[5] The controlling purpose of the work is an inquiry into the *nature and end of human society as determined and achieved by Mind. The Republic is a philosophy of society, which is based on a social psy-*

[5] B. Bosanquet, *A Companion to Plato's Republic* is recommended.

chology, a logic, a doctrine of ethical values, a theory of education, and a metaphysics or philosophy of reality and religion. The work sets out, in Book I, from a preliminary examination of popular and sophistical notions of justice. All other virtues are applications of justice considered as a quality of individual character. It is to be noted that Plato uses the same word *dikaiosune,* for *justice* as involved in the right social relationships of individuals, and for *righteousness or goodness* as a quality of individual character. Since the word is usually translated "justice" the reader needs to be on his guard against confusion. The same double usage is found in the New Testament, though, of course, the latter is seldom concerned with questions of political or legal justice. The outcome of Book I is that an examination must be made of the nature of the state. So Book II begins with an inquiry into the origin of the state, which is found in man's economic needs. The conduct of the state, for the satisfaction of these needs, requires a differentiation of functions in its members. There must be guardians, and, in Book II, 374-376, the qualities which these must possess are stated. The problem of their education leads in 377 ff. to a criticism on the poets for their depictions of the Gods. In 379-383 it is insisted that God is not the author of the evil and shameful things found in human beings. Book III, up to 411, continues the examination of poetry, music and other means for the education of the guardians. In 420, at the beginning of Book IV it is insisted that the state is an organic unity, and the object of it is, not to make any one class preëminently happy, but to make the whole state as happy as it can be made. Therefore the guardians are not to have private property. From 428 to the end of Book IV the fundamental virtues are discussed, with reference to the various psychological functions of the soul. Book V, up to 471, discusses the position of women and children in the ruling class. Community is advocated and a similar education for both sexes. Plato then comes to the education of the philosophers, that is, the experts, or men wise in both theory and practice, who are to be the rulers of the state. Plato does not mean that the philosopher-kings should be mere "theorisers." A philosopher is one who loves and does the truth, one whose actions are based on a rational insight into Values and the means by which they can be realized. The distinction is made between *opinion,* which is all the many are capable of having, the *sciences of existents* (what we to-day would call "the special sciences"), and *Dialectic* or *Philosophy* proper, which involves insight into the being and nature of Essences or Ideas. From 505 to 535A there is developed, in outline, Plato's Theory of Knowledge and Reality (Metaphysics). The Supreme Essence, Idea or Form, is the Essential Form of the Good (505); it is the Cause and Ground of all things (508, 509, 517, etc.). It is the Sun of the world of reality and truth. It is not truth, but the condition of our seeing truth. It is not existence, but the condition of the being of existence and of that vision or apprehension of existence, which is truth for the thinker. Thus the good actually transcends existence in power and dignity (509). It is the limit of our inquiries and can hardly be perceived (517). Dialectic or philosophy is the science of the good (533-534). (In this connection should be read 596-7 in Book X where Plato makes the distinction between the "essential bed" the pattern or rule for making a bed, the manufactured bed, and the pictorial imitation of bed. From this section it seems clear that Plato admitted Ideas of artefacts.[6]) At the beginning of Book VII occurs Plato's famous figure of the mass of men as denizens of a cave, chained with their backs to the light, who can never see the true realities but only their shadows as reflected from behind them on the walls of the cave. The function of philosophy is to remove the chains from such as can be taught to see the Forms or Ideas. But the capacity for the gaining of wisdom must be inborn in the soul; otherwise, it cannot be developed by any training. (One cannot make a silk purse out of a sow's ear and most men cannot attain to any height of wisdom!) Note the unflattering portraiture of Greek democracy and Plato's defence of philosophy in 488-502. Dialectic is the *science of sciences,* and mathematics is the gateway to the palace of the royal science[7] (522-535). Book VIII discusses the various forms of political constitutions, and Book IX the character of the tyrannical man, in contrast with that of the happy and just man. Book X, after a discussion of poetic art, concludes with the myth of the Son of Er, setting forth a fable of future retribution for the souls of men. Thus ends the masterpiece of the master of all speculative seers and, with the exception of Jesus of Nazareth, the greatest spiritual creator in

[6] Much controversy has waged about this point. Professor J. S. MacKenzie thinks this passage a bit of playful humor directed by Plato against his misunderstanders.

[7] See the comparison of Plato's and Hegel's *Dialectic* in the note on pp. 266-7.

the recorded history of mankind. The Republic has not the orderly and progressive unity that we should expect from a Plato, were he creating to-day. But, in its interweaving of psychological analysis, ethical, logical, and metaphysical insight, with mystic vision, the Republic achieves a unity and ascends to an altitude that leaves it still peerless. The dominant motive of the entire work is the *perfecting of the human soul,* the fulfillment of the spirit in the beauty of holiness. To this end, the organization of society, the conduct of education, and the vision of truth itself, are all instrumental. Therefore the state is to be constructed and conducted after the analogy of the soul-life (*cf.* 368-9, etc.). Civic virtue or social justice is the fitting of every soul to its proper functions and the exercise of these functions by all souls "as members one of another." Note the æsthetic qualities of the Good (400-403). Rhythm, harmony, or order, in the soul, is the good. Throughout the dialogues of Plato there runs, like a golden thread, the theme that the good is the truly beautiful, that Righteousness, Beauty, and Truth have their concrete and living unity of being and action in the soul that is symmetrically developed and, therefore, functions in an orderly and harmonious manner. The soul that knows the truth and does it, shines with spiritual beauty and is in harmony with the perfect and eternal order—with the Cosmos. For the supreme truth of being is that Reality is a perfectly ordered and harmonious whole, which is the Absolute Good. The Cosmos is a righteous order and altogether lovely. Such is the final insight and message of Plato.

Philebus and *Sophist.* The two outstanding doctrines of these dialogues are—1. The Ideas or Universals constitute a system of forms or types that are in communion with one another, in other words are interrelated; for example, the One and the Many or the Limited and the Unlimited, the Same and the Different, Rest and Motion or Permanence and Change. Each member of a pair implies the other, and also members of other pairs. 2. Mind, or Soul is the Force or Power which is the First and Final Cause of all creation. Mind is the unitary ground of the Ideas.

Philebus. In this dialogue Plato discusses, in a more dialectical or metaphysical fashion, the central theme of the Republic, the Idea of the Good. Setting out from the question whether the good life consists in pleasure or wisdom, the doctrine is developed that the true good consists in a harmonious or symmetrical mixture of thought and feeling, in which thought occupies the ruling place. It is agreed that happiness or well-being of the soul is the good; and (in 12) Socrates suggests that happiness may be a third state of the soul, which is better than either wisdom or pleasure but more akin to wisdom. Both pleasures and sciences are many and diverse (12 ff.); the world of generation or sense experience is an indefinite Many (the Unlimited), but every kind of thing has its Idea or Universal (the Limit or principle of Unity); therefore the One and Many are present in all things (15). Thus the problem of the good involves that of the One and the Many. But we must not be content with this vague insight; in order to attain *scientific insight* we must determine the precise numbers or quantitative proportions which hold in every field. For example, the grammarian must know the *precise* number and relations of speech sounds and letters, the musician of the sounds which yield musical harmony and rhythm; just so with regard to pleasures and sciences (17-18). Pleasure is impossible without soul or mind, since without memory, hope, and knowledge there can be no desire (21). The good life is the union of pleasure and wisdom; it is a harmonious or symmetrical mixture, the union of the infinite and the finite, or the Limit and the more and less (22-23). Throughout the world the same principle obtains; health, music, good weather, involve a commensurable and harmonious intermingling of elements. Law and Order is the universal principle of the Good. The cause of the proper mixture is Mind or Soul (27). Mind is the King of all things good (28). The Whole is a Cosmos or Body, the Universal Organism, with a Soul which rules it. "In the universe there is a mighty infinite and a sufficient limit and a no mean cause which orders and arranges years and seasons and months and may most justly be called reason and mind" (30). There are four classes of existents—the Infinite (so Jowett translates ἄπειρον, it would better be called the Unlimited or Indefinite), the Finite (or Limit), the Mixed (compounded of the two first), and the Cause of the Mixture (23 *et al*). The Infinite is Matter, the Finite is Form, Actual Individuals and Particulars are the union of the two, and Mind is the Cause of the union. In this dialogue Plato clearly seems to identify the Cosmic Mind with God, to regard the latter as the Universal Soul, and the Author or Creator of all order, symmetry, beauty, and harmony in the universe, but he does not withdraw the doctrine elsewhere advanced that the Idea of the Good is above God, being the form or pattern by which he fashions the world. Perhaps Plato meant that God is identical with the Idea of the Good. But this is too large a question to be discussed here (*cf.* the Republic and Timæus).

Pleasures and pains belong to a mixed class. Pleasure is a harmonious mixture; pain is the destruction of a symmetrical union of the finite and infinite (31-32). From 33 to 53 there is an elaborate discussion of various kinds of pleasures and pains; the chief conclusions are: that there are false pleasures, that pleasures and pains are relative, that the most intense or violent pleasures belong to diseased states of the organism, and finally, that the purest pleasures are those of knowledge. The latter conclusion leads (end of 53) to the proposition that pleasure, belonging as it does to the realm of the changing and the many (of generation), has instrumental Value; it exists for the sake of Essence. This is the realm of eternal being, of the Good-in-Itself, of Intrinsic Value (54). In 54-59 the field of knowledge is divided into instrumental or technical knowledge and the contemplative insight into true being or reality. The only knowledge which has intrinsic value is that which yields to the soul some glimpse of Eternal Being. From 60 to the end there is a *résumé* of the argument. The life of true happiness consists in the interfusion of the sensuous by the spiritual, the temporal by the eternal, under the guidance of the ruling principles of Beauty, Symmetry, and Truth. In the good life, and in the Cosmos, the first is Measure, the second is Symmetry, the third is Mind or Wisdom, the fourth is Science, the fifth the Pure Pleasures of the Soul, and there is no sixth. Thus the Philebus emphasizes *symmetry* and *harmony,* or *order* and *proportion,* as being both the principle of the Good, and the ruling principle in the universe; the one, in fact, because the other, since the Good or Mind is the First and Final Cause of existence. Less imaginative and artistic than most of the other dialogues of Plato, the Philebus is very important, since it expounds the central principles of his matured doctrine of reality.

In the *Sophist* Plato argues explicitly that *the Ideas constitute a system.* There are certain fundamental ideas or categories which are involved in all others—such are Unity and Plurality, Identity and Difference (Sameness and Otherness), Rest and Motion, Being and Nonbeing. (These imply one another.) The Universals are in communion with one another. Not all things have communion with all, but some with some (251). In short, One and Many, Rest and Motion, Sameness and Otherness, and even Being and Nonbeing, imply each other.

Being is defined as Power, Life, Mind (247 and 248). "And, heavens, can we ever be made to believe that motion and life and soul and mind are not present with absolute being? Can we imagine being to be devoid of life and mind and to remain in awful unmeaningness an everlasting fixture?" (249). Thus the most significant thoughts in the Sophist are that Ideas are spiritual powers, that mind is dynamic, and that there is a unity or system *of the Ideas.* The ultimate realities are not a pluralistic aggregate. They are an organized totality. The Philebus and the Sophist are somewhat abstruse and difficult dialogues to follow. The style is technical and dry. The student would better omit them on a first reading of Plato and come back to them after having studied carefully the dialogues previously touched upon.

The *Timæus* is Plato's mythical or poetical story of creation. It calls for no special comment, beyond attention to the fact that Plato seems here to be giving an imaginative account of things beyond the reach of science. His insistence that the cause of the world's existence was the goodness or love of the Creator, which led him to desire that all things should be as like him as possible, seems to indicate that he identifies the Idea of the Good (the supreme idea in the Republic) with the Creative Ground of the world. We find here the distinction between three kinds of being: (1) *The Eternal Essences or Ideas;* (2) *Sensible Things, the empirical world of sense perception;* and (3) *Pure Space.* The actual world is due to the union of these three kinds of being. The creator put intelligence in soul and soul in body. The soul is made of three elements: (1) The unchangeable essence or Idea; (2) the changeable or corporeal; (3) an intermediate essence.

References

Adam, James, *Vitality of Platonism.*

* Avey, Albert E., *Readings in Philosophy,* Chapter VII.

* Burnet, John, *History of Greek Philosophy,* pp. 205-350.

Campbell, Lewis, *Introductions to the Sophist and Politicus.*

Dunning, William A., *History of Political Theories, Ancient and Modern,* 1-48.

* *Encyclopædia Britannica,* 11th ed., Article "Plato."

Grote, George, *Plato and the Other Companions of Socrates.*

Lutoslawski, Wincenty, *The Origin and Growth of Plato's Logic.*

* MacKenzie, J. S., *Outlines of Social Philosophy,* pp. 89-90 and 259-274.

* More, Paul Elmer, *Platonism* and *The Religion of Plato.*

Nettleship, R. Lewis, *Lectures on the Republic,* and *Theory of Education in Plato's Republic* (in *Hellenica*).

Pater, Walter, *Plato and Platonism.*

* Plato, *Dialogues,* translation by Jowett, especially Meno, Gorgias, Protagoras, Symposium, Phædrus, Theætetus, Phædo, Philebus, Sophist, Politicus, Parmenides, Republic, Timæus, and Laws.

The Republic, translation by Davies and Vaughan.

* *Histories of Philosophy* previously cited.

* Ritchie, David G., *Plato.*

Stewart, J. A., *Plato's Doctrine of Ideas,* and *Myths of Plato.*

Shorey, Paul, *The Unity of Plato's Thought*

* Taylor, A. E., *Plato.*

Windelband, Wilhelm, *Platon.*

Zeller, Edward, *Plato.*

CHAPTER VIII

ARISTOTLE (384–322 B. C.)

Plato had a large school called the Academy. Of that school Aristotle was the ablest member, and he in turn later established the Lyceum, an institution which became the most important center of learning in the ancient world after Plato's demise. Aristotle was a tutor of Alexander the Great, and it is supposed that Aristotle got money for his school from Alexander. Aristotle made great collections in the departments of botany, zoölogy and other fields of science. While Plato was a man of poetic inspiration and great speculative insight, Aristotle was a great intellectual organizer. He systematized and developed the doctrines of Plato. His great aim was to transform the Socratic-Platonic philosophy into an organized body of theory that would systematize and interpret the world of experience. Aristotle's greatest achievement consists in the methodizing or ordering of science. He analyzes and classifies his materials, separates and formulates the problems, and coördinates the results into a coherent whole. His logic has remained the basis of logic to the present time, and his ethics is still full of sound instruction. He wrote on politics, anatomy, botany, and poetics. He also wrote treatises on metaphysics, or the first principles of reality, and psychology, which are still very important.

I. ARISTOTLE'S LOGIC

Aristotle was the first to organize into a coherent body of doctrine the various outcomes of logical investigation on the part of his predecessors. Some of the most fundamental principles of logic, such as the principle of contradiction, the principle of sufficient reason, the dictum concerning all and none (*dictum de omni et nullo*) and others, had been already formulated. What Aristotle did was to weave all the logical principles and rules into a coherent whole and to formulate a system of deductive logic or logic of proof that has, in the main, stood until the present.

Aristotle regards logic as the theory of scientific method; that is, as the formulation of the systematic procedure of the intellect, by which it apprehends particulars in the light of universals or concepts. Logical thinking is the *organon* or *instrument* by which truth is reached. The two chief divisions of this organon are the *Analytics* and the *Topics*. The *Topics* is devoted to the consideration of *induction* or *Dialectic,* which ascends from particular facts of experience to the universal propositions that explain the particulars; induction is a method of research which attains to only probable conclusions; the degree of certainty of these increase, however, in so far as they explain particular phenomena; in the special sciences only relative universality is attainable. We shall give no further space to his treatment of induction, since it does not compare in value with his theory of deduction, which is expounded in the *Analytics*.

All scientific knowledge, according to Aristotle, consists in the subsumption of particulars under class concepts or universals, and in the combination of concepts into a system. Deductive Logic is the theory of proof or inference by which, starting from given propositions, we may reach conclusions that are absolutely certain. A correct syllogism is an inference from a combination of concepts. A proposition consists of two terms, *subject* and *predicate,* and the *relation* between them; for example, S is P, or S is not P. Propositions may be either *affirmative* or *negative* in *quality,* as in the above examples; they may be either *universal* or *particular* in the *quantity* of the terms; for example, all S is P, and no S is P, are both universal, some S is P and some S is not P, are both particular, with reference to the quantity or extension of S. In order that, by a combination of two propositions, a third may be inferred with certainty, there must be a *universal* which is shared in common by the two propositions which constitute the premises. The term for the common universal concept is the middle or mediating term designated by the letter M. Thus—All M is P, All S is M; therefore, All S is P; or All living beings are mortal, All men are living beings, ∴ All men are mortal;—are examples of the syllogism.

Aristotle enumerated and gave rules for correct inference in three figures of the syllogism; the *figure* being the combination of terms in the premises which depends on the position of M. These are

M — P	P — M	M — P
S — M	S — M	M — S
∴ S — P	∴ S — P	∴ S — P

Later logicians added the fourth figure, which is the reverse of the first. It will be obvious that the quantity and quality of the propositions inferable from the given premises, depend upon the special combination of terms in the various figures. The first figure is the perfect one, since one can infer all four kinds of propositions by it.

Syllogism for Aristotle is not merely deductive; it is a means of induction. Beginning with particular possible or probable conclusions in the imperfect figures, we may, with increase of insight, proceed to universal affirmative conclusions in the first figure.

Aristotle held that scientific knowledge involves: (1) particular data to be investigated; 2, certain essential or universal properties in the data; and (3) certain general principles of all reasoning. The latter are presupposed in all science; we come gradually, through reflection, to a knowledge of them; thus our knowledge here, as everywhere, depends upon the intellectual development of our experience. But the first principles of reasoning, when we become aware of them, are recognized as *axiomatic* or self-evident. They are, the *law of contradiction* (A cannot be both B and not B), and the *law of the excluded middle* (A must be either B or not B). In special fields, such as geometry, there are special axioms; for example, in regard to space relations, Aristotle held that, while it is through experience that we become aware of universal propositions, the highest universals are *presupposed* in the possibility of our understanding experience. There could be no science were not the highest universals *first in order of being,* although *last in the order of the psychological growth of knowledge* in the individual mind.

The beginning and the goal of science is *definition.* We must begin with tentative universals, with propositions which define the terms whose content we are investigating. The goal of science is a definition which explains the nature of the subject by its *essential properties* and by the *differentiating properties* by which it is marked off from other groups. Thus the final goal of science would be a complete classification of objects of knowledge into class groups, exhibiting all the resemblances and differences in the properties of the various classes. And the beginning of science is made with those empirical and tentative classifications which common sense makes. We might, for example, begin an investigation of man's place in the universe with the tentative definition, "Man is a two-legged erect animal who uses speech and invents tools." The goal of the science of anthropology would be a complete grasp of man's relations to all other classes of beings. This conception of science was clearly formulated by Aristotle. He says that the definition of a term or a class concept must be: (1) a complete statement of the *essential attributes* of the class, for example, man is an animal with powers of rational speech; (2) the *peculiar attributes* of the class, for example, man is capable of laughter; (3) the *next higher genus,* for example, man is an animal; (4) the *properties which differentiate* man from all other animal species, for example, man is capable of speech; (5) *accidents,* that is, properties not part of definition but common to the class and other classes, for example, man is a material object.

II. Aristotle's Theory of Realitty—(*Metaphysics*)

Aristotle accepts the Platonic conception of knowledge, that is, knowledge comes only through universals, concepts, forms. Yet Aristotle thinks that Plato erred in separating the universals from the particulars. Aristotle's fundamental doctrine is that the *Supersensible Realm of Ideas or Forms is in and one with the realm of sensuous existence.* He agrees with Plato that the task of science and philosophy is the deduction or derivation of particular facts from universal principles or laws; and, thus, that all knowledge consists in seeing and interpreting the particular, sensible datum in the light of the universal or concept. The following scheme illustrates Aristotle's conception of reality.

The individual being (ἐντελέχεια)

Matter (δύναμις) Form (ἐνέργεια)

The individual is the union of matter and form, or the passing of potency into actuality.

By matter Aristotle means the potentiality of forms. There is one pure form, namely, God. There is no matter in God. 'Εντελέχεια is that which is the fulfillment of an end. Thus we see that Aristotle has a teleological conception of nature.

Δύναμις or matter is the *possibility* of being an individual, while the form is the shaping, the organizing, the dynamic principle. For Plato, the ultimately real world is the realm of eternal forms. Aristotle, however, maintains that reality is a development of individuals through the immanent, indwelling force of the forms. The universals do not exist apart from the particulars; they exist only in the individuals. The formative principles, therefore, are immanent, not transcendent. We may illustrate this doctrine as follows: We say the child is father to the man. We mean by this that the possibility of the statesman, poet, or artisan, is in the child, and the realization of that possibility is the coming into being of the individual man. The oak tree is the realization of the matter or potentiality latent in the acorn. Thus throughout nature there are operative purposive entities, and the realization of the end is always due to the activity of the form *in* the matter. Thus, too, whether any individual is to be regarded as matter or form depends on whether one is considering it in relation to stages of existence *below or above it* in the whole scale of existence. A *baby* is *form* in relation to an *ovum* which is its *matter;* but the *baby* is *matter* in relation to a *youth* which is its realized *form;* in turn the youth is the *matter* of a *statesman, poet,* or *artisan;* and the latter are realized forms.

Aristotle criticizes Plato on the ground that he separated ideas from the sense world.[1] Aristotle himself seeks to make ideas the immanent, indwelling or shaping princi-

[1] It is a debatable question whether, on this score, Aristotle's interpretation of Plato is justifiable. I doubt it.

ples in the world of sense experience, and he develops this view as follows: matter, he maintains, is the potentiality or the possibility of form. Matter does exist, but not by itself. Matter is not *nonbeing* or *absence of being* as Plato seems, according to some of his expressions, to have held. Matter is a positive existence. It is the "promise and potency" of all individuality. It is actuality in the making, and subservient to the formative and dynamic purposes which are the animating powers of reality. There is no such thing as formless matter, a primeval stuff which is pure chaos. The notion of pure matter is for Aristotle a limiting concept. Matter which is to some degree shaped by forms is what actually exists. Thus his conception of matter represents an advance over the view of Plato. The forms or universals of Aristotle are called *entelechies*. They are the realization of the possibilities of matter to be formed. Reality, what is real, is the individual. There is no such thing as either pure matter or pure form except in the case of God, who is pure form—Form of Forms.

The world is a system of development in which there are an indefinite number of stages or levels. On the lowest level we have an individual that has the fewest forms embodied in itself, for example, clay. This lump of clay may be taken by the sculptor and shaped into the figure of an Apollo Belvedere, or a Venus de Milo. Then the lump of clay, under the guiding mind of the sculptor, becomes the embodiment of the Greek ideas of manly and feminine beauty. Into the making of any individual, according to Aristotle, there enter two causes, the material cause and the formal cause. The material cause of the statue is the clay or the marble, the stuff out of which the individual is shaped. The final cause is the purpose or idea. In a broad sense, the final clause is identical with the formal cause. For the *end* is the expression of the form. There are three phases or aspects of the formal cause:

1. The end—τέλος: the manifestation of beauty.

2. The formal cause, that is, the shape the individual takes in the mind of the sculptor.

3. The efficient cause, the instrument by which the end is realized.

Thus the formal cause is a dynamic, purposive principle. The true nature of anything is revealed in its *end*. Nature, as a whole, is a system of ends, a hierarchy of ascending *values*. Thus, to the *mechanical* nature philosophy of the atomists, Aristotle opposes a *dynamic* and *teleological* and *vitalistic* nature philosophy. For him, *qualitative* distinctions of *value* and *meaning* in nature cannot be reduced to quantitative differences between the masses, figures, and spatial configurations of atoms. Aristotle's individualized forms are *qualitatively different centers of purposive energy*, which determine the course of reality.

The idea of artistic creation was very influential with Plato and Aristotle. They were both Greeks, and these above all other peoples were endowed with a high order of artistic powers and appreciation.

Aristotle's interpretation of nature is both humanistic and artistic. His Philosophy of Nature is what may be called an artistic teleology, that is, he gives us an interpretation of the processes of nature in terms of artistic purpose. God is a cosmic artist. Among all the natural sciences, biology is the one which interested Aristotle most. His conception of the relation of life and matter is teleological and artistic. This comes out clearly in Aristotle's conception of the soul and its relation to the body.

III. Aristotle's Psychology

The soul is the entelechy, the principle of life which shapes the body to its ends. Only potential life belongs to bodies. Actual life is due to the influence of the soul, the body is the instrument of the soul. The actuality of the body is derived from the soul. Aristotle distinguished between three levels in the soul:

1. *Nutritive soul:* This is the principle of life and reproduction, and is common to all plants and animals.

2. *Sensitive soul:* This is common to all animals. It is the soul which has sensation and feeling. Aristotle thinks that plants do not have sensation. Among the senses, he makes touch fundamental and the source of all the others.

3. *Rational soul:* Through this soul knowledge and reflection come.

In man these three interact. Reason gets all of its material through the senses and the imagination. At this point Aristotle gives us a *psychology* of knowledge, which we did not get in Plato. While the materials come from sensation, the separate senses have not the power of discriminating and reasoning. Both the analysis and synthesis, by which knowledge is built up out of sensation, are functions of *nous* (νοῦς) or thought.

Aristotle is the first to definitely formulate a theory of the nature, structure, and function of the judgment. So far as the rational soul is influenced by the lower grades, it is relatively passive. But reason itself is active, creative, synthetic, and its activity enters into all true knowledge, and true knowledge consists in knowledge of the universal concepts. In the act of knowing, which is always *judgment,* whether it be of sense perception, memory, or inference, the mind is one with what it knows. Thus the objects of sense perception are, in the moment of perception, identical with the process of perception; and, in the absence of the latter, exist *potentially.*

Reason is pure activity, whose work is guided by the laws of thought. Aristotle holds that, while our knowledge of the world is derived from the senses, yet there is no *knowl-*

edge except in so far as the materials of sense are judged by reason.

IV. Aristotle's Theory of Knowledge

In the moment of knowing, mind is one with the object known. The knowing process is one with what it knows. Aristotle's theory of knowledge is *monistic*. The mind knows reality in its very nature or essence, not a mere copy or shadow of reality. In true knowledge, the apprehending mind and the apprehended object come immediately to grips with one another. This view of knowledge is to be contrasted with all theories of dualism. Dualistic theories maintain that in knowledge we deal with symbols or copies, and not with the object directly. In Aristotle we have the realistic position—mind knows the objects as they really are—which is opposed to phenomenalism. In phenomenalism the mind is said to know appearances, symbols, copies of things, and not things as they are. In Aristotle we have this, one of the most persistent of philosophical problems, explicitly formulated. In this realistic position, mind and object known are held to be one in the moment of knowing.

All forms of phenomenalism agree in saying that mind knows only appearances. There are, to be sure, several types of phenomenalistic theories. These types range from those which insist that the knowledge copies are fairly good copies, to those views which urge that through our copies we get to know nothing whatever about the object. Realism denies that knowledge is concerned with copies. It rests directly upon the assumption that, for example, in the moment of my perceiving this desk, there is no real distinction between my perceiving and what I perceive.

Aristotle held that sense perception is a genuine source of knowledge, and that the reason is dependent on perception for its knowledge of objects in nature. There is a gradual transition from sense perception to rational thought. In the lowest stage there is direct perception of objects; after this there comes the process of forming images, and then the forming of conceptions; but in all this reason is active. To illustrate this point, suppose that you visit some strange region never before visited by man, and in that region you see unfamiliar animals. You begin to gain control of the situation by classifying the animals in question, and you form images and class concepts into which the objects fall, and then you make a definition of the class thus discovered. It is in the formation of the definition that the mind is most active, and it is upon the basis of such definitions that the reason can further work deductively. This threefold process eventuates in scientific knowledge only through the unifying power of the reason. It is through this power that all our concepts are synthesized into a well articulated system, and this takes place under the guidance of the first principles of thought. These first principles we intuitively perceive, and while they do not have their origin in sensory experience, they do have application in experience; that is, these first principles are not *of* experience, but their application *in* experience yields scientific knowledge.

Aristotle's theory of knowledge is more carefully elaborated and systematized than Plato's. He also pays more attention to the psychological process by which knowledge is constructed. It is often said that Aristotle is an empiricist. This is not true, although it is true that he gave far more consideration to empirical data than did Plato. Aristotle holds positively to the existence of intuitively known principles. For him all knowledge is not derived from sense perception. The individual mind is not purely passive. He differs greatly from the English empiricists who maintain that the individual is a passive organism on which the world writes or perchance scribbles. Rationalism holds that the fundamental principles of knowledge are not derived from sense experience. Rationalism need not deny that the senses give the materials of knowledge. A rationalist of the Aristotelian variety does not excogitate the data of perception out of his own inner consciousness; but he holds that the reason is creative, and it is the source of the fundamental principles of thought. There is an oft forgotten and withal important distinction which Aristotle makes when he points out the difference between priority in the psychological order and that in the logical order. Psychologically, sensation is prior to conception, that is, the child has sensations before it has concepts; it has particular experiences before it has general ideas. Our scientific knowledge begins with crude data and proceeds only gradually to the refined results given us in scientific formulæ. By logical priority, Aristotle means that there is implied, or actually used, universal principles in the organization of our sense experience. In the organization of sense experience into science the mind uses these fundamental principles, even though it may never know what these principles are. In short, Aristotle is a rationalist who gives experience its due; a realist, with respect to the relation of knowledge and reality, whose realism rests upon the metaphysical doctrine that the structure of the world is determined and controlled by intelligible Forms, Ideas, or Ideals, and Values. Reality for him is a process in which Form or Meaning and Value, is forever taking on more and fuller *individuality*. And, notwithstanding their difference in temperament and method, Aristotle is really carrying out, in more systematic fashion, the fundamental insights of Plato. Their basic harmony of view is deeper than even Aristotle saw.

V. Summary of Aristotle's Theory of Reality

Aristotle's conception of reality is that of an endless procession of passing from potentiality to actuality, or, from the formless to the formed. Forms are the dynamic principles that operate in the natural order. All individual beings, from the simplest crystal to the very highest individual, are the results of the operation of the entelechies or formative principles in nature. Reality is the constant process of the actualization of forms.

Nothing in the natural world is created all at once. Everything develops, grows. Broadly speaking, therefore, Aristotle's philosophy is that reality is an evolution. It is an evolution towards progressively higher types of individuality. It is a teleological evolution including in its purposiveness a realization of a multitude of purposes or ends. Such a conception of nature implies that the all-inclusive purpose is operative through all the stages of the process. In other words, such a theory implies that, while the purpose of the whole is realized in time, this purpose must be eternally existent. There must be a form of forms, a pure and all-inclusive form, free from any admixture of matter; and this form of forms must be presupposed in order to account for the process, and indeed, for any stage of the process. This form of forms, this eternal purpose, this universal mover, is God. He is the source of all movement, of all actuality.

Matter has a contingent, irrational character. It is not wholly subservient to the realization of form and purposive reality, and it is this character that matter has which is the cause of all failure in nature. God is the final cause, and as the final cause, he is the eternally first cause of all movement. He is eternal, being without parts or passion, and unmoved by the phantasmagoria of the world of sense. He is pure thought, pure activity—pure thought unhampered by any admixture of sense. He is the eternally tireless, active thought of the universe. As to why there is one and not a plurality of gods, Aristotle replies that God is one because the world is one. The beauty of the world, the intelligent and harmonious connections of its parts are evidence of a supreme purpose operative everywhere in nature. The splendor of the stars point to one being from whom comes all unity, harmony, and splendor of the world. This one God is transcendent, self-conscious spirit, the eternally first cause of all change and development.

Aristotle believes in divine providence, but that God works through natural means. At the time of Aristotle there were two ideas in Greek religion which he readily accepted:

1. Recognition of the existence of gods.
2. The divinity of the stars

As to how God acts upon the world, Aristotle holds that there is a longing of matter after God. In matter is the desire to become pure activity. It is this longing of the world to become like God that is the immediate cause of the whole world process. God does not move the world by acting on it directly. The world is moved by the desire of the imperfect to attain perfection, by the longing of all other individualized forms to become as like God, the pure Form or Forms, the Absolute and Perfect Entelechy, as possible. God is pure actuality, completely self-contained and self-moving Activity. His alone is the pure and passionless delight of eternally unhampered self-contemplating thought. He does not strive nor suffer. He knows no pain nor any sorrow. How sharp the contrast with the Christian God who ever strives and suffers, sorrows and rejoices with men! Aristotle's God is the apotheosis of an intellectual aristocracy, the God of Jesus, a humanized spiritual ground of the ideal community.

VI. Aristotle's Doctrine of the Good (*Ethics*)

The good of anything, on the basis of the Aristotelian conception of the Good, consists in the actualization of all the functions that belong to that being. Every type of being has its own modes of activity, and it is the realization of these that constitutes the Good. That which distinguishes man is his reason, and therefore, the Good of man is the activity of reason unfolding itself in all the virtues. When man exercises his functions as a human being, he is happy, but the desired end of such functioning is not pleasure. Pleasure is the result but not the motive. Welfare is the energizing of the soul according to virtue. Nowhere in the whole range of ethical literature is there a better definition of the Good for man. Aristotle does not have the ascetic strain of Plato, at least not to anything like the same degree. The body is not a prison house for Aristotle.

Aristotle gives a twofold classification of the virtues, namely, practical and theoretical. By practical, Aristotle means the fundamental social virtues, and, like Plato, he holds that the good life can be realized only in society: ethics and politics for Aristotle are inseparable. This is a fundamental truth—politics is nothing but applied ethics. These practical virtues are courage, self-control, liberality, high-mindedness, friendliness, truthfulness, justice, et cetera, and each of these, it is evident, is a functional means between two extremes. Right action is, with respect to the satisfaction of the ordinary human wants, always a mean between the extreme of excess and the extreme of defect, between too much and too little. For example, temperance, or self-control, consists in satisfying the bodily appetites in moderation; courage is a mean between foolhardiness and cowardice, liberality is a mean between prodigality and miserliness. The theoretical virtues have to do with the exercise of thought. Judgment here assumes two forms:

1. Judgment as to means
2. Judgment as to ends or intrinsic values

The highest virtue of all is wisdom. Applied to life as a whole, it is self-knowledge and understanding of things in relation to God. It is pure contemplation. This is the sweetest and best of all things. This contemplation of all things as dependent on God—thinking the thoughts of God after him—of this one never grows tired. When freed from the vicissitudes of chance, this is the highest delight of man.

References

* Aristotle, *Nichomachean Ethics,* translations by Chase, Welldon, and Peters; especially Books I, II, V and VIII-X.
* Avey, Albert E., *Readings in Philosophy,* Chapter VIII.
Grant, A., *Aristotle.*
Grote, George, *Aristotle.*
* *Metaphysics,* translation by Ross; especially Books VII or Z and XII or Λ.
* *Politics,* by Weldon and Jowett.
* *Psychology,* by Hammond, Hicks and Wallace; especially Book II, Chapters 2-5 and Book III, Chapters 4-7.
* Taylor, A. E., *Aristotle.*
* Wallace, Edwin, *Outlines of the Philosophy of Aristotle* (for students who read Greek).
Zeller, *Aristotle and the Peripatetics.*

CHAPTER IX

STOIC PANTHEISM

I. The Decline of Greek Speculation

The spiritual conditions of the last centuries B. C. and the first centuries A. D. in Greece and Rome, can be but briefly touched upon here. It is the task of the historian of social life to work them out more fully. What we do see is that there is an organic connection of the problems of philosophy with the life problems of a people. Philosophy is a statement of the spirit of the time. The old city state, which was the social and political form of Greek life, was passing away and now large heterogeneous empires, first the Macedonian, which split up into fragments, and then the Roman, threatened to absorb all these smaller states. As these empires grew larger they presented more and more a confusion of races, tongues, customs, beliefs, and superstitions. By means of this confusion, the morals of the city states were broken down, and this was done on a much larger scale than in the age of the Sophists. The Romans were a formal, utilitarian people, who adjusted themselves to certain grossly practical needs, but they were never able to adjust themselves to the finer intellectual and spiritual demands without importing ideas. The Roman Empire became a great melting pot of moral, practical, and intellectual interests. The Romans were not a speculative people, and with the single exception of law, they made no great creative achievements in the world of thought. This period is characterized by the growth of an intense feeling for both practical guidance and emotional consolation. Out of this developed the Epicurean and Stoic schools.[1]

After the Hellenic philosophical efflorescence in Plato and Aristotle, atomism exercised considerable influence through its adoption by the Epicureans, but the interest of this School was not in scientific inquiry. The two centers of scientific inquiry were the Academy and the Lyceum. It is possible that atomistic philosophy was a factor in the scientific work that was carried on after the time of Aristotle in Alexandria and other places. It is well known that in geography at this time the sphericity of the earth was taught. The heliocentric theory was also advanced, by Aristarchus and others, but through the influence of Aristotle and other causes, this theory died out. In this period Euclid's *Elements of Geometry* was composed. Archimedes laid the foundation of mechanics, while in medicine certain important discoveries were made.

Experimental science, however, after flourishing for several centuries, died out. It had made auspicious beginnings; nevertheless, although it had also achieved, through the progress of Greek mathematics, a firm mathematical basis, it did not, until after the lapse of over fifteen hundred years, make any fruitful application of the method devised by Democritus. The spirit of independent inquiry gradually died out. The old Greek world of city states, with their keen intellectual atmosphere, was submerged in the all-devouring imperial Roman world. This world of Roman imperialism was the melting pot of the ancient world. It was a polyglot world, a world of all sorts of races and nationalities, a world of intellectual and religious confusion, and a world of political and economic confu-

[1] The two great postulates of Greek thought are: (a) psychological—all desire the good; (b) metaphysical—nature is good, the good is sovereign. For the Romans, *law* is sovereign.

sion. It was largely through the functioning of this last form of confusion that the Empire's disintegration resulted. There was no spirit of individual inquiry to speak of—the Romans were neither philosophically nor scientifically minded. They were empire builders and rulers, they were city builders, they were road builders—in short, they were practically minded. They did not make even second-rate contributions of the creative intelligence in philosophy or science. After the disintegration of the classical Greek world, the minds of men turned more and more to the questions of conduct and religion. In all ages of confusion, in periods of lack of unified culture, in epochs where there is an absence of stable, political and social life, when the lives of local communities are merged in the vast welter of some extensive empire, when the old religion is losing its regulative power—in short, when the old traditional life in all its diversified forms is passing away, there may be nothing positively constructive and able to replace it. At such junctures, the minds of men turn from philosophy and science to the practical questions of the hour. And so we have, at this special period under discussion, an eclipse of the spirit of philosophy and science.

There is a superficial, optimistic faith as to progress. Some think that progress continues in a straight line. This is a childish faith. Magnificent Greek culture with all its bewitching splendor died out and was succeeded by centuries in which the independent thinker never dared raise his head and look with open eye at nature and see things as they are. There is a story told to illustrate this point. It is of an incident that occurred in a monastery about the year 1600. A monastic student of astronomy discovered the spots on the sun, of which there was no mention in Aristotle. He was told by his master that if it was not mentioned in Aristotle then the spots were either in his eyes or his glasses.[2] This illustration shows the blind obedience to authority which prevailed through the Middle Ages.

II. Ethics and Speculative Religion—the Stoic System

Epicureanism is a doctrine of prudent amiability. It teaches the individual the advisability of avoiding all entangling alliances. Pleasure is the only good, but true pleasure or happiness is to be found, not in the pursuit of the coarse and violent pleasures of sense but in the equable, moderate, and enduring pleasures of the mind and of friendship. Everything in nature, including the soul of man, is composed of material atoms (*cf.* Ch. IV, Atomism). But the atoms have spontaneity; hence, man has free will. There are gods. They are like glorified men. They did not create the world, and they do not care for men or interfere in the course of things. They live, happy and care free, in the interspaces of the world. Man need not worry about the gods or the hereafter, for death ends all. Let man live wisely, temperately, justly, in the congenial society of friends. Let him be guided by intelligent self-interest, and avoid giving hostages to fortune. The wise man will eschew public life, because of its risks. This is a prudent and enlightened gospel of selfish amiability. It did not appeal to the nobler feelings and aspirations in man. It had no tonic effect.

The best forces of the Roman world rallied under Stoicism. Zeno, 336-264 B. C., was the founder of this School. He was followed by Cleanthes, 264-232; Chrysippus, 232-204; Panætius, 180-110; Seneca, 3-65 A. D.; Epictetus, first century, and Marcus Aurelius, 121-180. Stoicism is

[2] This story is told of Scheiner, circa 1600, who contests with Galileo the honor of having discovered the sunspots.

an ethics based on a religious metaphysic, namely, *pantheism.* Pantheism means the identification of God with the cosmos. God is the essence or the unity of the cosmos. He is wholly immanent, the *One in All. Theism* does not thus deny the transcendence of God. The theist holds that God is the *One above All,* the perfect and transcendent *Self,* on whose ceaseless conserving will, nevertheless, the universe depends. For the Stoic, the world is pervaded and penetrated by one spirit, the universal Reason, and this world reason or world soul is interpreted in other than idealistic terms. On the whole the Stoic conceived this permeating principle as a fine, all-pervading, fiery medium or ether, a sublimized breath, the cosmical *pneuma.* From it, all the elements and all the cyclic transformations of the universe emanate. The *pneuma* is present in all things, but it is present in a preëminent degree in man. Reason is the germinating principle of all things, but in man it exists as self-conscious reason. It is the universal *logos* of which there is a spark in every man. Man is an individual expression of the world-soul, and because of this he is capable of communion with God. Man's destiny is to realize himself as a rational individual in communion with God. Man is to become what he is capable of becoming, namely, a rational, self-determining spirit, living wholly in harmony with the universal Spirit, *pneuma,* Soul or Reason.[3] It is given to man to live a life according to nature. Such a life is one of self-sufficiency, of independence from all the mutations of life. It is a life of complete imperturbability of mind. In such a life man realizes the divine image.

[3] In the Stoic conception of God there is interwoven, without any attempt at logical consistency, the ideas of God as an impersonal, necessary, rational, and dynamic soul or spirit of nature; and as a personal and loving providence who cares for the human individual and, by his will, orders all things for good.

The "pneuma" in man and animals is part of the fiery cosmical spirit. The soul is a unity whose ruling principle is reason. The Stoics persistently emphasized the activity of mind in knowing. Knowledge arises in perception, but for perception to become knowledge there must be an active attitude of mind. The act of perception is the transmission of the perceived quality from the object to the mind—and the mind reacts to this quality.

Thus images and concepts, or general ideas, are formed, by the mind, from sensations. From the universal experiences of mankind there are formed, unconsciously, *common notions;* that is, notions which are common to all persons and are universally true. Our scientific ideas are produced consciously. While the Stoics hold that all knowledge is derived from sense perception, they also hold that thought is the active and reflective principle, by means of which the mind lays hold on, organizes, and generalizes from, those qualities that are transmitted to it from the physical objects.

Each act of perception involves apprehension, *katalepsis,* the laying hold of things. This active apprehension involves general notions, or concepts, or types, which are unconsciously and spontaneously present in the mind. The mind is adapted by virtue of its nature to grasp truth. This, the act of perception, is one which involves, on the part of the percipient, a laying hold on the object. Isolated perceptions do not constitute science. They must be bound together by reason. And it was to characterize this prerequisite that the Stoics used the word "conscience." For the Stoic, the highest criterion of truth is *self-evidence,* or the *feeling* of *certainty.* True ideas are those which adequately *copy* their objects. An idea will give one the conviction of self-evidence, when it is clear and distinct, and first impressions have been verified by repetition. The Stoics emphasized, also, the importance of correct inference and paid a good deal of attention to formal logic.

Reason is the highest quality in man; it is the divine spark. Reason unites men, reason is social. Hence the Stoics emphasized the social nature of man so far as he is rational. We were made for coöperation, but by our passions we are divided and sundered from each other. By the reason we are united. Hence the Stoics lay stress on the duty of man to fulfill his social obligations. The duty of man is to live according to the real nature of things, and, in so far as men do this, they are brothers. Earth is our dear fatherland, and we men are all brothers. The world is our home.

Man is man, not because of his language, or the color of his hair, or skin, or by any other physical accident, but solely through the exercise of reason. This is an anticipation of the Christian doctrine of the universal brotherhood of men. By virtue of this notion of a common, rational nature in man, the Stoical philosophy became the rational basis of Roman law. When Rome passed from being a city state to the form of an empire, the practical Romans were confronted with the problem of nationalization. The problem of the Parthian, Mede, Greek, Jew, Gaul, Briton, Teuton, et cetera, pressed for solution. All these tribes were parts of the Roman government. Now the Stoical philosophy suggested the solution in that it had developed the idea of humanity as distinct from that of Greek, Jew, et cetera, and on this basis Roman Imperial law was constructed. Man as man was seen to be worthy of rights. It was on this Stoical principle that Roman law was made to rest. This idea of free personality as the subject of rights and duties has its development in Roman Imperial law, resting ultimately upon Stoical philosophy. This step was a most tremendous one for the organization of civilization.[4]

Stoicism became the rallying point for the strongest spirits of the Roman Empire, and in addition to its appeal to these spirits, it had a very widespread influence. Teachers of Stoicism traveled about like itinerant preachers. They were both the teachers and preachers of morals. These itinerant teachers were domiciled in the homes of the great. It was the work of such as these that really prepared the way for Christianity. St. Paul's sermon on Mars Hill undoubtedly refers to the Stoical hymn to Zeus, and throughout the New Testament many terms and expressions of stoical origin are used, as, for example, "in him we live and move and have our being."

Stoicism has deeply influenced many modern thinkers. Descartes was really a Stoic in his ethical attitude; so were Spinoza, Leibnitz, and others.

Why was Stoicism not the salt which was to save Roman society? Why was it not sufficient? The answer is, it was too cold and lofty for the masses of men. It did appeal to the high-minded man, but it did not supply any dynamic that could lift the average man above the range of his senses. It did not generate any consuming passion for humanity. The Stoic proclaimed that the masses were fools and only the few were wise. Stoicism thus, with all its optimism IN THEORY, did not supply a strong dynamic and a transfiguring hope as the days of the Empire's fall drew near.

---

[4] There are three stages in the development of the Roman conception of *law*, which meet the developing needs of the Roman state: 1, the law of the city, *jus civile*, founded on custom and having to do with the citizens alone; 2, the laws of nations, *jus gentium*, which applied to all freemen; and 3, the law of nature, *jus naturale*, which applied to all human beings.

References

ARNOLD, EDWARD VERNON, *Roman Stoicism.*
* AVEY, ALBERT E., *Readings in Philosophy,* Chapter IX.
* BAKEWELL, CHARLES M., *Source Book in Ancient Philosophy,* pp. 269-289, 317-339.
BEVAN, E., *Stoics and Sceptics.*
* EPICTETUS, *Discourses,* translation by Long, Higginson.
HICKS, R. D., *Stoic and Epicurean.*
* MARCUS AURELIUS, *Meditations,* translation by Long.
PATER, WALTER W., *Marius the Epicurean.*
* ROGERS, ARTHUR KENYON, *History of Philosophy,* pp. 137-159.
* SENECA, *On Benefits.*
* STOCK, ST. GEO., *Stoicism.*
* THILLY, FRANK, *History of Philosophy,* pp. 104-116.

References on the General Spiritual Development in the Græco-Roman World

* BRETT, G. S., *The Government of Man,* Chapters VI, VII and VIII.
* CUMONT, F. V. M., *Oriental Religions in Roman Paganism.*
DILL, SAMUEL, *Roman Society from Nero to Marcus Aurelius.*
FOWLER, W. WARDE, *The Religious Experience of the Roman People,* Lectures XVI and XVII.
MAHAFFY, JAMES P., *Greek Life and Thought, Greek World Under Roman Sway.*
* MARVIN, WALTER T., *History of European Philosophy,* pp. 164-191.
* MURRAY, GILBERT, *Four Stages of Greek Religion.*
PLUTARCH, *Morals.*
* THILLY, FRANK, *History of Philosophy,* pp. 94-97.

CHAPTER X

MYSTICISM—NEOPLATONISM

I. The Meaning of Mysticism

This too is a distinctive type—it is a new type of religious philosophy. Many attempts have been made to define mysticism. As I understand mysticism it is a doctrine which holds that it is possible for the human soul to have direct access to divinity. Mysticism rests on the assumption of the possibility of a direct and immediate communion with God, without the intervention of any intermediate agency. It is the sense of the "immediate presence" of the Divine to the soul of the experient; in other words, the presence of a Reality whose being is not mediated by either sense perception or rational inference.

Mystical experiences are not confined to what are ordinarily called religious states of mind. In the broadest sense of the term "mysticism," any intuition or immediate apprehension of a being that exists beyond the data given by the senses, may be regarded as a mystical experience. When the lover claims to have an intuitive sense of the soul of his beloved; when the mother "feels" the soul of her child; when the nature lover feels, in any aspect of nature, "a presence far more deeply interfused"; or when, contemplating nature in its entirety, he has a "cosmic emotion"; all such attitudes are forms of mysticism. Nature mysticism is characteristic of the poetical and prose literature of the Romantic movement and of the American transcendentalists including Walt Whitman. Any sense or feeling of the presence of a "Beyond," of a Life not apprehended through the senses, nor inferred from perceptions, is a form of mysticism. And there is, obviously, a close kinship between the "feeling" of life and beauty in nature and in human beings, and religious mysticism. Moreover, since the sense of beauty is closely connected with sex feeling, it is not strange that the mystic's language should be deeply tinged with erotic symbolism. Indeed, Plato has set the pattern for this symbolism in the *Symposium.*

In specifically religious mysticism the Beyond may be pictured or conceived as a personal being, Jesus, Buddha, or God; or as an impersonal and cosmic life or spirit, the World Soul, the Universal Spirit, Brahman.

There are degrees of mystical experience. We can distinguish the milder form of mysticism, in which the experient feels at times an ineffable Presence without being rapt out of himself into an ecstatic condition of mergence in the Presence, from the extreme form, in which the mystic is snatched away from all sense of his earthly surroundings and of his own body, and may even lose all feeling of his own distinctness as an individual. St. Paul had such ecstatic seizures. (*Cf.* II Corinthians XII; Galatians II, 2; Acts XVI, 9; XVIII, 9, 10; XXII, 17-22; et cetera). Indeed, the Pauline doctrine of the "witness of the Spirit" and the indwelling Christ, as well as the entire trend of the Johannine writings, is mystical. Other greatly influential, Christian mystical writings were those of St. Augustine, John Tauler, the *Imitation of Christ,* the *Theologica Germanica;* and, among Protestants, Bunyan's *Pilgrim's Progress* and George Fox's *Journal.*

The milder form of mystical experience has been very widespread. We find it among Christians of all denominations, Hindus, and even Mohammedans and Jews; and also among many, like Shelley, Walt Whitman, and Dr. Bucke, who did not count themselves members of any sect. With some it has been chiefly a vague, and withal delightful, emotional exaltation, with a slight imaginal and conceptual content. With others the imagery and concepts have been well defined, and it has seemed to them a cognitive experience of superlative value. The character of the experience depends, of course, upon the mental individuality and cultural environment of the mystic.

The ecstatic raptures and visions of Christian mystics, such as St. Teresa, St. Bonaventura, St. John of the Cross, Julian of Norwich, St. Catherine of Siena, Meister Eckhart, and Madame Guyon, as well as of Plotinus, the greatest of pagan mystics, are more concentrated, intenser and, therefore, much rarer cases of the same phenomenon that occurs frequently in the milder forms of mysticism. If the latter have any cognitive value superior to sense perception and rational inference, there is no good reason for disallowing the claims of the ecstasy to be a first hand illumination of ultimate reality. The difference between the two types of cases is one of degree, not of kind.

The mystic way, *Mystica Via,* of course varies with the different types of mysticism. Quietistic mysticism, emotional mysticism, sensuous mysticism, et cetera, all elaborate various technic for achieving the communion with the Godhead. The mystic may conceive the Godhead *theistically* or *pantheistically;* either as the Supreme Person who is yet "closer to us than breathing and nearer than hands and feet"; or as the superpersonal all-inclusive Divine Spirit or Over Soul, the Over Soul who, as Self of and in all selves and things, is more than a Self. The Christian mystics, such as St. Paul, Origen, St. Bernard of Clairvaux, Thomas Aquinas, Bonaventura, St. Teresa, St. John of the Cross, Boehme, George Fox, Henry Vaughan, conceive God personalistically; the modern nature mystics, such as Shelley, Wordsworth, Tennyson, Novalis, Emerson, and Walt Whitman, are pantheistic in tendency. I think that the drift of the mystical experience is always, when it is reflected upon, towards pantheism, towards the mergence of the individual soul and all else in the all-including One or Superpersonal Unity. In its ethical implications mysticism may be individualistic or social. The notion of God as the Sustaining Spirit of the perfect society, or ideal community, would seem to afford the best synthesis of the ethical or social and the mystical motives. (See further, Chapters XXIV and XXXI, 4.)

It is impossible here, by reason of space limitations, to give even a summary account of the rise and development in the ancient and medieval Christian world of the practice of the mystical life and the formulation of mystical theology or philosophy. It must suffice to say that mysticism played a great rôle in the cultivation, both within and without the limits of Church dogma and discipline, of personal and experiential religion, and of philosophical speculation. And, at the beginning of the modern age, the reformers of institutional religion, from Luther to Loyola, were nurtured on mysticism. The mystical theology of Dionysius the Areopagite, John the Scot, St. Anselm, Meister Eckhart, Bonaventura, and Nicholas of Cusa, were the forerunners of the great idealistic systems of Schelling and Hegel, as well as of the earlier modern pantheisms of Bruno, Boehme, and Spinoza.

The first and still, perhaps, the greatest philosophy of mystical experience (with the possible exception of Hegel and F. H. Bradley) is that of Plotinus, a pagan Greek. He is the true father of philosophical mysticism in the West; and his system the fountainhead of speculative mysticism. Therefore his system is worthy of extended consideration, even in so brief an outline as the present one.[1]

[1] The one adequate work on Plotinus in English is *The Philosophy of Plotinus* by Dean W. R. Inge, who is, so far as I know, the greatest living exponent of mysticism, with the possible exception of Baron F. von Hügel.

It is possible to trace down to the present the various lines of influence which he initiated. St. Augustine, John the Scot, Thomas Aquinas, Bruno, Boehme, Spinoza, The Cambridge Platonists (Whichcote, Smith, Culverwell, Cudworth, and More), Fichte, Schelling, Hegel, the German Romantic School, Berkeley, the English poets—Wordsworth and Shelley—Bradley, Royce, Emerson, Bergson, and many more reveal this mystical motive.[2]

Mysticism as a movement in Greek thought goes back to both the Orphic Mysteries and the Pythagorean brotherhood. The Pythagorean brotherhood was a society which had politicial, as well as ethical and religious, tendencies. For us their chief interest is in their ethical tendencies. The reputed founder of this school is said to have taught at Crotona and to have died about 500 B. C. His life is veiled in legend. Plato is said to have visited this brotherhood, and was much influenced by it. For Pythagoreanism, reality consists of numbers. Numbers are the ungenerated principles of things. They seemed to find in the properties of numbers analogies to the facts of experience. They investigated the mathematical basis of music, and were greatly influenced by the results of their researches in this field. These numbers are akin to the ideas of Platonism. The Pythagorean brotherhood, by dietetics and purgation, and by speculation, aimed to develop the soul to where it could have the mystical union with the divine. Such, too, was the motive of the Orphic Mysteries. Pythagorean writings had increased influence in the last century B. C. and in the first centuries A. D.

The failure of the rationally grounded ethics of Sto-

---

[2] Of late years there has been a pronounced revival of mysticism, and many books on the subject have appeared. *Studies in Mystical Religion* by R. M. Jones, *The Mystic Way* and other books by Miss Underhill, *Christian Mysticism* by W. R. Inge, and *The Mystical Element in Religion* by Friedrich von Hügel, are some of the principal works on this revival.

icism to satisfy the longing of the time, as shown by the violent reaction against sensualism and the protest against the social corruptions of the time, brought about an intense feeling of the opposition between the soul and the world, and between the spirit and the flesh. The developing influence of Pythagoreanism, and of oriental cults brought to Rome, all point in the direction of the increasing craving of the best spirits of the time for direct union of the soul with the Divine. There is an insatiable craving for an immediate experience of the Godhead. In Platonism there was much to fall in with this tendency, and so the influence of Platonism increased, and it was this movement which was carried on to its completion in ancient times by Neoplatonism.

Neoplatonism was thus prepared for by Pythagoreanism. The Neopythagoreans and Neoplatonists were eclectics who tried to fit together into a harmonious whole the fundamental elements of the preceding theories. This was the form of speculative mysticism that was prevalent in the time of Plotinus. In various quarters we find that the mystical and religious side of Plato is eagerly taken up even long before the time of Plotinus. The estimable Plutarch uses Platonic philosophy to interpret religious differences. Philo Judæus is also seen interpreting Jewish religion in terms of Platonic philosophy. In doing this Philo posits the Logos as the creative principle of the world. The Logos is the unity from which come all ideas or logoi. It is the divine, creative word, by which the world was fashioned. This creative word, the immanent, dynamic reason of God, operates in the world, and it alone stands between God and the world.

For mysticism the goal of life is the vision of God—it is deliverance from the world of sense—it is ecstatic union with God. This type of thinking was given its classic formulation at Alexandria, the city which was the next greatest center of philosophical activity after Athens. In this great, populous, rich, manufacturing city, all the streams of higher thought met, and here the foundation was laid for Christian philosophy by Origen.

II. The System of Plotinus

Plotinus, 204-269, was a native of Egypt, and a pupil of Ammonius Saccas. In the year 244 A. D., he established a school at Rome, and after a period of ten years his famous school had the Emperor Gallienus and the empress aligned with it. Plotinus himself was a man of strong personality attested to by the fact that many noble Romans made him the guardian of their children. Having weak eyes, he did not like to write. It is for this reason that his works have not the clearness and the well-rounded symmetry which is characteristic of many other philosophies. His fundamental thought is that reality is through and through spiritual, and that it is One. The One or Monad is God, the Absolute. Below the One or the absolute Spirit is the "nous," and below "nous" is "psyche." Lowest of all, in the scale of being, is Matter—the formless or indefinite, the principle of plurality, ugliness and evil. Plotinus, like Plato and Aristotle, does not regard matter as nonexistent but as the source of change and manyness and imperfection; in short, as the indefinite potentiality of all things finite, imperfect, and changing. Matter exists in many forms as bodies. The Idea or Notion of matter exists in the mind. But matter, as the metaphysical principle of plurality, without which the realm of individual souls and the world of the senses would not exist, is simply the lowest stage in the necessary emanation of the world from God. Without matter, although the latter by itself is darkness, impotence, nothingness, there would be no distinction between human souls and the world soul. The One, or God, is above definition or conception. He is the source from which irradiate or emanate, *first, Thought or Nous* (which is the unity of the Ideas, in the Platonic sense, and which, hence, is the intelligible pattern of the world of phenomena); *second, Supersensuous Soul* or *Psyche,* which, as thinking the Ideas, is World Soul, and, as seeking to express itself in matter, is Nature or the world of space and time; *third, Matter* or *Hyle,* on which individual souls, themselves parts of the world soul, act, fashioning it into bodies in the likeness of the ideas. The whole process of emanation is an eternal and inevitable descent from Unity, through Duality, to Plurality. The existence of a world of incarnate souls is the necessary result of a fall from the supra-intelligible One. Thus, the *Incarnation* is the fall of God himself into material forms, although Plotinus holds that God does not lose anything of himself in this process of world formation. Salvation, or redemption, as we shall see, is the reverse movement of *Discarnation,* or release from fleshy matter and plurality into heavenly or spiritual body and unity.

In man are "nous" (Spirit), "psyche" (soul), and "sarx" (flesh or body). Thus there is a trinity in man, which epitomizes the trinity of Thought or Spirit, Soul, and Body, in the world at large. Man is the microcosmic reproduction of the macrocosm. Objectively, *body* is the world as it is perceived through the senses; the *soul* is the world interpreted as a spatial and temporal order by the discursive reason, while *spirit* is the world as apprehended by direct intuition. Reality is really a trinity in unity. It is the intuiting "nous," the objects apprehended, and the act of intuition. The summit of knowledge is the attainment of a divine insight, in which spirit is at one with the object. This fruition is the vision of God; it is the contemplation of God that is the ultimate goal of knowledge.

The world of appearance is of scattered, disconnected, diverse, data. It is what William James called a big, blooming, buzzing confusion. But, as this world is illuminated by mind, it is seen to manifest a unity. In the theory of Plotinus, there are two aspects which in a rough way correspond to the two phases of scientific analysis, that is, to the inductive process of discovering the universal, and to the deductive process of applying the same. The first of these aspects in Plotinus is that which tells of the descent of existence from the Absolute. By the second aspect, Plotinus shows the mode of ascent of the soul to the Absolute. The Absolute, the One, is above existence, it is without form, it is before motion and rest; and to reach the Absolute one must pass beyond knowledge. One must pass to the unity which is implied in duality. The Absolute is also the one universal good, which is above all things and the cause of all things. It cannot be named. It is above thinking. It is the first principle of thinking: it is the root of the soul. In brief, it is the absolute unity of truth, beauty, and goodness. In this way the highest form of reality is seen to consist of these ideas as a unity. This unity, this oneness of all things, is the indivisible root of subjectivity and objectivity, of thought and things. We thus see that this doctrine is a metaphysics of moral, æsthetic, and intellectual values.

How do the many arise from the One? This is the most difficult question in all philosophy. This is the question as to how we are to conceive of the embodiment of universals in particular existences. To this question Plotinus replies: The many arise by effulgence, by irradiation from the One. As light radiates from the sun, so by reason of his very fulness of being, individual objects emanate from the One. The One first expresses himself in "nous." This is the first step down from the Absolute to the many. "Nous," in turn, expresses itself by an outflow or a shining forth in the cosmic world. The world comes from the divine spirit or "nous." The soul of the world is the cause of all *things*. This world soul is unmoved and eternal. The One in thus manifesting itself remains undiminished.

In brief, then, the system of Plotinus is one of dynamic outflow from, and reunion with, the One. God, the One Exhaustless Source of all being, is above all definition. He cannot even properly be named One (monas); this term is the best symbol for him. He is the source of all forms, but without form; the source of all good, but above the good; the fountain of all beauty, but above all finite forms of beauty; the ground of all ideas and knowledge, but above all ideas and knowledge. He is the inexhaustible spring of life and mind, the principle of being, the cause of the good, the root of the soul. All these flow forth from him but he remains undiminished. He is above Thought or Mind (Nous), since the latter involves the duality of Knowing and the Object Known (of Nous and Noeton). Nous is his first Image, since Nous is, in itself, undivided and the ground of the Ideas or forms, and is the unity-in-duality of Thought and the Objects thought. As being the Universal Mind or Spirit, Nous is the Logos, the unitary ground of the Ideas, which fills the soul of the world with itself. The world soul is the Image of the Nous. (*Cf.* Plato, *Timæus,* from which this doctrine is derived.) The world soul is the cause of the existence of the plurality of things, and of all their life and movement. It is the cosmical principle of life. From it come all souls. The human soul is a fragment of the world soul. From the desire of the finite soul to live the life of sense, together with the desire of the world soul to fashion matter, arise bodies. The soul is the principle of life and movement in the body. Thus the individual soul is the meeting-place of mind or spirit and body. The soul is free, either to choose to abide in the sense life or to retrace its way back to God. As to matter Plotinus makes a distinction between the particular sensuous matter, which forms the body for the individual soul, and the ethereal matter which is the product of the Cosmical Mind or Spirit. Celestial souls, free from the thraldom of sense, have ethereal bodies of light (*cf.* St. Paul, I Corinthians, Ch. XV, on bodies celestial and bodies terrestrial). Thus it is erroneous to say that Plotinus was a dualist for whom all matter or body is evil. Evil for him consists in the isolation of the individual from his fellows and from God, which is a consequence of the pursuit, by the soul, of the life of the senses. Evil is separation, egoism, or selfishness.

It is interesting to ask, what does Plotinus mean by the distinction of spirit and soul? The cosmic soul is a vaguer principle than the cosmic spirit or *nous*; in some respects it seems to be less self-conscious than spirit. From the cosmic soul come all individual souls. All souls are derived from the universal soul. Plotinus conceives of the soul as the meeting place of intelligence and body, and he holds that there are three orders of souls, namely:

1. Heavenly souls
2. Souls enmeshed in matter
3. Souls that waver between these two

Our souls have preëxisted in the celestial world; they have fallen. Why did they fall? At this point Plotinus is not unambiguous. In some parts of his works, the view taken is the same as that in certain of the Platonic dialogues, namely, that the fall is a part of the divine purpose, while in other parts he holds that the fall is due to acts committed by the soul. The lowest step of existence is ensouled flesh. In this way we see the descent from the One to the many.

The prime interest of ethics and religion is to point out how the soul may ascend to God. In giving his interpretation, Plotinus rests continuously on the validity of his assumption that nature is the expression of the cosmical soul. And when the human mind begins to get its orientation in experience by ordering things in space and time, it begins to make its way back toward the Absolute. Space and time are both modes of discovering the One in the many. Now the universal soul is not in the world, but the world is in it. The world is in the universal soul; the universal soul depends upon the universal spirit; the universal spirit, in turn, depends upon the One. Only by contemplating the One is it possible for the individual to realize his true destiny. Man has in him a fragment of the Absolute, and, through insight and spiritual contact, he becomes one with the Absolute. The individual passes through several stages. The first step in this ascent is the practice of social virtues such as wisdom, courage, justice, and self-control. The second step is the practice of purification (katharsis). At this stage there is effected a complete subjection of the flesh—a freedom from all thraldom to passion is attained.[3] At this point Plotinus uses the Platonic idea of philosophical love. Every soul by nature loves and desires oneness with another. But there are stages of this form of love. True love, as opposed to earthly love, is kindled by the vision of all things in one. The living soul through this love is transformed and embraced in the unity of the whole. The final step, and this is one which requires intense concentration, is the direct union with the One. This stage Plotinus calls "ekstasis." It is an absolute self-surrender, "epidosis." The experience is that to which we referred above as being higher than knowledge. It is beyond knowledge; it is oneness with the One. This union with God is attainable through concentration and self-surrender. It is a spiritual contact in which we reach the fountain of being, and in this experience the soul is alone with the Alone. Through these three types of experience, the individual is led to God; and in this beatific experience, the emotional aspect of which is characterized by Spinoza as "intellectual love of God," there is a contemplation of beauty, truth, and love. In this experience all separate existences have van-

[3] Compare the Four Noble Truths of Buddha: 1, suffering is the accompaniment of change; 2, desire is the cause of suffering; 3, the suppression of desire is the only means of escaping suffering; 4, the three stages in the achievement of this suppression are uprightness, meditation and wisdom.

ished as being illusory, and all individual souls have merged into oneness with the Godhead.

Thus, for Plotinus, the Highest Good is progressively attained in so far as man achieves, step by step, first, through the practice of the ordinary and civic virtues, control of his body and harmony with his fellows, then speculative or contemplative union with the cosmical mind or spirit, and, finally, ecstatic union with the Godhead. Thoroughly Platonic is his doctrine of the ascent of Love from the vulgar and fleshly love to the love whose consummation is contemplative union with the universe and with God. Love, he says, is union of souls. But earthly love, in which this union is accomplished through bodily union, is mortal and easily passes into its opposite. The true love, the love of God, is a spiritual embrace, by which the mortal soul is wholly transformed, through being wholly laid hold upon by the Divine. This is the true being, the pure and unmixed actuality, of the soul, the union with God who is the beginning and the end. This experience is not a spectacle, but an ecstasy and a self-surrender, above beauty and above virtue. In it we reach the invisible sanctuary and fountain and principle of all, and attain a life, passionless, blessed, and divine. No finer attempt to satisfy man's spiritual needs, by a fusion of speculative and ethical motives, since Plato, can be found than the system of Plotinus. He uses the basic doctrines of Plato and Aristotle, but his system is not a mere patchwork. It is an original and well-knit synthesis. There is not space here to consider the successors of Plotinus in the school. It declined before the increasing influence of the Christian system. But Neoplatonism has had an immense, and still continuing, influence, both on Christian theology and independent philosophy.

This Neoplatonic view is the last speculative and religious effort of Greek genius. It is a universal philosophy, having incorporated into itself elements from all preceding philosophies save Epicureanism. It has already been stated that the growing demand of the social tissue was for union with the Godhead. The way to this union is here charted. This system also represents the consummation of Greek thought. Many modern systems of philosophy are at heart the same as Neoplatonism. This is preëminently true of the systems of Spinoza, Fichte, Schelling, Hegel, F. H. Bradley.

Neoplatonism failed. Christianity conquered. Why? Neoplatonism was unable to tell men how to make the state of peace endure. It was unable to make its philosophy take hold of the masses. Its method or way of ecstatic union with the Godhead was too hard for the ordinary man. It did not, and indeed by the nature of the case, it could not, present its way of life and salvation incarnated in a historic personality able to stir men's affection and command their loyalty. But this is precisely what Christianity did. The story is told of a certain propagandist of a new rose-water religion of universal philanthropy in the days following the French Revolution who, disappointed at the failure of his religion to make headway, asked advice of that old cynic Talleyrand. The latter replied, "I recommend that one of you be crucified and rise again the third day."

References

* Avey, Albert E., *Readings in Philosophy,* Chapter X.
* Bakewell, *Source Book in Ancient Philosophy,* pp. 340-393.

Bigg, Charles, *Neoplatonism, and Christian Platonists of Alexandria.*

* Dill, Samuel, *Roman Society in the Last Century of the Western Empire.*
* *Encyclopædia Britannica,* 11th ed., Article "Neoplatonism."

Fuller, B. A. G., *The Problem of Evil in Plotinus.*

Guthrie, Kenneth S., *The Complete Works of Plotinus* (Translation, to be used with caution).

* Hastings, James, *Encyclopædia of Religion and Ethics,* article, "Neoplatonism."

Inge, W. R., *Christian Mysticism,* and *The Philosophy of Plotinus.*

MacKenna, Stephen, *Translation of the Ethical Writings of Plotinus.*

TAYLOR, THOS., *Selections from Plotinus* (translation).
* WEBER, ALFRED, *History of Philosophy,* pp. 167-184.
WHITTAKER, T., *The Neoplatonists.*

ON THE GENERAL PSYCHOLOGY OF MYSTICISM

* BOUTROUX, E., "The Psychology of Mysticism" in *International Journal of Ethics,* Vol. XVIII.
* COE, GEORGE A., *Psychology of Religion,* Chapter XVI.
* CUTTEN, GEORGE BARTON, *Psychological Phenomena of Christianity,* Chapters III-XI; XXIV.
DELACROIX, H., *Études d'histoire et de psychologie du mysticisme.*
HÜGEL, VON, F., *The Mystical Element in Religion.*
* JAMES, WILLIAM, *The Varieties of Religious Experience,* Lectures XI-XVII.
* PRATT, JAMES BISSETT, *The Religious Consciousness,* Chapters XVI-XX.

CLASSICS OF CHRISTIAN MYSTICISM

BOEHME, JACOB, *The Signature of All Things* (in *Everyman's Library*).
BUNYAN, JOHN, *Pilgrim's Progress.*
FOX, GEORGE, *Journal.*
ST. AUGUSTINE OF HIPPO, *Confessions, City of God.*
ST. IGNATIUS LOYOLA, *Spiritual Exercises.*
ST. JOHN OF THE CROSS, *Ascent of Mount Carmel.*
ST. TERESA OF JESUS, *Life, Way of Perfection.*
TAULER, JOHN, *Life, Sermons.*
Theologica Germanica (translation by Susanna Winkworth).
THOMAS À KEMPIS, *The Imitation of Christ.*

A very interesting work by a forgotten English Mystic, Thomas Traherne, *Centuries of Meditation,* was discovered and published a few years ago. The poems and books of visions of William Blake belong in the category of mystical writings.

CHAPTER XI

EARLY CHRISTIAN PHILOSOPHY

The original Christian Gospel was not a system of philosophy. It was a religion claiming the definite authority of a revelation from God, and it appealed primarily to the emotions and consciences of men. It enjoined certain principles of conduct. The motives to enable men to obey these principles were offered in the feelings of gratitude and love for the Savior who died for them and arose again, in the promise made of an immortal and blessed life for the faithful, and in the fear of divine judgment upon the disobedient.

So long as primitive Christianity was a religion of the lowly and made popular appeal on these grounds, and while it continued, as in its origin it was, a movement within the Jewish Church, it did not make much use of philosophy. As soon, however, as it began to spread in the Roman world and came into contact with the civilization of the day, and indeed, even before it thus began to spread, it came into contact with the all-pervading Greek philosophy. The highest culture of the Empire was Greek in character, and in Alexandria the Jewish theologian, Philo, 30 B. C.—50 A. D., had already been deeply influenced by Greek culture. The Logos was conceived by him as the creative and revelatory Word of God, the immanent Divine Reason, operative in the world, and the unitary principle of the world of Ideas, Universal Types or Patterns, according to which all things were made. The early Christian philosophy is a synthesis of the Christian religion and Greek philosophy, for which the Jewish-Greek philosophy of Philo paved the way. It was an attempt to state the fundamental principles of Christianity in terms of Greek philosophy. Just so in every age, religion must either remain dumb or speak in terms of that age's concepts, if it is to speak to the cultured.

The ethical content of Christianity is, in some important respects, closely akin to the ethical teachings of Plato and the Stoics. The Hebrew and the Christian conception of God as the Supreme Good is thoroughly Platonic, while the conception of God as overruling Providence is Stoic. It was because of the incorporation of these basic principles in the more spiritual forms of late Greek philosophy, that Philo and others recognized an identity of Doctrine in Plato, Moses, and the prophets. The Apologists of Christianity went further than this and held that the Logos was manifested in Socrates and Plato. Justin Martyr, who flourished about 140, the first one of these Apologists, was a philosopher dissatisfied with the results of Greek philosophy, and he turned to Christianity because of its practical fruits. He did not, however, give up Greek philosophy. He showed the harmony of Greek philosophy and Christianity. He regards Greek philosophy as being a preparation for Christianity.

I. Ethical Content of Christianity

The ethical content of Christianity may be subsumed under the following eight heads:

1. God is the spiritual Father of men.
2. Human souls are of supreme value in the eyes of God, because men have within them by birth the capacity for realizing divine sonship.
3. Men should treat one another as brothers.
4. Divine sonship implies the practice of sympathy, service, coöperation, forbearance, and forgiveness.

5. The quality of man's character for good or ill and the judgment passed upon him by God depend upon motive and intent, and not upon external acts.

6. Nothing in the world has any value as against the right life of the soul.

7. The Christian ideal of life is to be realized in a new social order, The Kingdom of God, in which we shall treat all men as brothers in God.

8. This kingdom is to be ruled, not by force or external authority, but by motives of good will and love.

Christianity takes its origin from the life of an historic person who was believed to have sacrificed his life for men and to have arisen from the dead. His resurrection was taken to be the final authentic seal of the divine character of his mission. Jesus was held by his followers to have been, in a unique sense, the Son of God. The promise which he made to send to his disciples, after his departure, the Holy Spirit to guide and inspire them, was believed to have been fulfilled. Thus the Christians believed in a triune God—Father, Son, and Holy Spirit. It is this connection of Christianity with an historic person that fundamentally distinguishes the Christian religion from Greek philosophy. As against this association with an historic factor, Greek philosophy dealt with eternal truths which have nothing to do with time and place. As time goes on in the last centuries B. C., there becomes manifest in the Græco-Roman world an increasing hunger for an authoritative revelation and way of redemption. Indeed, it was taught later that both Socrates and Plato were divine revealers. It was because of this general demand for the revelation of a divinely authenticated method of redemption that Christian teaching found ready response in the Greek and Roman world. Plato dealt with abstract principles and not with historical processes originating in specific individuals and going forward in definite places and times. The Logos was the connecting link for integrating Greek philosophy and Christianity. The Logos is the divine reason which manifests itself in the creation and the order of the world. God in his fullness of being transcends the world, but is immanent in the world through the Logos. In the Gospel of St. John, Jesus is identified with the Logos or creative Word or Reason of God. The divine creative Word which issues from the Father is held to have been fully incarnated in Jesus.

The Holy Spirit is the continuously immanent activity of God in history. Thus the Christian religion unites the transcendent and eternal God, the Creator-Father, with the social and historical life of man. God is, at once, the eternal Creator of Nature and Father of men, and the ever-living and energizing ground of the spiritual life of humanity. Thus Christianity synthesizes the august notion of an Eternal and Transcendent Spirit, with the humanly warm and inspiring notion of an immanent, divine, spiritual Energy which ever keeps company with man in his pilgrimage through time, which comforts him and guides him (The Spirit which guides men into all truth, the Paraclete or Comforter). No other religion is, at once, so equally just to man's impulse to revere the Majesty and Mystery of the Universe, to bow his spirit in the presence of the Eternal, and to his longing to feel that the Eternal is present in his own life; that it is "closer to him than breathing and nearer than hands and feet," ever ready to comfort, forgive and guide him. The doctrine of the Trinity arose to meet this dual need, to find God in human life, in the individual's experience, and in the social and historical order, without reducing Him to a mere apotheosis of human aspiration, to an illusory projection of human wishes on an unfeeling and inexorable Cosmos.

II. The Doctrine of the Trinity

The foundations of Christian philosophy were laid by Origen of Alexandria (185-254 A. D.). God, says Origen, is pure spirit, the Absolute Creative Will, and the Logos is his expression. The Logos is a hypostasis, a being, distinct from the Father, but eternally generated from the Father. The Platonism of Origen is evident in his conception of the Logos as being the unity of all ideas. It is the *idea of ideas*. The creation of the world by God is an eternal process. It is really the eternal procession of spirits from God. Sin is the result of freedom, and the fall into matter is the result of sin. Origen maintains that all souls shall finally be redeemed. Salvation is the eternal procession of spirits from their alienation back to knowledge of and union with God.

As to the relation of the Father and the Logos, it must be said that there was a long controversy before the question was settled by the Council of Nicæa, A. D. 325. The Arian party, so called from Arius its leader, maintained that the Logos was a second divine principle, created by and subordinate to the Father, and that it was not of the same substance. The Son therefore is an independent being and is not *very God*. The Son is a creature who, by his own will, raises himself to moral unity with the Father. Athanasius, who flourished about 338, and his party contended against the Arians that God verily entered humanity through Christ. They held that the work of Christ would be lost if God had not entered into Christ. Christ is of the *same*, not of *like*, substance with the Father-God. Christ has come to make us divine. Therefore the Son is God. The Logos is eternally begotten of the Father, and not created in time. The Godhead is a unity. Eternally the Father implies the Son, as the spring implies the brook or as the sun implies the light. Therefore Christ is the veritable incarnation of God. He is of one and the same substance; his nature consists of a duality in unity, humanity and divinity in one self. The intent of this doctrine was to save the full value of Christ's work of revelation and redemption for humanity. The Logos, the second hypostasis or person of the Trinity, was fully incarnated in Jesus the Christ.

The Athanasian view triumphed. Its final triumph took place in the year 325 at the Council of Nicæa. Most of those who passed upon the question were utterly ignorant of the finer points of the controversy. But the influence of the Emperor on the Athanasian side meant the overthrow of the Arian party. This triumph of the orthodox doctrine now raised new questions. If God the Father was in Christ, then he suffered when Christ suffered. From this position (patripassionism) many recoiled. The discussion at this point gave rise to the question of the relation of the two natures in Christ, the Monophysite party holding that there was but one nature in Christ, the Docetic party maintaining that the incarnation was only in appearance. The view finally adopted at the Synod of Chalcedon in 451 was that there are two natures in one personality in Christ. The next problem was as to whether there are two wills or one will in Christ. The doctrine established as orthodox was, that there are two wills corresponding to the two natures, the human will of Christ being subordinate to and in harmony with the divine will. This doctrine is called *dithelitism,* the heretical view *monothelitism.* Finally, since the Holy Spirit was recognized as a distinct being, the immanent Spirit of God working in individuals and in the community of the faithful, the question arose as to the relationship of the three Divine Beings. The orthodox view of three distinct persons or beings, but so united as to form but one God, was finally accepted. This was a hard saying and the school of thought which gave the most plausible meaning to it, the Modalists or Sabellians, held that the three beings in the Trinity were only three distinct modes or relationships or phases of the life activity of the one God.[1] St. Augustine, 353-430, the greatest and most influential theologian of the Christian Middle Ages and possibly of all Christian centuries, was a Modalist. He explained the Trinity as Divine power, wisdom, and goodness, after the analogy of the human soul which is a trinity-in-unity of will, thought, and feeling. For us, as students of philosophy, the important point is that the doctrine of the Trinity was the vehicle by which the Platonic philosophy was transmitted to the Celtic, Teutonic, and Slavic peoples, and thus entered into the thought of the whole Christian world.

References

AVEY, ALBERT E., *Readings in Philosophy,* Chapter XI.

* *Encyclopædia Britannica,* 11th ed., Article "Christianity."

HARNACK, ADOLF, *The Expansion of Christianity in the First Three Centuries,* and *History of Dogma.*

* MARVIN, WALTER T., *History of European Philosophy,* Chapter XVIII.

* MCGIFFERT, ARTHUR CUSHMAN, *The Apostolic Age.*

* THILLY, FRANK, *History of Philosophy,* pp. 120-125, 133-155.

WERNLE, PAUL, *The Beginnings of Christianity.*

---

[1] The Greek terms for *person,* Latin *persona,* are ὑπόστασις and πρόσωπον. *Persona* was an unfortunate translation of ὑπόστασις. The latter meant, for the creedmakers, an essential character and function of God. The Nicene creed was concerned to affirm the *identical quality* of Christ's essential character or being and function with that of the Father; to maintain, in other words, that, while Christ had a distinct function and, therefore, a distinct being, he was of essentially the same nature or quality, *ὀυσία,* with the Father; not merely of similar nature. The word *persona,* and its modern equivalent *person,* however, came to mean a separate and distinct center of conscious experience and deed. Thus, if we take "three persons" in the modern sense of the term, the doctrine of the Trinity is tritheistic. If, on the other hand, we take it in the original sense, it means three characteristics or functions of one superpersonal Deity, who might be described as a community of persons in the modern sense.

CHAPTER XII

MEDIEVAL PHILOSOPHY

I. The Spirit of Scholasticism

The period called the Middle Ages extends approximately from 450 to 1500. It is a period characterized by the gradual development of a new civilization. The Roman Empire of the West had suffered disintegration from internal complications and the impact of the Teutons. Even in its original home the march of Roman civilization was arrested in many vital respects. The medieval civilization was built in part on the ruins of Roman civilization, and it gradually developed into a type of civilization which has maintained itself on into modern days.

Modern culture is more like Greek culture than it is like medieval culture. It is rationalistic in that it rejects the authority of organizations like the Church, custom, and tradition, and in that it critically examines facts, beliefs, and theories. In medieval culture the principle of authority rules. Spiritual values are a miraculous contribution from a higher and supernatural source coming into human life by way of a Divine Revelation, by the grace of God, whom it pleased to send his unique or only Son to redeem men from their sins. Modern culture is, by contrast, on the whole naturalistic or THIS-WORLDLY in its attitude. It looks with open-eyed interest at the facts of nature, which it regards as worthy of consideration and proving. Medieval culture, however, regards the world of nature as tributary to a world of grace. The supernatural, spiritual realm is the real realm. Such hymns as *Oh Mother Dear, Jerusalem* reveal for us the main features of the medieval attitude. There is embodied here that profound sense of otherworldliness, we are but "strangers and pilgrims here below." Our true home is in the transcendent realm of the spirit—the kingdom of God beyond the world of nature, and into which we may enter by means of the instruments of grace. For the child of modern culture this point of view has largely lost its validity. Our eyes and interests are fixed on another realm, this present world. Furthermore, modern culture is humanistic in the pagan or classical Greek sense; it aims at the fullest development of human powers here on earth. *This* world is the *locus* of the modern man's interest. For the medieval thinker, man is a dual being whose earthly interests are to be completely subordinated to the heavenly; he is a brand to be snatched from the burning. This is the dominant *motif* of the whole period.

Man's vocation is not viewed as being the process of developing and enjoying all his powers and interests. Man is to subordinate the so-called natural man to the spiritual, the supernatural, and the superrational. It is no exaggeration to say that the spirit of Neoplatonism and medieval Christianity are identical. Both involve the dualistic conception of man and the world, the ceaseless conflict between fleshly and spiritual interests and powers, and both explain the presence of spirit on earth as the result of its sin and consequent fall. The way of redemption is the way of escape from the prison house of the body by a superrational process. It is no accident, but part of the logic of thought and history, that St. Augustine, whose thought dominated the whole medieval Church, was a dualist. Before becoming a Christian, he was a Manichæan, and still later he was a Neoplatonist, and even in his latest stage he adhered to the refined dualism of Neoplatonism.

Medieval culture was begun and built up chiefly through the Church. This development was peculiarly facilitated by the disintegration of the Western Roman Empire. The Church was well organized and the Bishop of Rome, by virtue of the political and historical prestige and power of Rome, became the head of the Church. The Church remained the one stable, continuous form of cultural organization during the long period of transition from the ancient to the modern civilization. The Church was the vehicle by which there was preserved something of Græco-Roman culture, and through which that culture was effectively brought to bear upon the barbarian peoples. The Church was the instrument by which the education of these crude tribes was carried on. Deeply indeed were they impressed and awed by the Church; by its far-flung organization and activities, its control over the moral and spiritual life of its adherents, its vigor and its splendor. It was thus the Church that laid anew the foundations of civilization and began building up a new culture. It was the one all-embracing social institution. It claimed authority over all principalities and powers; it controlled the individual from the cradle to the grave, and beyond the grave.

There were no sharp lines between political, religious, scientific, and philosophical thought for the medieval mind. Theology was held to be the queen of sciences and philosophy was but her handmaid. Political and other species of social authority were held to be derivative.

The Church built up a splendid civilization, one in which industry and trade, no less than political and social life in general, were subjected to the control of the moral principles of Christianity. For several centuries the Church successfully asserted the right of religion to control and give guiding principles to every department of human life. The great religious foundations, the great cathedrals, and the scholastic philosophy remain as monuments of a period when Western Europe came nearest to realizing that complete moralization of life under the régime of one governing institution, which Plato dreamed out so coherently in the Republic.

The materials which the Church employed for educational purposes were the following: Trivium, which gave instructions in grammar, logic, and rhetoric, and Quadrivium, which was a course in music, arithmetic, geometry, and astronomy. These were taught from compilations. There was no direct acquaintance with the original Greek. There were, it is true, translations of parts of Aristotle's Logic, together with commentaries by Bœthius. Plato's *Timæus* and the writings of Cicero and of the Church Fathers were also available in the Latin tongue. From 500 to 1000 A. D., a period which is called the Dark Ages, there was only the most elementary form of education, and in this long period there was only one isolated intellectual phenomenon that relieved the blackness of this dark night. He was John Scotus Erigena, a profound thinker who flourished about 850. After 1000 A. D., a distinct revival of intellectual activity took place. Scholastic philosophy began to develop at this time. It developed rapidly and culminated in the thirteenth century. The first great Scholastic philosopher was Anselm, who flourished about 1075 and who struck the keynote of Scholastic philosophy when he said: *Credo, ut intelligam,* "I believe so that I may understand." Abelard showed himself to be a heretic by assuming the standpoint: *Intelligo ut credam,* "I understand so that I may believe."

Scholastic philosophy means, *first,* the philosophy taught by the *School men,* the great teachers of the Middle Ages. *Second,* since in their teachings they aimed to be in harmony with the faith of the Church, Scholastic philosophy came to mean a system of thought in which, while much free play is given to the analytical and speculative activity of *reason,* the starting points and results are always checked up by reference to the fundamentals of Christian faith. The Scholastics by no means confined themselves to the problems set by the faith. They debated, with great acuteness, on all the basic metaphysical and logical problems.

The Church had settled all fundamentals as to man's origin, nature, and destiny. The Church had fixed the metes and bounds of all knowledge. God created the world good; man fell, the Son of God was sent to redeem the world; the Church was the one custodian of all the instruments of salvation. Philosophy was to move and operate only within the limits of Church dogma. First of all the Scholastic philosopher bows to the authority of the Church; he then proceeds to defend the whole doctrine of the Church. The Church gave an intellectual map which charted all things, the origin, destiny, and nature of everything in earth, below the earth, above the earth, and in heaven above. This doctrine culminated in the *Summa Theologiæ* of Thomas Aquinas (1225-1274). He was the great organizer of Scholastic thought, and he shows that, when reason reached its limits, then revelation completed the edifice of truth. There is no opposition between faith and reason. The former supplements the latter. By reason we can prove the existence of God and the immortality of the soul. But the mysteries of the Trinity and Salvation are known only through revelation.

It was about this time that first-hand knowledge of Aristotle was to be had for the first time in western Europe. The Greek text was now brought in. This system quickened the mind of Scholastic thinkers and gave them method and scope which they had not had before. It is christianized Aristotelianism that we have in St. Thomas Aquinas. Although in 1215 Aristotle was condemned, he was, about ninety years later recognized as the precursor of Christ, and was made the supreme authority in philosophy.

At the very time that Scholastic philosophy culminated, the seeds of decay were beginning to germinate. In England, the Ionia of modern philosophy, Duns Scotus (1265-1308) denies that philosophy has the scope which Aquinas maintained, and he struggles to separate religion from reason. He says that the reason cannot prove either the omnipotence of God or the immortality of the soul. The function of theology is the purely practical one of promoting the soul's salvation. This brilliant dialectician was followed by William of Occam,[1] who went still further in attacking the philosophical presuppositions of the Scholastic system. He holds that reason is confined to the analysis and combination of the facts of sense perception. Therefore no articles of faith can be rationally demonstrated. At about the same time Roger Bacon turned his back on the *a priori* method of Scholastic philosophy and forcefully advocated the open-eyed study of nature and humanity, by empirical and common-sense methods.

II. Realism, Nominalism, and the Problem of Individuality

The preceding section has emphasized the outstanding characteristics of medieval culture, by contrast with Greek culture. In the twelfth, thirteenth, and fourteenth centuries, which are the great centuries of medieval philosophy, the Scholastic philosophers debated with great vigor three great doctrines, namely, *realism, nominalism,* and *individuality.* The relation of the universal to the particular is the quickening motive of the problem of individuality. This problem is involved also in the application of the first two doctrines to human nature. As a correlate to these, is the problem as to whether the intellect or will is central to human nature.

The question at issue between realism and nominalism

[1] Also spelled Ockham.

seems to us very much like hair splitting, but such feeling is due to our ignorance of the real nature of the controversy. The same problem is to-day the very core of the most controversial aspects of our basic problems. Medieval realism is the doctrine which argues that the universal, in the Platonic sense, has an existence superior to the particular, that it exists eternally, and that it is the *cause* of the particular. The universal, or type, is not only logically prior, but is also existentially prior, to the particular. The universal "humanity" is the cause of the particular human beings. The logical and existential priority of the universal to the particular is expressed by the realist in the phrase, *Universale ante rem.* How do these universals exist before the things? The opinion of the Scholastic is that they are the forms, or types, according to which God creates particulars. They exist before particular things in the mind of God. The second position of realism as to the nature and status of the universals is expressed in the phrase, *Universale in re.* These universals are the common nature or the common essence of particulars. If we have a given lot of particulars, we discover that the universal is that which exists in them as their common nature. The third phrase, *Universale post rem,* means that our knowledge of universals follows our perception of things, in the sense that, through reflection upon sense data, we gradually arrive at a knowledge of the eternally existing, universal real. We first perceive particulars, and then get their common nature. We do not start out with a ready-made kit of universals in our minds.

The position of St. Thomas Aquinas is that the universals first exist in the mind of God. The name Moderate or Aristotelian Realism has been applied to this standpoint. Extreme realism maintains that all individuals are illusions. It argues in an Eleatic fashion that there are no separate individuals; universals alone exist. The extreme realist is therefore a pantheist, and the fact that such a position is incompatible with Christianity doubtless deterred many from espousing this standpoint. Why was this question of such consuming interest? To show the interest of it *then* and *now,* it is necessary to contrast the standpoint of moderate realism with that of nominalism. Realism views the universals as being superior realities. *Nominalism* says that universals are nothing but words, *flatus vocis,* empty sounds. Roscellinus, the first nominalist, said individuals alone exist. Applied to the Trinity this meant that there were three Gods. It was not till the time of William of Occam, who flourished about 1330, that nominalism had its next great advocate. He says that only the particulars are real; the universals are mere names. There is no such thing in reality as *goodness, justice,* or *triangularity.* The world consists of an aggregate of particular instances, and what we call universals are names that we attach to the similarity between objects. We see objects and we note that they have certain common features. The generic term *humanity* is a name for those that have certain common features. We give these generic terms not only to objects, but also to various acts and processes which are like each other. Nominalism is not a defunct doctrine. It is what is known in modern thought as extreme empiricism. Such empiricism holds that what we perceive through the senses is the only reality that exists. What you think is but a *copy* of what you perceive.

Realism is a term frequently used with regard to a movement in literature, and in this connection it means that art is to embody things as they are without selection or evaluation. Medieval realism has a different meaning from this. It means that *universals are real.* Realism in literature is just the opposite of this type of realism. The fundamental doctrines of the Church were given a philosophical basis by the realistic formula. God is one substance in three persons. The Church also taught that the whole of humanity was involved in the consequences of Adam's transgression. Humanity is one, and so the fall of Adam entailed the whole human race. "For as in Adam all die, even so in Christ shall all be made alive." We are all parts of a whole, and not separate individuals. All men are saved in Christ. He is the typical man, the universal man, present in all men. The Church holds that it itself is made after a pattern laid up in heaven, and, because of this, the Church is more real than the individuals which compose it. This realistic motive is also the philosophical basis of the Church's doctrine of the Lord's Supper.

The culture of the Church conceived all existence to be arranged in hierarchical order. At the top of the hierarchy is God, and next, the angels. In God and the heavenly world are to be found all the types of earthly existence. After the fashion of Dante, our earthly existence is viewed as being only an allegory of the divine order. The earthly order is only a preparatory stage for the celestial order.

If the world of universals is thus so much more real than the particulars, the latter order is to be saved only by the descent of the universals into this order, and thus is the earthly order transfigured into the semblance of the divine. If the universals are so much more real than the particulars, then what is to become of the particulars? We feel ourselves to be separate beings. We have each his own inaccessible citadel of personality. Each person is an isolated, unique being. How often do we feel that nobody understands us! Uniqueness, isolation, privacy—these are marks of our personality. What becomes of this if the universal is the more real? Our feeling of freedom and our sense of responsibility point to the reality of the individual. How can this be? Aquinas said that *matter* is the principle of individuation. As forms, all souls will be identical, but as *embodied* they are different. We are individuals, therefore, in consequence of our bodies. To this position Scotus replies, that when we slough off this mortal coil, then we must lose our individuality. Scotus said that it is not in the fact of the mere embodiment of the soul that individuality is effected. It is not body that makes individuality, for God has no matter in Him. Each individual is real as a soul. Each soul has its *hæcceitas,* is an individual *this*. Each thing is a unique thing and has its own being. The fundamental thing in individuality is will, says Scotus, and in this he anticipates current psychology and philosophy. But Aquinas held that intellect is prior to will, and in doing this he is doing just what we would expect him to do in the light of the rest of his system.

The question as to the primacy of the will or the intellect comes out of the preceding inquiry, that is, as to universals. Will is primary for Scotus, and in consequence of this he defends free will, taking the indeterministic position, man has the power of free choice. As time went on nominalism gathered constantly increasing momentum and in William of Occam we have one of the acutest and subtlest thinkers championing the cause of nominalism. Universals exist only in the thinking mind, says Occam. Individual things alone are real. Universals are formed in the mind by abstracting the common features of the particular concrete things perceived, and by making linguistic symbols to denote the results of abstraction. A universal is a mental artefact, necessary for discourse. Occam is an out-and-out empiricist. With the increasing interest in the study of nature and with the development of nationalities, which involved the throwing off of ecclesiastical and political authority, there is a constantly growing interest in the nominalistic standpoint. The great development of dialects and languages, and the emergence of the empirical study of nature fostered nominalism, or empiricism.

The empiricist regards concepts as artificial abstractions which are derived from the inspection of particulars. Concepts are mere names for the empiricist. The basic motive of this view is the fact that he is prone to say that the psychological steps by which we get knowledge is all there is to knowledge. He does not seem to be conscious of the difficulty involved in the assumption of laws and abstractions which are valid for our own experience, but which have nothing in nature, as perceived through the senses, corresponding to them. In science we constantly classify facts and correlate them causally. Every exact law of science presupposes that nature is a kind of crystallized mathematics. We generalize so as to forecast and predict, and this certainly implies that there is a rational structure in nature. But nominalism reduces science to a set of symbols that do not represent reality. It makes reality a chaotic mass or aggregate of isolated particulars. Many people to-day smile at these old controversies. They do not realize that the same controversy is involved in the existence of the state. Are we isolated individuals? Is society simply a mass of separate individuals? This is the position of anarchy. There are thousands in our own republic who do not realize the significance of this conception with reference to the nature of the state. For very many the state is only a milk bucket. On the other hand, there is the equally vicious and defective view that all individuals exist *for* the state. The question to-day is as to where lies the seat of a rational and just authority of society over the individual. Thus the old question of Scholasticism is the central question of to-day. Are the state, justice, merely empty names? Is society only a horde of self-seeking individuals? Plato represents the state as the magnification or projection of the individual. It is the great instrument for the development of the soul of man. The anarchist would achieve the welfare of man by shattering the state and all social authorities into fragments. He would get harmony through the spontaneous action of the individual atoms in society.

References

* AVEY, ALBERT E., *Readings in Philosophy,* Chapter XII.
* *Catholic Encyclopædia,* articles on all above-mentioned subjects.

DANTE, *Divine Comedy,* and the *New Life* (translation by C. E. Norton).

* DE WULF, MAURICE, *History of Mediæval Philosophy.*

Essays Commemorative of Roger Bacon, edited by Little.

HASTINGS, JAMES, *Encyclopædia of Religion and Ethics,* articles on *Abelard, Anselm, Aquinas,* and *Scholasticism.*

POOLE, R. L., *Illustrations of Mediæval Thought.*

RASHDALL, HASTINGS, *Universities of Europe in the Middle Ages.*

* RICKABY, JOSEPH, *Scholasticism.*
* ROGERS, ARTHUR K., *History of Philosophy,* pp. 197-222.

ST. ANSELM (translation by Deane), *Proslogium and Monologium* (Open Court Series).

ST. THOMAS AQUINAS (translation by Rickaby), *Of God and His Creatures,* and *Summa Theologiæ* (translated under direction of the Dominican Order).

TAYLOR, HENRY OSBORN, *The Mediæval Mind,* Chapters XXXV–XLIV.

* THILLY, FRANK, *History of Philosophy,* pp. 155-163, 166-172, 188-218.

THOMAS À KEMPIS, *Imitation of Christ.*

* TURNER, WM., *History of European Philosophy.*
* WEBER, ALFRED, *History of Philosophy,* pp. 201-261.
* WINDELBAND, W., *History of Philosophy,* pp. 263-347.

Note.—Scholasticism has had a vigorous revival since about 1880. This is especially true of *Thomism* (the system of Thomas Aquinas). Its most active center up to August, 1914, was the University of Louvain. This revival is confined to the Roman Catholic Church.

PART II

THE CHIEF PROBLEMS AND STANDPOINTS OF MODERN PHILOSOPHY

CHAPTER XIII

MODERN PHILOSOPHY: ITS SPIRIT, ITS CHIEF PROBLEMS, AND ITS STANDPOINTS

Modern philosophy did not come into being suddenly. Even back in the thirteenth and fourteenth centuries, men like Roger Bacon, Duns Scotus, and William of Occam, advocated the separation of philosophy from theology. In this way these men claimed for philosophy the right of free and independent inquiry, while at the same time they recognized the practical value of theology.

The first really *modern* system is that of Giordano Bruno, a man burned at the stake in Rome in the year 1600. He was burned as a heretic, and thus suffered martyrdom for the cause of free knowledge and science. Three hundred years later, a great bronze statue was erected to him. His work is penetrated through and through by the idea of the infinitude of the universe. God is held by him to be the immanent unity of the universe, the all-pervading soul of things. God is the unity of opposites, the one in the many. He conceives of the material world as being made up of indivisible monads, and that there are physical and psychical monads. These monads are the elements of which the world is made.

The first scientifically developed system is that of Descartes, 1596-1650. The poetic impulse of Bruno is lacking in Descartes, who is a rigorous thinker. Soon after Descartes developed his system, Hobbes worked out his materialism, and, in rapid succession, we have given us the system of Spinoza, Leibnitz, Locke, and Berkeley. The seventeenth century was a period of great metaphysical systems.

All modern philosophy is rationalistic. It rejects the authority of tradition and works independently of ecclesiastical dogmas and religious beliefs. Its one standpoint is that of rational inquiry into nature and the meaning of experience. This revolt against authority and tradition is seen in other fields than science and philosophy. In the Reformation movement we have the rejection of the authority of the Pope in ecclesiastical and religious matters, and particularly the rejection of his right to interfere in matters of state. The Reformation is thus partly religious and partly political. This revolt goes hand in hand with the development of nationality and of regional government, and the beginnings of movements toward democracy.

The demand for representative government was successively successful in England, France, and America. Out of this movement developed the doctrine of the natural and inalienable rights of man, a doctrine which was expressed in its most classic form at the time of the French Revolution and the American Revolution. The democratic movement, in politics and industry, is the offspring of the same spirit, which rejects traditional forms of authority and proclaims the right of the individual to free thought and self-development. The doctrine of the natural rights of man goes back to Aristotle, the Stoics and Roman Imperial Law.

The chief social and cultural influences which resulted in modern thought are the following:

1. The influence of the Crusades in bringing Western Europe into contact with the culture of the Saracens.

2. The culture of the Renaissance. Here we have the spirit of humanism and naturalism quickened by first-hand acquaintance with the classics of Greece.

3. The growth of the spirit of nationality, or a sense of the rights of the local, social, and political organizations.

4. The influence of the Reformation in the matter of the rejection of papal authority in matters of religious observance and belief.

5. The influence of the doctrine of natural rights.

6. The new discoveries in geography and natural science.

Of these influences, the new natural science is by far the most potent.

The second great characteristic of the spirit of modern philosophy is that it develops in the closest association with special sciences. Until the end of the eighteenth century, mathematics, astronomy, and physics not only exercised a great influence upon philosophy; they even determined the very structure of philosophy, and in the nineteenth century the biological sciences, with their all-embracing generalization of evolution, molded new types of philosophical doctrine. This close relation of the sciences and philosophy in modern times is shown by the fact that many of the leaders in the development of science have been philosophers. Descartes was a great mathematician and physicist. Analytical geometry is largely a creation of his genius. Leibnitz, an eminent mathematician, geologist, physicist, chemist, comparative philologist, philosopher, invented the calculus, and in this way we see the organic relation between philosophy and science in his case. Locke and Hume were analytical psychologists, and furthermore, they were political thinkers or social philosophers. It is not until William James that we have another English-writing psychologist who ranks with them. Hume was an eminent historian. Kant was a mathematician and a physicist; he formulated the nebular hypothesis. It is only our second or third rate philosophers and scientists that fail to see the close relation between science and philosophy.

Another outstanding characteristic of modern thought is the marked development and emphasis of *empirical* or *inductive methods of inquiry.* In the ancient schools, particularly the Aristotelian and, later, the Alexandrian schools, the collection and interpretation of the facts of nature were not neglected. But the Romans were deficient in free scientific curiosity, and in the Christian Middle Ages it was generally assumed that the church had in its possession a complete set of universal propositions from which could be inferred, by deduction, all the most important truths.

The coincidental disintegration of the principle of authority and the discovery of the manifold complexity and interest of nature brought the problems of the correct methods of observation and classification of particular facts, and of drawing general conclusions from them, into the foreground. These are the problems of *inductive* or *empirical logic,* as contrasted with the formal or purely deductive logic which Aristotle had, with such marvelous completeness, formulated.

It is interesting to note that, while continental thinkers contributed most, up to the time of Newton, to the development of mathematical instruments of inquiry, it was English thinkers who gave the most powerful impetus to the theory of inductive inference. Roger Bacon (1214-1292) and Francis Bacon (1561-1626) in his *Novum Organum* and *The Great Instauration* were the prophets of the new inductive science. Their work was continued by Locke and Hume in the seventeenth and eighteenth centuries, and by William Herschel, William Whewell, John Stuart Mill, and others in the nineteenth century.

The two chief problems of induction are: (1) What are the conditions of correct observation? and (2) What are the conditions of correct generalization or the formulation of universals, from the facts? Francis Bacon, by his discussion of the four types of *idols* or mental blinders which distort human observation, contributed much to classify the conditions of correct observation. These are the *idols of the tribe* (the prejudice of the human species, due to passion, haste, habit, et cetera); the *idols of the market-place,* due to the current shibboleths or catchpenny phrases; the *idols of the theater,* due to false systems of philosophy which, he says, are so many plays; and the *idols of the cave,* or personal weaknesses of the individual. Bacon counsels us to be on the lookout for negative instances and go slowly in theorizing. He opposes speculation and deductive logic; in these respects he swings too far in his reaction against medievalism.

Bacon did not contribute much to the formulation of methods of generalization; indeed he underestimated the importance of hypotheses as a stimulus and guide in scientific inquiry. To David Hume, Sir John Herschel, and John Stuart Mill belong the credit of having formulated the specific methods of determining causal relations. In his "Rules by which to judge of causes and effects" in the *Treatise of Human Nature,* Book I, Part II, Section XV, Hume formulated with remarkable clarity and conciseness the canons for the methods of agreement, difference, and concomitant variations which are recognized as being, with the method of residues, the fundamental methods of causal determination.[1]

The significant, new thing in the background of modern philosophy—the novel standpoint in thought that shapes the point of view of much of modern thought, is the development of a mechanical view of the world. It is the conception of nature as a vast mechanism, infinite both in extent and in the complexity of its details. At the same time it is a mechanism whose fundamental principles of

[1] Compare any elementary treatise on logic, for example, Creighton, Sellars, or Hibben.

operation are known. Nature is viewed as a self-running mechanism. Four men of the highest importance have elaborated this doctrine. They are Copernicus, Kepler, Galileo, and Newton. Copernicus, in his astronomical theory, originated what is perhaps the most revolutionary thought of the ages. His theory loosened all the foundations of science and religion. Kepler formulated the laws of planetary motion. Galileo gave an experimental foundation to this theory and established many principles of modern physics. In addition to this he made many inventions of apparatus for better observation. One of the many things which he worked out was the determination of the concept of acceleration. In this way he showed that the rate of falling bodies is not a function of mass. Thus, at this time, a dogma which was accepted from the days of Aristotle was shown to be invalid. Newton, by his formulation of the laws of motion and the principle of gravitation, was able to bind all into one comprehensive synthesis. His formula is a generalization which involves the result of the researches made on falling bodies, the pendulum, and the planets.

Galileo had a clear conception of scientific method. He argues that what we can measure we can know. The book of the universe is written in mathematical characters. All changes in nature are the results of movements of atoms, but the secondary qualities of bodies are only subjective. In the year 1633, Galileo was forced to recant, but after having made his recantation, he raised his eyes to the stars, and while looking into that far off region which he knew so well, he involuntarily exclaimed, "And yet it moves." The background of modern philosophy is this development of the mechanical conception of the universe. The medieval philosopher viewed nature animistically and teleologically. A problem that becomes acute for the modern philosopher is this: If nature is blind and insensate;

if all that takes place in nature is the result of mechanical movements, and if all the motions of the heavenly bodies and all the changes that take place in the universe can be explained without assuming any interference of mind, then what becomes of mind, of the soul and spirit, in the universe? Are these not superfluous and antiquated conceptions? The first and greatest problem of modern philosophy is this: What is the character of reality? and how are the soul and body to be related? If nature is only an infinite machine, if this is all that there really is, then spirit seems to be a mere by-product of this machine, and science, language, art, music, and religion, seem to be reduced to the status of glandular secretions. If nature is only mechanism, then there is no ground for assuming that purpose operates, and we must abandon entirely the teleological conceptions.

In the physics and cosmology of scholastic philosophy, as in those of Plato and Aristotle, things and events in nature are conceived and explained in terms drawn from human purpose and will. Brute matter is subservient to purpose, to a good. In modern physics and cosmology all changes are explained in terms of the push and pull of blindly operating mass particles moving in space. Whereas in the former system, events are due, chiefly, to conscious or unconscious *striving for a good,* in the latter system, natural occurrences are the mathematical and inevitable resultants of the previous configuration of mass particles and their motions. In the former conception nature is impelled to achieve ends foreseen, or, at least, felt, to be *good.* In the latter conception whatever happens now is the inescapable consequence of a blind push from the past. The future is not a real factor in determining the character of the present; the latter is the inevitable echo of the past.

The great seventeenth century systems are attempts to

answer, in all the logically possible ways, the question as to what is the relation of mind and body, spirit and matter.

References

Berry, *Short History of Astronomy,* pp. 76-409.
Burkhardt, J. C., *The Civilization of the Renaissance in Italy.*
* Bury, J. B., *History of Freedom of Thought.*
Cajori, F., *History of Physics,* and *History of Mathematics.*
Cambridge Modern History, Vol. I.
Galileo, *Dialogues Concerning Two New Sciences.*
* Höffding, Harald, *History of Modern Philosophy,* Vol. I., pp. 103-148, 167-183.
* Lecky, W. E. H., *History of the Rise and Influence of Rationalism.*
Lindsay, T. M., *History of the Reformation.*
* Marvin, W. T., *History of European Philosophy,* Chapter XXI.
Rogers, A. K., *English and American Philosophy Since 1800.*
* Sedgwick, W. T., and Tyler, H. W., *A Short History of Science,* Chapters X-XIII.
* Thilly, Frank, *History of Philosophy,* pp. 221-240, 250-254.
Whewell, Wm., *History of the Inductive Sciences.*

CHAPTER XIV

THE PROBLEM OF REALITY

In this problem, which occupies the center of the stage in all the great epochs of modern philosophy, there are two main questions at issue: (1) What is the nature or character of that which is real? (2) What is the relation of the part to the whole, or, what is the place of the individual in the Universe? The central interest in this latter question for us is, What is the place of personality in the universe? In connection with this latter question emerge the problems of the meaning of personality, freedom, and immortality.

The first problem is to determine what is the abiding *substance* of things, or, what are the *substances?* It is in terms of the concept of substance that the four typical answers to this question were given in the seventeenth century. By substance was meant that which is permanent, that which exists on its own account. Substance is conceived as independent and self-existent. "Substance is that which exists in itself and requires nothing else in order to exist" (Descartes). In the textbooks on metaphysics, the ordinary classification of problems and theories is as follows: ontology, cosmology, and psychology. Ontology is the theory of the nature of being or reality. Cosmology is the theory of the structure of the universe. I find it unprofitable to thus separate ontology and cosmology. The questions of the nature of being and of the structure of the universe are obviously but two ways of stating the same problem. Metaphysical psychology is the theory of the structure and nature of the soul or self. But the problems of the self are evidently subordinate divisions of general metaphysics. While we may fix our attention, for the time, on the general problems of metaphysics, or on the special problems of external nature or human nature, all these problems are interlocked as parts of metaphysics.

What is the substance or permanent qualitative nature of things? We have five types of answers to this question:

1. Dualism.
2. Materialism
3. Spiritualism or Idealism
4. The Identity Theory
5. Neutral Monism

Dualism is the common sense theory, and has its classical formulation in Descartes (1596-1650). This theory is held by Locke (1632-1704), Kant (1724-1804), McDougall, Bergson, and many others. This theory rests on the assumption that there are two substances, namely, mind and body in man, spirit and matter in the universe at large. The three remaining theories are all monistic. Materialism is the view which we find in Hobbes (1588-1679), Priestley (1733-1804), Holbach (b. 1789), La Mettrie (1709-1751), Büchner (1824-1889), and Haeckel (b. 1834). There is one substance, namely, matter in motion. Spiritualism or Idealism assumes that the substance of things consists of minds, their activities, and their contents. The leading representatives of this view are Berkeley (1685-1753), Leibnitz (1646-1716), Fichte (1762-1814), Hegel (1770-1831), Schopenhauer (1788-1860), Lotze (1817-1881), Green (1836-1882), Bradley (b. 1846), Bosanquet (b. 1848), and Royce (1855-1915). The Identity theory is the doctrine that reality is neither physical nor mental—it is both physical and mental. Reality has these two aspects, and these two aspects are parallel manifestations of the same underlying substance. Representatives of the identity theory are Spinoza (1632-1677), Schelling (1775-1854), and Spencer (1820-1903). These views are all designated *qualitative monisms,* inasmuch as they maintain that there is only one kind of being.[1]

Somewhat remotely akin to the Identity Theory is the doctrine of Neutral Monism, or reality, as "pure experience" of which the physical and the psychical are but special configurations or complexes. This view is advanced by Avenarius (1843-1896), Mach (1838-1916), and James (1842-1910). It has been further developed by certain of the New Realists of to-day, and is favored now (1922) by Bertrand Russell. See Chapter XXI.

The second question referred to above is that as to the relation of the parts to the whole. What is the relation of the unity of the universe to the parts that are in it? We find here two main types of theory, namely, Monism or Singularism and Pluralism. Here the question is not, *how many kinds* of being there are, but *how many beings* are there. Spinoza is a monist of both kinds. There is for him only one ultimately real being and only one kind of being. In many respects this Spinozistic view is the doctrine of Hegel, Royce, Bradley, and Bosanquet. For all of these there is only one, ultimately real, absolute, all-inclusive being. The pluralistic theory is that finite beings, especially human personalities, have a distinct and separate existence and that they are not parts of God. They are private and unique beings, but not, however, without relations to one another. It is from this point of view that we see the metaphysical significance of the different types of philosophy of the State. The State for the

---

1 It should be said, in qualification of the above statements, that Bergson, in his doctrine of *pure duration* with its degrees of tension or condensation into images, tries to bridge the chasm between mind and matter; and that Bosanquet, like the present writer, recognizes the reality, though not the separate or independent existence of nonmental being.

singularist view is the *all-inclusive social unity,* an all-inclusive social sovereignty, to which all other social groupings are subservient. The democratic or pluralistic conception, however, is that the State is a human device set up to enable us to get along. The State is an instrument, a tool. *We are not its tools, it is our tool.* Among the great Pluralists are Locke, Berkeley, Leibnitz, William James, and Bergson.

The second central problem of modern philosophy—the problem of the nature of the unity of the universe and its relation to the diversity or plurality of the empirical world—takes on a different coloring and emphasis, according to whether the world is looked at statically or dynamically. It would not be a great exaggeration to say that modern philosophy, before Fichte and Hegel, was, with the exception of Leibnitz and eighteenth century evolutionists in France, prevailingly static in its outlook. The truly real world was not looked upon as having a history. Change, growth, evolution, struggle, and effort were foreign to the true reality, which was an eternal order, an unchanging Substance or Substances. In the nineteenth century, philosophy became increasingly dynamic, historical, or evolutionary in its outlook. Thus, whereas before Kant we find the principal stress laid on some sort of changeless elements, such as *extension, primary qualities, thought, ideas, truths of reason, material particles,* in recent philosophy the concepts and problems that predominate are those of *force, development, will, life, individuality, evolution, change, and time.*

Before proceeding to the consideration of the chief problems of modern philosophy, in the general order of their emergence, it may be well to outline the scope of philosophy to-day. Man and his physical environment are the two ever abiding terms for reflective thinking, however much human interpretations of these terms may change. *Physical*

Nature, Human Nature, and their Interconnections—here we have stated the whole vast, intricate, and significant problem of philosophy. Thus, systematic philosophy or *Metaphysics,* as I would employ the term, falls, logically, into three principal divisions, (1) *Philosophy of Nature* or *Cosmology:* this involves the consideration of the constitution or structure of matter and life, the place of life, consciousness, and individuality in nature, the respective meanings and relations of mechanical causality and purposiveness or teleology, the characters and place of space and time. (2) *Philosophy of Man, or of Society and Values:* this involves the consideration of the structure or constitution of personality and society, the place of self-hood and society in the evolutionary order, the nature of knowledge and truth, the nature of the other values which, like truth, are functions of social individuality or personality, namely the æsthetic values, the ethical values, and the interpersonal, affectional values, and, finally, the interrelationships of all the principal forms of values. (3) *Philosophy of the Cosmos, or Metaphysics of Ultimate Reality:* this consists in gathering up and interweaving the results of the two previous parts; it includes such problems as the ultimate relations of Unity, Plurality and Individuality, of Continuity and Novelty, of Evolution and Permanence, of Law, Order and Freedom, and, finally, of the place of Personality and its Values in the Universe conceived as a Totality.

It is impossible to discuss thoroughly the fundamental problems in any main division of philosophy without, at the same time, taking account of problems in other divisions of the subject. Thus, for example, the problem of the relation of mind and body in man, or of the mental and the physical in the universe at large, cannot be considered thoroughly without entering upon the problems of the general structure of organisms and of matter, the nature of our knowledge both of mind and body, and the nature of volition and human individuality. It is impossible to consider the problem of the Unity of the Universe, without taking into account the natures of space, causality, purpose, time, evolution, human individuality. Since, in philosophy, one big problem always leads us into others, the justification of such a division as that proposed above is that it affords the plan for an orderly conspectus and treatment of the whole field. The following treatment aims only at a discussion of the central problems in an elementary fashion. Therefore, I shall not spread it out rigidly upon the lines of the above division. I shall aim rather to discuss the central problems and theories, in the order of their emergence into prominence in the history of modern thought, and with regard to the way in which they lead into one another. The attentive reader will note that, broadly, the treatment does correspond to the order outlined above. This order corresponds, roughly, to the development of modern philosophy. The great seventeenth century systems on the continent of Europe were primarily cosmologies, Locke and Hume emphasized psychological, ethical, and political problems, with Kant the emphasis, in continental philosophy, shifted to psychology, theory of knowledge and ethics. Kant's successors, Fichte and Hegel, attempted psychological, ethical and social cosmologies. They sought to read the meaning of the universe in terms of a broadly and profoundly conceived philosophy of human nature.

References

Höffding, H., *History of Modern Philosophy.*

* James, William, *Some Problems of Philosophy,* Chapters II and III.

* Rand, B., *Modern Classical Philosophers* (judiciously chosen selections from all the great modern philosophers).

Windelband, W., *History of Philosophy.*

CHAPTER XV

DUALISM

This theory assumes that there are two distinct substances. In the human individual they interact. This is the common sense view. It is based on what appear to be glaring distinctions. When we will, a mental process, we determine a bodily movement. In tight places we frequently discover that we can do things with our bodies that we never thought we could do, for example, in situations of fright, and in athletic contests, et cetera. Conversely, bodily conditions influence mental processes.

When, however, we consider the respective properties of mind and body, we find that they are sharply contrasted. While body is a *divisible mass, extended* in space, mind is an *indivisible unity,* having *no mass* or *extensity*. Again, body seems at all times to be determined from without, while mind is a self-determining, self-directing principle. Mind has interests and seeks to realize values. It is purposive and develops new interests and values, and continually devises new means to realize its values. The dualistic theory thus seems to be based on obvious facts and contrasts in respect to the relation of mind and body. The Cartesian dualist says that the body apart from mind is mechanical, a system of juxtaposed points moving in space. The living organism is a machine. If there were in it no mind, it would still exhibit the same motions which it now manifests. Heat, as agitation of particles, is the cause of motions of the heart. Fine particles of blood pass to the brain. Thus, the heart gives rise to fine ethereal flames forming the "animal spirits." The nerves are tubular vessels which conduct the animal spirits. Animals are pure automata, since they have no souls. Except for the influence of thought, men are likewise automata.[1] Such was Descartes' view.

Thus, extreme Dualism affirms the substantial reality of two sharply contrasted kinds of being, which may interact at specific points, to wit in human organisms. These beings or substances or entities are—

MATTER OR BODY, which	*MIND OR SPIRIT,* which
is Extended in space,	is Unextended,
Consists of juxtaposed parts,	A Unity whose various aspects are
Hence is Divisible,	Inseparable features of the
Ponderable, and	One, Indivisible,
Moves through the impact, pressure, and pull of other bits of matter or by virtue of its own weight.	Imponderable, and Self-active pulsation of Thinking itself.

[1] See, especially, Descartes' *Principles*, IV, and the sixth *Meditation*. The brusque opposition of Body and Soul, in the Cartesian system and its congeners and descendants, is motivated by the conflict between the new naturalistic and mechanistic conception of Nature and the animistic and spiritualistic view of Nature which was the heritage of the Christian world from the Middle Ages. Descartes accepts and develops the doctrine that the human body, like all other animal bodies, is a machine, and, hence, a causally determined part of the world machine. On this hypothesis, reality and efficacy can be saved for the Soul, Spirit, or Mind of man only by assuming that it is absolutely different in character from the bodily machine, with which it is associated and which it influences. If the living body is merely a machine, then either the mind is its by-product or is an absolutely different kind of entity which interacts with the machine, however inconceivable interaction may be. On the mechanistic theory of life, either mind is an epiphenomenon or the true relation is Dualistic Interactionism. From this dilemma there is no logical escape. The doctrines and arguments of "psychical researchers" to-day, who accept the veridicality of telepathy, telekinesis, levitation, communications from the souls of the departed, *et hoc genus omne*, are usually based on the premises of Dualism.

It is necessary to distinguish clearly between *Naïve* and *Sophisticated Dualism.* Common sense or Naïve Dualism holds that body or matter is just what we perceive to exist in the external world, by the means of our senses. Likewise Mind is just what we are conscious of being when we feel and think and will. But a little reflection suffices to show that what we perceive depends in part: (1) On the momentary condition, as well as on the permanent structure, of our sense organs; (2) on the images and concepts which embody the results of social and racial experience, handed down to us through tradition, and which are to some extent supplemented by the previous findings of our individual experience, reflection, and memory; and (3) on the fact that our perceptions are also influenced by our spatial positions and our emotional prejudices and desires. *Thus sophistication begins, and, with it, the process of drawing into the mind or subject what naïve belief puts in the object.* The first step in this process of sophistication is exemplified in ancient Atomism and in the Dualism of Descartes and Locke.

I. Cartesian and Lockeian Dualism

Descartes and Locke are in substantial agreement as to the respective natures and relations of bodies and minds. Bodies are made up of minute particles of space-occupying substance. These cannot be atoms, says Descartes, for anything which occupies space must be indefinitely divisible. But they are mass particles. These differ in shape, size, and rate and figure of motion. Magnitude, extension, figure, and motion are clear and distinct ideas of matter, and, therefore, true (Descartes, fifth *Meditation*). Gross bodies, perceived through our senses, consist of configurations of mass particles. For Descartes, space is the same as material substance, and thought is the same as mental substance. Locke holds that solidity also is a property of bodies in themselves. Thus, for him, the qualities which mass particles (the term he uses is "corpuscles"), the constituents of bodies, possess in themselves are size, shape, mass, and movement. Because of the grossness of our senses, we do not perceive the mass particles, but there is a rough correspondence between the spatial qualities that we perceive in bodies and the primary qualities of real bodies.

Body and mind interact in man. As to the *how* of interaction Descartes vacillates. The view which he seems to favor most is that the *animal spirits,* a purely mechanical process generated in the heart, is carried to the brain and, in the pineal gland, influences and is influenced by the mind; and thus, in turn, enables the mind to control physiological movements. Locke simply accepts interaction as a patent though an inexplicable fact. He says that it is possible, though not probable, that a certain system of matter might think. It is improbable, since thought seems to be more than the effect of the mechanical interaction of particles juxtaposed in space. But, on the whole, he believes in two different substances which interact. But we do not know the natures of substances; we assume them as "the unknown support of known qualities." Material substance is the unknown support of the primary qualities of empirical bodies; mental substance is the unknown support of thought and volition. With respect to matter, Locke approaches very closely to the position of Kant; the critical difference between them being that Kant makes space a mental form of perception, whereas Locke makes it a physical reality. With respect to the ultimate natures of substances, both are agnostics. Both say that while we cannot help believing in substances, we do not know what these are in themselves. We have genuine empirical knowledge only of their appearances to the mind. Locke holds that we do not know how one body can act on another body any better than we know how mind and body can act on one another. We must simply accept the inexplicable facts in both cases.

II. Kantian or Agnostic Dualism

Kant, the main features of whose philosophy are best considered in another connection, is significant here, because his dualism is a halfway house on the road to Idealism or Spiritualism. Cartesianism puts the *secondary qualities of bodies, such as sounds, colors, tastes, and odors, in the subject, and leaves space and time as objectively or physically real determination of bodies;* thus laying itself open to the criticism, as we shall see, of inconsistency. *Kant puts space and time in the subject, and leaves only an unknown something, an X, as the objective ground of sensation. Space and Time are in the mind; the mind is not in space and time; thus we escape the difficulty of attempting to conceive how the mind can act on or be acted upon by spatial objects. We do not and cannot know the nature of the objective ground of our sense experiences. But we do know that the whole order of bodies, as these exist for common sense and science, is phenomenal reality, not ultimate reality.* The difficulty with Kant's doctrine is that he fails to explain by what right, on his premises, we assume at all that experience has an objective ground. In order to do so, we must apply the concept of *causality* beyond the limits of experience; that is, we ask for a cause of our sensations, and, according to Kant, causality, like our other mental forms, has no proper application beyond sense experience.

Berkeley, the Idealist, is more logical than Kant at this point. He argues that, since all sense qualities depend on a mind, and since I cannot explain my own sense perceptions as created by my own mind, while, at the same time, I know that I am a true cause of changes in the world, therefore my sense perceptions must be produced in my mind by the activity of some other mind. *Thus the process, begun in Cartesianism, of taking the sense qualities into the mind or subject, ends in Berkeley in the whole world being regarded as a society of interacting or intercommunicating subjects or selves.*

III. Criticism of Dualism

What are some of the objections to this theory? First of all, it is inconceivable and inexplicable how an unextended principle can act upon an extended principle; because of this it is said that the relation cannot be explained. To this objection, however, the dualist may reply that many inconceivable things are facts, and he will urge that it is our province to be guided by facts rather than by considerations of inconceivability. The second objection to dualism is this: That if mind acts on body, then the principle of the "conservation of energy" is violated. This principle is the statement that, in all changes or transformations of energy in the physical series, there is a mathematical equivalence. So much energy of one kind produces so much energy of another kind. Throughout the series there is a constancy, there is a strict quantitative equivalence, thus precluding either the creation or destruction of energy. Now, in the interaction of the dualist, there is energy injected into the physical series by the action of the mind on the body, and this injection means the destruction of the principle of the conservation of energy.

To this objection the dualist may reply: The amount of energy injected into the physical series by mind is too small to be detected by our most refined instruments. The objector would object again to this reply by saying, that, though such a position is plausible, it does violate the principle of the conservation of energy. A still further dualistic reply might be something like that which Lotze indicated, namely, the passage from the one series to the other is on the whole balanced, and there is thus no loss or gain. This also is very plausible, but it entangles the dualist in a further difficulty and one of such a character that, if the dualist adheres to it, he ceases to be a dualist. If energy can thus be interchanged, then energy is the common denominator of both series, and mind and matter are only forms of a common principle. The dualist has still a third answer, which is to the effect that the mind directs the body but uses *no* energy in so doing. The advocate of this view might point, for example, to an engineer directing a great engine by a small lever, or, to such an incident as President Wilson pressing a button at Washington, thus setting in motion all the machinery in a large exhibit on the Pacific Coast. But the President did use energy—he pressed the button—so this answer also is invalid. Still a fourth reply might be given by the dualist. He may argue that the principle of the conservation of energy is a working hypothesis for the physicist, when dealing with strains and tensions, and with the mathematical relations of mass particles. He finds that the principle works, but his point of view, says the dualist, is abstract, and from a total point of view there is no reason for assuming that the physical series is a closed one. The standpoint of physics is *partial* or *abstract,* that of philosophy *total* or *concrete.* When we take the whole of experience into account, it is seen to be too complex for one to be justified in saying that the principle of the conservation of energy is absolutely valid.

This principle when considered in connection with the second law of thermodynamics (the entropy of a physical system tends to increase) breaks down as an ultimate principle for interpreting experience. In actual physical changes, work and motion are effected only through the loss of available heat energy. In the doing of work, energy is passing from available to unavailable forms, from unequal to equal temperatures. Energy generated by a waterfall may be harnessed and made to drive wheels or other types of machines. But a large proportion of the energy of the waterfall is dissipated in the form of heat. If the sum total of energy in the universe is constant, and if the doing of work always involves the passage of energy from available to unavailable forms, then either the universe is finite in duration, or there is a creative source of energy which compensates for the passage of available into unavailable forms. If we do not assume this, then we must assume that the universe is running down, that is, is tending to equilibrium, and that the time is coming when there will be *nothing doing*. If the universe has existed through infinite time, then it must have run down long ago. Infinite energy, in amount, is not a sum total; it is not a so much. The term "infinite sum" has no meaning; a universe consisting of a definite quantity of energy, however great, would be finite. A universe which had no beginning is not finite and it can have no ending. Thus we are led to the view that the universe cannot be a perpetual motion machine containing a definite quantum of energy. The second law of thermodynamics, when thought out, requires us to assume, if the universe is endless in duration, a Creative Source of Energy.

The discussion of the above point brings us directly to another problem, namely, what do we mean by matter? Common sense dualism holds the view that matter is what we perceive. When the dualist believes in interaction, he means to say that an unextended entity is seated somewhere in the brain and directs it. Descartes got himself into inextricable difficulties in trying to square the theory that the human body is a pure machine with the recognition of the soul or mind as an original source of volition and thinking. The scientific conception of matter is not identical with the common sense view, and the difference is seen in the fact that the man in the street is a *naïve realist* as regards the problem of our knowledge of reality. He believes that the real, external world is just what we perceive, and exists, just as we perceive it, independently of our perceptions. The *idealist* points out that what we perceive does not exist independently of our perceiving it. The world of experience is, he shows, a world of sense qualities. It is a congeries of sense qualities having temporal and spatial relations. Now sense qualities are just things perceived by minds. The idealist asks this question of the naïve realist. If sense qualities, which are all that you perceive, are independent of the mind, how do they exist when no mind perceives them? Is there color when no one is looking? Is there sound when no one is listening? Sometime ago I read a book entitled, *Light, Visible and Invisible.* Such a title is really tantamount to the expressions, untasteable taste, unhearable sound, or unseeable light. This is nonsense. If the naïve realist says that he thinks the perceived sense qualities are independent of mind, what is the nature of these qualities when not perceived? If I were to bring before a class a band of colors, without a doubt the girls would recognize the differences between them better than the boys. Were there a number of musical instruments played here now, many of you would recognize distinctions which others would not hear at all. We do not all agree either as to the number of sense qualities perceivable, for example, in the case of colors or music; nor as to the relations of space, time, and intensity in sense qualities. Sense qualities are variable functions depending on variations in the senses, mental and physical habits, interests, et cetera. That which exists apart from our perceiving is nothing but the abstract possibility of further perceiving. Then what exists in the moment of perception is not matter, but experience. The physical world is just this *possibility of experience* for all. *It is social possibility.* What we mean by the physical world, the idealist argues, is something that can be perceived, if there be someone to perceive it, and can be perceived by all percipients. Now, we do not all agree as to its qualities and relations, but we attempt to overcome this subjective perceptive standpoint by means of quantitative ratios which serve as tests of commonness or social perceptibility, and it is this that is the basis of our belief in the external world. The latter is the realm of common or social percepts and perceivables.

Now the question arises what is matter in itself, or as it is apart from perception and experience? The scientific dualist, who believes in an independent matter, says to the idealist, you must admit that something independently real is the cause of what we perceive. To perceive there must be an objective cause or ground of our perception. We do distinguish, says the dualist, between perceptions and images, between realities and illusions.

Were I to say to this class, look at that striped tiger in the back of this room, you would immediately think I am experiencing illusions. The victim of delirium tremens sees snakes crawling about him, but we can neither see them nor touch them. We do not have the same images and perceptions that he has. His visual images are incoherent with tactual percepts and with all our percepts. Thus we say he is in an abnormal condition, whereas we are normal. Illusion is thus a test of the distinction between appearance and reality. We say that that which resists our wills, our purposes and intents, is reality, but objects which do not resist or modify our wills, we say are illusions. We say that the thing which we cannot resist is real. The meaning of this is that we call that real wherein the qualities of our sense organs are confirmed by the experiences of the other senses and, more especially, by the experiences of other selves.

The scientific dualist, who differs radically from the scientific materialist, says that what really exists independent of percipient minds is a world of mass particles having no secondary qualities. He conceives a world of no color, no taste, no smell, no temperature, no sound. It is this world that really and independently exists. It is a world of mass particles moving in space and time. But, impressed by the fact that mind or thought and volition do seem to be real causal factors at some points in the physical process, and unable to conceive, either how mind can be produced, by the motion of mass particles, or how mind and body can interact, the scientific dualist is content to affirm the facts, and to admit that he does not understand the *how* or particular *go* of the interaction. He is unwilling to let the passion for intellectual unification ride roughshod over facts and obliterate what seem to him fundamental distinctions and relations.

References

* Avey, A. E., *Readings in Philosophy,* Chapter XV.
* Descartes, *Meditations.*
* Locke, *Essay Concerning Human Understanding.* Especially Books II and IV.

McDougall, W., *Body and Mind.*

* Russell, B., *The Problems of Philosophy,* Chapter II.

CHAPTER XVI

MATERIALISM

I. The Scientific Notion of Material Substance

The scientific dualist, naïve dualist, materialist, and idealist, all agree with the man in the street in that they unanimously admit the existence of the external world. When we perceive, they assert, *there is* something outside our own minds. A disagreement emerges, however, as to what this something *really is* and, consequently, as to how that external something is known, how it acts upon, and is acted upon by the human mind.

The lecture desk before me is as I perceive it, urges the man in the street. Its existence is independent of me. We know, however, that the desk as I perceive it is in some fashion a function of many variables, to wit: sense organs, nerve currents, my position, my interests, my attention, my previous experience and ideas. An African savage could not perceive this desk before me just as I perceive it. It would not *mean* "desk" to him. What we perceive is largely determined by our *already* achieved mental structure and outlook. In view of this, what is the factor that is independent of my perceiving? Many say that this object before me is a mere appearance, and that the *real substance* is something different *in kind* from its appearances. The scientific dualist maintains, as against the materialist, that there are two kinds of being, mind and matter. The materialist says that there is only one kind of being, and that is matter. The attitude of the materialist is indicated by the old adage: What is mind? Answer: It is no matter. What is matter? Answer: Never mind.

The advocate of material substance admits that the qualities which we perceive in the external world are in part dependent on our organism. He admits that colors and other secondary qualities are phenomena. They are the joint resultants of external substance and of our percipient organism. What then is the nature of this independent substance or matter? In many of the older forms of the substance theory, it consists of mass particles in motion. It is an aggregate of minute bodies having mass, density, and varying in size, and perhaps in shape. In terms of the distinction between primary and secondary qualities, the secondary qualities are subjective, they exist only where there is a percipient organism for which they exist. Body in itself consists of these minute particles in motion. In perceiving primary qualities, we have a copy of being as it is. Molecules in motion is thus the make-up of matter. Recently this Lockian notion has been greatly modified and we now have a more dynamic conception. In place of mass particles in motion, we now have the view that mass particles are but nodal points of energy. Matter therefore is the result of the action, on our sense organs, of centers of electrical charges. In the highly elastic, frictionless, imponderable ether are centers of strain, and these strain centers are the electrons. Our sense organs and brain are themselves constellations of electrons. This newer theory makes matter to consist of *nonmatter in motion*. There are, however, many difficulties involved in this notion of the enormously strong ether, as well as in the assumption of an independent substance different in kind from what we perceive and yet assumed to be the cause of what we perceive.

My criticisms of this theory are in part identical with Berkeley's. The first difficulty is as to how the advocate of an independent material substance is justified in his conception that, while secondary qualities have no correlates in matter itself, the primary qualities do represent properties that are inherent in matter. Locke and Descartes are in agreement on this point. The secondary qualities, they both say, are produced in us by the action of particles that actually possess the primary qualities. This is an assumption, and is for many purposes highly convenient. But this assumption is not thoroughly logical. Why not? No one ever perceived primary qualities without secondary qualities, neither did anyone ever perceive secondary qualities unaccompanied by primary qualities. There is no such thing as one set of these qualities without the other. The disjunction seems forced upon us that either all the qualities are in the percipient organism or all are in the object.[1]

The advocate of material substance says that primary qualities are in the object, for the reason that they do not vary as do the secondary qualities. The secondary qualities do vary and therefore are in me. But primary qualities are perceived by us just as are the secondary, and the primary qualities do vary, although less markedly than the secondary. Either none of these qualities testify to independent substance or all of them do. The Lockian distinction is illogical. The advocate of material substance is not yet silenced. He will say, "I admit that,

[1] Practical and social motives are responsible for the distinction between primary and secondary qualities. The so-called primary qualities of bodies—space occupancy, mass, inertia, motion—are the perceptible qualities which, being *relatively least variable*, human beings can *agree upon as being, for practical and social purposes, constant*. Moreover, since vision and touch are the two senses through which our active intercourse with the world is chiefly guided, the visual and tactual qualities which have most constancy are *convenient* substrates for all the other qualities.

but there must be *something* external which exists, some cause independent of our will and imagination. What is it?" The advocate of an independent substance insists that there is something independent of the mind.

Let us look at the most serious difficulty involved in this assumption of a material substance. Naïvely, we all assume and believe in an independent substance. We believe in it until we reflect a moment on the difficulties that are involved. But most of us after reflecting, forthwith go back on our reflection and still believe in an independent material substance. We are like the man spoken of by St. James in the Bible: "He is like unto a man beholding his natural face in a glass: for he beholdeth himself, and goeth his way, and straightway forgetteth what manner of man he was." We assume that the world as we perceive it, is a part of an independent reality. But the variability of our perceptions ceaselessly operates against this assumption. Two men in the same field do not see identically the same field. Two men before a great mountain do not perceive identically the same mountain.

We are told that what really exists is a material substance, but on analysis this material substance is not the common world of our experience; it is a substitute for it. It is something which by hypothesis can never be directly experienced. What then is the relation of this world of supposed substance to our common world? Here we get no cogent answer. John Locke says that our knowledge is a sort of poor copy of the external world. The huge assumption made here Locke never was fully conscious of. How do I know that my knowledge is a copy? A copy is a copy of an original. How do we know that our knowledge is a copy? If, by hypothesis, we never could know the independent material substance, then how could we ever tell that our knowledge is a copy of the material substance? This is the greatest difficulty with this standpoint.

By what transcendental sense could these men perceive the original?

Two further difficulties remain: (1) How can mass particles, or mass points, produce in us the sensations of color, sound, touch, taste, smell, heat? This difficulty is, perhaps, no more serious than the converse one as to how the mind can influence physical things. (2) The substrate or real external cause of visual sensation is wave motion in the ether, we are told; of sound, undulations of air particles; of touch, mechanical contact; of taste and smell, chemical changes; of heat, the rapid agitation of molecules. If, then, there be one real physical substrate, or substance, it must be the common ground of all these changes, which are specific causes of specific sensations. We have ethereal theories of the physical substrate of color, electricity, and magnetism; but none that are plausible as a physical basis for smells, tastes, and sounds. We have electronic theories of electricity and radioactivity, and an attempt at electronic theories of gravitation and inertia; but no well-worked out theory which makes it clear how all kinds of physical stimuli can be regarded as modifications of one substrate or substance. The reduction of the various types of quality in nature, *as we perceive nature, to one consistent type of spatial thing-in-motion,* is far from having been attained. Perhaps, it is better to admit that nature is not so simple and homogeneous as the doctrine of one and only one kind of ultimate material substance would imply; that nature has several qualitatively different kinds of thing, and that mind is a true and organic constituent of nature seems a reasonable conclusion.

Locke admits that we know nothing as to how the primary qualities, such as figure, size, or motion of parts, produce in us secondary qualities, such as a yellow color, a sweet taste, a sharp sound; further, that we do not know whether any mere material substance exists, or how it can interact with an immaterial substance. He thinks we do know that our simple ideas agree with things, since these ideas arise in us independently of our minds. But Locke admits that all that "this sensitive knowledge of particular existence" amounts to is that there is *something* corresponding to the idea; for example, something which produces in us the perception of a fire. (*Cf.* Locke, *Essay,* Book IV.)

The "somethings" or "objects themselves" are but *powers* to produce various sensations in us by their primary qualities. This is done "by single imperceptible solid bodies coming from objects to the ideas." Our ideas of primary qualities resemble the objects; our ideas of secondary qualities do not.

Hume reduces our knowledge of the external world to the confidence engendered by habit, in the routine succession and repetition of impressions seemingly similar and contiguous, buttressed by the mind's inveterate propensity to feign connections and existences. (*Cf.* Hume, *Treatise of Human Nature,* Bk. I, Pts. 3 and 4).

The Matter about which physicists theorize is a hypothetical something, a *construction,* a theory. Descartes saw clearly this difficulty, but he never succeeded in making much out of it. He was doubtful as to whether there is any external world at all. He says that it is possible that all of our perceptions are illusions. To guarantee the validity of our perceptions, he called in the veracity of God. If God exists, He is veracious—He won't deceive us and therefore there must be an external world.

II. Materialism

The scientific dualist, who assumes the existence of a matter different from the experienced world, has thus far not given us a clear and consistent conception as to what this matter is, nor can he give a plausible explanation of how it acts on mind and is acted on by mind. In actual experience we have sense qualities and mind interdependent. *Materialism* holds that *matter only* really exists and that mind is but an epiphenomenon, a by-product of matter. Like a tramp "bumming" his way on a train, it is not a real factor in the process of experience. The materialist argues that matter is the only reality. The causes of all the complex qualities of experience, both in the physical and the mental realms, of all thought, feeling and volition as well as of all physical and vital processes, are complex and microscopic movements of mass particles in space. This view is expressed by the saying that brain secretes thought as liver does bile and the expression "der Mensch ist was er isst"; "man is what he eats."

The arguments given by the materialist are these:

1. He adduces obvious evidences of the dependence of consciousness on physical condition such as: If the supply of blood to the brain stops, unconsciousness ensues; when in great fatigue, it is difficult to think; a blow on the head will produce unconsciousness; drugs and diseases have various effects in the way of heightening and lowering consciousness; mental disorders follow on lesions of the brain; old age comes from a running down of the bodily machine, and this is accompanied by a decline in mental power. Finally, the cessation of bodily functions results in the extinction of thought.

2. The materialist reënforces his first argument by pointing to the development of consciousness in the biological series. He regards consciousness as a function which is dependent on the degree of development of the nervous system. There *seems* to be a one-one correspondence or co-relation between the vividness and apparent efficiency of consciousness and the organization or complexity of the nervous system. Man has the most complicated brain of all animals. The more organized the nervous system, the more organization of brain structure, the higher the degree of consciousness and intelligence. Mind, therefore, is simply a function of the nervous system, says the mate-

rialist. Consciousness is not an entity or an agent, it is only an attribute of the nervous system.

Let us examine these arguments. Both imply that consciousness is the effect of purely physical causes. What do we mean by saying that one set of conditions is cause of another set? In the sciences, by cause is meant an invariable and unconditional sequence; what always follows is the effect and what always precedes is the cause. This is the scientific notion of cause, save where the more rigid notion of quantitative equivalence is used. In so far as cause is identified with the idea of quantitative equivalence, the causal idea loses its significance in application to the relation of brain and consciousness. Materialism would be established scientifically, if the processes of mind, such as perceiving, imagining, analyzing, synthesizing, generalizing, forming universals, selecting, inventing, feeling, valuing, and willing, could be measured and equated, in terms of energy units, with other forms of energy. This cannot be done. Mind is in active power, and yet it cannot be identified as one form of physical energy. If it be an energy system, it is a wholly unique kind of energy. In measuring the equivalence of forms of physical energy, the physicist can find no place into which mind, the measurer and director, will fit. From the standpoint of mechanics, mind seems to be a troublesome interloper in the physical series. It will not submit to be formulized in terms of foot-pounds, ergs, or dynes. Futhermore, from the viewpoint that cause is invariable sequence, the materialist's argument is one-sided. It is true we do observe mind changes following upon bodily processes, but the converse is equally true, and it is on this converse that the strength of dualism and interaction reposes. In his first argument the materialist ignores one side altogether. His second argument is much more important. There is a correlation between the degree of the organization of the nervous system and the degree of consciousness and intelligence. We cannot, with our present technic, carry this out in a detailed way, but we must admit that the functioning of mind in this two-sided world of ours is dependent on a nervous system. Minds do not work without nervous systems, but we must not forget that, though the nervous system may be a causal condition, it need not be the *total explanation* of the operation of mind. The functioning of the nervous system may be an invariable condition of the function of consciousness in the present empirical environment, but we cannot explain mind entirely in terms of this one causal condition.

On the materialist's hypothesis, mind is useless, it does not really do anything, it is an otiose by-product, it is wholly passive. In the organism, bile does something physiologically, and we can analyze it. But thought escapes all analysis by physical means. The analogy between thought and glandular secretions is worthless and misleading.

The power of the mind to influence the body is just as well attested a fact as the converse. All our purposeful activities depend for their efficacy on this power. In critical situations, under the influence of strong emotion, conviction, faith, fear, pity, loyalty to duty, friends or country, the mind makes the body do unexpected and otherwise impossible things. The influence of faith, autosuggestion, heterosuggestion, and hypnotism, which is just an extreme instance of suggestion, in increasing and directing the bodily energies, in producing anæsthesia and actual bodily changes, and in healing effects, are cases in point here. That the set or attitude of mind, however generated, has a decided influence on the bodily condition and action cannot be gainsaid by an open-minded person.

As a matter of fact, animals with the greatest degree of consciousness are those which dominate creation. "Beware when a thinker is let loose on this planet,'' said Emerson. Pictures, poems, tools, states, religion—these are the products of thought. It is not in accordance with plain facts to say that conscious intelligence does not do anything. Consciousness is efficacious both for good and for evil. In the recent World War, we have seen clearly this bifocal type of mental efficacy.

The scientific-minded materialist appeals to the doctrine of the conservation of energy as his last resort, and he assumes that this supports his theory. As we have stated above, this is only a working hypothesis and we do not take this as our *sole* guiding principle. But even if we do take the materialistic viewpoint, we yet have something outside the range of measurement. If we take the principle of the conservation of physical energy as the absolute truth, we can see no reason why there should be such a thing as mind appearing in the series of organic forms. Either mind is an efficient agent, and in that case the conservation of energy is not an absolute principle, or mind is without any efficacy and in that case the mass particles moving in space do not seem to behave in accordance with nature's principle of parsimony, since they generate a superfluous and useless illusion, that is, conscious intelligence.

On reflection it is clear that the materialist is unable to explain *how* mind can be a product of matter. Furthermore, it will be evident that the scientific conception of matter is itself a product of mind. The matter the scientist deals with is a conceptual construction, a product of the scientific imagination and not anything that anyone can ever experience. But how remote is this conception from that of the ordinary man? The ordinary man means by matter the organized qualities that we perceive. These, we have seen, in part depend upon our perceiving. What we experience are *grouped sense qualities*. Our world of experience is, therefore, a realm in which the percipient organism and the object mutually imply one another, and the world beyond what we perceive is only the real possibility of further experience.

In short, matter, in the scientific sense, is a moving configuration of mass particles in space; or, in terms of the latest theory, a system of electrically charged positions in space. It has none of the qualities which we perceive in the actual physical world, the realm of sense experience. It has not the colors, shapes, sizes, motions, sounds, odors, tastes, feels, and warmth and cold, which we attribute to physical objects. It is devoid of all "secondary" qualities and all "primary" qualities too, except, in exceedingly comminuted form, position, inertia, attraction, and relation in space. Even more strikingly is it devoid of the "tertiary" or æsthetic qualities of beauty, grandeur, picturesqueness, sublimity, majesty, or homely friendliness. Scientifically conceived matter is not the *nature* or *physical world*, which man, through his whole being, acts on, is acted on by, struggles and communes with, in part knows and masters and, in part, is mastered by. It is inconceivable that such a ghostly fabric, woven by the mathematical imagination however deftly, and however useful it be as a web on which to stretch physical calculations, should be the *ultimate and sole reality of which mind is but the shadow occasionally thrown hither and yon on the evershifting web—Mind, with its power to select, generalize, abstract, remember, invent, devise, imagine, purpose, and execute, with its power to remake its physical environment, to build up a new environment of social institutions and values, and to create a spiritual world of justice, integrity, love, beauty, and fellowship. To say that mind is the by-product of mass particles is to assume that the whole superphysical realm of human and cultural life and values, including the "Nature" of our common human experience, is the blindly produced, inexplicable, and super-*

fluous effect of impacts and tensions in a realm of ghostly entities which is itself the offspring of the constructive imagination of the physicist. Surely this is making the cart draw the horse with a vengeance.

References on the Conception of Matter

* Ames, J. S., *The Constitution of Matter.*

* Avey, A. E., *Readings in Philosophy,* Chapter XVI.

Fournier d'Albe, *The Electron Theory.*

Leighton, J. A., *Man and the Cosmos,* Chapters XV, XVI, XVIII-XXI and XXVII.

* Lodge, Oliver, *Electrons.*

* More, L. T., *The Limitations of Science.*

* Nichols, E. F., "Physics" (*Lectures on Science, Philosophy and Art*), Columbia Univ. Press.

* Pearson, Karl, *Grammar of Science,* 3d edition, Chapters VII–X.

Poincaré, H., *Science and Hypothesis.*

Poincaré, L., *The Evolution of Modern Physics.*

* Russell, B., *Our Knowledge of the External World,* Lectures III and IV.

* Soddy, F., *Matter and Energy.*

* Ward, J., *Naturalism and Agnosticism,* Volume I, Part I, especially Lectures V and VI.

References on Materialism

Büchner, L., *Force and Matter.*

* Calkins, M. W., *The Persistent Problems of Philosophy,* Chapter III.

Haeckel, E., *The Riddle of the Universe.*

Lange, F. A., *History of Materialism.*

* Paulsen, F., *Introduction to Philosophy,* pp. 60-86.

* Robertson, G. Croom, *Hobbes.*

* *Selections from Hobbes,* by Calkins, in Open Court Series.

* Seth, James, *English Philosophers,* Chapter II.

* Taylor, A. E., *Hobbes.*

CHAPTER XVII

THE PHILOSOPHY OF KANT

The philosophy of Kant is an exceedingly difficult one to outline in short space. Nevertheless, it has proven so provocative of further speculation, and is still so stimulating, that its main ideas should be considered by everyone interested in philosophy. Indeed, it is not possible to understand fully the later developments in philosophy without reference to Kant. In this chapter I shall essay an outline of Kant's most significant theories in the hope of thereby sending the reader to Kant's own works,[1] and to more extensive discussions thereon.

Kant's philosophy defies classification. In his theory of knowledge he is a rationalist, and *a priorist,* and yet he holds that *possible experience* sets the bounds of knowledge. He rejects the subjective idealism of Berkeley, and he prepares the ground for and sows the seeds of objective idealism. He is an agnostic, with reference to a scientific, demonstrable knowledge of the existence of God, freedom, and immortality, but he justifies a rational faith in these three supreme interests of man. He holds that man is absolutely limited to a knowledge of *phenomena* or *appearances,* and yet he maintains that man unavoidably and justifiably assumes the reality of a *noumenal* or *spiritual order.* For Kant, man and all his deeds are, *empirically,*

[1] The best book for a beginner in the study of Kant is Watson's *Selections from Kant.* All quotations from Kant in this chapter are from that book. For further references see the end of this chapter.

mere links in the iron web of physical necessity, whereas, *morally regarded,* man is a free self-determining rational spirit. We cannot *know* God or the true self, but, in the light of our consciousness of our infinite moral vocations, we must *believe* that God exists as the Righteous Governor of the Universe and that the true self is immortal.

From the loins of Kant's philosophy sprang directly the moral idealism of Fichte, indirectly the logical idealism of Hegel, the voluntarism of Schopenhauer, the agnostic phenomenalism of Hamilton and Spencer. Through the study of Kant the spirit of speculative philosophy has been quickened once more, after an epoch of positivism, skepticism, and materialism, in Germany, France, England, and America. To Kant the idealism of Green, the Cairds, Bradley, Bosanquet, and Royce owes much. Even pragmatism may be regarded as, in part, an effect of the Kantian philosophy. The sensationalistic or "idea-istic" phenomenalism of Mach and Pearson is like the Kantian theory of knowledge, with the activity of the Ego left out. The same remark would hold true, with some qualification, of William James' later philosophy of pure experience.

Kant, who had been brought up in the rationalistic and *a priori* philosophy of Wolff, which constructed, by *a priori* definitions and deductions, the theory of everything under the sun (for example, of architecture), and who had been awakened from his dogmatic slumber by the skepticism of Hume, finds philosophy or metaphysics to be in a deadlock. It oscillates, he tells us, between extreme dogmatism and complete skepticism. Dogmatism assumes, offhand, the competency of the abstract reason to prove everything by a rationalistic procedure and deductive methods. This procedure leads, owing to the constant breakdown of these proofs and the ensuing conflict of reason with itself, to complete skepticism. But skepticism is equally one-sided, since there is undoubted knowledge, that is, mathematics and physical science. In order that philosophy may set out upon the path of progress, Kant proposes what he calls a revolution, namely *a critical inquiry into the presuppositions or foundation of knowledge as contained in the self.*[2] Before we can determine whether it is possible to have a *knowledge* of the great objects of metaphysical speculation—*God, freedom,* and *immortality* —we must first inquire—*under what conditions alone, scientific knowledge is logically possible.* And we must not set out in our inquiry from complete skepticism, since skepticism would prevent our taking a single step forward and, therefore, is self-contradictory.

By *criticism,* then, Kant means an analytic inquiry into the fundamental conditions of knowledge.

Now, says Kant, in pure mathematics and physics we have not only knowledge, but knowledge *a priori,* that is, *not derived from sense experience.* If we can find what are the rational or nonempirical factors of knowledge, and determine in what situation these factors are operative in the production of valid knowledge, we shall have solved the critical problem. *We can then determine absolutely the conditions of the knowable, and make a sharp separation between all possible objects of knowledge and the legitimate objects of faith.*

In his *Critique of Pure Reason, Kant's conclusion is that there are nonempirical factors in science, but that these factors have no valid sphere of application beyond the limits of possible experience or sense perception; and, since we can have no perception of God, of an act of freedom, or of an indivisible self, belief in the latter is based on faith.* On the other hand, he concludes, in his Meta-

[2] Locke, to a great extent, anticipated Kant in this enterprise. And Hume, who traces descent from Locke *via* Berkeley, seems to have given Kant the immediate stimulus to his inquiry into the foundations of knowledge.

physics of Ethics, that the implications of our *moral consciousness* not only entitle us, but require us, to *postulate* or *assume* the reality of God, freedom, and immortality. We will now consider, summarily, Kant's procedure in these regards.

Kant finds that there are always *two factors* in genuine knowledge—the raw materials, which are sense experiences, and the synthetic, organizing, or ordering, activity of the mind. The *content, stuff, or material* of knowledge is sensation. But sensation is in itself a chaotic manifold. It is devoid of form, that is, of arrangement and orderly sequence. The latter are supplied by the mind. The mind has a native or inborn structure, which functions in the forms of knowledge. To the mind's *sensibility,* or faculty of receiving sense impressions, belong natively the forms of *space* and *time.* Space and time are native to the mind, since we cannot conceive how the recognition of outness, side-by-sideness, or succession, would arise out of experiences in which they were not already present. Space and time cannot be obtained by generalization from particular sense perceptions, without presupposing them to be already there. Moreover, in arithmetic we have universal and necessary judgments or propositions, which involve the consciousness of time; and, in geometry, we have similar judgments which imply the consciousness of space. Now, from sense perception alone, we can never arrive at a truly universal judgment; a judgment based on perception alone can only take the form "So far as I have observed" or "So far as has been observed." The fact that, in mathematics and mechanics, we arrive deductively at whole systems of necessary and universal propositions can only be accounted for by supposing that space and time are forms of perception native to the mind.

To the *understanding* or *the faculty of making judgments,* that is, of forming the concepts and laws that constitute order and sequence, belong the native forms of judgment—the universal ways in which the mind synthesizes or orders the contents of sense perception. These forms are the *categories,* that is, the fundamental and universal forms of thinking objects and their relations. *Through the use of these categories, the mind builds up the material of sense perception into a systematized or orderly whole of intelligible experience;* that is, *it builds up science and, in so doing, builds up nature, as the latter exists for common sense and for science.*

The categories [3] of Kant correspond to the classification of judgment forms in the traditional logic. They are as follows:

1. *Quantity*
   Unity
   Plurality
   Totality
2. *Quality*
   Reality
   Negation
   Limitation
3. *Relation*
   Inherence and Subsistence, or Substance
   Causality and Dependence
   Community, or Reciprocity of Causal Influence
4. *Modality*
   Possibility—Impossibility
   Existence—Nonexistence
   Necessity—Contingency

In order to illustrate Kant's argument and theory it will suffice to show the application of a few of the categories: (1) *Unity.* The mind unites various sensations, for example, color, form, weight, size, odor, taste into the unity or

[3] The categories are the forms and activities of judgment as applied to the matter of experience. Thus there is a category, or form of unification, corresponding to every judgment form. Kant treats of all the categories fully, but it is not necessary here to summarize his entire treatment. As a matter of fact it is the categories of the third group—those of Relation—which play the most important rôle in Kant's Theory of Knowledge.

identity of an orange. (2) *Plurality.* The mind, in order to count a bag of oranges, must repeat, say twelve times, its identification of unity and add or synthesize each one to the previously recognized number, as it goes along. (3) *Substance.* The mind can recognize change only by reference to something permanent. Without consciousness of permanence there is no consciousness of change, and vice versa. Were we not conscious of the identity of our experiencing and thinking self, through changing experiences, we could never be conscious of change. Could we not recognize change in our experiences, we could never become conscious of permanence or identity.

So when we think of any object, for example, a table or a mountain, we can say its appearance changes, only if we recognize an identical "it" that changes. If we go back to the old boyhood home, we can say, "It is not changed much," only if we recognize that we and other things have changed, while remaining recognizably the same.

(4) *Causality.* A causal relation is one of necessary and irreversible sequence. A is the cause of B means that it is necessary that A should first occur if there is to be an occurrence of B. But from sense experience alone we could never derive the idea of necessary and irreversible sequence.

Now, the use or application of all the categories means always *synthesis, organization,* or *unification,* in some fashion, of the chaotic manifold of sense experience. Knowledge involves both analysis and synthesis; but there can be nothing recognized as individual, concrete, and persisting, for analysis, unless in experience there has already been synthesis—the putting together of sensations. *We must first see things together before we can take them apart, and we cannot see things together unless we put them together.* The sense organs alone will not make "things" by putting sensations together. The mind must do that. Now the basic condition of all synthesis is the activity of a *syn-*

thesizer, that can know itself as one and continuous in the successive steps of synthesizing activity. Thus, the prime condition of science is the activity of the *pure or transcendental Ego,* the synthetic activity of the nonempirical self. By calling this ego *"transcendental"* Kant means that it *transcends sense experience.* It cannot be experienced, but it is the logical condition of there being an articulate and intelligible experience. All the categories are *forms* of the pure self's synthetic activity. The "I think" must be presupposed as accompanying all judgment and conception.

Suppose, says Kant, I draw a line. In order to recognize it as one continuous line, I must synthesize or put together the succession of muscular sensations of drawing the line and the visual sensations of seeing the line as drawn. This presupposes that I, the thinker, continue to exist as such and can know myself. Suppose I go on drawing, beyond what I can see as one segment of the line. I must put together my consciousness of what I am now doing or experiencing with what I did or experienced a moment ago. Suppose I leave the room and, coming back to-morrow, say "there is the line I drew yesterday." This statement presupposes my memory or consciousness of my continuous identity in the meantime. Thus, in experiencing anything intelligible, seeing a single thing in a single relation, enlarging the scope of my seeing and relating, remembering and recognizing, there is presupposed always the permanently identical synthetic activity of the pure ego. But the ego itself can never be experienced. What I experience of myself is always of a changing self. But I could not ever know myself as a changing self, much less know anything else, if there were not functioning in me the pure unchanging and universal ego of synthetic thinking.[4]

"There could be no such unity of consciousness were the

[4] The mature student who studies the views of English and American new realists, notably those of Bertrand Russell, and

mind not able to be conscious of the identity of function, by which it unites various phenomena in one knowledge. The original and necessary consciousness of the identity of oneself is at the same time the consciousness of a necessary unity in the synthesis of all phenomena according to conception.[5] Combination is a spontaneous act of consciousness, and, as such, it is the especial characteristic of understanding as distinguished from sense."[6] "This act we call by the general name of synthesis to draw attention to the fact that we can be conscious of nothing as combined in the object which we have not ourselves previously combined"—"the resolution or *analysis*, which seems to be its opposite, in point of fact always presupposes it."[7] "It is only because I am capable of combining *in one consciousness* the various determinations presented to me, that I can become aware that in every one of them the consciousness is the same."[8]

And the human understanding prescribes or puts into sense experience the laws of nature. Nature is *objective,*

Perry, Marvin, and Spaulding and the other Americans who have collaborated in the work called *The New Realism,* will note that these writers seem to agree with Kant and the objective idealists in holding that the mind has a knowledge of logical, mathematical, and ethical universals or concepts as well as of sense percepts and that these universals exist (or subsist) in the universe. But, whereas Kant and the objective idealists argue that universals can exist or subsist only in and for an active or thinking Ego, the New Realists seem to deny that mind has any other function than simply to *see* or *recognize* the universals, which exist independent of it. Hence they deny that the reality or validity of universals constitutes an argument for the doctrine that the world of truth or existence depends for its existence on a mind. In this respect they claim to be true to the standpoint of Plato, but they differ from Plato in that they deny that the universals constitute a system or organized totality. Objective idealists argue, in the spirit of Kant, that Plato's doctrine of the systematic unity of universals, when thought through, leads necessarily to the hypothesis of a universal mind as ground of the order and connection of all things into a cosmos, which order and connection is involved in the reality of universals. (*Cf.* Chapter XXIV.)

[5] Watson, *Selections from Kant*, p. 62.

[6] *Ibid.*, p. 63. [7] *Ibid.*, pp. 63-64. [8] *Ibid.*, p. 66.

in the sense of being the same for all beings endowed with and dependent for their knowledge on the same senses and the same principles of thinking. Nature is not your individual dream or mine. But nature, or the world of space-time-causality, and all the sense qualities, is *subjective* or *phenomenal,* in the sense that there enters into its making the universal forms and activities of the human mind. Nature does not exist apart from mind. Of what exists apart from mind we can have no knowledge.

"Just as phenomena have no existence at all, apart from a subject that has senses, so there exist no laws in phenomena apart from a subject that has understanding. Things in themselves would of course have laws of their own, even if they did not come within the knowledge of the subject through his understanding. But phenomena are merely the manner in which things appear in consciousness, and give no knowledge of what things may be in themselves. As mere appearances they are subject to no law of connection but that which is imposed by the connective faculty. Now it is imagination that connects the various units of sensuous perception, and imagination is dependent upon understanding for the unity of its intellectual synthesis, and upon sensibility for the complexity of apprehension. But nothing can come under observation without synthesis of apprehension, and this empirical synthesis is dependent upon the transcendental synthesis, and therefore upon the categories. . . . In the categories, therefore, nature as a system of necessary laws has its ground and origin. . . . To learn what are the special laws of nature, we must go to experience; but it is none the less true that only the *a priori* laws imposed by understanding tell us what is necessary for any experience whatever, and what is capable of being known as object of experience."[9]

---

[9] Watson, *Selections from Kant*, pp. 80-81.

Thus, for Kant, science, and nature as the object of science, are constituted by the interaction of the pure Ego with the materials of sense perception. Where there is no sense experience, there can be no knowledge. "Thinking without percepts is empty." But sense experience means nothing without thought. "Percepts without concepts are blind." The categories have no application beyond the limits of possible sense experience. What lies beyond? We know not. There must be Something, the unknown ground of our sense experience, but what it is like, or how it produces sensation in us, we cannot know. We know only appearances, phenomena. Things-in-themselves are forever hidden from our gaze. Between the nature of things as they are in themselves and our knowledge there is always interposed the forms of our perceptions and thinking—space, time, and the categories. But Kant thinks that, though we can have no positive knowledge of the nature of things in themselves, we have negative knowledge. Since space and time are human forms of perception, things-in-themselves need not be subject to the laws of empirical causality and substantiality. There may, in the world of noumena, or ultimate reality, be a self-existent, eternal being, a causeless freedom and immortal souls. Kant, starting from the results of his analysis of knowledge, namely that space and time are human forms of perception and the categories human forms of synthetic thinking, and that these imply in man an active principle of intellectual synthesis, proceeds to the seemingly gratuitous assumption that space, time, and the categories do not apply to things as they are in themselves. Why did he not recognize that the real world must have something corresponding to spatial and temporal order and to causal relations? In fact he is inconsistent, for he does apply unity, plurality, totality, and substance or self-existent being to his own *thought* about Noumena or Things-in-Themselves. He even unconsciously applies causality, for he assumes that things-in-themselves cause our sense experiences.

The answer to these questions lies in Kant's *Dialectic.* He finds there that the attempt, on the part of Reason, to reach ultimate or total conceptions leads to contradictory conclusions. Attempt to conceive the universe as a totality in space and time, and as a total system or community of casual relations, says Kant, and you run into the following inescapable conflicts of reason with itself: (1) You can prove, with equal cogency, that the world must be infinite spatially and that it must be finite spatially; (2) that it must be eternal and that it must have had a beginning; (3) that there must be and there cannot be free causality; (4) that there must be and that there cannot be a self-existing being.

Now, if space, time, and causality have no application to the nonmental realities or things-in-themselves, then these contradictions are resolved. If the ultimate reality be spaceless and timeless the above contradictions are abolished. There may be freedom, creative beginnings, and a self-existent being, in the nontemporal and nonspatial realm of reality. It is clear that Kant thought he was, once for all, achieving the liberation of faith from the thraldom of skepticism, by rightly limiting the application of the forms of thinking to the field of sense experience. From the theoretical standpoint the noumenal world, the realm of things-in-themselves, is but the concept of a *limit* to man's possible experience and, hence, to the possibility of scientific knowledge. The reason demands *totality* or *completeness,* but scientific thinking cannot attain to any positive concepts of totality. We must *think* the ideas of God or a self-existent being, of freedom and immortality, but we cannot *know* them as objects either of science or metaphysics. They are necessary *regulative ideas.* In other words, they are *ideals,* toward which our knowledge may seek indefinitely to approximate, but forever and forever they elude the grasp of science.

"It may seem from this that the result of our critical investigation is purely *negative,* and merely warns us not to venture with speculative reason beyond the limits of experience. And no doubt this is its first use; but a *positive* result is obtained when it is seen that the principles with which speculative reason ventures beyond its proper limits, in reality do not *extend* the province of reason, but inevitably *narrow it.* For, in seeking to go altogether beyond its true limits, the limits of sensibility, those principles threaten to supplant pure reason in its practical aspect. Let us suppose that the necessary distinction which our criticism shows to exist between things as objects of experience and the same things as they are in themselves, had not been made. Then the principle of causality, and with it the mechanical conception of nature as determined by it, would apply to all things in general as efficient causes. Hence I could not, without palpable contradiction, say of the same being, for instance the human soul, that its will is free, and yet is subject to the necessity of nature, that is, is not free. But, if our criticism is sound and the object may be taken in two distinct senses, on the one hand as a phenomenon, and on the other hand as a thing-in-itself, there is no contradiction in supposing that the very same will, in its visible acts as a phenomenon is *not free,* but necessarily subject to the law of nature, while yet, as belonging to a thing-in-itself, it is not subject to that law, but is *free.* Now, morality requires us only to be able to think freedom without contradiction, not to understand it. . . . From the critical point of view, therefore, the doctrine of morality and the doctrine of nature may each be true in its own sphere, which could never have been shown had not criticism previously established our unavoidable ignorance of things in themselves, and limited all that we can *know* to mere phenomena. I have, therefore, found it necessary to deny *knowledge of God, freedom, and immorality,* in order to find place for faith.''[10]

The postulates of the practical reason, that is, the demands of a faith which has its origin in the moral will, carry us across the gulf impassable by theoretical reason. The Ideas of God, Freedom, and Immortality, which ever transcend the reach of science, become *immanent* for the practical or moral consciousness, on the guidance of which depends man's fulfillment of his moral vocation. The commands of duty are absolute, unqualified. The voice within us, the voice of conscience, utters the categorical imperative ''Thou shalt not do thus and so!'' and ''Thou shalt do thus and so!'' The Right is the Good-in-itself. There is nothing Good-in-itself except the Good Will, and the Good Will is the will of a rational self-determining personality which, in knowing and willing the Good, knows and wills into action its own true nature. In the last analysis, only moral personalities are absolutely the subjects and objects of moral volition and valuation. But, if thou oughtest unqualifiedly, then thou canst, *Du sollst denn du kanst.*

> So nigh is grandeur to our dust,
> So near is God to man,
> When Duty whispers low, Thou must,
> The youth replies, I can.

The absolutely binding character of the moral imperative involves moral freedom or the power to obey the imperative. Hence we have a practical consciousness of freedom. Through the sense of duty we know that we must be free; through freedom we are able to obey the commands of duty, and thus to fulfil the law of our spiritual being.

---

[10] Watson, *Selections from Kant,* pp. 5-6.

But the fulfillment of our moral vocation is an endless task. We must live eternally, since, if to strive ceaselessly after moral perfection be our true calling, the beginning that we make here on earth opens to our spiritual eye dim and distant vistas of the pathway which prolongs itself ahead into a future life in which we approach ever more nearly towards perfection. Thus *immortality* is the second postulate of the moral life.

And, if this moral vocation of man be not a mocking delusion, if it be a realisable ideal, then the whole of nature must be subservient to the moral order. Virtue and happiness, which by no means coincide here and now, must, in the long run, coincide. Righteousness must triumph and rule in the cosmos. And, since only a *will* is righteous and good, the third and crowning postulate of the moral life is that *God exists as the righteous will who governs the universal order.* Thus the highest objects of reason's quest which, from the theoretical standpoint, were problematical, become, from the practical standpoint of the moral life, the objects and abiding place of a *reasonable faith.* In our scientific knowledge we are strictly limited to the space-time world of sensuous phenomena, with its endless and iron-bound causal sequences. In this world our bodies and our empirical selves are but ephemeral fragments, whose origin, career, and decease are as inevitable as the course of a mote or a planet. We find, in the phenomenal realm, no freedom, no God, and no self, except the logically presupposed self of the pure universal thinker, the principle of intellectual synthesis. But this whole phenomenal order is incomplete and dependent. Through moral insight we are led to see that it is but the appearance of the noumenal or spiritual order, in which, for moral faith, God, freedom, and immortal souls are the supreme and abiding realities.

But, we ask, what is the relation of faith to science?

What is the positive relation of the phenomenal or space-time world to the spaceless and timeless world of the self-existent God and free moral causality? What is the relation of my empirical and ever changing selfhood to my spiritual or free selfhood? What is the relation between that timeless act of freedom, by which a moral will begins a series in time, and the temporal phenomenal causal order which has neither first nor last term? How can I be both creatively free and temporally determined? Empirically, my every volition, as well as my every bodily movement, is caused by antecedents. *When,* then, and *how,* can I, by an act of free obedience to duty, break through this iron sequence? What is the relation of God to nature? How can the world of time be the appearance of a timeless world? And is not the appeal to moral consciousness, as the key to the interpretation of the noumenon or thing-in-itself, an appeal to experience? Does not Kant himself depart from his narrow limitation of experience to what comes through the avenues of the outer senses, when he tries to analyze and to interpret the philosophical significance of man's moral life? Are not the moral experiences of the individual, and the moral history of the race, truly valid bases for philosophical construction?

Kant was feeling his way tentatively towards a richer and more unified concept of experience, when, in his *Critique of Judgment,* he argued, that in the judgments of æsthetic feeling, in other words, in the experiences and valuations of beauty, grandeur, sublimity, which we have in the contemplation of nature and of works of art, we have hints of how the gaps might be closed between the sensible and the supersensible worlds. We cannot help seeing purpose in nature, especially in living organisms, and we cannot help feeling beauty in nature and art. Beauty is the feeling of the perfect harmony of the world with intelligence. The judgment of purpose in nature gives us *the idea of the world as an organic system.* The perception of beauty in nature seems to show us an organismic teleology. It suggests a cosmic purposiveness, operating in ways other than the halting and circumscribed purposiveness of human endeavor. Thus, in judgments of purpose and of æsthetic feeling, we get suggestions as to how the world of nature may be a living and worthful whole, one organism and life, which owes its existence and its continuance in existence to the creative and intuitive intelligence of a Cosmic Thinker, who in thinking creates the objects of his thought, in whose mind there is no passivity, who is not dependent on the reception of sensory stimulations for the materials of his knowledge and who, hence, has no need of thinking discursively; that is, of proceeding step by step by synthesis and analysis from the particular to the universal. Art, the creation of human genius, is produced without deliberate design by an intelligence which works like nature. This notion of a cosmic Intuitive Intellect or Creative Reason, whose nature is adumbrated by the creative imaginative work of the human artist or genius, is evidently one to which Kant returned again and again. We find it in the early stages of the *Critique of Pure Reason* [11] and in the last pages of his last great work, the *Critique of Judgment*.[12]

This notion of a creative or intuitive thinker, put out tentatively by Kant, plays an important part in the philosophy of his followers, Fichte, Schelling, Schleiermacher and Hegel.[13]

---

[11] Watson, *Selections from Kant,* p. 67, "An understanding in which the consciousness of self should at the same time be a consciousness of all the complex determinations of objects would be perceptive."

[12] *Ibid.*, pp. 339-342.

[13] It will prove interesting to compare Kant's attempt to bridge the gulf between Nature and Spirit with that of Plato in his doctrine that particular and sensuous objects *participate* in or *imitate* the ideas or eternal forms, of which the essential form of the Good is the supreme and organizing principle; with Plotinus' doctrine

The philosophy of Kant is epoch making. It was the most powerful influence, along with the philosophy of the French enlightenment (which, in turn, was a popularization, by Voltaire and others, of the ideas of Locke, Hume, Newton, Lord Shaftesbury, and the English moral philosophers), and the social philosophy of Rousseau, in bringing to pass a shift of emphasis from the ontological problems of substance to the problems of human nature—from the problems of the Mind-body and Spirit-matter relationships, to the problems of human knowledge, human association, and the evolution of human culture. After Kant, philosophy in Germany was concerned chiefly with the interpretation of human society and the meaning of man's cultural development—with the evolution of human institutions and ideas. In other words, philosophy becomes, after Kant, primarily a study and interpretation of the meanings, for the development of the human spirit, of morality, law, the state, science, art, and religion, all from the historical point of view. Later idealism is an idealistic reading of man's cultural history, as being the most important key to the meaning of reality as a whole. This movement achieved, as we shall see, its greatest results in Hegel.

For Kant's philosophy of history see Chapter XXVIII.

References

• Adamson, Robert, *The Philosophy of Kant.*
• Avey, A. E., *Readings in Philosophy,* Chapter XVII.
Caird, Edward, *The Critical Philosophy of Kant.*

---

of the series of *emanations* or outflows from the ONE, through reason (spirit) and soul to body; with that of Spinoza in his argument that nature is the necessary expression of the eternal Divine substance which appears to us in two parallel ways as Body and Mind, but the key to the nature of which is found in the human mind's capacity to see all things natural under the form of eternity; and finally with the doctrine of Fichte, Schelling, and Hegel that nature is the unconscious or externalized expression of spirit.

KANT, *Critique of Judgment* (translated by Bernard).

* KANT, *Critique of Pure Reason* (translated by Max Müller).

KANT, *Ethical Works* (translated by T. K. Abbott), or *Metaphysics of Morals* (translated by Semple).

KANT, *Philosophy of Law and Principles of Politics* (translated by W. Hastie).

KANT, *Prolegomena* (translated by Mahaffy and Bernard).

KANT, *Religion* (translated by Semple).

KEMP-SMITH, NORMAN R., *A Commentary on Kant.*

* LINDSAY, A. D., *The Philosophy of Kant.*

MEREDITH, J. C., *Kant's Critique of Judgment.*

* PAULSEN, FREDERICK, *Kant* (translated by Creighton and Lefevre).

PRICHARD, H. A., *Kant's Theory of Knowledge.*

* WATSON, JOHN, *The Philosophy of Kant Explained,* and *Selections from Kant.*

CHAPTER XVIII

SPIRITUALISM OR IDEALISM

The basic thesis of this standpoint, in its principal modern classic forms, is that only minds and their contents exist. To my mind there are three chief forms of idealism, namely:

1. Berkeleyan or Subjective
2. Leibnitzian or Monadistic
3. Hegelian or Objective

I. Berkeleyan Idealism

The essence of the first is this: Berkeley argues that our knowledge consists of *notions* and *ideas* or perceptions. By *notion* he means an immediate awareness or intuition of the self. I know myself directly as an active being, thinking, perceiving, and willing. In addition to this immediate awareness of my activity, I also have ideas. Ideas are the sole contents or stuff of our experience when we perceive things by means of the senses. The being of things consists in being perceived. I am passive or receptive in having ideas. These two, Ideas and Notions, exhaust the whole field of knowledge. When I perceive any object such as desk, tree, snow, I have a congeries of sense qualities, united by the mind, and these congeries I call things. A cherry, for instance, consists of a specific roundness, smoothness, size, color, taste, odor, and interior structure, united by the mind into this thing. There is nothing behind the group of *sense qualities, which is,* hence, *the real cherry.* By things Berkeley means just what one perceives.

The field of knowledge includes, then, notions and ideas. Notion is a knowledge of the spirit as an acting subject. In perception we know that we are relatively passive. Our perceptions are received by us; they must, therefore, have a cause which is independent of ourselves. We are continually distinguishing between those images that are, and those that are not, under our control. We know that we do not cause our perceptions. I cannot help seeing, feeling, hearing, the content of my present field of perception. There is involved in perception a degree of constancy and a type of order which attests the independent character of the *cause* of our perceptions.

What causes our perceptions? We have seen that the materialist argues that the cause is matter, or a substance which is very different from our perceptions. The materialist argues that matter has the primary qualities in minute, imperceptible forms, but is eviscerated of all secondary qualities. This distinction, says Berkeley, is illogical. If the primary qualities are objective, so also are the secondary. Berkeley convincingly and irrefutably shows that all qualities are on the same footing, since they are perceived in the same manner and subject to the same conditions; and the one set of qualities is never perceived apart from the other. For instance, shape, size, texture, and motion are never perceived apart from color. The ordinary assumption of the believer in a material substance is that ideas are *copies* in our mind of the independent matter. Now Berkeley asks, if we cannot perceive matter, how can we know that there is matter? And if we can perceive matter, then matter is the content of the act of perception. We cannot know the relation between ideas and matter if we do not perceive matter. Berkeley says that the material world of common sense is only perception. Perception must have an objective cause. We have no knowledge of matter as a cause. We do know, however, that we, as *selves* or *spirits,* are causes. We are conscious of producing changes in the world, therefore the cause of our perceptions must be a spirit. As our perceptions show order, regularity, and an intelligible structure, so the cause of our perceptions must be the incessant operation of a spirit which has such an intelligible character, as being the rational and permanent source of the constancy and order in our perceptual experience. Since our spirits are progressively discovering ever more order and meaning in the realm of sense perception, the Ground or Cause of the latter must be essentially akin in nature to the spirit of man.

Mind I know intuitively—by a notion—as a thinking, acting principle. I thus know mind as the spiritual support of ideas. There is, therefore, no independent *material substance* for Berkeley. Nature is literally the living garment of the Deity. The world of nature, "the whole choir of heaven and furniture of earth," is a divine, visual language. Just as I infer from your looks that you are intelligent, so I infer that an infinite, omnipresent, intelligent principle is speaking to me through nature. Nature is not a garment that hides the Deity, nor is nature a body of thought forms which hide reality from the percipient individual. Nature is the direct revelation of God's intelligent and benevolent will.

I do not perceive my fellowman's spirit directly, but I do infer from his actions that there is a spirit. So I infer from the order, utility, and beauty of nature that there is a Supreme Spirit. There is also this important difference between our perceptions of nature and of other finite selves. Nature we have constantly before us as a manifestation of the power and intelligence of the Supreme Spirit, whereas human individuals do not bear this constant relation to us. Since nature therefore is a language to man, all he has to do is to study it and it speaks. Berkeley would say that the whole technic, both mathematical and experimental, of modern science are but elements in the process of learning nature's tongue. Do we eat and drink ideas when we eat and drink sense objects? Yes. But it is, however, only a question of names at this point. Berkeley insists that his view is the common man's view. The materialist philosopher says that what you perceive is not matter. Back of what you perceive, says Berkeley, the materialist postulates some thoughtless, stupid, unintelligible thing. It is the futility of this postulate that Berkeley is seeking to show. He argues that such a postulate will not explain the facts of perception. When Dr. Johnson kicked the stone and it hurt, he did not refute Berkeley. It is the materialist who deprives our sense impressions of their reality. *Esse est percipi,* this famous expression, which has often been taken to be the whole of Berkeley's system, is in reality only its beginning. The divine mind is the cause of our perceptions, and it is the cause of the continued existence of things when we do not perceive them. Mind is the only conceivable cause of our ideas and perceptions. God is the universal intelligence which we conceive on the analogy of our own existence as thinking, willing selves.

There are certain fundamental difficulties in Berkeley. Nature for him is simply the effect in human minds of the continuous activity of the divine mind. From this standpoint, what becomes of the past history of nature, of the genesis of the solar system; in short, what becomes of the whole world before man appeared? Nature is simply a continuous manifestation of the divine mind to finite minds, on Berkeley's premises. This continuous manifestation of the divine is all there is to nature. At this point we see, therefore, that Berkeley deprives nature of any existence on its own account. This is one of the two chief difficulties in his system. His doctrine is also unsatisfactory in the solution it offers of the relations of one finite mind to another and to God. Your body from your point of view is the effect of the divine will acting upon your mind. But your body as I perceive it is the effect of the action of the divine will on my mind. Here arises a serious difficulty. How can I distinguish between my body as I perceive it and my body as you perceive it? This question is not satisfactorily answered in Berkeleyan idealism. As James has said, my appreciation of my own body has a peculiar *warmth* and *intimacy* which I never experience in connection with my perceptions of your body. Never do I perceive your toothache quite as I do my own. Never do I perceive your difficulties as I do my own. Why feel in such an intimate way the action of the divine mind which I call my body, if the whole world is perceptual content? Why is there not the same emotional tang to all my experiences? If body is what I perceive and only that, then Berkeley's theory fails to account for this patent fact.

Berkeley argues that the constancy, coherence, and independence, in the order of our perceptions of things justify the inference that nature is the continuous expression of the Divine Mind to our minds, just as the constancy and independence of my will, in my perception of your body, leads me to infer that your mind speaks to me through your body. But your body is a part of the same total and continuous natural order of perceptions to which belong my perceptions of inanimate things. By parity of reasoning, then, one might infer a mind in every natural object, instead of One Divine Mind in all things. If the individual body is simply an effect of the action of one finite mind on another, it would follow that the whole of nature is but the sum of the effects of all other finite minds on the mind of the percipient. Thus Berkeley assumes the independent realness of our percepts of one another's bodies, and then argues that the remainder of our percepts (that is, the physical world) is the direct expression to us of God's mind. Thus his argument at once assumes and denies that human bodies, and the minds associated with them, exist independently of the divine mind.

In conclusion we may say that Berkeley's theory does not give us a satisfactory doctrine of nature, nor does it account for the uniqueness and the discreteness of selves.

II. Leibnitz's Monadology

Leibnitz's doctrine avoids one of Berkeley's difficulties. Leibnitz starts from the idea of substance. He is thus in agreement with the other chief thinkers of the time in making substance the central explanatory principle. He sets up a plurality of *monads,* or individual substances. Now a monad is a center of force or of desire and activity. We may almost say that a monad is an animated point. In this respect Leibnitz shows profoundly the influence of the mathematics of his day. Galileo, in describing the path of moving bodies, called the differential a point of tendency and at no time in the physical series does Galileo resort to rest, as did Archimedes, as the final point of explanation. So here Leibnitz comes not to a position of equilibrium or rest, but to force. The whole universe consists of an infinite number of centers of desire or striving. There are three kinds of monads, namely:

1. Body monad (animated molecule)
2. Soul monad (monad having memory or conscious continuity)
3. Spirit monad (a thinking center that reflects, thinks in conceptual terms, and sets up ends)

All physical bodies are made up of monads. All living bodies have soul monads. Human bodies are governed by spirit monads. These centers of force and feeling exhaust the whole content of the world.

The monad develops from within. The history of the monad is a consequence of inner impulsion and not of external impact. Here also we find employed the conception that Galileo, Huyghens, and other physicists of the time worked out, of the nature of a point of any function as expressed by the differential.

Every monad is in some degree a soul or self. Even the body monads are rudimentary selves, that is, they are low grade centers of feeling or desire. Each monad mirrors or reflects the universe, and its development is entirely from its own internal impulse. It is self-active. The monad produces no change in any other one. Each develops solely by the law of its own being. In this aspect, Leibnitz expresses the central core of the mathematics of his day. The monad, in addition to being a point expressing the law of an entire series, is also a complex unity. It is the true type of that which is both one and many, both unity and complexity. The best analogy of such a function Leibnitz finds in the self or soul. A human individual is complex; it includes a variety of impulses in a unity of feeling and purposive activity.

In the body monad there are only dazed flashes of consciousness, and from the lowest body monad there begins an infinite gradation of organization. There are no breaks in nature; and so we have an infinite series from the very lowest up to the most rational and self-conscious monad. This may be pictured as an ascending scale which leads up to the perfect monad, namely, God. God is the one perfectly organized monad. He is the governing monad, and is also the cause of the existence of all the others.

In conceiving of the relation of body and soul, Leibnitz

does not think that one term of the duality sends over any influence into the other term. Both members of the duality work together in harmony. There is in Leibnitz's view, no dead matter which serves in Lockian fashion as the unknown cause of our perceptions. On this point Leibnitz is in fundamental agreement with Aristotle. The soul is the entelechy of the body.

Leibnitz has propounded an original conception in psychology, to wit, the conception of grades of consciousness. There are all sorts of modes of awareness ranging from the most transient and evanescent feelings up to clear self-consciousness. The inner life of the monad is made up of *petites perceptions,* minute perceptions. In the very lowest type of monads there are but few of these minute perceptions and the unifying principle is least operative. Since Leibnitz conceives all force as being in the final analysis psychical, the physical spatial order is but the phenomenal expression of an infinite number of interrelated monads. Force is of the nature of a self-acting and desiring type. I am a body governed by soul. I perceive most clearly those monads which are nearest to me in kind, and I also perceive their interrelationships under the form of space. The world is a harmonious system of such monads, and these monads are not *in space,* but space is *in them.* The same relation is also true of time. The laws of mechanics are true, but they are not the ultimate truth. The Newtonian principles express the order and continuity between spatial phenomena. From the spatial point of view, the world is through and through mechanical, but this mechanical system is the expression of an inner purposive, teleological nature. The monads constitute a kingdom of spirits, a cosmical harmony of souls. In this way Leibnitz has incorporated into a single principle the teleology of Plato and Aristotle, and the mechanics of Newton, Kepler, Galileo, Huyghens, *et al.*

Spiritualism or idealism in Leibnitz thus assumes a form which does not deprive nature of reality—nature is real, apart from our minds. Nature is really alive, is psychical, and in this respect the Leibnitzian conception of nature is in perfect harmony with the nature-romanticism of Wordsworth, Byron, Shelley, and others. In nature there is an all-pervasive spirit akin to ours. Leibnitz is also in harmony with the most recent deliverances of physical science; for both nature is dynamical, is process, activity.

The doctrine of Leibnitz is one of the most original metaphysical conceptions of modern times.

This type of spiritualism does not really account for the fact that the world of our experience has two aspects. This view may be true, but it fails to convince us that the whole of nature is alive and psychical. It does not tell why there should be this double aspect to experience and why, if physical nature really consists of souls, we commonly fail to be conscious of their presence and are usually incapable of communing with them. Royce, our late notable American idealist, and also Liebmann,[1] have tried to rectify this one defect. Royce says that the reason why we do not apprehend the psychical life of nature is because the souls distributed throughout nature have different time-spans. Our own consciousness has a certain beat, so to speak; attention wavers and wanes at a fairly constant rate. Our consciousness has a certain rhythm. If we had a more rapid rhythm of consciousness, we might live in a minute as much as we now live in a hundred years. As compared with the elephant and lower forms of animal organism, and still more so with inorganic nature, our consciousness has a much more rapid rhythm. Now if we had different rhythms of consciousness, we could perhaps hold commu-

---

[1] In *Zur Analysis der Wirklichkeit.*

nion with stars, mountains, trees, yes, even with stones. Our failure to apprehend the all-pervading psychical life in nature is thus, according to Royce, due to the differences in time-span between their lives and ours.

This seems unlikely to me. If all parts of nature have an indwelling consciousness, then our scientific formulæ for the regular behavior of objects should be reducible to a common type, and all the different sciences could be shown to be only parts of one science, namely, psychology. Not only logic and ethics, but physics and chemistry, would be merged into psychology. As science develops, we discover that the rules of the behavior of stones, rivers, and clouds are not the same as the rules of the behavior of psychical beings. And, among psychical beings, those with the most highly organized individuality have the most unique and significant ways of behaving. Moreover, we also discover that the difference is not reducible to variations in the time-span. It is a difference in kind. There is a constancy, a regularity, that differs in kind in these different levels—namely, the physical, the animal, and the rational—and I fancy that the time is not even relatively at hand when the only technic of the social engineer will be a book of log tables and other mathematical formulæ. I see no promise of the reduction of the psychical and the physical to a common basis.

III. Objective or Absolute Idealism

Berkeley's Idealism is designated subjective, since for him only subjects—God and finite spirits, human and superhuman—really exist. For him Reality is a *plurality* of selves. Physical nature exists only in the minds of selves. Leibnitz differs from Berkeley in that he gives to nature a quasi-independent existence. Nature for him consists of low grade centers of feeling and will. Nature and man constitute elements in a harmonious system. Their existence and harmonious working together is constituted by God, the Governing Monad. Thus for Leibnitz nature is not, as it is for Berkeley, the mere effect of God's direct action on human minds. Nature has a real existence. More recent objective idealism does not regard nature as being necessarily an assemblage of finite souls. Nature is unconscious mind. It does not exist as such independent of all mind. But it has forces and ways of behaving that are different. From the standpoint of objective idealism the physical world has a character of its own. In fact, it is only because the physical is "opposite" to, or "other" than, finite mind that the latter can realize itself, or develop to full consciousness. On the other hand, physical nature and finite mind, ultimately, really exist only as elements in the unity of the whole, which is *absolute mind* or *spirit. Thus the unity of the universe is that of one self-active, self-developing, self-expressing being, God or the Absolute —which differentiates itself endlessly into nature and finite mind, but which never loses itself in the processes of the finite or for an instant ceases to be any less a unity.* When we think of the universe, from the standpoint of its unity, it is the eternally self-active, self-differentiating One, that manifests its life in the ceaseless process of the finite—in physical attraction and repulsion, in the play of the polarity of magnetism and electricity, in the analytic and synthetic forces of chemism, in the endless or circular process of self-reproduction, self-development, death and birth of living organisms, in the ceaselessly recurring and yet ever progressing conflicts of the human spirit in history. When we look at the universe from the standpoint of any finite member thereof, whether it be a physical atom, a living organism, a human being, a nation's history, or the evolution of art or religion, the finite member in question is seen to find its being in *process*—in attracting and repelling other atoms, in growing and dying, and thus furthering the race life, in realizing its destiny or making way for the destiny of another nation, or another phase of art or religion. Thus reality is at once a self-differentiating unity and a struggling and conflicting procession of many finite and transitory elements. The key to the interpretation of the whole of reality, as having these two aspects which mutually imply one another, is to be found in the nature of *mind—not in the mind of the individual, as he thinks himself to be, but the racial mind, the cosmic mind.*

The names of chief importance in the development of objective idealism are J. G. Fichte, who took the first step in transforming the dualism of Kant into a system of objective idealism; Hegel, who developed it, with systematic completeness, into a rounded-out system, and who applied his central insight to all spheres of existence, to nature and the social order, and the whole of man's cultural history; the English objective or absolute idealists, T. H. Green, E. Caird, F. H. Bradley and Bernard Bosanquet, who give to the doctrine a freer and more elastic form than it has in Hegel's hands; but who, in fundamentals, represent a kindred standpoint; and, finally, Josiah Royce, in whom it takes a decidedly original form.

In the following exposition of the fundamental standpoint of objective idealism I shall follow Hegel chiefly, only noting briefly some of the later divergencies from Hegel's standpoint. The present exposition of objective idealism cannot be understood without reference to Chapter XXIV, for objective idealism is essentially a *singularistic* or *monistic* system. Indeed it is the most logical form of singularism.

J. G. Fichte was an enthusiastic disciple of Kant. But he soon became dissatisfied with the impassable gulf that yawned in Kant's system between the world of phenomenal knowledge, built up by the activity of the pure ego out of the raw materials of sensation, and the unknown world of the Thing-in-itself, the realm of noumena, forever hidden behind the impenetrable (by any scientific thinking) veil of phenomena. Kant had said that the human understanding, by its analytic and synthetic activity, fashions the nature known to science, that is, the realm of things causally connected into a system in the space-time world, out of the materials that come through the senses, out of the ceaseless stimulations that come to the mind through the organs of sense perception. *But what causes these sensations or how the cause is related in character to the human mind,* Kant said we cannot know. Fichte, dissatisfied with this agnostic dualism, boldly undertakes to show *why* there is a sense world or physical world. He says that there are only two consistent systems of philosophy, *dogmatism* or *materialism* which affirms minds to be products of things, and *idealism* which affirms things to be products of minds. Either one or the other system is true. Neither can explain *how* that which it takes to be causally dependent is produced. Idealism cannot explain *how* mind produces matter. Materialism cannot explain *how* matter produces mind. Still less can it explain why mind, if the by-product of matter, should be self-conscious.

Fichte holds that a man's philosophy is the expression of his character. One who has a sense of man's moral worth and spiritual freedom will choose idealism. One who, with the "pigsty philosophy" of hedonism, regards man as merely an animal, will accept materialism.

Fichte chooses idealism on grounds of moral insight and faith. Then he proceeds to explain *why,* if idealism be true, there should be a sense realm at all. (Note that he explains *why,* not *how,* the world of the *senses* comes into being). *His standpoint is teleological and moralistic, not causal in the scientific sense at all.* The explanation is as follows. The finite moral will, in order that it may develop into a fully conscious, rational self-determining will or ego, must be confronted by an *opposite* or *other,* which challenges it and stimulates it to free self-activity. The rational or spiritual life of man can be developed only in conflict with, and in the overcoming of, the physical. *Nature,* the realm of the sensuous or material in experience, *is that apparent other-than-mind,* in the conquest of which mind comes into conscious self-possession.

Nature is the sensuous material for the fulfillment of man's moral vocation. This vocation, in turn, consists of *free, rational self-activity.* The individual wins his freedom through control of his sensuous impulses. The race wins its freedom and finds its vocation in subduing nature to cultural or spiritual ends. Thus the opposition between nature and reason is set up in order that in every finite self and, therefore, in the whole of the human race, reason may develop from unconscious latency to rational-self-consciousness. The eternal meaning of the universe is that there shall be a world of rational selves, hence the opposition between self and nature, ego and non-ego, is set up (*posited* is Fichte's term) by the universal or cosmic will, in order that there may be an ever developing world of finite wills which shall express his being. Reason's world, the world of the cosmic will, is an infinity of self-production. All finite willing is to realize the infinite will, the universal ego, which is infinite activity. There is no real world but *will.* There is no destiny but the ceaseless self-realization of rational will by finite selves, as organs of the world will, as sparks of the world reason.

The moral vocation of man is the supreme clue to the meaning of reality. This moral vocation involves a *dialectical* or *triadic* process. First, is the *universal will* or *ego.* Second, in order that the universal ego may come to consciousness in a world of finite egos, there must be set up, by the universal will, a *non-ego,* an opposite which is nature, the sense world. Third, is the process of overcoming the opposition, in which process the finite ego wins rational freedom and becomes a conscious member of the universal moral world order. The triadic process, thesis-antithesis-synthesis, is the essential or true process of mind or spirit.

Hegel takes up this basic insight of Fichte's and works it out, with unwearied assiduity, profound insight and comprehensive knowledge and great synthetic power, in all aspects of existence. Later forms of objective idealism are chiefly commentaries on, or emendations of, Hegel.

In the following exposition of Hegel's doctrine I shall pass lightly over Hegel's philosophy of nature, as being the least interesting and least fortunate part of his system. Hegel works out the principles of absolute or objective idealism in all directions. His is a system of evolutionistic or dynamic idealism, into which is woven the whole content of the historical life of the human species. Reality is process, and process is essentially spirit or mind. Human history is the progressive expression of the supreme spirit, reason or purpose. He holds that the starting point for philosophical interpretation is experience, but says that, in interpreting experience, everything depends on the mind we bring to the task. Experience, in its true character, is a logically articulated system, not a heap or disconnected sequence of isolated particular facts. The scientific development of this system is the task of logic which, for Hegel, is identical with metaphysics, or theory of reality: "The science of things set and held in pure thought. Logic develops the system of the pure types of thought, not of the individual's thought but of universal objective thought, the world reason." Applied philosophy consists of two parts: (1) Philosophy of nature, which traces out the stages in the materialization or concretion of thought unconsciously operative in physical nature; mind alienated from itself; (2) philosophy of mind, which traces out the stages in the ever increasing coming-to-more-adequate-consciousness of the universal reason in human thought and social culture. Philosophy of mind has three divisions: (1) Philosophy of subjective mind, the science of the individual mind operating in the bodily organism (anthropology and psychology); (2) philosophy of objective mind, the science of the mind as it objectifies itself in the social institutions of family, law, property, economic, civil, and political life; it is through social institutions that the individual mind becomes moralized and rationalized, in short, attains personality; (3) absolute mind. In art, religion, and philosophy, human mind attains a higher and more adequate consciousness of itself as the organ of the absolute mind, and of the identity of itself with the absolute mind, than it is able to reach in social life. Thus the final and highest task of philosophy is to interpret the meanings of art and religion for the self-realization of Spirit.[2]

For Hegel *the true is the whole.* Truth is the self-comprehension of reality. When we say "true" we are thinking of that which is comprehended, that is of the contents of thought. Hence the test of truth for him is not agreement of thought with anything independent of thought. Truth is the agreement or coherence of thought with thought. The absolute truth is the self-consistent totality of truth. The absolute reality is the self-coherent whole of being. Absolute reality is the perfectly harmonious order or system which is at once subject and object, Knowing that knows itself. (How reminiscent this is of Aristotle!) The utterly coherent or harmonious cosmical order, which is the absolute mind, is a *living process;* it contains within itself the whole endless variety of finite events. It includes, and

---

[2] The word that Hegel uses for mind is *Geist,* which means *spirit* or *mind.*

ever subdues into its eternal harmony, all the clashes of physical forces, all the conflicts of history, all the striving and suffering of human life. It is eternal calm in the midst of the world storms, eternal harmony that runs through all the cosmical discords. The untrue, the bad, the transitory, is that which is discordant, that which is at war with itself and is, therefore, forever passing over into something other than itself. But the untrue, the bad, the apparent, the transitory, is ever being transmuted or transfigured into content of the true, the good, the real, the eternal. The one in the many, the infinite in the finite, the absolute in the relative, the real in the apparent —such, according to Hegel, is the final insight attained by speculative philosophy. Such he thinks is the true meaning of mysticism. Hegel's philosophy is a system of speculative mysticism, worked out with extraordinary industry, knowledge and insight, in application to all spheres of human life. *Nowhere else in the history of Western philosophy does one find such a blending of mystical vision with logical vigor and wealth of concrete knowledge of man's cultural history as in Hegel.*

The paradoxical union of opposites is achieved by the *dialectic method*. We have seen that Hegel was indebted to Fichte for the suggestion of his method. But he was also much influenced by Plato's use of dialectic, especially in the *Parmenides* and *Sophist*.

Reason, says Hegel, is the faculty of true speculative knowledge, the *understanding* only sets up oppositions. It is the reason which overcomes them by showing that they are united in a higher synthesis. Kant had argued in his antinomies that, on equally cogent grounds, one must affirm and deny that the world in time and space is finite and infinite, is and is not made up of simple parts, and that there is and there is not freedom and a self-existent and free first cause. Kant could find no solution for this conflict of reason with itself but to deny that time and space were ultimately real. Hegel thinks the statement of the antinomies the best thing in Kant's philosophy, but he holds that Kant failed to find the right solution which is this: "The true and positive meaning of the antinomies is that every actual thing involves a coexistence of opposed elements. Consequently to know, or in other words, to comprehend an object is equivalent to being conscious of it as a concrete unity of opposed determinations." (Wallace, *The Logic of Hegel,* p. 100.) Thus "by dialectic is meant the indwelling tendency outwards by which the one-sidedness and limitations of the predicates of understanding is seen in its true light." (*Op. cit.,* p. 147.) "For anything to be finite is just to suppress itself and to put itself aside. Thus understood, the dialectical principle constitutes the life and soul of scientific progress, the dynamic which alone gives immanent connection and necessity to the body of science."

"When we look more closely, we find that the limitations of the finite do not merely come from without; that its own nature is the cause of its abrogation and that by its own act it passes into its counterpart." (*Op. cit.,* p. 148.)

Man is mortal means not external circumstances cause death but life, as life, involves the germ of death; "everything finite, instead of being stable and ultimate, is rather changeable and transient and this is exactly what we mean by that dialectic of the finite by which the finite, as implicitly other than what it is, is forced beyond its own immediate or natural being to turn suddenly into its opposite." (*Op. cit.,* p. 150.)

Thus everything finite, from the humblest sense object to the greatest man or nation, implies always an "other" or "different" on which its meaning and very being depend. For every being is specific or individual. Mere being, undefined being, is the same as nothing. To be is to be something and hence not to be some other thing. Everything concrete is a unity of differents or opposites. Let us take an orange. We say an orange is a yellow spheroid with a rough skin and a soft interior with an acid juice. But yellow is not spheroidal, rough is not yellow, softness is not acidity and juiciness is not acidity. So on we might go. The orange is a unity of *differents* or *distincts*.[3] Moreover, an orange is *not any other finite object*. There are on my desk paper, inkstand, books, pipe, pens, pencils. No one of these things is any other, and yet any one is definable and can exist only in relation to the others. Let us take, says Hegel, the spiritual world and we shall find everywhere illustrations of the dialectic. "Pride goeth before a fall." "Vaulting ambition o'er leaps itself and falls on the other side." "Too much wit outwits itself." "Push a right to an extreme and it becomes a wrong"; for example, Shylock and his pound of flesh. Men cannot live without one another or peacefully with one another. Thus, as Kant said, the chief cause of society is man's unsocial sociableness.

---

[3] Hegel's *Logic* is not free from the confusion between predicates that are *differents*, and predicates that are *opposites* in the sense that they are incompatible and, hence, to attribute them to the same subject is to do violence to the nature of experience and thought. There is no contradiction between an orange being both yellow and round at the same moment, but there is a contradiction between its being both yellow and not yellow, for example, green, at the same moment. Hegel, in his arguments on the "othering" process, has two aims in mind, which he does not always keep distinct. One of these is to show that reality is a concrete whole of interrelated elements; the other is to show that reality is a living process and that, therefore, things are incessantly passing beyond themselves into their opposites, or becoming other than they first appear to be, for example, life into death and death into life, one generation into another, body becoming individual mind and individual mind becoming socialized, God becoming Man and Man becoming divine, etc. The power of negation or contradiction, of which Hegel is so fond of talking, is the nerve of the latter or dialectic process. See Hegel, *Logic*, translated by Wallace, and B. Croce, *What is Living and What is Dead in Hegel's Philosophy.*

Reasonableness, says Hegel, *consists just in embracing these opposites as unsubstantial elements in the concrete unity of the whole system of reality.*

Heraclitus said: "All Being is becoming." This, says Hegel, means that Hamlet's question "to be or not to be" is posed at the level of the mere understanding. The truth is that to be is not to be, and not to be is to be; for all life and mind are process, a passing from one stage of being to another. In any and every such transition, *if the earlier stage is taken as being, in relation to that the later stage is nonbeing, and, if the later stage is taken as being, the earlier stage is nonbeing in relation to that. But the true insight is that being consists just in the continuous transition from one form of finitude to another.* Everything finite is relative, transitional, in process and *the infinite* is the totality of the process, the absolute is the total system of the relative.

Hence, says Hegel, it is a superficial and indeed a false philosophy which makes such assertions as these: "We know only appearance; the essence of reality is hidden and unknowable." "We do not know what force really is, we know only its manifestations." "We do not know what electricity or life are; we know only their phenomena." "We do not know true causes, but only apparent effects." The essence is simply the whole system of appearances. The noumenon is the systematic totality of phenomena. Force, electricity, life, are what they do. Causes are causes only in relation to effects. So, too, says Hegel, to make God a being beyond the stars and inaccessible is to make him nothing, a mere abstract essence, a mere name with three letters. God is what he appears to be. *He is essentially the being who manifests himself, and the whole world is his continuing manifestation.*

Thus far one might suppose Hegel's view identical with Hindu pantheism or that of Pope,

> All are but parts of one stupendous whole
> Whose body nature is, and God the soul.

But Hegel's doctrine is much more profound. God, the absolute mind, is nothing apart from the universe. He is the unity, the coherent totality of which all finite forms and events are manifestations. *In* him these live and move and have their being, and *through* these he lives and moves and has his being; but not all appearances are on the same level. *The dialectic process of reality is an ascent,* from physical movements of attraction and repulsion, through living organisms and species, to mind's or spirit's summit of self-comprehension in art, religion, and philosophy. One star differeth from another in glory, and just so one finite form differeth from another in the degree of its adequacy of manifestation of divinity or of reality.

There are three chief stages in the process:

1. *Being-for-another.* In the physical world all things exist only in relation: for example, a thing and its properties, negative and positive electricity, the acid and the base, cause and effect. But until conscious life is reached, everything seems only to have being *for* another, that is, it can exist and be defined only in relation to another which is external to it. It is not a self-determining center of being and action. It has no inner life, no power of return into itself. The significance of things physical, existing side by side in space and following one another in temporal succession, is exhausted in their external relations. Nature, indeed, has neither kernel nor husk. She is both at once. But nature seems to flow on endlessly without achieving any inner self-possession.

2. *Being-in-itself.* In conscious life we have a phase of existence that indeed depends upon the other, but also has a self-returning, self-possessing unity. Living organisms are not exhausted in their external relations. Life

maintains itself, enhances itself, reproduces itself. The individual is prolonged and perhaps enhanced in the life of the species.

Thus *individuality,* as the centralizing operative power of relationship, appears. Still the individual organism is dependent on another, and is but a link in the endless chain of the life of the species which, since it is an endless procession, nowhere enables the principle of individuality to be fully realized. "Life," says Hegel, "is the Idea (or mind) which has not yet realized its true purpose." (*Op. cit.,* 255.)

3. *Being-in-and-for-itself.* It is first in self-conscious or rational individuality that the true purpose of the dialectic process is achieved. By this Hegel means the individuality that goes out into and lives in all the relations which constitute the world, but which, in that ceaseless out-going, realizes itself as the central and conscious focus of these relations. Thus the true individual is an organized rational unity, a system of elements existing in conscious relations. The mechanical view of reality is inadequate, because it gives no real unity, only an external juxtaposition of parts related in space. The organism is higher, but single organisms are the prey of the environment, and the species is a mere succession of living individuals. The true whole. the true reality, is a self-differentiating unity, a self-unifying plurality. It is the absolute Spirit operative in nature (blindly) and coming to ever fuller self-consciousness in Humanity.

From the standpoint of the unity, reality is the eternal ground of the endless procession of spirits. From the standpoint of the plurality, reality is the society of selves realizing in time its unity with the eternal ground. The absolute is the universal spirit that lives and moves in the whole system of finite spirits. He is the perfect self or ego who lives in and through all imperfect selves.

Hegel is very emphatic in his expressions as to the supremacy of selfhood. He says that Kant's criticism, which denies that we can know the self, takes the self as a mere abstract essence. It is objected that in order that the ego may know itself it must make itself object and that this is a circle. Hegel remarks that it is true that if one thinks a stone is a stone, the stone does not stand in the way. But surely, he remarks, this does not mean that a stone is superior to a self, because it has no self-consciousness to stand in the way of its being thought by another. He affirms that it is the very nature of the ego or self to be subject-object. "In thinking itself the absolute, eternal nature and notion of selfhood is revealed in the immediate empirical consciousness, since self-consciousness is precisely the existing and therefore empirically perceivable pure notion, the absolutely self-relating, which as distinguishing or separating judgment makes itself its own object and thus alone is able to constitute a circle, that is of knowing and known in one." The concrete self or ego is subject-object. It is that which moves and lives and knows itself in differences or otherness. The single living individual lives and knows himself through the species, and the species lives through being transformed into spirit. The unitary and eternal ground of the whole process is the *absolute spirit:* the absolute all-inclusive individual. For Hegel the individual, the concrete self is real, but there is only one *absolutely real individual—God.* God is the eternally realized absolute idea or purpose, the perfect individual or personality. He is the absolute spirit, in whom finite spirits live and move and have their being. In terms of feeling, God may be defined as Love, as a play of differentiation, together with the consciousness of the unity which dwells in the differences. God is the universal self-consciousness which comprehends within itself all concrete differences. He is the unity of spirits. The society of finite spirits exists as the object of his thought. In him the scattered rays of light, which form the multitude of finite selves, converge to a single point—to the unstained purity and translucence of an absolute self-consciousness.

It has been maintained that God or the Absolute, for Hegel, is simply the impersonal unity of a perfect society or community of selves.[4] I have not space to discuss this view fully here. Hegel frequently refers to the absolute as an individual, nay *the* individual. We have just seen the high estimate he places on selfhood as at once subject and object. Again he says, speaking of the dialectic process or activity of selfhood, "Every new step in the going-outside-itself, that is, in the farther determination, is also a return-into-self; the wider extension, is at the same time, the higher intensity. The richest is the most concrete and subjective, and the mightiest and most comprehensive which goes back into its own simplest depth. The highest, extremest summit is pure personality which alone, through the absolute dialectic, which is in its nature, grasps and encloses everything in itself—since it makes itself the freest—makes itself the Simplicity which is the first Immediacy and Universality." (Hegel, *Werke*, V, p. 339.)

In short, God, for Hegel, is the conscious unity which lives and acts, thinks and feels, in and through the whole system of finite being. He is the unity of subject and object, the living one in and through which the many have their being. As the unitary totality of all related beings he is the absolute. He is the universal all-including, all-sustaining self-of-selves.

Thus far we have been outlining Hegel's conception of

---

[4] For example by Mr. J. M. E. McTaggart. See his *Studies in Hegelian Dialectic* and *Studies in Hegelian Cosmology*.

reality, and indicating how he reached it. We have seen that he regards everything finite and transitory as a phase of the eternal self-manifestation of the Absolute Self or Spirit. This spirit is dynamically and progressively immanent in the works of nature and the whole political and cultural or social life of man. But this absolute Spirit, as the *eternal* ground of the finite, *transcends* nature and human history. Man's highest knowledges of him are attained through art, religion, and philosophical speculation. (Like many other features of Hegel's doctrine this is reminiscent of Plato and Aristotle.)

Hegel carries out his fundamental insight by tracing out the evolution of human culture; that is of art, religion, political history, and philosophy as, from one side, aspects in the progressive self-manifestation in time of the Absolute Spirit and, from the other side, the progressive self-realization by humanity of its spiritual destiny through the growth in self-conscious possession of reason, beauty, social order, and individual freedom and unity with God. It is beyond the scope of this introduction to outline these. The beginner in the study of objective idealism will probably profit most by studying this aspect of Hegel's work. In fact *his philosophy of history* is probably the best introduction to the study of his system. I shall have occasion to refer to some of these parts of Hegel's Philosophy in later chapters. (*Cf.*, especially Chapter XXVIII.)

The reader will find it interesting and profitable to compare the dialectic method of modern idealism, especially Fichte and Hegel, with the dialectic of Zeno the Eleatic, and of Plato. Zeno's aim appears to have been purely negative—to refute the common assumption of the reality of motion, number and multiplicity in things, by showing that those who make such assumptions fall into hopeless contradictions. Thus the belief in motion, change and multiplicity is reduced to a logical absurdity. The dialectic of Plato has a positive, as well as a negative, purport. Plato aims, (1) to refute the dogmatic assumptions of common opinion and, more especially, of the Sophists, by showing up their inherently self-contradictory character; (2) to lead the mind of his hearers and readers up, from the unreflecting status of persons in whose minds a heterogeneous collection of unexamined and unrelated beliefs find lodgment, to an insight into the rational and systematic or "ideal" structure of reality. To this end Plato sets out from many different points of departure in common "opinion," from ordinary views concerning moral qualities, æsthetic qualities, natural and artificial kinds or classes, mathematical relationships. Hegel's aim, in his dialectic, seems to be the same as Plato's; there is, however, this fundamental difference —whereas, for Hegel, the dialectic process is the moving spring of reality itself, since reality is spirit and spirit lives and functions in the process itself, Plato does not seem to admit that reality, in its total truth and nature, is a process that is forever transcending itself and returning to itself. Plato's insight into the nature of spirit is not so profound as that of Hegel, who had behind him the results of nearly eighteen centuries of Western civilization impregnated with Christianity. Plato, I think, taught that true reality is spirit and that spirit is one-in-many. He did glimpse the dynamic and dialectic character of spirit, but he failed to see clearly the consequence that, from his premises, *spirit must be the immanent dynamic activity of the whole of being.* He does say that Ideas are powers, but he does not see that, if this be so, Ideas must be functions or phases of personality. Plato does not plumb the full depths of personality or spiritual selfhood, and, therefore, there remains a dualism for him between the Ideal and the Actual. Hegel boldly says that this dualism is a moment in the eternal process of spiritual self-realization. Whether we agree with his interpretation of reality or not, we must admit that it was he who has most nearly sounded the full depths of the philosophy of spirit. I do not mean that Hegel was infallible, nor that tnere is nothing more to be done in the interpretation of personality. I mean that he sketched the main outlines. In this sense all objective idealism, every interpretation of reality in terms of spirit, must follow in his path, though not in every one of his footsteps.

The most important recent statements of objective idealism are those of F. H. Bradley and B. Bosanquet in England, and Josiah Royce in America.

Mr. Bradley's *Appearance and Reality* (2nd Edition) is the most brilliant and incisive piece of metaphysical writing in English that has appeared since Hume. He shows a quite extraordinary power of putting subtle dialectical argumentation into clear English. Here I shall only state briefly wherein he seems to modify the Hegelian statement of absolute idealism. The criticism most frequently directed at Hegel is that he reduced the whole of nature and human experience and life to a cobweb spun by pure thought. It is charged that his absolute is the hypostatisation of *pure thought,* and that he is one-sidedly intellectualistic or panlogistic, ignoring the dominant part played by *will* and *feeling* in human life. As a consequence of this vice, it is said, Hegel attempts to reduce nature, history, and human life to a network or mesh of logical relations spun out by the spiderlike intellect of the Absolute. I do not regard these criticisms as wholly justified. Hegel's *Thought, Idea,* or *Notion* (*Begriff*) includes feeling cultivated by the reason, and will as rational activity. But there is some measure of justification in the criticisms—just how much is beyond the scope of this work to determine. Mr. Bradley holds that thought necessarily involves *duality*—the *distinction* between thinking or knowing and its objects; and that volition involves a similar duality—the contrast between purpose or striving and the ends or objects thereof. The same duality infects the entire lives of selves or persons. One can think a self only in relation to that which is not-itself. The absolute unity cannot then be thought, volition, or even a self. It must transcend the oppositions or dualisms by which these are necessarily beset. An immediate experience, analogous to love or æsthetic feeling, an experience in which thought, desire, and will are all taken up and transmuted into a perfect, harmonious and stable unity of feeling, is the Absolute. The Absolute then is a living, single, and seamless whole of experience, in which thought and will find their fruition, in which every flame of passion chaste or carnal burns, not in separation, but as an element in the perfect and utterly harmonious whole of experience. Outside this experience nothing can maintain itself. In it all changes and histories, all sufferings, evils, imperfections, errors, all ugliness and discords, are transmuted into the eternally perfect harmony of the One. Thus Mr. Bradley's view is a speculative mysticism. His nearest of kin, in spirit, is Plotinus.

The most obvious difficulties that are suggested by this view are:

1. How an experience can exist that is not felt nor owned by a self. All experience seems to belong to a self. Mr. Bradley might appeal to the poet Tennyson's words:

> "Love took up the harp of Life, and smote on all the chords with might,
> Smote the chord of Self, that, trembling, passed in music out of sight."

2. How are we to harmonize the eternal and timeless perfection of the absolute with the facts of change, instability, evolution in nature, and striving, change, development, and progress in human life? Here Mr. Bradley would say that the goal of all change, the bourne of all progress, the cessation of suffering and striving, lies in the awakening of man to a consciousness of his true being in the absolute. These points are more fully developed in Chapter XXIV.

Mr. Bosanquet's view does not differ essentially from Mr. Bradley's except that he seems to admit a greater *relative* reality to the physical order. His works give, perhaps, the best balanced statement of objective idealism, or "speculative philosophy," as he calls it, in English. I have not space to compare in detail his standpoint with those of Hegel and Bradley. Mr. Bosanquet dwells less on the contradictoriness of finite lives and experiences and more on their positive contributions to the whole or absolute than does Mr. Bradley.

Josiah Royce, our late American Idealist, has emphasized the volitional element in man and nature and, therefore, in the Absolute. For him the Absolute is the self of selves, the eternal all-knower, the solver of all problems, the fulfiller of all volitions. He is the all-inclusive self or individual. Our temporal and fragmentary lives are fragments of his eternally whole and complete life, our ideas, our volitions (Royce insists on the active or practical character of ideas) find their eternal and perfect fulfillment in his perfect insight and will.

The chief difficulties of objective or absolute idealism, regarded as a form of singularism, will be discussed in a following chapter. In the meantime, may I suggest that, if objective idealism, which seems on the whole to be the doctrine which squares best with the postulates of knowledge and science and with man's practical, social, and æsthetic interests, is to meet the criticisms which are leveled against it, it must broaden its base and become *dynamic*. Let us imagine that the universe of finite, temporal, developing multiplicity, the universe which is thronged with living organisms, selves, histories, with all the struggle, passion, and pathos of humanity, with planets and star systems in evolution, is the ceaseless manifestation of the energizing life-force, not a mere cosmic consciousness of self-revolving thought but an eternally creative life, will, spirit; and yet the central peace that abideth at the heart of things, the inexhaustible fountain of energy, life, and thought, the source and conservator of values, life of our lives, bone of our bone, flesh of our flesh, thought of our thought, feeling of our feeling and yet transcending all finite energy, will, feeling and thought, as being the eternally creative self-existent fountain, ground and goal of all life, will, thought, aspiration! Might we not thus dimly see that there may be peace in the midst of strife, harmony ruling through discord, values victorious through the striving, struggling lives of men and animals, a good that overcomes and is richer for evil, a joy that swallows up and is deeper for suffering, a truth that is fuller and more concrete for all the fragments, which, seen apart from one another, seem error?

References

* Adamson, R., *Fichte.*
* Avey, A. E., *Readings in Philosophy,* Chapter XVIII.
* Berkeley, *Three Dialogues Between Hylas and Philonous,* and *Principles of Human Knowledge* (Open Court Series or Fraser's Selections).

Bosanquet, B., *The Principle of Individuality and Value,* and *The Meeting of Extremes in Contemporary Philosophy.*

Bradley, F. H., *Appearance and Reality,* Second Edition.

* Calkins, Mary W., *The Persistent Problems of Philosophy.*
* Caird, E., *Hegel.*

CAIRD, E., *The Evolution of Religion.*

CARR, H. WILDON, *A Theory of Monads.*

* CROCE, B., *What is Living and What is Dead in Hegel's Philosophy?*

* DUNCAN, G. M., *Philosophical Works of Leibnitz.*

* FICHTE, *Vocation of Man* (Open Court Series).

* FRASER, A. C., *Berkeley.*

GREEN, T. H., *Prolegomena to Ethics.*

HEGEL, *Philosophy of Mind, and Logic* (translated by Wallace).

* LATTA, R., *Leibniz, The Monadology,* etc.

* LEIBNITZ, *Monadology* (In Open Court Series).

* LEIGHTON, J. A., *Man and the Cosmos,* especially Chapters VIII, XVII, XXII-XXXIII, and XXXV-XXXVIII; and *Typical Modern Conceptions of God.*

ROGERS, A. K., *English and American Philosophy since 1800,* Chapters V and VI.

* ROYCE, J., *The Spirit of Modern Philosophy,* Part II, and *The World and the Individual,* Vol. I, Lectures VII and VIII, and Volume II, Lectures II, IV and V.

RUSSELL, B., *The Philosophy of Leibnitz.*

* SETH, JAMES, *English Philosophers,* Part II, Chapter I.

* SINCLAIR, MAY, *The New Idealism.*

* SMITH, WM., *The Popular Works of Fichte.*

* SORLEY, W. R., *History of English Philosophy.*

* THILLY or ROGERS' *History of Philosophy,* Chapters on Leibnitz, Fichte, and Hegel.

WINDELBAND, W., *Geschichte der neuern Philosophie,* and *History of Philosophy.*

CHAPTER XIX

THE IDENTITY OR DOUBLE ASPECT THEORY

The identity or double aspect theory of the relation of soul or mind and body in man and in the universe was first formulated by Spinoza. It has since been advanced, with various modifications, by Schelling, Fechner, Paulsen, Herbert Spencer, Heymans, and others. Fechner, Paulsen, Strong, and others give it a spiritualistic twist and Haeckel gives it a materialistic twist. It has found favor with many psychologists. According to this theory, reality consists of two irreducible and absolutely parallel aspects. They do not interact; they are the two aspects of one principle or substance. *Ordo idearum idem est atque ordo rerum.* The order of ideas is the same as the order of things, that is, Spinoza means to say that the mental and physiological processes are parallel orders. Each one constitutes a causal nexus uninfluenced by the other; but each of the two orders is, down to the minutest and most momentary event, an expression of the single determined order of the one substance—God. Therefore the correspondence between the two orders of events is complete. This psycho-physical parallelism rests on the assumption that the degree of mental organization and perfection corresponds to the degree of bodily organization and perfection but the one does not cause the other. They are two-faced expressions of the one substantial being. This standpoint, starting as a metaphysical interpretation of the relation of soul and body in man, is generalized into a theory of the relation of mind and matter in the universe at large. It thus passes from a psychological doctrine into a cosmology. Reality is one, but it has two faces or aspects, known to us as mind and body. In itself the one substance is neither mind nor body; to us it appears as both.

One who thinks clearly, and follows it through, cannot stay in this double aspect view. There is an inevitable tendency to emphasize the one or the other term of the parallelism, to shade off from a monism with two faces into either spiritualism or materialism. Nevertheless, as regards the relation of body and soul there is an element of truth in this view. Mental and neural processes do exhibit a considerable degree of parallelism and can be thus fruitfully regarded. But the mental self is not literally parallel with the nervous system, notwithstanding the fact that it operates in the closest connection with the nervous system.

The self is a more intimate and unique kind of unity than even a living organism.[1] It is a unity whose constituent parts are not parts in any spatial, or even numerical, sense; they are distinguishable, but not separable, aspects or phases of a living and indivisible unity. Each moment of a self's life is the single pulsation of a continuous activity. The elements of a self completely interpenetrate one another. Furthermore, self-consciousness, the consciousness of being conscious, of feeling, acting, and thinking, is a property possessed by nothing in the world except thinking selves; a property that, strictly speaking, has no physical parallel.

If psychological parallelism be taken to mean that mental and physiological or neurological processes run parallel to one another, but never influence one another, it is open to three fatal criticisms: 1. It is not a fact that bodily and mental processes do not influence one another, and the supposed parallelism cannot be worked out in minute

---

[1] *Cf.* Chapter XXV, The Self.

detail; for (a) we cannot identify mental processes corresponding to every sort of bodily process; events are constantly occurring in organisms (metabolisms, secretions) to which no corresponding mental process can be shown; (b) there is no balanced correspondence or equivalence between the physiological correlates and the mental manifestations, social and individual (consider the mental and social differences between receiving, by telegraph, the news respectively of an invitation to play golf, of the death of one's beloved child, of a bequest of a million dollars, of the capitulation of the German army); (c) the self functions as a unity, not always in the same degree, but at its best moments very fully; what, then, is parallel in the physiological series to this dynamic unity of thought and volition? Parallelism is atomistic in principle and can, logically, have no place for the unity of the self; (d) the mental and bodily processes that correspond should be synchronous, if parallelism be strictly true, but they actually follow one another in time.

2. If parallelism be true then there must be mental processes corresponding to everything that goes on in atoms or electrons. We should then have a doctrine of the feelings, thoughts and volitions of the atoms and electrons, their loves and hates, joys and sorrows—in short, an electronic psychology and sociology. This is simply the utter confusion of thought and science.

3. Parallelism sets out from an extreme dualism and then violently converts it into an abstract monism. The parallelism of mental and physical would be inexplicable, unless these are two aspects of one substance which is the *real reality*. What, then, is this one substance? If it be an unknown third or X then we have a doctrine which explains the relatively unknown by the absolutely unknown. We do not know the inner "go" of the relations of mind and body. But, certainly, it is no illumination, but rather

a further darkening, of this mystery, to be told that mind and body are absolutely parallel aspects of an unknown third; that this is the real reality. If it means that reality is psychical, that is true of some, but not of all, actual forms of being. And, if it means that the real reality is the physical, parallelism is then a specious name for materialism.

Summary View of the Mind-Body Problem

The following seems to me the most reasonable hypothesis. There are three grades of individua: (1) *Inorganic* or *Physical Individua* or *Monads.* These are dynamic centers, which yield sense qualities when they are in interactive relations with percipients. All that can be said about them, when they are not being perceived, is that they have the real possibilities of yielding sense qualities. Physical individua attract and repel one another and they form aggregates, varying in complexity and coherence from a heap of sand to a crystal or a magnet. (2) *Vital Individua* or *Monads.* These develop and maintain themselves by processes in which they utilize inorganic monads. They reproduce their kinds, but, especially by sexual reproduction, with constant variations. Thus, vital monads have a plasticity both of adjustment, self-maintenance and reproduction much greater than inorganic monads. Some, perhaps all, of them have sentience or feeling. Inorganic monads are instrumental and constituent to the organization of life and thus, indirectly, to the operation of mind. (3) *Mental Individua* or *Selves.* These develop and function in organized bodies. They are centers of awareness, memory, reflection, selection, valuation, invention, and rational or purposive conation or volition. They are in space and time, in the sense that they are associated with spatial configurations and have histories. But they are not bounded by space and time in the same sense in which physical bodies are; for they have the power to know at great distances, and, partially, to conquer space, as well as to span time by making records and executing purposes.

Inorganic monads do not, as such, develop into selves; but, on the other hand, there is no absolute dualism of character such as would prevent a mutual influence. If inorganic monads actually became selves, then there would be no real grounds for distinguishing between their respective characteristics or modes of behavior. Then we should have, not only a psychology and sociology of the electron but, as well, a logic, ethics, æsthetics of electrons and molecules. The distinction between physical science and the moral and social sciences would vanish. Some monistic fanatics look for this happy consummation. To my mind, it is to blot out, rather than to fill in, the lineaments of genuine science.

The realist[2] is correct in his contention that no convincing argument has been advanced for the view that all that exists is psychic content, stuff, or "ideas." And the burden of the proof is upon him who assumes that every thing in the universe is simply psychic stuff; for, on the face of it, as well as when its behavior is probed by science, the physical realm does not appear to be psychic stuff. On the other hand, we can know nothing about anything that is not either actual or possible matter of experience, or, that, as *law, universal, concept* or *value,* does not belong to the texture of experience. But to say that, in order that anything may be, or may become, known, it must be psychical stuff, seems like arguing that he who would drive fat oxen must himself be fat.

The contemporary objective idealist does not mean that

---

[2] I suggest that, after reading this chapter, the student read Chapter XX on Recent Realism, and then return to the consideration of the above paragraphs.

the stuff or content of reality is all psychical or mental. He means that the structure and drift or meaning of reality, taken as a whole, is the partly actual, and partly possible, expression and instrument of purposes and ideals. He means that values and ideals are not the blind products and playthings of mass particles in motion. In this sense of teleological or axiological idealism, there is no halfway house open to man between idealism and materialism, except the frail shelter which accepts a final dualism between the order of nature and the order of values, and, declining either to affirm or deny that ideal values are mere human allusions, is, nevertheless, constrained to regard them as homeless and unparented waifs adrift in the cosmic storms. (See further Chapter XXVII.) Thus realism in epistemology leads, according to the weight attributed to the values of personality in relation to the physical world, either to materialism, idealism, or agnosticism, in metaphysics.

In view of the varied and misleading meanings of the word "Idealism" it would, perhaps, be better to call the view which I have stated, as my own, "Organic experientialism." I will now summarize this view.

Reality is experience (actual and possible). It is an organized whole having many degrees of individuality. So far I go with Leibnitz. The whole world is a dynamic process, but the physical world is not psychical in itself. Selves are true parts of the world. The physical order is the substructure of the social order. There is therefore nothing real which is not subject or object of either actual or possible experience. Furthermore, experience is social. What we mean by the physical is that which is accessible to all selves. Of the individual self we can have no adequate conception apart from society. The individual lives and develops only as a member of a social order. Now the physical is the real, common ground of our social activities. But the social and spiritual is also a true part of the real. The physical is intelligible and is to some extent subject to human control. And because of this we may say it is a part of a teleological system, but it is not a figment of the ego's imagination, as Fichte came perilously near saying. Nor is nature the mere subservient tool of purpose interpreted in a narrowly humanistic or supernaturalistic fashion, as was done by older naïve and pre-evolutionary teleologists in their watchmaker theories of design. (Of this matter more anon.)

In the real world of actual and really possible experience, which is the only world that has concrete meanings for human beings, selves-in-societal-relations and physical nature are in organic or functional interdependence. They are coördinates and therefore functions one of another. Reality contains nonmental individuated centers of force or dynamic relationship, vitally organized and psychical individuals of various grades of wealth of content, degree of organization and harmony. All these various types of individual or monads live and function in what, for want of a better term, I call "organic or functional" interrelation and interexistence. The highest type of individuum that we know is a rational human individual or personality. In human individuality the functioning of mind is conditional upon the functioning of a central nervous system, but, as I have already argued, we are not compelled, since we have not sufficient grounds for the assumption, to say that mind and nervous system are absolutely identical. An individual mind is a conscious, active, and selective center of meanings and values expressing itself through, and therefore conditioned by, a physiological organization. The mind is the dynamic meaning and purpose of the body. The relation between them is not properly described as "causal." It is the functional interdependence of two systems which, together, constitute a teleological whole and in which body is the teleological instrument of mind.

Such, with reference to the soul-body and mind-matter problems, is the standpoint which may be called "organic experientialism" or "dynamic idealism."

References

* Avey, A. E., *Readings in Philosophy,* Chapter XIX.
* James, William, *Essays in Radical Empiricism,* especially, *Does Consciousness Exist?*
* Leighton, J. A., *Man and the Cosmos,* Chapters XIX, XX, XXI and XXVII.
* Mach, Ernst, *Analysis of the Sensations.*
* Paulsen, F., *Introduction to Philosophy,* Book I, Chapter I, pp. 74-111.
* Spinoza, F., *Ethics,* especially Book I.

Strong, C. A., *Why the Mind Has a Body.*

CHAPTER XX

RECENT REALISM

I. The Meanings of Realism

The term "Realism" has a variety of meanings; in this respect it is in the same boat with the antithetical term "Idealism." Plato's philosophy is realistic, in the sense that it affirms the enduring reality of the Ideas or universals, by contrast with the transitoriness of their phenomenal embodiments. Aristotle is even more realistic, in that he seems to accord to matter a shade more reality than does Plato.

Modern realism includes a variety of doctrines, but common to them all is the assertion of the existence of realities of some description independent of and other than, minds. Taken in this sense the proper contrast is between Realism and Mentalism or Spiritualism. In metaphysics a realist may be a materialist, or a dualist, or a neutral monist, or a multiplicist (one who believes in more than two kinds of real being); a realist may have a theory which affords a permanent place for human values, if he be not a materialist.[1]

With the exception of Thomas Reid's *Philosophy of Common Sense*, and Herbart in Germany, realism played an insignificant part in modern philosophy until near the end of the nineteenth century. Since then it has grown in volume and influence and is one of the three major tendencies of contemporary philosophy; the other two being

[1] Thomas Aquinas, and in present-day philosophy, S. Alexander, R. B. Perry and E. G. Spaulding are epistemological realists who affirm the validity of spiritual values.

objective idealism or "speculative philosophy," as Dr. Bosanquet calls it; and pragmatism or instrumentalism.

All forms of the new realism agree in holding that many of the objects of knowledge exist independent of their being known; for example, the physical world and other minds than that of the knower. Many realists also contend that universal principles, such as the principles of logic, mathematics, and the exact physical sciences, exist or "subsist" independently of their being known. Some realists assert that even moral and æsthetic values subsist independently of their being known or felt.

All realists reject Berkeley's argument that, because what is perceived implies a mind perceiving it, therefore, what is perceived can exist only in and for some mind. The realist says that the idealist is guilty of equivocation in his use of the term "experience." Because what I experience seems to me real and because my experience implies myself as ego or experient, the idealist argues, says the new realist, that all reality must be experience, and therefore dependent on an ego. Because everything actually known is, as an actual item of knowledge, present *to* the mind of a knower, it is illegitimately assumed that the *being* of everything must be being *in* and *for* a knower. In short the idealist converts the proposition "All *known* being involves a knower or mind," into "*all being* involves a knower or mind," dropping out the essential qualification "*known.*" But there may be many things and qualities existing which are not known to any mind. Certainly the physical conditions of perception, such as vibrations in the ether or the dance of electrons are not perceived at all; they are inferred to exist as *pre-conditions* of perception. We may be in doubt as to what precisely are the physical conditions of perception in the external world. We may not even know what goes on in our nervous systems. But we can scarcely doubt that some sort of physical or *non-*

mental events are the indispensable conditions of mental events. If this be so in the case of human knowing, we have no right to jump to the conclusion that the physical conditions of knowledge are acts of other minds. To argue that, because known-being implies a mind, therefore all being is being in and for a mind, is to ignore the mass of evidence which goes to show that a mind is a function of a certain type of physical organization, namely, a nervous system. The realist can admit that minds are important items of reality, but not that they are the all-important items.

Indeed, says the realist, in the very act of knowing an object (whether that object be a physical thing, a scientific principle, or a mind) it is implied that the *existence* of the object is independent of the act of knowing it, otherwise there would be no difference between imaginary beings and real beings. Even in knowing my own mind, what is known is different from the knowing of it. If I know that I am in love or unhappy, I must first be in these states before I can know them. By the reality of a physical thing, or the truth of a rational principle, *as known*, I do not mean that I have invented it out of whole cloth, but that I have discovered or recognized its reality.

On the latter point there is no need for quarrel between objective idealists (such as Leibnitz, Hegel, or Bosanquet) and realists. Indeed, the gist of the objective idealists' argument for an absolute mind or cosmic experient is, as we have seen, that reality must have an organized structure or texture, since the more we interpret experience in terms of thought the better we apprehend its rational organization. Against this argument many realists retort that the statement that reality is one complete whole or *individual* is an assumption without warrant. It is more in accord with the facts, say these realists, to affirm that reality is simply an aggregate of many examples of several kinds of entities, some of which are interdependent, but many of which are independent of one another. Thus they are metaphysical pluralists. Dr. S. Alexander, we shall see, is a singularistic realist, B. Russell a pluralistic realist.

With respect to what entities or "things," in a broad sense of the term, exist independent of minds, all realists are not in agreement. Some approach the position of naïve realism that everything perceived or conceived has physical existence. S. Alexander attributes physical existence even to images, illusions, and hallucinations. Others (and these are the great majority) hold that the perceived qualities are the results of the interaction of minds and nervous systems with the microscopic motions of minute physical things (atoms, electrons, ether waves, et cetera). In the absence of percipients only the latter things exist. Those who admit the independent existence of minds are dualists. Others (especially certain American neorealists) regard the mind as simply a function of the nervous system, but they avoid materialism by the hypothesis that all minds and bodies are compounded of one sort of stuff, which in itself is "neutral" in character; that is, neither mental nor physical.[2]

I shall examine in this order the doctrines of neutral monism, of Bertrand Russell and S. Alexander, and conclude with some critical remarks on realism.

II. Neutral Monism

Among American thinkers, instrumentalism in particular (in John Dewey and his congeners) has become more or

[2] In the most recent realistic work, *Essays in Critical Realism*, by Drake and others, the writers do not seem to agree as to what the stuff of reality may be. They are content to agree that what the mind knows, through sense data, are *essences* which are different from the sense qualities. For them the sense qualities are signs or representatives of these independent essences.

less *behavioristic,* in its conception of the mind and, thus, has become increasingly realistic. (See Chapter XXII.) For realism, beginning with the denial of the privileged position of mind in the universe, sometimes leads on to minimizing the function of conscious mentality in man regarded as a biological organism; and the further step is a short one to the assertion that consciousness either does not exist, or, if it exist, does not play any other rôle in life than that of an impotent spectator of the game.

In general the ultrabehavioristic conception of man is that he is to be regarded as a bundle or complex of physiological reflexes. Thought is viewed simply as a complex of speech reactions, built up out of elementary reflexes in a similar fashion to those in which walking, dancing, and other forms of skill are built up. From the standpoint of ultra behaviorism we must substitute, for the statements "Man is a rational animal" and "Man is a mental and physical individuality," the statement "Man is a complicated, physico-chemical mechanism built up out of elementary physiological reflexes evolved in the struggle for existence and transmitted through the germ plasm."[3] Short of this *ultra behaviorism,* which finds no useful function for consciousness or mind, is *moderate behaviorism,* which admits that consciousness makes a difference in human behavior.[4]

The reduction or elimination of "mind," as a causal factor in behavior, naturally leads to a metaphysical monism which must be either materialistic or neutral. The ultra behaviorist is possessed by the irresistible desire to get

---

[3] *Cf.* J. B. Watson's *Behavior, An Introduction to Comparative Psychology,* New York, 1914; and *Psychology from the Standpoint of a Behaviorist,* Philadelphia, 1919.

[4] H. C. Warren's *Human Psychology,* Boston, 1919, is a good exposition of moderate behaviorism. R. S. Woodworth's *Psychology,* New York, 1921, seems to me to include whatever is of essential value in behaviorism.

rid of dualism; this is his dominating "complex." If consciousness does not perform any unique function in the world, why should we suppose that there is any unique distinction between sentient and insentient stuff? Why not say that everything is made of the same stuff, complicated in various ways? Behavioristic realists shy at a crass materialism and in general incline to regard the physical and the mental as two different ways of taking the same "neutral" stuff. By calling this fundamental stuff "neutral," they mean that *in itself* it is neither physical nor mental; it will appear as either the one or the other, according to the way in which it is conceived. *The world of physics,* on the one hand, *and the world of psychology* (including in the latter all human reactions, attributes, and activities in social and cultural, as well as individual life), on the other hand, *are just two ways of looking at what is in essence the same stuff of reality.*

This neutral tendency was given a great impetus by William James' three essays entitled "A World of Pure Experience," "Does Consciousness Exist," and "The Place of Affectional Facts in a World of Pure Experience," et cetera, collected together in his volume, *Essays in Radical Empiricism.* It has affinities with Avenarius' concept of pure experience and with the sensationalistic phenomenalism of Ernst Mach.

James proposed to get rid of the duality of consciousness and its objects by taking a radical step and thus rightly called his doctrine "radical empiricism." He says there is no such entity as consciousness. The standing assumption of common sense is that there is a duplicity in experience—knower and known, thought and things. James says "*Experience, I believe, has no such inner duplicity*";[5] "*thoughts in the concrete are made of the same stuff as things are.*"[6]

[5] *Essays in Radical Empiricism,* p. 9.
[6] *Ibid.,* p. 37.

"The instant field of the present is at all times what I call 'pure' experience."[7] The sum total of all experience "is a *that,* an absolute, a 'pure' experience on an enormous scale, undifferentiated and undifferentiable into thought and thing";[8] "experience as a whole is self-containing and leans on nothing."[9] It is "the selfsame piece of pure experience, taken twice over, that serves now as thought and now as thing."[10] I am writing at a desk. The paper, the desk, and the pencil are bits of pure experience. If they are taken in their spatial relations in the house, they thus become physical things; but, if they are taken as items in my personal biography, they thus become thoughts. As virginal experiences they are neither thoughts nor things, and their being taken as either the one or the other is an addition to their original natures as just pure experiences. As for the relations which seem to do the taking and thus the dualizing or dichotomizing of the world of pure experience, they too are experiences of transition which no Ego has or makes. They just happen. The relations are empirical data like the substantive bits of pure experience between which they are transitions or passages.

In short, the color, shape, and touch qualities of the desk *are the physical desk,* when taken in their space relations; the color, shape, and touch qualities *are my mind,* as perceiving the desk, when these qualities are regarded as events which happen in the history of a living body. It is all a question of how you take them. The paper on which I am writing is physical, as a patch of color and touch quality on the desk; the paper is my mind, when the sense qualities which are the paper are viewed as happening to this series of events which is called a human body.

This seems a beautifully simple way of circumventing all the difficulties which arise from the duality of Ego knowing

---

[7] *Essays in Radical Empiricism,* p. 23.
[8] *Ibid.,* p. 134.
[9] *Ibid.,* p. 193.
[10] *Ibid.,* p. 27.

and object known. It solves the problem of the self by saying it consists of certain transitional experiences. Consciousness becomes a clumsy and misleading name for certain empirical groupings. There is no longer any problem of mind and body on our hands, since mind and body are merely the same pure experiences connected by other pure experiences of relation or transition. Knowing, affection, and willing consist of certain transitional feelings, and material movements consist of other transitional feelings. No Ego feels the feelings or knows the knowledges. All things flow and all things, including the rates and kinds of flowing, are simply experiences. A personal history is simply an experience of continuous transition.

James' doctrine has been taken up by certain American neorealists, especially by Perry and Holt. According to the latter, the world consists of *neutral elements,* that is, elements that are neither physical nor psychical. These elements are numerically many but qualitatively of the same substance. They are *logical* "terms" and "propositions," but active and generative of more complex entities. These elements constitute an indefinite variety of complexes, since they may enter an indefinite variety of group or class relations. They are the foundation stones of the universe. Mind is a class or group of neutral entities, as a physical object is another class or group. A mind makes a cross section of the world which is always a group of the neutral components of the object and its immediate relations. Consciousness is any part of the field of neutral entities that is illuminated. Mere illumination makes no change in the natures of the entities. They may exist the same in relation and out of relation to consciousness. Consciousness is like a searchlight that plays over the entities.[11] The work of selection and illumination, which results in con-

[11] Holt in *The New Realism*, p. 352 ff.

sciousness, is done by the central nervous system.[12] The processes of the nervous system are of a mathematical and neutral structure,[13] like all physical processes. Holt would even define a collision between two railroad engines as a contradiction between two groups of logical entities. In short, reality is resolved into an unearthly ballet of bloodless terms and propositions. Neutral monistic realism thus turns around into a pluralistic logicism.

Neutral monism seems to be but a philosophical aberration for the following reasons:

1. It can offer no explanation of why we should make a distinction between consciousness and its objects, between knowing and the thing known, without invoking the nervous system as the real agent. Much less can it account for the fact of self-consciousness. Can a searchlight search for its own searchings?

2. It cannot account for the felt difference between perception of objects as present to the percipient and imagination of objects not so present.

3. It cannot account for memory since the latter involves the conscious continuity of the self.

4. It cannot account for error. If consciousness be but the passively illuminated field of objects selected by the central nervous system, how can there be wrong judgments? The theory of error requires the assumption of an active thinker.

5. Since consciousness is the illuminated field of the *present,* how can one believe in *nontemporal* propositions such as those of logic, mathematics and natural science?

6. Neutral monism involves phychological atomism. The self is resolved into an ever shifting phantasmagoria of neutral entities selected by the brain.

---

[12] Holt in *The New Realism*, p. 352 ff., and Perry, *Present Philosophical Tendencies*, p. 299, etc.

[13] Holt, *The Concept of Consciousness*, p. 255, etc.

7. Since the brain is the real selective and attentive agency, the searchlight that makes the illumination which is consciousness, *neutral monism is but a new and specious name for materialism.* It has no right to be called *neutral monism.*

James' standpoint of radical empiricism is simpler and not open to all the above objections, because it evades all troublesome problems as to *how* the "inner duplicity" arises in experience and would make philosophy a mere description, without analysis and reconstructive interpretation, of the flux of experience. James fails to offer any account as to why or how it happens that identically the same bits of experience get taken, respectively, in physical and personal contexts of relations. Personal biographies, appreciations, judgments, feelings, volitions just appear and disappear mysteriously, hither and yon in the flux of experience. It is simpler and more reasonable to admit that experience involves an experiencer, and, hence, a self, especially in view of the fact that one is not only conscious but may be conscious of one's being conscious, that is, be self-conscious.

III. Bertrand Russell's Realism

The realism of Bertrand Russell has changed a good bit in the course of his publication. In his earlier works, *Our Knowledge of the External World* and *The Problems of Philosophy,*[14] he makes a sharp distinction between the world of *sense data* and the world of *physics.* Among the data of our ordinary experience, a distinction is made between "hard" data and "soft" data. "Soft" data are those data which become, when subjected to critical scru-

[14] See especially *Our Knowledge of the External World,* Chapters III and IV.

tiny, more or less doubtful;[15] "hard" data are those data which resist the solvent influence of criticism. "The hardest of hard data are of two sorts—the particular facts of sense, and the general truths of logic."[16] The belief in the existence of sensible objects when not perceived, and the belief in other people's minds, are soft data. The *sense data* or *sensa*—that is, the actually perceived colors, shapes, sounds, et cetera—are hard data. A *sensation* is a mental event which consists in our being aware of a sensible object. A *sensible object* is one of which we are aware. If I believe I see a real table, the *sensible object* is a patch of color which is a "perspective" of the table. I do not see a physical table. What we call "things" are series of perspectives, for example, the series of views one may have of a table or a teacup, from different situations. Since these perspectives are related to the percipient, and to one another according to certain laws which are formulated in the science of physics, "*Things are those series of aspects which obey the laws of physics.* That such series exist is an empirical fact, which constitutes the verifiability of physics."[17] But physics presupposes one common space. Now the individual does not *sense* one space—the space of sight differs from the space of touch. The one space for the individual is an intellectual construction, into which he fits both sight and touch sensations. Moreover, each individual has his own "private" world of space. No two men perceive precisely the same spatial world. So many percipients, so many private worlds. But several men may perceive *similar* worlds. Suppose two men sitting in a room. Then two similar worlds are perceived by them; enter a third, who sits between them, and he perceives a world intermediate

---

[15] *Our Knowledge of the External World*, pp. 70 ff.
[16] *Ibid.*, pp. 70-71.
[17] *Ibid.*, p. 110.

between their worlds. We may suppose, not that what he perceives existed before he came in, but that *some aspect* of the universe *from that point of view* existed. So we may think an infinite number of possible points of view, some perceived, many not perceived. These aspects constitute the system of perspectives which makes up the real world of physics.[18] It is to be noted that, in order to get from the "private" world of each separate individual into this public space-system, Russell has to assume the existence of other minds. He admits that we cannot offer very strong proof of the existence of other minds, but holds that we cannot help believing in them.

In a similar fashion Russell gets from the private "times" of individuals to the notion of one time which is an intellectual construction.

Russell, thus far, is a dualist. He holds to the *existence of minds* and their activity; the existence of *sense data,* which are *for* minds but cannot be explained as caused by them; and the existence of *something independent of mind,* which is the physical ground of our perceptions of sense data, and of our intellectual construction of physical space, time, and matter.

Russell rejects the arguments of idealists on behalf of the interdependence of terms and relations. The nature of a thing is identical with the thing. The relations do not make the thing nor the thing the relations. Relations are real as such; the particular terms or entities which they relate have their "natures" or qualities independent of the relations which relate them in manifold ways. Thus Russell is a pluralist or "logical atomist." The business of philosophy is logical analysis, and its work consists in resolving the complexes of naïve experience into their atomic elements. Analysis shows us that there are three

---

[18] *Our Knowledge of the External World,* pp. 87-97.

kinds of entities: (1) general relations; (2) physical things, and (3) minds. These may exist independent of one another or in partial dependence on one another.

In his latest work, *The Analysis of Mind,* Russell tentatively advocates the doctrine of neutral monism. He proposes to dispense entirely with the subject, or self, as being a gratuitous hypothesis. (*Analysis of Mind,* p. 142.) When we do so, there is left no distinction between sense datum and sensation, because of course there is no ego to have a sensation. There are data, but no selves for whom the data exist. "The stuff of the world, so far as we have experience of it, consists of innumerable transient particulars, such as occur in seeing, hearing, etc., together with images more or less resembling these." (*Ibid.,* p. 143.) A "perception" becomes the appearance of an object from a place where there is a brain. The person is constituted by relations of the thoughts to each other and the body. "It would be better to say it thinks in me" like "it rains here," or better still, "there is a thought in me." "To say that it is Jones who is walking is merely to say that the walking in question is part of the whole series of occurrences which is Jones." (*Ibid.,* p. 195.) In brief, whether Jones thinks, walks, or falls in love, it is simply a case of certain bits of the neutral stuff of the universe happening to fall into a peculiar arrangement in a certain temporal series.

Russell does not go the whole way with behaviorism. Minds for him are composed of sensations, images, and a variety of feelings (of *familiarity, pastness, expectation,* et cetera). Even our emotions of pain and pleasure are composites of sensations and feelings. But *images* and *meanings* cannot, he thinks, be accounted for in purely behavioristic terms. And the outstanding psychological fact is *mnemic causation,* which means that the present experience of a mind is determined by the past experience, as well as by the present stimulus. Thus there does, after all, seem to be something rather unique about mind, although there is no active ego or self. The "active self" Russell regards as the disappearing ghost of the "soul."

He sums up his views as follows:

1. Physics and psychology are not distinguished by their material, but by their relations. Physics groups particulars by their active places, psychology by their passive places.

2. The two most essential characteristics of the causal laws which would naturally be called psychological are *subjectivity* and *mnemic causation.*

3. Habit, memory, and thought are all developments of mnemic causation. It is probable, though not certain, that mnemic causation is derivative from ordinary physical causation in nervous (and other) tissue.

4. Consciousness is a complex and far from universal characteristic of mental phenomena.

5. Mind is a matter of degree, chiefly exemplified in number and complexity of habits.

6. All our data, both in physics and psychology, are subject to psychological causal law. Physical causal laws, strictly speaking, can only be stated in terms of matter; which is inferred and constructed, never a datum. In this respect psychology is nearer to what actually exists. (*Ibid.*, p. 307-308.)

In short, the neutral stuff theory reconciles a materialistic psychology with the immaterialistic tendencies of physics. But, if the reconciliation is achieved by reducing the self to a mere momentary complex of unconscious unthinking "stuff," I think its "neutral" monism is only a new and specious name for materialism. The quintessence of materialism is the reduction of the mental self to an epiphenomenon or by-product of nonmental entities.

Russell finds an irreconcilable opposition between human ideals and the physical universe. The actual physical world is "omnipotent matter," "blind to good and evil," reckless of human life and human ideals.[19] Justice, fellowship, coöperation, love, exist only as human ideals. They have no cosmic support. Nay, the cosmos grinds these dreams to powder with man their maker. "Brief and powerless is man's life; on him and all his race the slow, sure doom falls pitiless and dark."[20] "The life of man is a long march through the night, surrounded by invisible foes, tortured by weariness and pain, towards a goal that few can hope to reach, and where none may tarry long. One by one, as they march, our comrades vanish from our sight, seized by the silent orders of omnipotent Death."[21]

To us is left only the stoic and heroic endurance to be faithful, in the face of a pitiless and insensate universe, to human values. Our freedom lies in the will to help, to pity, and to love one another, to renounce, and to endure, to be free in the empire of the spirit even while we are being crushed to powder, to cherish, while we may, beauty and sublimity, resignation and love. "For Man, condemned to-day to lose his dearest, to-morrow himself to pass through the gate of darkness, it remains only to cherish, ere yet the blow falls, the lofty thoughts that ennoble his little day; disdaining the coward terrors of the slave of Fate, to worship at the shrine that his own hands have built; undismayed by the empire of chance, to preserve a mind free from the wanton tyranny that rules his outward life; proudly defiant of the irresistible forces that tolerate, for a moment, his knowledge and his condemnation, to sustain alone, a weary but unyielding Atlas, the world that his own ideals have fashioned despite the trampling march of unconscious power."[22]

---

[19] Russell, "The Free Man's Worship," in *Mysticism and Logic*, Chap. III, or *Philosophical Essays*, Chap. II.

[20] *Mysticism and Logic*, p. 56.

[21] *Ibid.*, p. 56.

[22] *Ibid.*, p. 56-57.

A most eloquent and classic expression of immitigable pessimism and the proud courage of utter despair; and of the worship of ethical values, abstract logical essences, and visions of beauty and grandeur, created out of nothing!

IV. S. Alexander's Realistic Metaphysics

There are certain striking contrasts between Russell's latest position and that developed by Dr. Samuel Alexander in his massive, elaborate, and highly original work, *Space, Time, and Deity.* It is impossible, in the present work, to do more than sketch very briefly some of Alexander's main theses.[23] Alexander rejects the pluralism held by other neorealists. Coherence is the test of truth, and indeed of all values. There are no purely external relations in reality. Some relations are *extrinsic,* others *essential.* For example, it is extrinsic to the nature of a man as man whether he be or he be not in the relation of king, father, or slave; but even extrinsic relations and the natures of the things related by them are not wholly indifferent to one another.

Reality is one whole—it is a system. The whole reality, the one stuff of all things, the one all-sustaining matrix of finite existences and values is *infinite space-time.* All things are finite configurations or complexes of space-time; it is the absolute. Space and time are intuited as infinite continuous wholes of parts; the limiting cases of bits or elements of space-time are *point-instants* or pure *events.* Point-instants do not exist, except as the logical limits of our analysis of concrete space-time. Space-time is the primordial stuff or matrix out of which things and events are made, the medium in which they are precipitated and

---

[23] For a fuller summary *cf.* the present writer's review of Dr. Alexander's work in *The Philosophical Review,* Vol. XXX, 1921; pp. 282-297.

crystallized. Mental space and time, mathematical space and time, and physical space and time, are just the one reality *space-time,* considered under different aspects.

Space is the "body" of which time is the "soul." Space is generated in, or by, time. Space is the trail of time. The history of the universe is a continuous redistribution of instants of time among points of space. (*Ibid.,* Vol. I, p. 63.) What we actually perceive are "perspectives" of space-time. Total space-time is the synthesis of all partial perspectives of space-time. (*Ibid.,* Vol. I, p. 76.) At any moment in its real history space is not all of one date, and time is not all at one point. It is possible, because time is repeated in space, and space in time, to speak of time and space as existing by themselves. But this language is the result of an arbitrary selection from the space-time whole. "In order that time should linger, space must recur, a point must be repeated in more than one instant." (*Ibid.,* Vol. I, p. 49.) "If Time were bare Time it would consist of perishing instants. Instead of a continuous Time, there would be nothing more than an instant, a now which was perpetually being renewed. But Time would then be for itself and for an observer a mere now, and would contain neither earlier nor later." (*Ibid.,* Vol. I, p. 45.) Time gives distinction to the parts of space; we are able to distinguish the parts of space, because different instants of time occupy the same point of space and different points of space occur at the same instant of time. Space gives continuity to the successive instants of time.

Empirical finite existence consists of a series or hierarchy of levels of "empirical qualities." Each level is built up by a selection and complication from the qualities of the next lower level. This complication generates a new simplicity of qualities—a unique group of qualities, which in turn become the bodily basis for the next higher group of qualities. The new level may be called the "soul," of which the bodily basis is the group of qualities next below from which the "soul" emerges. The "soul" or higher set is not caused by the lower or bodily set, but "emerges" from them. The empirical levels are, in order of their complication and emergence: the primary qualities of pure space-time; the secondary qualities, such as color, sound, taste; the qualities of life, which is a selection from a larger whole of physico-chemical processes; mind, which is a selection from the larger whole of the life processes. Life thus *emerges* from matter, and mind emerges from life. Life and mind are extended and in time. (*Ibid.,* Vol. II, p. 71.) Everything that is empirically real, is a complex of space-time.

Mind, *as contemplated,* is a vital process; specifically it is a process of *innervation.* Mind, as *enjoyed innervation,* is *consciousness.* Alexander uses the peculiar term "enjoyment" for mental awareness, or what is commonly called "introspection." Mind is identical with those complex neural processes from which consciousness emerges. But mind is not an epiphenomenon or by-product of the body; it is the enjoyment of themselves by those neural processes which are mental. Mind consists of *Acts;* it is essentially *selective* and *attentive.* Mr. Alexander's psychology is conational or volitional. Even purely speculative knowledge is for him delayed or suspended conation or action. (*Ibid.,* Vol. II, pp. 120, 121, 124, 125, et cetera.) Thus, he differs radically from Russell, who reduces the activity of mind almost to a vanishing point.

Knowledge is a *selection,* by the finite mind, of some "aspects" or "perspectives" of the real world. All finite things are configurations of space-time. The *objects,* which are the "aspects" of real things as contemplated by a finite mind, are selected perspectives of the real things. The *sensa* or *sensory appearances,* in which the mind contemplates the *things* as *objects,* are of the same kind as the things themselves. All that the sensory appearance owes to mind is their selection. Illusions "are perspectives of the real world as seen by a mind in abnormal condition." (*Ibid.*, Vol. II, p. 216.) The illusory object is nonmental; the mind chooses illusions from the world of reality. (*Ibid.*, Vol. II, p. 211 ff.) The real thing is the totality of its perspectives. (*Ibid.*, Vol. II, p. 196.) Thus even images and memories are physical objects; in imagination and memory the innervation processes are contemplated. (*Ibid.*, Vol. II, pp. 90, 91, 94, et cetera.) All appearances of things are thus nonmental. The appearances which conform to the standard of social normality, for example, the table and the teacup as they appear to a group of normal persons, are *real appearances;* the appearances which result from the influence of one thing on another, for example, an object seen in an artificial light, are *mere appearances;* the appearances which are due to some abnormality in the percipient in his relation to the thing, for example, color blindness, are *illusory appearances.*

Truth, we saw, is belief that conforms to the social standard of normality. A true belief is one in which the mind believing is coherent with itself and with other finite minds. So it is with all other *values.* The *goodness* of an act or disposition is the coherence of the volition or intent of the individual person with the conditions of personal satisfaction by normal minds. The *beauty* of an object lies in the coherence of its parts, as felt coherently by several minds. Thus all values are social. In the self-coherence of the individual mind and its coherence with other minds is the home of values. The reality of values is the reality of socialized minds. Values are, then, the felt relations of minds as members of the community of minds. Values are real, since mind is the highest finite empirical reality we know.

We have every right to believe that there are higher

empirical qualities than finite minds. *Deity is the next higher empirical quality than mind.* An infinite or perfect God cannot exist. What exists is the infinite universe's tendency towards deity. God is the ideal God in embryo, always becoming deity but never attaining it. (*Ibid.*, Vol. II, p. 365.) The striving of the universe towards deity is God. God must include mind, which we may say is his body, since the whole universe is the body of God. The values which our minds realize are the materials for the making of deity. Thus God is a metaphysical name for the qualities-higher-than-finite-mind, which, presumably, emerge in the endless life of the infinite motion-stuff, space-time. Deity is the coming into being of new complications in the order of finite qualities. God is not and never will be a perfect existence; but space-time goes on enriching its qualitative wealth, and therein lies the divinity of things.

So highly elaborated and original a system as Alexander's requires a more thorough examination than I have space for here. I must content myself with suggesting, for the reader's consideration, a few objections:

1. To say that all finite existences are generated from space-time by "emergence" or "complication," and to deny that this is materialism, seems to me an equivocation. *If* all things emerge from pure space-time or motion-stuff, and if "mind" is not coeval with this motion-stuff, then not only living beings but minds are mechanically caused.

2. How can a mind be said to act *as such*, if it be merely the awareness of a neural process? The neural process is physico-chemical, and therefore the real agent is physical.

3. I do not see how illusions and errors of all sorts can be said to exist *physically*, unless the minds which hold them as true be *merely* physical complications? Again we have the same fundamental equivocation.

4. If space-time be the absolute, I do not see by what

right we speak of one set of qualities as "higher" than others, or of any value as better than another.

5. The striving of the infinite motion-stuff towards higher qualities that are never fully realized is so Pickwickian a God that, I think, perhaps, Alexander would further clearness of expression by expunging the terms God and Deity from his system altogether.

6. I am unable to see that the whole world of human and spiritual culture can be regarded as merely an emergence from, or complication of, so thin and poor a motion-stuff as space-time.

V. Metaphysical and Religious Implications of Realism and Speculative Idealism Compared

If one follow the excellent suggestion of Dr. Bosanquet and employ the phrases, "speculative philosophy" or "speculative idealism," in place of "absolute idealism" or "objective idealism," to designate the doctrine that reality is a coherent whole or universe to whose structure mind affords the best clue available, then the metaphysical realism of Dr. Alexander and the speculative idealism which is best represented by Dr. Bosanquet are not so far apart as at first blush they seem. For Dr. Bosanquet, like Professors Creighton, Seth Pringle-Pattison, MacKenzie, and others (including the present writer), who have deep sympathies with the idealism of Plato and Hegel, rejects the "mentalism" of Royce and Calkins as well as that of Berkeley and Fichte.[24] Both Dr. Alexander and the speculative idealists, as I shall hereafter call them, are agreed that reality is one coherent whole, and that the most comprehensive and adequate criterion of the truth

---

[24] The reader is reminded that "mentalism" means the doctrine that nothing really exists but minds; that so-called physical world of common sense is but the appearance of minds to other minds.

of any human apprehension of reality is the coherence of beliefs with the facts of experience and with one another.

Of course these two philosophies differ with regard to the position assigned to mind in the total scheme of things. Dr. Alexander denies to mind that privileged position in the universe which the speculative idealist assigns to it; but it is noteworthy that, as his scheme of things unfolds, from mere space-time and physical qualities to the richer empirical qualities of reality, mind takes up more and more the burden of the tale. Human minds and their values—beauty, truth, and the ethical values of justice, love, and other forms of goodness—*are empirical realities of a higher order than mere animal life;* and life, in turn, is a higher order of reality than physical qualities. Furthermore, the universe, as a whole, possesses Deity, in its everlasting movement towards the realization of higher empirical qualities and values than those which finite minds enjoy; and the Deity (I would prefer to say "Divinity") of the universe includes, while it transcends, the qualities and values of human minds. It seems to be the difficulty of conceiving the concrete character of that which is higher than human mind, and yet includes it, in terms of mind, that leads Dr. Alexander to deny that God is the universal mind. He is not able to see how the whole range of empirical qualities can be conceived to be included in a universal knower and will, or experience, or absolute logos or problem-solver. A self for him is essentially finite and conditioned. The limitation of mind or selfhood to a conditioned place in the finite empirical order, in which it rises from, and is the enjoyment or awareness of itself by, a complication of neural processes, lead Dr. Alexander to say that Deity must be more than mind; since finite mind is its "body" it must be richer than this, just as finite mind is richer than its own bodily basis. The Deity of the universe, which is space-time, includes and transcends all the meanings and values of the hierarchy of empirical qualities, from color and form up to sentient life, which we contemplate; it includes and transcends all the mental and social values which we enjoy.

I do not see why the limitations of mind in ourselves should prevent us from concluding that the Divinity, which includes and carries on to higher levels our finite lives and their values, must be mind—the immanent spiritual community and ground of values, which in its perfection transcends the empirical natural and social orders. Nevertheless it is clear that Dr. Alexander's intent is that reality has many degrees of meaning and value, and that the total significance of the universe is always much richer than the best that human beings are or may become. The universe for him has Divinity, and is worthy to be held in reverence. It is the all-inclusive, omnipotent, and eternal dynamic order, in which all values are realized and conserved. Thus, his position approaches very closely to speculative idealism. Moreover, in the emphasis he puts on the social character of values—truth is socially normal believing, goodness is socially coherent willing, beauty is coherent feeling—Dr. Alexander approaches the idealistic notion of God, or the Universal Spirit, as the spirit of the beloved community, the principle of the ideal social order. Royce has made most of the latter motion, but it seems to be implied in all speculative idealisms from Hegel to the present.

The new realists in general are not materialists or mechanists; although I think that those of them who are neutral monists, if they followed out the logic of their position would come to materialism. For the neutral monist is in a position of very unstable logical equilibrium. If it is difficult to stand long on one leg, as the mentalist and the materialist try to do, it is still more difficult to remain suspended in mid-air, as the neutral monist tries to do. But the new realists, in general, not only affirm vigorously the reality of values and the power of man, through reason and imagination to achieve higher social and spiritual values; they are not, as a rule, hostile to the hypothesis of a supreme ground of values. Professor R. B. Perry, a leading American new realist, gives a high place to the claims of spiritual religion on the thought and allegiance of men.[25] Prof. E. G. Spaulding, in his carefully elaborated book, *The New Rationalism,* commits himself more specifically to a belief in the existence of God as the ground or totality of values. He says: "God is the totality of values"; He is "justice and truth and beauty, both as these are 'above' our world and as they are in it"; "He is thus both transcendent and immanent."[26] He believes in "a Power that works not only side by side with man, but also in him and through him, flowering in that freedom which is given to his reason to get at truth, to his emotions, to love the beautiful, the good, and the true, and to detest the ugly, the evil, and the false, and to his will and manhood to engage in the struggle."[27] The principal exception to this attitude is Bertrand Russell. Religion for him is possible only as a stoical and heroic devotion to the highest human qualities, the cherishing of love and pity and fellowship, and the contemplation of the beauty and truth created by the human reason and imagination; but all in this in the face of a brutal and unmeaning universe. His metaphysical attitude is one of thoroughgoing scientific materialism; or, rather, was up to the publication of his *Analysis of Mind.* Just what it may be now I do not know. I am unable to find any inevitable logical connection between Russell's realism in theory of knowledge and his atheistic materialism, except that the atomistic

---

[25] See his *Present Philosophical Tendencies,* and *The Moral Economy.*

[26] E. G. Spaulding, *The New Rationalism,* p. 517.

[27] *Ibid.,* p. 521.

pluralism or logical atomism, which he adopts as a method, if consistently carried out would negative the admission that there may be a cosmical ground of values. No one can be a thoroughpaced pluralist and find any place in his metaphysics for the hypothesis of God as the unity and ground of human values. Hence, while a realist may start from extreme pluralism as a working hypothesis, he has abandoned it as soon as he sets up the notion that truth, goodness, beauty, and whatsoever other values there may be, have a cosmic ground. It is not inconsistent to recognize that the cosmic ground of values is limited in some way, and that there is an evolution in which values are progressively enhanced; in other words, a God limited by the conditions in which he must work to achieve the highest values is not a foolish notion. But if, as the extreme pluralist holds, reality does not consist of a whole of interrelated members, the idea of God is childish nonsense.[28]

VI. A Critique of Realism

The neorealistic movement arose as a protest and criticism against subjectivistic tendencies manifest in idealism, sensationalistic empiricism, and pragmatism. Realism protests against the narrow humanism manifested in certain forms of idealism, as well as in pragmatism. Realism stresses the *objectivity* and *determinate structure of nature and of reason or thought.* Nature is not the mere reflection of the subject; nor are our true ideas and modes of thinking the expression of our individual, or even our social, wishes and aims. There is a real and determinate order of nature and a real and determinate order of thought. In these regards the position of the realists is wholly sound and must be included in a genuine specula-

[28] See, for further discussion of pluralism and the idea of God, Chapter XXIV, *Singularism and Pluralism.*

tive philosophy. Realism also criticizes the position of absolute or objective idealism that reality must be, and is, a coherent and harmonious *system or relational organization,* the clue to which is to be found in the nature of mind. The absolute idealist argues that the structural texture of reality and of mind are identical in character and, therefore, no truth is absolutely true and no finite reality absolutely real, except when referred to and taking their due places in the absolute systems of truth and reality. The realist replies that, from this standpoint, since we do not know, and indeed, cannot know, in detail the character of these supposed absolute systems, every specific proposition which we believe to be true is thereby cast in doubt and we have no means of knowing what its ultimate status may be. He asserts, on the contrary, that we may know directly by perception and intuition the truth of some propositions. The absolute idealist replies that we can know the general character of the system of reality and, therefore, can tell, approximately, the position of some of our human truths in it.

The realist is right, it seems to me, in holding that we can know some truth directly, by reflective intuition, and that, for us, these truths are absolutely true. We have such true propositions in pure logic and mathematics; perhaps, there are some ethical values which are absolutely valid, too. If we had to wait until we knew the whole nature of reality, even though only in outline, before we could be sure that we had any truth, we should be in a very bad fix. On the other hand, the most comprehensive test of truth seems to me to be the coherence of intuitively known propositions, and their deduced consequences, with one another, and with the inductively established interpretations of perceptual experience. Progress in any field of knowledge, and, consequently in the whole field of knowledge, consists in weaving our perceptions of fact into bodies of conceptual systems consistent with the fundamental logical laws of identity, coherence, and sufficient reason. In so far as we succeed thereby in knowing and in controlling nature, this success implies that nature and human nature are reciprocating members in one universal order or system. It makes no difference whether we say that the structure of reality corresponds with or reflects the structure of mind, or that, since mind is a live focus of reality, the structure of mind must reflect or embody the structure of reality. Whichever side we start from we must come to the other. So far as reality is intelligible, it must be coherent. So far as mind expands in rationality and practical control of its data, it does so by taking the structure of reality into itself and thus becoming more rational. The universe is a living and dynamic whole which comes to awareness of itself in mind. Minds are effective centers in reality, in so far as they become alive to the fact that their function is to grasp the lines of force which center in them and radiate from them as *awaring members of the whole.*

The ever recurring controversies and misconceptions which arise from the equivocal meanings of the terms "idealism" and "realism" suggest that it might be better to discard their use altogether, and to call our standpoint "rationalistic" or "organizational experimentalism." Briefly, this standpoint involves the following propositions: (1) Things perceived are selected and organized groupings of sense-qualities in relation; such relations as spatial, temporal, numerical, qualitative (degrees of likeness and unlikeness), quantitative (equality, greater, less, etc.), dynamical (physical, purposive). (2) In knowing, true relations are *discovered,* not *made* by the mind; in willing, man does, to a limited extent, *make* new relations. (3) The known world, as a complex of things and events in relation, involves three factors: (a) the mind, with its definite structure, history and interests; (b) the physical or "objective" grounds and perception; these I conceive to be energy-complexes; (c) the central nervous system and the sense organs, which are at once parts of the physical order and the immediate basis of the mental processes of perception, et cetera, and hence are the intermediating links between the mind and the rest of the physical world. (4) Percepts are not copies of things but partial and fragmentary aspects or "views" of the real external world selected by the mind and the sensory system. (5) The mind is the "ultimate" active selective and analytic-synthetic principle which discovers and takes note of qualities-in-relation, and which constructs and organizes a larger context of reality, in which it sets and interprets the immediate data of experience. The relation of a perceived thing or event, or even a scientific law, to reality is that of a partial selected and interpreted aspect or fragment of an indefinitely complex totality of things, processes, qualities, and relations. Reality involves much more than any experience, but that "more" is a construction by the human mind from the structure of actual experience and the nature of the construction is determined by the joint natures of the experienced reality and of the mind's own structure. 6. In error and illusion the mind misinterprets or places in its wrong setting some bit of experience or generalization from experience. It may either fail to determine and analyze the data correctly or it may fail to set the data in the right connections with other items of reality. There can be no unreal experiences, only untrue, that is, wrongly related, experiences.

References

Alexander, Samuel, *Space, Time and Deity; Natural Piety,* in *Hibbert Journal,* Vol. XX, pp. 609-621.

Bosanquet, B., *The Meeting of Extremes in Contemporary Philosophy.*

Broad, C. D., *Perception, Physics and Reality.*

HOLT, E. B., *The Concept of Consciousness.*

LAIRD, JOHN, *A Study in Realism; Problems of the Self.*

LEIGHTON, J. A., *Man and the Cosmos,* Chapters IV-VIII, XVIII-XXI and XXIV.

* MARVIN, W. T., *A First Book in Metaphysics; The History of European Philosophy,* Chapter XXVII.

MOORE, G. E., *Ethics; Principia Ethica.*

* PERRY, R. B., and others, *The New Realism.*

* PERRY, R. B., *Present Philosophical Tendencies.*

* ROGERS, A. K., *English and American Philosophy since 1800,* Chapter VI, Sec. 3, and Chapter VIII.

* RUSSELL, BERTRAND, *The Analysis of Mind; Mysticism and Logic; Our Knowledge of the External World.* (Title on cover in American Edition, *Scientific Method in Philosophy*); *The Problems of Philosophy.*

SPAULDING, *The New Rationalism.*

Essays in Critical Realism, by D. Drake, A. O. Lovejoy, A. K. Rogers, G. Santayana, R. W. Sellars, and C. A. Strong.

HOBHOUSE, L. T., *The Theory of Knowledge; Development and Purpose.*

SANTAYANA, G., *The Life of Reason; Egotism in German Philosophy.*

SELLARS, R. W., *Critical Realism; The Essentials of Philosophy.*

CHAPTER XXI

TEMPORALISM

Temporalism is, in broadest terms, that philosophical doctrine which insists on the reality and significance of the time process. In its extreme form it asserts that all being is becoming. Thus, Heraclitus was a temporalist. Temporalism has gained ground steadily since the beginning of the nineteenth century when Hegel's historical idealism, with its strongly temporalistic coloring, appeared. Temporalism, however, received its greatest impetus from the rise and spread of the theory of evolution. Philosophers otherwise so diverse as Herbert Spencer, Josiah Royce, James Ward, F. Nietzsche, A. Fouillée (a French idealistic evolutionist), Henri Bergson and William James, John Dewey and S. Alexander, are all, in some sense, evolutionists.

I. Bergson's Temporalism

In this chapter I shall treat of Bergson and James as the major prophets of a temporalistic philosophy. Bergson's great influence has come chiefly from his bold and persuasive interpretation of evolution as the endlessly creative psychical process. His doctrines of the relations of space and time, mind and body, intelligence and intuition, are all contributory to his theory of evolution. He has promulgated and carried out, with great consistency and elaboration, the doctrine that reality is duration and that duration is identical with the creative activity of psychical life.

Setting out, in his first book, *Time and Free Will*,[1] from the contrast between the extensive or spatial order and the intensive or temporal order he builds his system of metaphysics thereon. He makes liberal and telling use of the facts of immediate experience and the theories of the special sciences.

The space order is the realm of pure quantity, of homogeneous elements. All quantitative measurement consists in reducing that which is measured to similar units spread out in space. To count any multiplicity is to picture it as spread out over space. We count by putting the units side by side. For example, to count the successive strokes of a bell one imagines them as extended in space. *But this entire conception of a pure homogeneous space order is an abstraction which has been fashioned by the human intellect as an instrument by which the self can grasp the similarities or repetitions in events and thus, by foreseeing, in part, the future, can deliberately plan its future conduct. In reality there is no pure homogeneity, no repetition of absolute similars. In reality there is only an endless succession of heterogeneous or different states of duration. Reality is incessant mobility, action, life. In reality there are no two moments which are absolutely alike.* The reality which is life or mind energy is a ceaselessly creative process of differing events or durations, which interpenetrate one another through memory. Age cannot wither nor custom stale the infinite variety of events in the onward movement of the vital impetus (*l'élan vital*).

The conventional clock time, conceived to be an absolutely even or rhythmical flow, is a bastard time, pictured

---

[1] French title, *Essai sur les Données Immediatés de la Consciénce.*

in terms of homogeneous space, in order that the intellect may count and measure its successive moments. Duration or real time is life's experience of its own creative process. Each self, each pulsating fragment of the vital impetus, has its own unique experience of duration or temporal flow. And in every self the successive moments of its duration are severally unique; by reason of memory, which is a unique property of the self, its successive moments, as they pass, are conserved and absorbed in the enduring, growing, or self-creating reality which is the vital impetus, the essence of every self. "Life is the invisible progress of the past gnawing into the future." "There are no two identical moments in the life of a self. A consciousness which could experience two identical moments would be a consciousness without memory. It would die and be born again continually." Thus the only real continuity is that of memory. (*Introduction to Metaphysics,* translated by F. E. Hulme, p. 13.) We think that there are a space and a time of which all the parts are similar, and which can be infinitely extended and infinitely divided. But this space and this time are not realities; they are but abstract mental diagrams, framed by the intellect for the purpose of perceiving continuities and uniformities in nature and the self. The intellect is a tool for operating on solids arranged side by side in space. All its logic is modelled on geometry. The uses of the intellect are limited to the reduction of the real qualitative diversity of life to equations of identity. Thus it sums up the never ending variety of actual changes in terms of the quantitative rearrangement of changeless units. Thus the goal of the intellect's apprehension of reality is to conceive it all as a spatial mechanism. But life belongs to an entirely different category.

It follows that psychical processes are not in themselves measurable. And, with regard to the critical problem of free will, Bergson argues that the common fallacy of physical determinism and psychological determinism lies in the transformation of the actual creative, living process, which we are, into a dead mechanism. Since life is creative psychical process and this is real duration, no one could predict what another self would do unless he were that other; and even thus, in important crisis, when the whole self acts, he could not predict his own action, since at the very moment of choice the creative urge of the self is issuing in a new fact. "To conceive all the conditions as given is, when dealing with concrete duration, to place one's self at the very moment at which the act is being performed." (*Time and Free Will*, p. 220.) "The free act takes place in the time which is flowing, not in the time which has already flown." (*Ibid.*, p. 221.) It is plausible, after the event, to say that a man could not have done otherwise, being what he was, because we infer what he was from what he did; whereas, in truth, what he did, especially in a great crisis, was an act of creation, by virtue of which he became to some extent a new being. The self is not determined to act by sympathy, aversion, love, loyalty, et cetera; as though these were forces which acted on the self from without. The self is what it is, and it becomes what it becomes, by giving creative expression to the moral attitudes signified by such terms.

We are free when, and in the degree in which, our acts emanate from our entire personality. Until a decision is made action is indeterminate and accurate prevision impossible. Psychical causation differs from mechanical causation in two respects: (1) In psychical causation the cause and the effect are not mathematical equivalents. (2) In psychical causation there is a feeling of *effort* in passing from the idea of action to the action. Mechanical causation is but the superficial relation between *events* as seen by the intellect. Retrospective analysis transforms a living progress into a dead thing. Psychical causation is the deeper reality immediately lived and experienced. The more we live on the surface of life the more adequate mechanical causation is to explain our actions though it is never wholly adequate; the deeper and fuller we live out our vocations, as creative selves, the freer we are.

In his second principal work, *Matter and Memory* (French, *Matiére et Memoíre*), Bergson applies the above principles to the solution of the mind-body problem. Matter and mind differ in degree, not in kind. Pure matter would be inert homogeneous space; pure mind would be absolutely inextended quality, pure heterogeneity. The self moves incessantly between these two extremes, which have no existence as such but are mere limiting concepts. The human body is a center of action living in relation to other centers of action. Bergson's conception of body is thoroughly dynamic. *Perception is a means of action, not of theoretical knowledge. It does not tell us what matter is like; it only furnishes images of surrounding things, as a guide to the outer action of our own bodies therewith.* "*I call* matter *the aggregate of images, and* perception of matter *these same images referred to the eventual action of one particular image, my body.*" (*Matter and Memory*, p. 8.) Realism and idealism both err in assuming that perception has a wholly speculative interest, that it is the mental representative of an external world; whereas perception is the lowest form of intellectual activity and is but a means to action. (*Ibid.*, p. 17.) Matter is precisely what it appears to be. (*Ibid.*, p. 80.) "There is in matter something more than, but not something different from, that which is actually given in perception." (*Ibid.*, p. 78.)

The brain is a kind of central telephonic exchange, whose office is to allow communication, or to delay it, between the mind and the surrounding world. (*Ibid.*, p. 19.) The more choices open to a living being the richer its perceptions The self, endowed with a power of creative choice, cuts out, within the material world, the center of action which is called its own body. (*Ibid.*, p. 45.) In the body, which is a system of images, the central image, the brain, is an instrument of action.

Actual perception is a fusion, in varying degrees, of percepts and memory images. The extended and more or less inert and homogeneous world, which we perceive, is so perceived because our sensations are overlaid with memory images, retained and recalled, since they guide us to action by emphasizing similarities between present and past. The survival of the past through memory is a condition of our survival and welfare.

There are two kinds of memory: 1. *Motor memory*, which is exemplified by every instance of our employment of a habit or skill acquired through repetition; for example, walking or talking. This sort of memory depends on the formation of motor diagrams or mechanisms in the brain. 2. On the other hand, when we recall, recognize, and place distinct events in our past; when, for example, we recall when and where we first saw the young goddess, our first love, swim into our ken, we have a case of *pure memory*—of the revival and identification of images from the past. Since images cannot be stored up in enormous numbers in the brain, and even if they were we could not pick out and recognize instantaneously the correct one of the quadrillion or so there, pure memory is independent of the brain. *The power of retaining, restoring, and identifying the images from our past, each in its individual flavor and setting, is a function of pure spirit or mind.* Bergson enforces this doctrine with a very acute use of cases of aphasia and amnesia to show that we cannot localize pure memory in the brain. In fact he holds that the past and present are not *in* the brain; the brain is in them, since past and present are functions of mind

Our lives oscillate between the planes of pure action and of pure dreaming. If we led only dream lives we should be living in pure memory alone; and our lives would consist simply of the endless phantasmagoria of individual images. If we lived in action alone we should be mere unconscious machines and the passive creatures of our environments. We oscillate between the two. In action, only so much of our past is brought to bear on present perception as will enable us to act successfully. The whole of our past psychical life conditions our present state, but we select only so much of it as we need to facilitate action. (*Ibid.*, p. 191.) Pure memory is essentially detached from the life of action; it is reverie. When action is imperative pure memory is latent and in abeyance. The past has not ceased to exist; it has only ceased to be useful. (*Ibid.*, p. 193.) Our ordinary consciousness embodies the materiality of our lives, the urgency of action. Our body is that part of our representation which is ever being born anew, for the purpose of action. True memory "retains and ranges alongside of each other all our states in the order in which they occur, leaving to each its place and consequently marking its date." (*Ibid.*, p. 195.) When action is not urgent pure memory surges up and we live almost as pure spirits. But it is our body which keeps our spirit in connection with the external world, and thus gives sanity and poise to life. Let the fusion between the mind and the external world, which the nervous system mediates, be relaxed and dreams and, at the extreme, insanity, occur.

Bergson concludes that the difficulties of the mind-body problem, in its traditional formulations are due to regarding the physical and mental as representations or duplicates, the one of the other. He treats them as differing only *in degree*. There is no pure space; there is only an extended mobile continuum in which we carve out our bodies as centers of action. Memory is spirit, but spirit must act, and therefore carves out a body from the stream of incessant becoming which is the real world or nature. In nature there are all sorts of degrees of extension and tension, in inverse ratio to one another. The body is a high-tension selecting and condensing medium, by which pure spirit, which is pure inextensive tension, is able to divide and subdivide extension by the use of intellect, and to subtilize it in the affections. The spirit effects the contraction of the less heterogeneous or more extended and physical into the more heterogeneous, or vital and spiritual, by degrees of tension. Thus Bergson thinks he has bridged the chasm between mind and body by the notion of degrees, in inverse ratio, of extension and tension.

In his third and most popular work, *Creative Evolution,* Bergson applies the fundamental ideas worked out in the two previous works to the theory of evolution.

After an acute criticism of both radical mechanism and radical finalism or teleology as involving the same error—that the whole of reality is eternally given all at once, and that the history of the world is but the inevitable unfolding of this whole—Bergson develops his own theory that evolution is a continuously creative vital and psychical process. The true reality is the vital impetus (*l'élan vital*); it is the creative current of being, the urge towards increase of individuality. But there is a counter current, the downward tendency towards inertia, sameness, immobility, exemplified in habit. This is matter; life and matter are thus two opposing tendencies, the one driving towards creativity and individuality, the other dragging it down towards immobility and mechanism which is death.

I am unable to make out what is Bergson's theory of the origin of matter. He assumes it as an original datum, when he is depicting the nature of the vital impetus as unceasing effort to mount higher against the current of matter. At other times he speaks as though matter and the intellect have been cut out, by an identical process, from a primal stuff that contained both. Intellect and matter, he says, have been evolved *together*. Matter is spatialized intellect. But again intellect was evolved by the vital impetus, as a means for successful action on matter. Therefore intellect presupposes matter.

Matter and Intellect have "progressively adapted themselves to one another in order to attain at last a common form" (*Creative Evolution,* p. 206). This common form is a homogeneous and static whole of parts juxtaposed in space. Essentially, *Matter* is a downward flux, "a reality that is unmaking itself"; *Life* is an upward flux, "a reality that is making itself" (*Ibid.,* p. 248). Life and Matter are opposing currents in the total stream of Becoming. Life cannot create absolutely, because it is confronted with matter (*Ibid.,* p. 250). Life in itself is an immensity of potentiality, in contact with matter it is limited and becomes an impetus (*Ibid.,* p. 258). The increase of materiality, the expansion of the current that is unmaking itself, takes place through the relaxation of tension, through a *detension* which produces *extension.* Thus matter extends itself in space, without being absolutely extended therein (*Ibid.,* pp. 202ff). The more inert and spread-out the downward movement becomes, the more materialized it becomes; for space and matter are identical. Because of the initial duality of movement, the *vital impetus,* in order to survive and move upstream against the pull of the downward current, evolved *intellect.* The latter has helped the vital impetus to survive and grow, but at a great cost. For intellect has rendered materiality more material, that is, more spatial. At the same time it has made the vital impetus, whose servant it is, more spatial. For the intellect has suffered from a natural inability to understand its master, life. Even intuition had to shrink into the narrow forms of the instincts, in order that the impetus might make headway.

This mechanization, this shrivelling up and ossification of the vital impetus, through its intellectualization, is reflected in philosophy and science, from the ancient Greeks to the present time. The movement of Greek philosophy, from Zeno the Eleatic to Plotinus, with its elevation of the *one eternal and changeless Reality* above *the many temporal Phenomena,* is the effect of the intellect's inveterate habit of taking static *snap-shot* views of the ceaselessly mobile and ever heterogeneous flux of real *Duration.* The *Ideas* or *Forms* of Plato, the *Forms* or *Entelechies* of Aristotle, are intellectual snap-shots of the ever-moving reality in which there is constant change of form. The mechanistic concepts of modern science, and of such a philosophy as Spencer's, are of the same origin.

In brief, Bergson holds—(1) That reality is a perpetual flux of two opposing currents, one of which becomes the world of living organisms and the other becomes, or tends to become, the world of inert space-occupying matter. (2) In order that life may persist and increase, it must become materialized. In doing this it loses something of its original spontaneity and creativeness; it becomes mechanized as intellect and narrowed as instinct. (3) There is in man vestiges of a power, by developing which he may restore, enlarge, and deepen the lost sense of life, and may even conquer matter and put on freedom and immortality. This power is *Intuition*—but that is another story. Meantime, if the reader finds himself perplexed as to the respective places and relations of *matter, space* and *intellect* in Bergson's philosophy, I confess I share his perplexity, and can only refer him to the original works. How a downward current, not in space, extends itself in space, I do not understand. Nor do I see why it should be necessary for the vital impetus to fabricate the intellect to aggravate the situation in which the impetus already finds itself, by making matter more spatial and imprisoning life more completely in it; since the impetus has produced intellect in order to free itself from this downward current. The liberator seems, in this case, only to have made the prison bars more secure.

The main types of living organisms are divergent lines of evolution, struck out by the vital impetus in its efforts to surmount the downward current of matter. The whole history of life is a cosmic obstacle race. The vital impetus has tried, here one device, and there another. Thus the evolution of life is the product neither of mechanical necessity nor of the necessity imposed by a single predetermined plan. The main divergent lines of evolution are expressed in the following diagram:

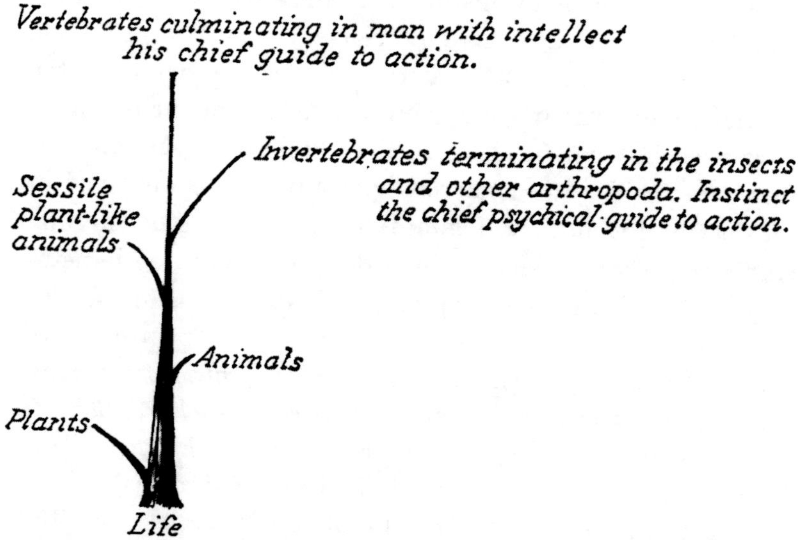

Thus the evolutionary process is like a tree with a few branches shooting out at irregular intervals. Life is a current sent through matter.[2] The whole history of life has been the effort of consciousness to raise matter. There are two orders—the physical order which is automatic or mechanical, and the vital order which is voluntary or psychical. Life is a reality which is making itself in a reality which is unmaking itself.[3] In the advancement of the vital impetus two things are necessary: (1) a gradual accumulation of explosive energy; this is achieved in plants through the chlorophyllian function; (2) an elastic canalization of this energy in variable and indeterminable directions.

The three divergent lines of animal life represent the three main experiments of the vital impetus. The sessile animals, such as the zoöphytes, represent a kind of plant life, a failure of the vital impetus to get forward. The second main line of animal evolution has reached its highest achievement in the arthropoda, particularly in the insecta. Here we find mobile animals adjusting themselves to the environment by instincts or inherited reflexes which display a marvellous degree of accuracy. *Instincts are fine, highly specialized tools.* Bergson cites particularly the Hymenoptera which sting their live prey and bring them, paralyzed but not dead, as food to their own young. But this great skill with a narrow specialization is achieved at the loss of the power of adaptability to changing circumstances. What is needed, in order that the vital impetus may go forward in the complementary directions of increasing individuation and association, is that *the capacity should be developed to fashion tools to meet changing conditions. This capacity is intelligence or intellect, which reaches its highest power in man, who is preëminently the toolmaker.* Whereas an insect is a very limited set of fine tools, man, with the unspecialized capacity of intellect, becomes the

---

2 *Creative Evolution*, p. 265.
3 *Ibid.*, p. 248.

maker of tools, of material tools and mental and social tools (language, social order, custom, law, morals, science). Thus man is capable of indefinite progress by virtue of his adaptability and inventiveness.

But this triumph of the intellect, as the power of indefinite adaptability to the material conditions of living, is achieved at a loss. The intellect is at home only in mechanical affairs.

Bergson conceives of the power of intelligence as rigidly limited to dealing with inorganic solids, with mere matter. Intelligence is able only to comprehend and formulate abstract geometrized equations of identity. It turns the mobility, warmth, manifold heterogeneity, individuality, creativity, and freedom of the *life force* into frozen concepts, into inert, motionless, and skeletal travesties of the rich and ever moving reality. Life is ever active and creative, reason is static and uncreative. Thus life, which is reality, transcends thought. The *vital impetus,* creative, mysterious, unpredictable, and uncontrollable, is the power which moves the world. Reality, as life, is not only incalculable and inconceivable in its secret tendencies, movements, and results, its secret essence can not be communicated, for language, an instrument of intelligence fashioned to meet the exigencies of social intercourse, is utterly powerless to express the multitudinous variety and novelty of life's manifestations. Words are pale and colorless abstractions, little more than geometrical marionettes. Thus intelligence trails along helplessly in the wake of life, picking up superficial uniformities and overlooking the spontaneous diversities and novelties with which life teems.

But Bergson holds that man's metaphysical thirst for reality must be slaked. In order to apprehend reality as it really is, man needs to develop another power—one akin to instinct in its immediacy and sureness of grasp, but vastly wider in range. This power is *intuition.* In order to know life and spirit we must divest ourselves of the prejudices engendered by perception and action. "To touch the reality of spirit we must place ourselves at the point where an individual consciousness, continuing and retaining the past in a present enriched by it, escapes the law of necessity, the law which says that the present shall simply repeat the past." "The point where we feel ourselves most intimately within our own life is a duration—in which the past, always moving on, is swelling unceasingly with a present that is absolutely new."[4] "The more we succeed in making ourselves conscious of our progress in pure duration, the more we feel the different parts of our being enter into each other, and our whole personality concentrate itself into a point, or rather a sharp edge, pressed against the future and cutting into it unceasingly."[5] This feeling is intuition. "By intuition is meant the kind of *intellectual sympathy* by which one places one's self within an object in order to coincide with what is unique in it and consequently inexpressible." (Bergson, *An Introduction to Metaphysics,* p. 15, Hulme's translation.) Analysis expresses a thing as a function of something other than itself. It translates the actual thing into symbols. Analysis is a representation of a thing from successive points of view, and thus goes on to infinity. But intuition is a simple act of direct, intellectual sympathy. We can certainly sympathize with our own selves. By dilating this self-intuition we can grasp reality outside ourselves; since all reality is action, movement, becoming. God, says Bergson, is unceasing life, action, freedom. Creation is free activity.

Intuition or the immediate feeling of, the direct listening to, the face-to-face vision of, our inner selfhood is the key to reality. In the supreme moments of life, in great

---

[4] *Creative Evolution,* p. 200.
[5] *Ibid.,* p. 201.

passional and volitional crises, when man feels his whole personality surging up from the deeps or feels that he is putting his whole self into an act: "Intuition is there, however vague and above all discontinuous. It is a lamp almost extinguished, which only glimmers now and then, for a few moments at most. But it glimmers whenever a vital interest is at stake. On our personality, on our liberty, on the place we occupy in the whole of nature, on our origin and perhaps on our destiny, it throws a light feeble and vacillating, but which none the less pierces the darkness of the night in which the intellect leaves us."[6] The function of Philosophy is to unite, to deepen, and dilate these evanescent intuitions and thus to enable man to continue consciously the work of self-creation. Intuition has lagged behind intelligence because of the insistent pressure of practical needs. The more philosophy advances the more it will perceive that intuition is mind itself, is life itself. A complete and perfect humanity would be one in which both intelligence and intuition should attain their full development.[7] "Thus to the eyes of a philosophy that attempts to reabsorb intellect in intuition, many difficulties vanish or become light. But such a doctrine does not only facilitate speculation; it also gives us more power to act and live. For with it we feel ourselves no longer isolated in humanity, humanity no longer seems isolated in the nature that it dominates. As the smallest grain of sand is bound up with our entire solar system, drawn along with it in that undivided movement of descent which is materiality itself, so all organized beings, from the humblest to the highest, from the first origins of life to the time in which we are, and in all places as in all times, do but evidence a single impulsion, the inverse of the movement of matter, and in itself indivisible. All the living hold together, and

---

[6] *C. E.* (*Creative Evolution*), pp. 267, 268.
[7] *Ibid.*, p. 267.

all yield to the same tremendous push. The animal takes its stand on the plant, man bestrides animality, and the whole of humanity, in space and time, is one immense army galloping beside and before and behind each of us in an overwhelming charge, able to beat down every resistance and to clear the most formidable obstacles, perhaps even death."[8]

This new irrationalism announces the failure of thought or intelligence to understand life and reality, and its subserviency to the native impulses and emotions. Intelligence trades in abstractions, we are told; reality is concrete. Intelligence is static. Life is dynamic. Intelligence is passive and receptive. Life is active and creative. In all its operations thought is tied up to space forms and space metaphors. Its greatest achievement is geometry. Life, on the other hand, is a flowing process in time. Thought always attempts to reduce the new to the old, differences to sameness, the individual to the universal. Hence, thought's attempted transcripts of life are petrifactions. It endeavors to transmute into frozen conceptual forms the warmth and "go" of life. It gives us in its concepts only inert, motionless skeletons of the living reality. "Gray, dear friend, are all thy theories; and green the golden tree of life." Life and reality transcend thought. They move forward with ever increasing acceleration and in imprevisible directions. The *vital impetus,* creative, mysterious, unpredictable, and uncontrollable, is the power which moves the world. Intelligence trails along in its wake, picking up superficial uniformities in experience and overlooking the teeming diversities and novelties of life. The reason is utterly inadequate to understand or depict the nature and directions of the *vital impetus.*

In order to live truly and be in touch with reality we

---

[8] *Creative Evolution,* pp. 270, 271.

must leave reason or intelligence behind. We must take to feeling, impulse, and a mysterious intuition. We must put our psychical ears to the ground and listen to the current of instinctive life, as it sweeps through us and by us, although we can neither understand it nor communicate rationally what we hear. We shall hear unutterable things, but what we hear will be the mysterious ebb and flow of life's secret forces. Let us divest ourselves of all our ordinary intellectual habiliments and plunge naked into the living turbid waters of reality. Only thus shall we genuinely live. Only thus do we escape from the ghostland of thought into the warm flesh and blood of real change and life. Thus speak our most philosophical irrationalists, of which Bergson is the chief. What is the nature of this intuition or feeling of life, this ineffable sense of *rapport* with reality? Foolish question! It is incommunicable and indescribable. It cannot be stated in terms of the intelligence, since to understand is to *immobilize* that which is essentially *mobility,* is to arrest and fixate that which is essentially process and change. It cannot be communicated, since language is a product of the reason which only skims over the surface of life and can never represent its depths.

II. A Critique of Bergson's Doctrine of Intuition

Reality must be directly perceived or felt, by an immediate contact or union of the contemplating soul with the reality contemplated. If Bergson means that there must be immediate data of experience at the basis of all genuine knowledge, thus far he is right. He is right, too, in holding that the data for the understanding of the nature of the self and of all psychical and spiritual life must be found in the living contemplation of the Ego's own life. I can only understand and appreciate another Ego by recreating his experiences and attitudes within myself. The key to the meaning of life is to be found in the experience of living.

Bergson holds that there need be no conflict between science and intuition. We must use the resources of intellect to enrich our intuitions. Intuition is a sort of instinct, rendered more comprehensive, penetrating and elastic. It is an intellectual sympathy with the most intimate part of reality (*C. E.*, pp. 89-91) . . . by intuition I mean instinct that has become disinterested, self-conscious, capable of reflecting upon its object and of enlarging it indefinitely" (*Ibid.*, p. 176). There is no way of passing from intelligence to intuition; we cannot win to knowledge of the reality of life by the highest exercise of intelligence. But there is a way of passing from intuition to intelligence. Hence, if we begin with intuition we may enrich it from the work of intellect. Bergson tells us that intelligence and instinct differ in *kind,* not in degree, although they never occur entirely separate (*Ibid.*, pp. 135, 136, 142). Intelligence knows only the *immobile forms* and *relations* of things. It cannot comprehend life (*Ibid.*, pp. 145-155). Instinct knows *things in their immediate characters.* It would seem to follow that the knowledge won through intuition, a dilated form of instinct, must differ entirely from it in kind. As a matter of fact, Bergson contrasts them in the sharpest manner again and again. But, when he wishes to save a place for the results of the intellect's work, that intuition may utilize these, he hedges. Thus he tells us that the knowledge yielded, respectively, by instinct and intelligence differ in *degree* not in kind (*Ibid.*, p. 145). How can two cognitive powers, differing in kind, produce knowledge differing only in degree? But Bergson's conception of intelligence is altogether too narrow. Intelligence is not tied up to abstract spatial forms. It does not traffic alone in barren identities, static formulas, and concepts. It has other modes of operation than geometry. The business of intellect is to interpret and organize the data of experience. These data have connections, relations, meanings, and, thus, are intelligible. If diversity, novelty, dynamic change, increasing individuality and freedom are facts, the intellect does not commit suicide in recognizing them nor does it try to reduce them to a dead monotony and colorless sameness. The intellect operates in this variegated moving world. Science is organized common sense and philosophy is common sense organized and interpreted as completely as possible. The intelligence is the power of reflectively organizing the perceptions, the impulsions, the deeds, the feelings, the valuations of the self, and so interpreting and interrelating the whole life of the self in its organic interplay with nature and humanity; so that thereby our impulses become dynamic elements in a harmonious personality, so that thereby our deeds take on a social and universal significance, so that thereby our dumb and blind feelings learn to speak the language of reason and become refined and transformed into the higher sentiments of a well articulated personality; and so that thereby, too, our valuations as the guides to our deeds and the finest fruits of our experiences become the universalized and harmonious instruments by which the individual self at once comes into fuller self-possession as a richer and more significant personal unity and comes into fuller union with man, with nature, and with the universal order. Perhaps this is what Bergson means; but it is unfortunate that he plays into the hands of irresponsible irrationalism and emotionalistic mysticism by offering us, as a foundation for his metaphysics, such an erroneous, ridiculous, wooden image travesty of intelligence or reason. By all means we must seek reality first-hand in living, in acting, in feeling. But by all means, if the universe be not a crazy patchwork, or a madhouse, we shall find our true selves, we shall understand and control nature and we shall organize our lives into richer and more meaningful internal and social harmony and attain union with the universal meaning of things, only by the unremitting exercise of the analytic-synthetic, organizing, and interpreting activity of intelligence.

III. Summary of Bergson's Temporalism

Bergson has shown very skilfully the defects in the mechanistic interpretation of organic evolution, and in the older form of absolutistic teleology which regarded the origin, growth, and functioning of living organisms as simply the unfolding of a predetermined plan. Mechanism assumes that there is nothing in evolution but the blind shifting of material particles in space. The origin and infinite diversification of living organisms is a purely accidental consequence of the permutations and combination of an infinite multitude of mass particles tumbling about in infinite space through endless time. The mechanistic view assumes that the whole is given all at once, and that nothing really new can ever be achieved. All changes and novelties are simply blind readjustments in the parts. The older teleology assumed that everything which takes place is the necessary consequence of a predetermined plan. All that takes place in the process of evolution has been foreseen and timed to occur just when it does occur in fact. Thus the older teleology has no explanation for failures and wastes, for the blind alleys, for the strange and bewildering diversities of nature's life. Like the mechanistic theory, it assumes that the whole is given all at once. In the one case this whole is the mechanical predetermination of mass particles in space, in the other case it is the equally necessary predetermination of an absolute design unerringly carried out. Both views deny the real significance of novelty, growth, variation, and individuality. Both are alike incompatible with the belief in the freedom of the personality of man. For both the course of evolution is like the rattling off of the links of endless chains forged from all eternity.

Against both views Bergson sets his own view that the evolution of life is a progress, resulting from the struggle of the creative activity of the vital impetus or life force, which is the source of individuality, of all variation, growth, and novelty, against the obstructive tendency of inert matter. Pure matter, if there were such a thing, would be the wholly static arrangement of things in space. A world of pure matter would be dead and motionless. Juxtaposition of parts in space is the essence of materiality. By contrast the essence of life and mind is development or movement in time. Life, soul, and time or duration—these are identical. No two instants of time are absolutely the same; no two moments of life are completely identical; no two successive phases of the soul are entirely the same. Ceaseless activity, constant mobility and creativity, a living and evergrowing present in which the past is conserved in so far as it aids in the production of the future—such is the nature of the *life force,* the creative soul of things, the essence of time and duration. Life and soul are the invisible progress of the present and past growing into the future.

Evolution is a creative psychical process, a ceaseless effort towards novelty, individuality, and freedom, carried out in the face of the obstructive counter current of materiality, against the downward tendency which is making for the absolute equilibrium of death. The world is neither wholly dynamic nor wholly static. It is the theater of the cosmical struggle of the dynamic and the static. The life force is mind. For the vital impetus, the moving spring of all evolution, is immaterial. Nay, it is the very essence of immateriality. All finite forms of individuality are the resultants of the unceasing endeavor of the vital impetus to insert itself in and to master matter, to subdue matter to its ends. The varieties of living forms, with all their complexities and imperfections, are the unforeseen but useful results of the struggle of the life force with the counter tendency to inertia, equilibrium, and sameness which is matter. Thus there is novelty, contingency, imprevisibility in the temporal process of evolution. This process is the very secret essence and substance of reality. Man, its highest product, is the fullest, the most successful, accomplishment of the vital impetus. He has most individuality, freedom, or creativity, power of adaption to and modification of the environment, the greatest range of action, because of the superior plasticity of his intelligence, the greatest capacity to conserve the results of the past in the present and to bring them to bear in giving birth to a richer future. He can grow without ceasing, because of the rich endowment of his soul life. His life comes down, nay is a very part of, the stream of time, freighted with the past which interpenetrates with his present. His vivid consciousness and intelligence illumines, from the immediate and remoter past, that zone of the environment on which successful action depends. Thus conscious intelligence, while but a small part of the soul's life, fulfills the important function of enabling a man to act with prevision, and thus to liberate himself from the fetters of the past as *fait accompli* and from the dangers of the present. Consciousness lightens his pathway through time and his labors in time and thus gives to the vital impetus a higher potency in man than in any other organism. Thus the true reality for Bergson is dynamic, creative, psychical.

Bergson has not yet published anything on the philosophy of religion. According to his expressions to correspondents, for him the life force is the creation of God. At any rate it is of the very substance and soul of reality; it is essentially mobile, dynamic, and creative. The general effect of Bergson's philosophy has been to strengthen the conviction of the positive reality and value of growth and evolution and to find the key to the meaning of evolution in the creative activity of mind.[9]

IV. The Temporalism of William James

James' conception of reality has much in common with Bergson's. James protested against the idea of a "block universe" or eternally complete and timeless world. He argued repeatedly and powerfully for the evolutionary and dramatic or historical conception of reality as a growing universe, a world whose future never could be wholly foreseen by even an infinite mind, since it consists of a plurality of individual centers of will who have the power of self-determining or free activity. James' picture of the universe is one in which men are real agents, not puppets either of a blind aggregate of mass particles or of a Divine, despotic Absolute. The world is a vast assemblage of finite agents, whose fates are in some degree in their own hands.[10] Each member of the world has his own part to play in the making of the world's future. God is the great companion or other self, a superhuman but finite, conscious will with which our human lives are probably continuous. In our religious and moral experiences we probably are in touch with the supreme other self. But God is not all-embracing; he is finite either in power or knowledge, or in both at once.[11] God "is himself a part (of the universe) when the system is conceived pluralistically," as James conceived it. "Having an environment, being in time, and working out a history just like ourselves, he escapes from the foreignness from all that is human, of the static, timeless, perfect abso-

---

[9] See William James, *A Pluralistic Universe,* pp. 262, 263 ff.
[10] *Ibid.,* p. 317.
[11] *Ibid.,* p. 318.

lute."[12] James, in the interests of fidelity to actual human experience, and especially to the moral and dramatic significance of the common human lot, embraces the pluralistic alternative. His reaction to the tangled facts of human life, its struggle, pathos, and mystery, led him to elect a spiritual creed, a world-view, in which there is room for possible free self-determination by the individual soul; wide possibilities of good and evil in a universe which evolves by the synergistic and antagonistic efforts of God and men; and, with reference to the ultimate outcome, a *melioristic* outlook, a gospel of hope, by contrast with *pessimism,* the gospel of despair, and *optimism,* the gospel of quietism or nonothingism.

In short, choose the temporalistic universe and life and history become freighted for you with infinite zest and meaning; the world becomes the field for the fashioning of souls and of civilizations. It becomes a place of high adventure, a romantic universe. But it becomes a risky place, no finished perfection anywhere, no absolute retreat from the fretful stir unprofitable and the fever of this world. Always the supreme command is

> Speed on, Fight on, Fare ever,
> There as here.

V. The Temporal and the Eternal

In the light of the last two chapters, we cannot accept any theory of reality which denies or even minimizes the reality and significance of time, duration, or change.

On the other hand, temporalism, raises a very serious

---

[12] James, *A Pluralistic Universe,* p. 318, "The only way of escape," etc., pp. 310, 311, "Monism, etc.," pp. 322-328. See also his *Some Problems of Philosophy,* especially Chapters VII to XIII. This work, left unfinished at his death, expresses James' maturest treatment of the problem.

theological and metaphysical problem. If God actively participates in history, if he lives and energizes in time, does he not grow? And if he grows, is he not always imperfect, suffering from the lack of completeness? If the history of the world is the working out of the drama of the divine purpose by the synergistic deeds of God and finite wills, then, until this purpose be fully achieved, there is want or deficiency in God as well as in man, although, of course, in very different degree. And one who replies that the divine purpose is eternally or timelessly realized is surely talking nonsense. A purpose timelessly fulfilled is no purpose.

On the other hand, if the whole sum of perfection is now and always timelessly present or real, then all the growth and struggle of time, the whole course of natural and historical evolution, and all the innumerable histories of finite personalities, constitute a tale devoid of meaning. The whole time process with all its burdens and its burgeonings becomes an inexplicable illusion. Such is the dilemma of metaphysics and theology before the problem of time and evolution.

Choose the static timeless perfection of the Absolute One and you gain perfection or completeness at the cost of making time, evolution, all the innumerable histories of worlds and living beings, all the tragic dramas of nations and of individuals, dissolve into phantoms of the morning mists.

> The cloud-capped towers, the gorgeous palaces,
> The solemn temples, the great globe itself,
> Yea, all which it inherit, shall dissolve,
> And, like this insubstantial pageant faded,
> Leave not a rack behind. We are such stuff
> As dreams are made on; and our little life
> Is rounded with a sleep.

Is there any way of escape from between the horns of this

dilemma? The problem of reconciling the belief in a perfect reality with the acceptance of the reality and meaning of the temporal order is the knottiest of all the knotty problems of metaphysics and theology. James showed a keen scent for the vital issues when he laid such stress on this issue.[13] There can be no question that, in contrast with speculative Hindu mysticism and pantheism, temporalism is in affinity with the ethical and religious consciousness of Hebraism and Christianity, except where the latter has been deeply infected with neoplatonic mysticism. The average Christian religionist believes in the serious and dramatic quality of the volitional life. He believes that the things that men feel and think and do, as individuals, count for something in the world and have some significance in the eyes of God. He does not think of God as the absolute motionless unity, in which all human feelings and deeds are literally parts or elements, and in which their dynamic and poignant diversity is mysteriously transmuted beyond all recognition into a timeless and static harmony.

The whole philosophical background of the Hebrew prophetic and the Christian world view is the conception of a governing spiritual will, a dynamic ethical intelligence which ceaselessly functions in time; a Being distinct from and related to other beings; an overruling providence who continually energizes in the natural world, but more fully and significantly in the human historical and social world. The world view of Christianity implies that serious and vital issues, issues fraught with high import from God's standpoint as well as from man's, are at stake in individual lives, in the social order, and in the ongoing history of humanity. Thus, temporalistic pluralism is very close to the heart of the common Christian heritage. Temporalism is a doctrine which summons to choice, to action, to hope.

---

[13] Especially in *A Pluralistic Universe* and his unfinished *Some Problems of Philosophy*.

It is a philosophy that makes room for freedom, individuality, and progress. It does not distort beyond recognition the face of our common humanity or derealize our most strenuous moments. It has its roots in the facts of human volitional experience. It does not cause all the variety and complexity, all the tang and color, in human individuality to disappear in the lion's den of the Absolute. It is disposed to estimate human deeds and experiences at something near their face values, whereas from the standpoint of eternalistic monism it is impossible to tell what value, if any, this mixed, confused, and mutable realm of human life can have. For no one, not even the philosopher of the Absolute, can raise himself to the point of vantage of the Absolute; and, if he could, he would have undergone such a metamorphosis that he could no longer hold converse with the denizens of time.

I offer the following suggestions as to how the reality of a perfect being might be reconciled with the imperfections of the temporal order:

1. The ideal of perfection as consisting in a timelessly complete and changeless reality is a false ideal. If reality were a static eternally complete Unity the universe would be a dead and lifeless one. *The best type of perfection is the ceaseless and tireless energizing of an intelligent will.* Self-activity is the authentic sign of perfection.

2. Eternalistic monism can give no intelligible account of the existence of the temporal world of selves, with their growth through self-activity and purposive striving. If one start with the timeless Absolute there is no way down to the temporal plurality of finite and growing souls. The existence and the striving and suffering of a multitude of individuals becomes an impenetrable enigma. It becomes an unaccountable fall. Therefore, in order to understand the actual world, we must start from the standpoint of temporalism, from a recognition of the significant reality

of dynamic centers, of living organisms and souls. On the other hand, temporalism can find an adequate substitute for the timeless absolute unity, one that meets better the ethical and religious needs. From the standpoint of static eternalism, all growth, evolution, history, and purposiveness are illusory. We must hold to their reality and therefore we reject eternalism.

3. There must be change and growth in God's experience or intuitive consciousness of his world, if life and history have any positive meaning. He must feel the losses and the gains, the failures and achievements, of finite souls. He must, as energizing and directing and guiding spirit, bear a part in the travails and the sufferings, the victories and the joys of his creatures. He must share in the processes of temporal growth. He must soil his hands in the grime of this muddy universe. A world which is the place and means for the growth of individualities and for the perfecting of personalities must be an evolutionary or historical world. "My father worketh hitherto and I must work." "I have yet many things to say unto you." "First the grain of seed, then the corn in the ear." The Christian doctrine of the sympathy and suffering of God implies the continuous presence and activity of God in the world of time and history.

4. Change and growth in God's experience, as due to the historical and evolving character of his world, does not imply that his character, will, or intelligence, undergo any alteration. If the evolution of matter, of suns and star systems, of living organisms, and the historical development of souls and peoples, be self-expressions of his unvarying will, then although there is change in his experience, his nature or character, that is his will and purpose, may remain unchanged. He is, as Aristotle said, the perfect energizer, the ceaselessly actualizing will who determines the conditions, directions, and goals or standards of

natural evolution, and human growth. If the realization, through temporal changes, of finite individuality, be part of the central and enduring purpose, be the self-utterance of the creative will, certainly the progressive fulfillment of that purpose does not change the nature of that will. It only enlarges its field of operation and increases the fruits of its operations. Indeed, an enduring purpose or intelligent will is implied in the fact that matter has determinate properties that make possible the evolution of living forms, that these living beings can respond in specific fashions to relatively fixed environments, that life has certain determinate or individual capacities, such as sensitivity, reproductiveness, mobility, intelligence, and that in man these capacities enter upon new levels of development, resulting in morals, social order, science, art, and culture generally. Without permanence of cosmical conditions for evolution, and definite capacities in the evolving elements, which determine the persistence of directions and goals of evolution, there would be no continuity in change, and hence no genuine evolution. For blind chaotic discontinuous change is not evolution. Evolution in nature, progress in history, development in the individual—all these features of the temporal world involve the reality of an enduring intelligent power, purpose or will, since they involve specific directions and goals.

There is much loose thinking abroad in regard to God's infinitude. God cannot be infinite in the sense that he can be anything that we can think of. We can think of many possibilities that cannot be realities in his nature, since they would contradict the idea of a perfect being, and would even be incompatible with the idea of a normal human being. God cannot be a liar. He cannot think things that are incompatible with the logical principles of correct thinking. He cannot will things that contradict his fundamental purposes and aims. He cannot, for instance, will that a world of selves should be both existent and non-existent. He cannot will that what for him is the supreme good should not be realized. God must be a determinate being, with a definite character. He must be the perfect individual if he be anything meaningful. But these are not limitations imposed upon him from without. His limitations are self-limitations which are the self-expressions of his individuality. He is a determinate individual but not finite. A being that might be anything imaginable, a nest of contradictory possibilities, is actually nothing. God's purpose towards the world must be the continuous actualization of his character, and, if this be unchanging, so will his purpose be. If he be the creator of finite selves, whom he endows with power to err, to struggle, to choose, and thus to develop into fuller selfhood, and if he be the originator and sustainer of the evolving physical and vital world in which these finite selves are generated and grow in time, then, in calling into being and sustaining such a world, the only limitations on his action are the self-limitations involved in his own creative love and providence.

As the director and sustainer of the whole process of temporal succession, and the source of the standards or ends by which the endless succession of stages in evolution and in the origin and development of individual lives are connected into a continuous movement, God must be an unchanging being, the changeless ground of the coherent and intelligible order of change.

5. As to God's relation to time and all that takes place in time I would say, not that he is timeless, but that he is the unitary and enduring ground of continuity and order in the time-process. Only the "now" or actual present is "really" real. The past has now the amount of reality which is involved in the conservation and activity of a part of that past in the present. The future has the amount of

reality which is involved in the dynamic quality of the present, by virtue of which there will issue from this present further presents which will be its active outgrowths. Such is the time-order for every finite self—a succession of dynamic "nows" or energizing presents, which blossom into one another and of which pasts and futures are functions. Each self's own present sums up and carries forward its pasts and is big with its future. The self's life now is charged with its vital pasts and blossoms into its futures. Both the tragedy and the promise of our pasts lie, not in the fact that they are irrevocably gone, but in that they really constitute functional activities of our presents.

But since time, evolution, and history are real, there must be, underneath all finite temporal processes, an objective and universal time-order, which sustains, includes, and unifies the infinite multitude of finite time-orders. There must be a universal "Now" or Infinite Present, of which all the variety and succession of finite presents are but broken lights. God's life, I would say, is that Infinite Present, that universal Now. His will and his intuition constitute the continuous dynamic ground, the vital functioning activity or will which conserves the past of the universe and guarantees its future. There can be no actual universal past unless there be a universal will and intuition in which all finite pasts are conserved. God is now, as always, that Universal Self. There can be no real futures, unless there be a continuously enduring and unvarying will, which, in the orderly succession of its presents, is the intelligent ground of the endless succession of finite presents. God's conserving will is thus the enduring ground of the future, as well as of the past and present.

6. Finally, as regards the question of the predetermination of the future, each finite self has given, within its own nature in relation to its specific environment, certain defi-

nite and limited possibilities of future choice and action. The number and nature of these possibilities must be predetermined, since they are determinate. Thus each self's will is limited to its possible choices. Therefore God, as the unifying and continuous ground of all possible future events, must foreknow all that is possible to every finite agent in every situation which that self will ever face. Does he also foreknow what the actual choice of every self will be in every case? This is the ancient problem of determinism and indeterminism. The question is whether, invariably and throughout all time, there is really only one course of action open to every individual at every juncture in life. Could a self ever have done otherwise, than, as a matter of fact, it did? The determinist answers, No! The indeterminist answers, Yes, sometimes!

The scientific conception of the world makes for determinism, since if determinism is never wholly true to the facts thus far causal explanation has reached its limit. I may point out that causal explanation does always reach limits in science—the limits set by the ultimate and not further reducible properties of space and time, matter, life and, indeed, by the ultimate qualities of sensation and the laws of selective thinking. Why not then, too, by the ultimate qualities of selfhood or personality? There are irreducible qualities in the elemental facts of experience. For example I see with my eyes and hear with my ears. No one science has yet explained fully these elementary facts.

The common sense belief in man's power to choose between alternatives, the belief in responsibility and guilt, the common idea of freedom, is that sometimes at least the issues of voluntary choice are not wholly predetermined, and that the power of spontaneous choice is no illusion, although its field of operation may be limited. The common sense belief may be but the reflection of man's ignorance of his own fatally fixed nature and of his environmental determinants in their complex interplay. It may be that, for an infinite knower and will, everything in the temporal order is predetermined down to the last iota and that all our apparently free choices are but the rattling off of the successive links in the chains of our fates, predetermined throughout the beginningless pasts and the endless futures. But, if temporalism be true, if individuality and history be more than mere phantasmal appearance, if all the toilsome and devious struggles along the pathways of evolution, if all the labors and the sufferings, all the tragedies and failures, all the joys and triumphs of human history, all the zest and poignancy of individual lives, are really worthful and significant in some measure, if these multiform and tingling facts of human experience are not mere hallucinations, born of human phantasy, there must be in human nature a fragment of creative will, a finite but nevertheless authentic reproduction in time of the Infinite and Enduring Will. If once in a lifetime, or in a whole series of lifetimes, man can perform a creative deed that springs spontaneously from the deeps of his spiritual selfhood, then determinism as a metaphysical hypothesis is false, and the course of man's temporal pilgrimage is not the fatal rattling off of the links in the chains that bind him fatally in the iron meshes of the web of time. Then God, who determines and foresees all the possibilities of choice open to man at all times, God, who determines the fundamental directions of time and history, does not wholly predetermine the acts of individual wills and cannot wholly foresee which way his human child will always elect to go. Then man's future, in its concrete and living actuality, cannot be known to God in precisely the same way as is his past. God can know the real possibilities of the future, but not the actualities which are not yet actual. He cannot now know my future in the same way in which he knows my present. Then there is an element of spontaneity, of novelty, of creativeness in the life of man, and possibly of other finite selves. Subject to the directing creative purpose of God's enduring will, there is creative freedom of self-determination for some of his creatures. As James Ward puts it, God creates creators, and, if he does I would add, he must conserve the fruits of their creativeness in the spiritual order. Such, as I understand them, are the final religious implications of temporalism—a dynamic universe of orderly spiritual creativity, reality a society of selves moving towards richer harmony of rational and coherent spiritual personalities, the real world a society or Republic of Selves—the Republic of God.

These problems are discussed further in Chapter XXIV.

References

* Bergson, H., *Creative Evolution; Introduction to Metaphysics; Matter and Memory; Mind-Energy; Time and Free Will.*
* Carr, H. W., *Bergson, the Philosopher of Change.*
* James, William, *A Pluralistic Universe; Some Problems of Philosophy.*
* Kitchin, D. B., *An Outline of Bergson.*
* Leighton, J. A., *Man and the Cosmos,* Chapters XVII, XXI, XXXV, XXXVI, XXXVII, XXXVIII.
* Le Roy, E., *A New Philosophy, Henri Bergson.*
* Lindsay, A. D., *The Philosophy of Bergson.*
* Lovejoy, A. O., "The Problem of Time in Recent French Philosophy," *Philosophical Review,* 1912, Vol. XXI; "The Place of the Time Problem in Contemporary Philosophy," *Journal of Philosophy,* 1910, Vol. VII.
* Miller, Lucius H., *Bergson and Religion.*
* Royce, Josiah, *The World and the Individual,* second series, *Nature, Man and the Moral Order.*

Ruhe, Algot, and Paul, Nancy M., *Henri Bergson.*

* Seth, Pringle-Pattison, Andrew, *The Idea of God in the Light of Recent Philosophy.*

Stewart, J. McK., *A Critical Exposition of Bergson's Philosophy.*

Ward, James, *The Realm of Ends.*

CHAPTER XXII

INSTRUMENTALISM OR THE NEW PRAGMATISM

The philosophy of William James has many sides, but it is not a unified whole; it could not be called a system. His widest influence, apart from his great work, *Principles of Psychology,* was undoubtedly as the first influential spokesman, and the leader of *pragmatism.* Briefly, this is the theory that the only criterion of the truth of ideas or beliefs is that they lead to satisfactory consequences; the sole proof of the intellectual pudding is in the eating thereof. All sorts of consequences—emotional and practical, social as well as individual—are tests of truth. No ideas or beliefs are inherently or absolutely true or false; they become true or false, are made so, by the issue of events. The pragmatic criterion of truth is thus bound up with the temporalistic conception of reality. Reality is always on the move, and truth is the apprehension by a mind of some phase or moment of its movement. The detailed examination of pragmatism is reserved for a later chapter (XXX). I have stated its fundamental principle here, because, in its later development, frequently known as "instrumentalism," from its stress on the instrumental character of intelligence, it has become, under the leadership of John Dewey, one of the most influential movements in American thought. Its influence is particularly strong and increasing in the philosophy of education and in social ethics and philosophy. It fits in with the practical and energetic temperament of the average American, with his disregard of tradition and his lack of deep interest in either the æsthetic or the contemplative life. The average American likes doing things; he does not like to muse or meditate; he has little interest in ultimate problems; he shies off from metaphysical questions and he wishes religion to concern itself wholly with "social service." Moreover, the increasing flux and confusion of civilization confirms the American in his distaste for attempting to take long views of things. Instrumentalism figures in the popular magazines and weeklies, even in the daily press, as no other philosophical standpoint does or ever has in the United States. Moreover, it seems to harmonize with the positivistic spirit of natural science, and with a civilization dominated by things and passing events.

I shall give a brief account of the most significant features of the philosophy of John Dewey, since he is the leader of the new pragmatism or instrumentalism. Dewey's chief interests lie in social psychology, ethics, social philosophy, and the theory of education. He and his followers have no use for the notions of anything absolute or final. They are contemptuous of finality of any sort, whether it be in ethics, social philosophy, or metaphysics. Indeed they seem to ignore metaphysics; they identify philosophy entirely with empirical logic, psychology, ethics, and social theory.

In connection with the following paragraphs the reader is advised to read Chapters XXIX and XXX, especially Section II of the latter chapter. Instrumentalism claims to be primarily a theory of thought and knowledge.

I. Dewey's Conception of Intelligence

In instrumentalism the Jamesian conception of the flux of experience is a characteristic feature. Dewey insists that we should abandon the old problems of the relation of knower and known, the self and nature, mind and body, freedom and determinism, the one and the many, the problem of evil, et cetera, and turn philosophy into an instrument for the better organization of human experience and activity by making it a tool for solving practical, social, educational, political, and personal problems. The time-honored problems and theories of metaphysics, he thinks, are evaporating. The truly useful and creative function of intelligence is the enrichment and harmonization of man's individual and social experience. And we are to take experience at its face value. Everything is what it is experienced as. But Dewey lays great stress on the active organizing function of intelligence in enhancing the values of experience. He seems to regard it as the chief instrument of human progress and individual, as well as social, welfare. Thus, while James seeks pragmatic justification for the contemplative side of life as found in religion, especially in mysticism, Dewey's standpoint is more that of a crusader on behalf of the practical, and especially the social, efficacy of intelligence. Bergson reduces intelligence to the level of a mere tool for action on matter and has recourse to intuition to satisfy man's passion to experience reality. Dewey elevates intelligence to the place of the supreme instrument which will enrich the whole of human life, while he seems to deny the value for life of the investigation of the classical problems and theories of philosophy in the past.

In short, while for James, Bergson, and Dewey, reality is flux, and intelligence is a biological instrument to improve human behavior and the behavior of nonhuman nature, James and especially Bergson offer, in immediate experience, feeling or intuition, a way of escape for the religious longing of man, his metaphysical craving for the experience of union with the universe; whereas Dewey apparently would have man give all the energies of his intellect to control and adjust himself to the flux of experience in which he lives and of which he is a part, thus relegating the problems of ultimate reality and man's place in it to the position of adolescent dreams left behind by the mind that has attained intellectual maturity.

According to Dewey—"We think not for the sake of thinking, but as a stage in the business of living. Reason is not something handed down from above to constitute experience rational; it is something which *happens* to experience under certain conditions."[1] These conditions are always conflicts between our native impulses. So long as life moves smoothly in the satisfaction of impulses, there is no occasion for thinking and the latter does not occur. "The business of science is to analyze the given, with the intent of discovering cues to action more dependable than those which a crude unanalyzed experience can supply."[2] The specialized work of the scientist is justified solely by his success in supplying tools for successful action, "knowing has reference only to the future, and is neither a contemplative survey of existence, nor the working out of a timeless, dialectical process."

"And here comes in the fundamental motive of Dewey's whole philosophy; it is an attempt to furnish a sound logical basis for progress—progress in the individual, but still more in the social world. Pragmatism is an experimental use of intelligence to liberate and liberalize action. It looks to a growing rather than a static world; thinking is not the reduplication of reality already complete, but the actual method of social advance, a method that is to free us alike from the unchanging ideals of obscurantism, and from the spasmodic demand for novelty or freedom working under no principle of control from the past. It is the logic of rational evolution, where, along with a constant alertness to the novelties in the situation, and an

---

[1] A. K. Rogers, *English and American Philosophy Since 1800*, p. 390.

[2] *Ibid.*, p. 390.

absence of undue subservience to the past, the new is at the same time connected with the old in an orderly and sober fashion."[3]

Reality is what it is experienced as, it is the whole content of experienced process, for experience is always a flux. Thinking is a part of the flux of experience. We are not to start from the assumption of the independent existence of either physical things or selves, either minds or bodies. The external world and the individual self are simply parts of the flux of perceptual experience. We are not to begin with the belief in an individual or ego who knows a reality that exists apart from him, and who acts by some mysterious effort of will on that world. As the Buddhist puts it—"There is no self or Brahma world; constituent parts alone roll on." The self exists in the moment of self-experiencing; for example, in the moment when I feel and value and choose, I exist as just that moment of feeling, and when I cease to feel I cease to exist as a self.

But what is a self really? One cannot make any progress in thinking, even for practical purposes alone, unless one has some realistic belief and conception. Experience must be *of* some thing, and *by* some experient. Even Dewey is forced to transcend the passing moment of "pure experience" (in the sense of William James and the neutral monists), in order to find a standing place, a point of departure and return, for a theory of the nature and functions of thought or intelligence. The world of pure experience in the philosophies of James and Dewey is like the "thing-in-itself" in the philosophy of Kant; without it one cannot get into their philosophies, and with it one cannot stay in them. The place occupied by the self in idealistic systems is taken, for Dewey, by the *organism*. The conscious and rational self is episodical, but the organ-

---

[3] *Ibid.*, p. 391.

ism with its neutral mechanisms is an objective and relatively permanent reality. All sentient life is a function of the organism. Thinking is a form of organic behavior, like walking, swallowing, and digesting. Thinking is a more complicated form of animal behavior than these other functions. At times, namely, in critical situations when impulses conflict and the organism is "up a tree," thinking becomes the most important form of animal behavior. But since it is simply a peculiar complication in the flux of experience, not the act of a being differing in character from the other items of experienced content, there is no metaphysical problem of knowledge or volition. There is no really significant distinction between "inner" and "outer," "mind" and "body," "individual" and "physical world."

Since thinking is purely a practical instrument, not the expression of an agent in any sense ultimately real, the terms "self," "soul," "spirit," "ego," lose their meaning. There are no ultimate or intrinsic ends and values, since to suppose these is to presuppose an ego or self. The ends followed are problems that occur or happen in the flux of experience. Life cannot help seeking its own expansion, fulfillment, continuance. Agreeable experiences have a way of striving for their own perpetuation, and disagreeable experiences of seeking self-annulment. Therefore all values are instrumental. Value belongs to whatever furthers life, unvalue to whatever hinders it.

The fundamental categories of Dewey's philosophy are biological. If we ask, what is reality for him, the only approach to an answer seems to be that reality is what is experienced in and by organisms. Something must have experience, must do and suffer, and this something is the organism. To the question, what antedated organisms, and more specifically, neurally endowed organisms, there seems to be no answer. The reality of the world thus implies that sentient organisms were coeval with the universe—eternal members of the ceaseless flux. Thus his philosophy is a reduction, a watering-down, of the fundamental presupposition of idealism to biological terms. Instead of saying with his former idealistic friends—"In the beginning was, and always is, mind," Dewey seems to say—"In the beginning was, and always is, organic life and behavior." However, his increasing expressions of sympathy with mechanistic behaviorism suggest that his philosophy is in a state of unstable equilibrium; perhaps, his antipathy to any relics of dualism would lead him to say that the organism is nothing but a special complication of mass particles. If instrumentalism does not move towards some form of teleological metaphysics, it must logically become a materialism. The present uncertain position of the theory illustrates two points—(1) the transitional and unstable character of much present philosophizing; (2) the truth that no one can set out seriously on the philosophical road, no matter how he may purpose to limit his interests, without arriving at some sort of metaphysics. The problem of reality will not down, and it cannot be waived aside by any amount of talk about the paramountcy of the practical or biological life. A metaphysics is implicit in every serious effort to think.

II. Dewey's Ethics or Social Philosophy [4]

Ethics, for Dewey, is the gateway to social philosophy, and social psychology is the key to ethics. He begins with the thesis that the conduct of mature or socialized indi-

---

[4] I have based this summary on Dewey's latest work, *Human Nature and Conduct*, because it is, in many respects, the best statement of his position in ethics and social philosophy. His part in Dewey and Tufts' *Ethics* is very hard reading for the beginner.

viduals is controlled chiefly by habit. And, of course, we are concerned only with individuals who live in society, the isolated individual is an unreal abstraction. The individual at birth possesses, or rather is, certain congenital capacities or powers of responsiveness to the various situations in which the human organism finds itself. The individual does not consist of a number of fixed instincts. The raw unsocialized or uneducated self consists of a number of impulses, which are very plastic or modifiable by social patterns. The sex impulse, for example, may run the ordinary course of courtship and marriage; it may undergo perversion; it may be "sublimated" and thus discharge itself in art, romantic devotion, religion or some other form of "spiritual" activity. Impulses are blended and irradiate in various ways, under the influence of social pressures and excitations. The common notion that human nature is unchanging is a fiction. Until the native impulses have been set and hardened into habits, by the canalizing power of social customs, human nature is very capable of change. The really stubborn and unyielding factors in human society, those which prevent change for better or worse, and on which the ultraconservative relies in his defence of established social institutions, are just the institutions or customs themselves; such as the usages and laws in regard to property, industry, marriage, et cetera. Human nature seems unchanging because, once the fluid impulses of the biological self have been shaped and set by social custom and usage, the *habits* thus formed are hard to modify. The habits, which, by their interpenetration, make up the character or personality of the developed individual, are the resultants of the incessant play of custom on the original impulses. Persons vary in the relative intensity of their native impulses. But human nature in the raw is much the same everywhere; the differences between persons is largely, and the differences between cultures is chiefly, due to the differences in social customs, by which habits are formed out of the raw impulses of human nature.

Habit is identical with will. A man's will is simply the system of his habits. If he have no unified will, if he be an abnormally divided self, that is because his habits do not jibe. Thinking is just as much a habit as walking, and is molded by social customs. There is no soul that thinks in general; "habits formed in process of exercising biological aptitudes are the sole agents of observation, recollection, foresight, and judgment"; "concrete habits are the means of knowledge and thought" (*Human Nature and Conduct,* p. 176). But habits do not *know,* do not reflect or imagine. *Intelligent thinking is born in the conflicts of habits and impulses.* Habit carried through to the limit of specialization ends in thoughtless action. "But only thought notes obstructions, invents tools, conceives aims, directs technic, and thus converts impulse into an art which lives in objects. Thought is born as the twin of impulse in every moment of impeded habit" (*Ibid.,* p. 171). Habit is vital only in so far as it is animated by impulse, and the function of thought is to liberate impulse from the thraldom of ossified habits. Through intelligence alone is man able to free himself from the automatic routine which custom engenders upon impulse.

How thinking can be at once a habit and the liberator from the thraldom of habit is not explained.

Intelligence, the power to set up, coördinate and guide to successful issue, conscious aims born of reflection on impulse, is the great agency for the realization of the good. Dewey rejects the notions of final ends, absolute values, infallible intuitions. The true ends of conduct are the definite concrete ends-in-view here and now, not remote and abstract ideals or values. Means and ends cannot be separated. A good means is part of the good end, and a good end is simply a series or totality of means. An end cannot be good and the means to it bad, or vice versa. Intelligence is the power to devise means which are steps in the gaining of the end, and also to generalize aims, to view them impartially, and thus to universalize and harmonize them.

Good conduct is intelligent conduct, aimed at satisfying human desire in a concrete, harmonious and progressive fashion. The good is the progressive increase in depth, multiplicity and extent, of the meanings of life. The good is always unique, never to be exactly repeated. It is the best attainable meaning of every single situation in life. It is new every morning, fresh every evening. Each moment has its own possible imperishable value, as each individual life has its own unique series of attainable good moments. Moral progress is not to be measured by approximation to some remote goal. "Progress is present reconstruction adding fullness and distinctness of meaning" (*Ibid.,* p. 281). Thus morals has to do with all activity into which alternative possibilities enter (*Ibid.,* p. 278). For wherever there are alternative possibilities there is occasion for deliberation and choice, for the exercise of intelligence to determine how meanings may best be realized. Thus moral conduct covers every act that is judged with reference to better and worse. "Potentially conduct is one hundred per cent of our acts" (*Ibid.,* p. 279). "Every situation has its own measure and quality of progress" (*Ibid.,* p. 282). "Progress means increase of meaning, which involves multiplication of sensed distinctions as well as harmony, unification" (*Ibid.,* p. 283). "Happiness, reasonableness, virtue, perfecting, are * * * parts of the present significance of present action. Memory of the past, observation of the present, foresight of the future, are indispensable. But they are indispensable to a present liberation, an enriching growth of action" (*Ibid.*, p. 265).

Since morality consists in the intelligent achievement, increase, and unification of the meanings implicit in impulse; since each moment in life, as well as every impulse, counts as one inherent value in its own good right, all dualisms, all two-world theories of morals, are to be rejected. The good does not consist in the sacrifice of feeling to reason, of sense to "spirit," of the present to a future Heaven or Nirvana. All popular dualisms and supernaturalisms, all romantic and transcendental idealisms, are forms of the same fallacy. Whether the good be conceived as a Christian supernatural Heaven from which all the present concrete impulses and interests of man's earthly life are banished, or as a transcendental Ideal of Reason which is contrasted, as the eternal self-identical life of pure spirit, with the concrete, active, changing, empirical, individual life, here and now; or, with still more logic, as the Buddhist Nirvana into which one enters by the cessation of all desire and the extinction of all interest, and the consequent total annihilation of individuality, the procedure is essentially the same. It is denied that there is inherent meaning and value in the present, actual, concrete situation of the individual here and now. In all these cases there is set up, "a goal of final exhaustive, comprehensive, perfection which can be defined only by complete contrast with the actual" (*Ibid.*, p. 260). Such a goal is a chimera, a psychological nonentity. It is only in the actual, the present dynamic moment of life, that intelligence can find concrete meaning or good. It is in the concrete transformations of what exists that the values of human existence are realized. The good lies alone in the progressing and harmonious satisfaction of all the concrete activities of the individual, as a member of society. Instead of seeking with Faust, the romantic idealist, some perfect future moment to which one could say—"Stay, fleeting moment, thou art so fair!"—Dewey's injunction is to use intelligence to make every moment as fair as possible, by the guidance of every impulse so that the maximum of depth and harmony of meaning is continuously realized. The only idealism that has place in this theory is that which consists in the idealization by intelligence of impulse, so that meanings are continuously achieved and enjoyed. Thus Dewey's conception of the good is empirical, concrete, relativistic, and temporal. The good is to be found in the intelligent guidance of the flux of daily impulses and interests.

Since intelligence is the universalizing and objectifying agency in the guidance of desires, the good is social as well as individual. Indeed it is the one because it is the other. It is false to say that morals "ought" to be social. They never are anything else. The true distinction is between better and worse social orders. And the best social order is one that gives the fullest play to intelligence to organize, interpret, and guide to deep and harmonious satisfaction, the native impulses and interests of humanity. Morals ought to be more intelligently social, and they will be when we have a more adequate science of human behavior, and when this science is used as the instrument to guide social institutions in such a fashion that social organization will afford the opportunity for the individual, by intelligent self-direction, to get richer meanings from the process of living itself, by ordering and integrating his native capacities. For the individual at birth is the whole of his impulses; and the adult is the whole of his habits and propulsions, as these have been able to shape themselves in his social circumstances.

The Kantian and, in general, the intuitionist doctrine that goodness resides in the will or intent, regardless of consequences, is rejected. The test of the goodness of any line of conduct is its concrete consequences, its total effects; not its economic consequences or its merely material consequences, to be sure; but its effects in enhancing the depth and range of experienced meaning in human life. "Morals means growth of conduct in meaning. * * * It is all one with growing" (*Ibid.*, p. 280). "In the largest sense of the word, morals is education" (*Ibid.*, p. 280).

"Morals is connected with actualities of existence, not with ideals, ends, and obligations independent of concrete actualities. The facts upon which it depends are those which arise out of active connections of human beings with one another, the consequences of their mutually intertwined activities in the life of desire, belief, judgment, satisfaction, and dissatisfaction. In this sense, conduct and hence morals, are social" (*Ibid.*, p. 329). Hence there is no abstract, and eternal Right or Good. "The belief in a separate, practically ineffectual, ideal or transcendental Right is a reflex of the inadequacy with which existing institutions perform their educative office" (*Ibid.*, p. 328). "For Right is only an abstract name for the multitude of concrete demands in action which others impress upon us, and of which we are obliged, if we would live, to take some account" (*Ibid.*, p. 326).

Individuality signifies unique connections in the whole. "Within the flickering inconsequential acts of separate selves dwells a sense of the whole which claims and dignifies them" (*Ibid.*, p. 331). The life of the community is the fit symbol of that sense of the whole which liberates us from the conceit of carrying the load of the universe. True religion is just the identification of the "sense of the whole" with the "sense of the community." It is the ideal of the community made the key to the total significance of life and reality (*Ibid.*, pp. 331, 332).

III. Dewey's Theory of Education

As I have already stated, Dewey conceives the function of philosophy to consist chiefly in fashioning intellectual tools or instruments for the furtherance of human happiness through social reconstruction, and more especially through education.

This is the burden of his most important work on education, *Democracy and Education,* and of his more recent *Reconstruction in Philosophy.*

Knowing is, we have already seen, entirely subservient to conduct—to doing and enjoying. We seek to understand in order that, by intelligent and therefore successful action, we may become happy. The surest way to a social reconstruction that will make general happiness possible is through education. For education is the whole system of means by which individuals may acquire control over their own natural impulses, by bringing these into harmony with one another and harmonizing the interests of the individual with the interests of other members of the social groups to which he belongs. Education is identical with the process of human growth, by the development of the individual and the coördination of his interests with those of the various social environments in which he lives.[5]

Philosophy is the theory of education in its most general form as a consciously directed process. It is the formulation of the social aims of education.[6] Its function is to integrate the aims of living.[7] Science becomes philosophy when it becomes a *general attitude towards the world.* Philosophy supplies the need for a total theory of action.

Dewey rejects the traditional dualisms, of empirical and rational knowing, activity and passivity, theory and practice. In particular, theory is the instrument for intelligent

[5] *Democracy and Education,* Chaps. II-IV.
[6] *Ibid.,* pp. 383 and 386.
[7] *Ibid.,* p. 379 ff.

practice, for consciously guided action.[8] "Education offers a vantage ground from which to penetrate the human, as distinct from the technical, significance of philosophic discussion."[9]

Knowing has to do with reorganizing activity. "The brain is essentially an organ for effecting the reciprocal adjustment to each other of the stimuli received from the environment and responses directed upon it."[10] The adjusting is reciprocal; the brain enables organic activity to be directed upon external objects in response to stimulation and this response determines the next stimulus.

The doctrine of biological evolution shows that the development of organs, from the simplest organic responses of the lowliest forms of life up to the intelligent responses of man, has been the fashioning of finer and longer range instruments of adaptation, by living beings, to the natural environment. The development of the experimental method is a further evolution of conscious activity directed towards still better adaptation.[11] The experimental method has two sides: (1) Nothing can rightfully be called knowledge, in which the conception entertained does not lead to physical changes produced by our activity in agreement with the conception. 2. The experimental method signifies that thinking is successful, and therefore true, "in just the degree in which the anticipation of future consequences is made on the basis of thorough observation of present conditions."[12] Experimentation is conscious intelligently-directed response. The scientific method is a trial of ideas. "In brief, the function of knowledge is to make one experience freely available in other experiences."[13] In habitual responses *freeness* of adjustment is absent. "In other words, knowledge is a perception of those connections of an

---

[8] *Ibid.*, p. 389 ff.
[9] *Ibid.*, p. 383.
[10] *Ibid.*, p. 392.
[11] *Ibid.*, p. 393 ff.
[12] *Ibid.*, p. 394.
[13] *Ibid.*, p. 395.

object which determine its applicability in a given situation."[14] "Genuine knowledge has all the practical value attaching to efficient habits. But it also increases the meaning, the experienced significance attached to an experience."[15]

From this conception of knowledge Dewey passes to the theory of morals.[16] He rejects the inherited dualisms or oppositions of the inner and the outer; that is, of intent and act, or the spiritual and the physical. These are not oppositions but two ways of looking at the same reality—the whole physico-psychical man. So, too, with the opposition of duty and self-interest. The interests of the larger or social self coincide with its duties. Thus, the social and the moral quality of conduct are identical with each other. The measure of the worth of all phases and types of "education is the extent to which they are animated by a social spirit." Education is the great moralizing agency, just in so far as it is the great socializing agency. *The human good*—what a man is *good for—is the social participation in a balanced experience,* one in which what he gets balances with what he gives. And what he both gets and gives "is a widening and deepening of conscious life—a more intense, disciplined, and expanding realization of meanings."[17]

All this is admirable, as far as it goes. But is it all? Are all values for the spirit of man to be measured solely in terms of their social utility or shareableness? Is the individual not something more than a mere social unit? And is nothing true or worth while which the individual feels or contemplates in distinction or isolation from the crowd? Is nothing true or beautiful or holy, except what can be put to work to produce obvious social results? Knowledge is indeed the most useful instrument of social action.

---

[14] *Democracy and Education*, p. 396.
[15] *Ibid.*, p. 397.
[16] *Ibid.*, Chapter XXVI.
[17] *Ibid.*, p. 417.

Knowledge is power, but is that all it ever is? Is that all beauty or the vision of holiness ever are? Simply instruments for social reconstruction! When we shall have reconstructed society to suit Dewey, what shall we have achieved? Millions of similarly clad, equally well-fed persons, thinking the same thoughts, enjoying the same amusements, feeling the same feelings? Is social reconstruction, through making intelligence solely a tool for action, and condemning all higher yearnings of the lonely spirit if they cannot be shared by all others, to result in the millennium of mediocrity? Spinoza said, "All things excellent are as difficult as they are rare." The instrumentalist theory of education and culture is, rightly or wrongly, taken to imply that all things excellent can be made easy and common. The contemplation of the history of humanity and the present plight of western civilization incline one to side with Spinoza.

IV. Critique of Instrumentalism

The conception of intelligence as an active organizing principle is the last remaining legacy of the objective idealists, from Plato to Hegel, which our newest instrumentalists have preserved. But surely the successful operation of intelligence as an instrument of control or successful behavior in a world implies that the world is, at least to a predominating degree, of similar structure. Mind can make itself at home in a universe only if the latter be in some sense a rational order. A philosophy which emphasizes the supremacy of intelligence as a practical agent, surely implies a teleological metaphysics. If the highest intelligence be the best guide to human welfare, then thought, at its best, is the most in harmony with the universe of all our human powers. Moreover, it is a narrow and unjustifiable limitation of the function of human intelligence to say that it exists only to exercise practical, technical, social, and volitional controls, and to invent makeshift adjustments between human emotional and biological needs and the daily and hourly flux of experience. The functions of consciousness and reason are not exhausted in meeting novel situations and controlling behavior by a reference to the future. When I am engaged in æsthetic contemplation of nature or art, when I am enjoying the companionship of a friend, when I am contemplating the logical symmetry, beauty, and impersonal grandeur of some scientific or mathematical construction, when I am living in some significant period of the past, for example Elizabethan England or the Athens of Pericles, when I am following the career and feeling myself into the life of some one of the race's worldly or spiritual heroes, my consciousness, keen, vivid, and expanding, may have no reference to my own future behavior or that of anyone else. The human spirit lives not by deeds of adjustment to external and future situations alone. It lives deeply in pure contemplation and free imagination. The instrumentalist errs by taking one important function of conscious intelligence and making it the sole function. Disinterested contemplation and enjoyment of the beauty, grandeur, meaning and order of things for their own sakes are for some human beings inherently worthful functions of consciousness. The philosopher, like Kipling's world wanderer, is moved by the passion "For to admire and for to see" the universe. To become, in however modest degree, the spectator of time and existence is a native human longing which philosophy exists to satisfy. Nothing is more truly a mark of the distinctively human life, nothing in human life gives more worth and poise, more inner strength and unshaken fortitude to life than the attainment of a contemplative insight in which the spirit's thirst for a reflective vision of reality is slaked, in which the *thinker* becomes, in however imperfect measure, consciously at one with the order of the universe. The truest mainspring of science and philosophy is not the discovery of "get-rich-quick" methods in either industry or social organization. Philosophy is more than a good economic, political, social, or even pedagogical tool. To make the guidance of the economic and social life of man its sole function would be to limit unduly the scope of philosophy. The theoretic or contemplative life is the crown and guide of the truly human life. The rational life is the coherent and harmonious life, in contrast with the random and disjointed life of blind feeling and impulse. Universality of meaning, harmony, organization into a coherent system—these are alike notes of the most true in science and of the highest type of social order and individual life. The mainspring of science and philosophy is the quest for a coherent and harmonious life, *including a coherent insight into the meaning of life and the nature of things.* Reality is more than reason, but without reason, without disinterested contemplation, without a life that seeks the reflective insight into the ordered totality, the coherent organization of the real, the deepest meanings and values of reality do not come into the possession of man. The truly human part of man is the rational and spiritual power in him which has fashioned and is ever fashioning, out of the materials supplied by nature, an objective rational order of social, moral, and spiritual life; and which creates science, art, religion, and philosophy, not for the satisfaction of man's belly needs but in order that reason and the creative imagination may find themselves at home in the spiritual universe.

The danger of overstressing the instrumental character of intelligence lies in covertly assuming that, since intelligence or reason is a practical instrument of behavior, it is nothing more. The instrumentalist *à outrance* condemns all pure speculation and contemplation, all imaginative musings over the problems of metaphysics and theology. He demands that philosophy come down into the market place, roll up its sleeves and go to work to prove its utility like the farm tractor or any other piece of human invention. He voices the severe utilitarianism of the practical American.

The instrumentalist philosophy has been embraced eagerly by radicals who would institute a juster society by overturning all existing social institutions and putting in their places the dictatorship of the class conscious proletarian minority, as the first step towards a communistic social order; it has also been embraced by the near-radicals of varying degrees of remoteness from sheer communism. It would be unfair to attribute such views to the leaders of instrumentalism, for they have some sense of the slow, difficult, and circuitous routes by which social order is built up and human progress made. Nevertheless, the radicals and near-radicals are not without justification in employing this philosophy, as better adapted to their purposes than any other. Since instrumentalism regards thought and all its works simply as tools for individual and social progress; since it stresses the fleeting moment and the endless flux of life and reality; since it well-nigh ignores the fundamental problem of religion, which is the question of the right relation of the spirit of man to the highest Reality; since it refuses to recognize any ultimate and intrinsic standards of value in the conduct of thought, the control of impulse, the relation of man to the universe; finally, since, by consequence, it can offer no well-defined criterion of social progress or individual goodness, instrumentalism can be used to justify any social attitude that an individual or a group may desire to identify with progress and the good. The class conscious moiety of the proletariat, the defenders of representative democracy, and the advocates of plutocratic governance can equally appeal to instrumentalism on the ground that their method is the most efficient tool for making progress. Unless we have well-defined standards of value, in regard both to the private life of the individual and his social relationships, "social progress" becomes a dangerous slogan, which can lead only to a social warfare in which the ultimate arbiters will be, not reasonableness and fair play, but the force of numbers and munitions. The militant leaders of the forces of both King Demos and King Plutos at the present moment are good instrumentalists.

Just now, society is divided too completely into the two camps of the unthinking reactionaries and the visionary radicals. What we need urgently is the vigorous growth, in numbers and influence, of a thoughtful *liberalism;* in other words, the increase of comprehensive and cautious, but fearless and open-minded, thinking and investigation in the social sciences and their applications. Perhaps this end is just what leading instrumentalists are aiming at.

The present writer has no faith in any agitation for social progress which does not recognize the rational and instructed *individuality* of the spirit as the ultimate standard; and which makes light of the teachings of man's cultural history. To me, history teaches that the only sure ways to lasting social progress and individual welfare lie through the selfless devotion of the individual spirit to truth, integrity, the highest quality of workmanship, and the spread of the spirit of free fellowship and coöperation among human beings who otherwise differ, and are unequal, in powers and functions. This devotion cannot flourish without *faith* in the supremacy of the rational spirit over all industrial, economic, educational, and other social "systems." Without a religion and a metaphysics, which is the intellectual interpretation of religion, no section of mankind has ever made progress. I see no grounds for believing that civilization will extricate itself from its present mess by instruments alone and without *faith and sacrifice for something higher than organic behavior.* When all due allowances have been made for the changes in cultural conditions, and when the traditionary excrescences that encumber our inherited spiritual idealism have been discarded, perhaps, in their essential insights with regard to the order of human values, Plato, Aristotle, the Stoics, Jesus, St. John, Origen, and Plotinus, and their modern interpreters, the great idealists, are not far astray.

The instrumentalist challenges all our social institutions to prove their humanistic values. He would liberate the human spirit from the thraldom of the past. His pole star is a better social order to-morrow. But, as yet, he has offered us no definite program for the attainment of a higher individual life in a better social order. He insists that the best experiences and values are those that are shared. But by what proportion of human beings? In the meantime, social unrest grows apace. The social mechanism is geared up to cater to the noisy, crude, commonplace, and sensuous life. One does not find, either in social administration or the business of industry and finance, any general or deep concern for the spiritual or ideal values. The life and death struggle between organized labor and organized capital seems, for the most part, to be a struggle over the fleshpots of Egypt. Neither party seems to be much concerned with the fate of spiritual values. We lack leaders who unite wisdom and courage. Many of them seem to hearken, not to their own rational consciences, but to the voices of the clique or the group interest. The notes of distinction do not grow stronger in our letters, art, or education.

The value of an instrument consists in what it is good for. In its own terms, what are the "practical fruits" of the instrumentalist philosophy? Is it aiding in the prevalent dissolution of our inherited ideals of æsthetic, intellectual, moral, and spiritual culture? Or, accepting this dissolution as inevitable, is it striving to put new goods in their places? And what does it put in their places? My questions are put in no carping spirit.

It is right to insist that the present, the *here-now,* should be filled with meaning; not sacrificed to some abstract beyond. This is precisely the attitude of all sane idealism. The idealist finds meaning and value in the present by joining it up with the realm of objective spiritual values which transcend every momentary here-now. The issue is this—how may the present life gain true richness, breadth, depth and harmony? The idealist answer is—by a transformation of the animal present through transfusing it with the spirit of devotion to the transindividual and transmomental values of intellectual and moral integrity, spiritual fellowship, and partnership in the striving for beauty and truth. Is this what the instrumentalist means? If it is, why does he take such a condescending attitude towards the high peaks in the spiritual history of the human race?

Notwithstanding its continual emphasis on the value of the concrete, the "here-now," instrumentalism is a most abstract philosophy. The instrumentalist tells us that the values of life and experience consist of the "meanings" to be distilled from the present. But he does not give us the slightest hint as to just what meanings, what values, contribute to the present fruition of life. He surely cannot mean just a life of momentary impulse, one that never looks before and after. For it is a pretty notorious fact that satisfaction is not found by human beings in this sort of jazzlike existence. What then does the instrumentalist mean by the enrichment of the present with meanings? What does he offer as a substitute for the life-views of, say, a Christian or a Hebrew?

The instrumentalist would exalt individuality. But what

is genuine individuality? It is realized by a strenuous and selfless devotion to spiritual ideals—to justice, integrity, and spiritual fellowship, in the service of those values that lift a man above the moment and out of his animal selfhood. Are we getting, by our prodigious educational activity and talk, a greater or a lesser proportion of wise, noble, and courageous individuals in our democracy? The instrumentalist rightly stresses the supreme importance of education. He makes education the one good key to individual happiness, social welfare, and progress. It is to supply individual guidance, social polity and religion. I share his faith in education as the one safe and effective means of social progress. But I question whether the "new education" is educating! It is part of the present mechanistic superstition to believe that moral character, intellectual power and ripeness of insight, can be "spoon fed" into the young, if only we have the right "system." And we are to get this system by an application of the "science of human behavior," that is, psychology. But such a science, pursued in indifference to the lessons of man's cultural history, will tend to turn us into noisy and commonplace machines, varying in our impulses but echoing the same thoughtless ignorance of the higher values and standards of human life. What we need is not so much a new system of pedagogical theory, as a renewed recognition of the fact that all the elements of education, culture, power, wisdom, strength of character, are won only by the arduous efforts of the individual expended in assimilating and turning into vital possession and use, the cultural goods that have survived the storms of time. It is a crime against youth and the future to cram the young with the raw or half-baked heaps of data and untested speculation of yesterday and the day before. All genuine education is self-education, the struggle of the growing mind to penetrate something of the meaning of those things that have endured. What our distressed time needs is more superior individuals in positions of public service—individuals whose exceptional native intellectual and moral endowments have been matured by a liberal humanistic and scientific education, in which stress has been laid on the individual's own efforts; and who are inspired with that fine and discriminating sense of spiritual values, which comes only from intimate and reverent communion with the heroes of man's spiritual history. We need, in place of the new education, a renewal of emphasis on hard work and individual responsibility and initiative.

Perhaps this is just what the instrumentalists mean by the new education. I have not been able to discover from their critical appraisals, largely depreciatory, of the works of culture and education up to the present, what they mean by the new education.

Nor can I admit that any democratic program of education will prove a sufficient substitute for the personal orientation of the individual towards the ultimate meaning and value of reality—an orientation by way of either religion or metaphysics. Educational processes may facilitate this individual self-discovery through the discovery of his true relation to reality. But the new birth which is a finding of one's real center and relationships, a coming to one's self, is essentially a process that belongs to what J. H. Newman called "the individuality of the soul."

I heartily agree that there is but one universe, and that, for us the meanings of life and nature must be found here and now, or not at all. But I insist that the one universe has diverse dimensions and planes of value. The creation and enjoyment of beauty for its own sake in nature and in man, and that disinterested union with the universe which is the quintessence of metaphysics, and spiritual religion and the higher poetry, which is the finer breath and essence of all knowledge; all these are forms of value which give grace and beauty to life's unquiet dream.

I must say, further, that the choicest goods are not accessible to all spirits, are not those of the common market-place and the popular taste. In his passion for raising the spiritual level of the democracy, the instrumentalist overlooks the fundamental truth to which the choicest spirits from Plato, through Spinoza, Shakespeare, and Goethe, to Nietzsche, have borne witness: Narrow is the way and straight the gate that leadeth to the highest values. Few there be that enter therein. Many are called but few are chosen. May many more be chosen in a juster social order! Nevertheless, the history of humanity does not support the assumption that an economic and industrial millennium would inevitably see all souls pressing eagerly into the inner temple to worship at the shrines of beauty and spiritual perfection—the twin forms of the good.

References

Bawden, H. H., *Principles of Pragmatism.*

* Bode, B. H., *Essentials of Educational Theory.*

* Dewey, John, *Democracy and Education; Ethics* (with J. H. Tufts); *How We Think; Human Nature and Conduct; Reconstruction in Philosophy; School and Society; Studies in Logical Theory.*

* Dewey, and others, *Creative Intelligence.*

* James, William, *Pragmatism.*

Moore, A. W., *Pragmatism and Its Critics.*

Schiller, F. C. S., *Humanism; Studies in Humanism.*

PART III

AN OUTLINE OF THE CHIEF PROBLEMS OF CONSTRUCTIVE PHILOSOPHY

CHAPTER XXIII

THE PROBLEM OF EVOLUTION AND TELEOLOGY

I. The Rise of the Doctrine of Evolution

Metaphysics or *Philosophical System* is the systematic and critical inquiry into the fundamental problems of philosophical thought. A system of metaphysics or philosophy is simply the organization of the results of a comprehensive and penetrating investigation of all the fundamental problems of thought and existence. A beginner must not be in haste, nor expect to reach a metaphysics by the study of one course and a few books. He must first survey carefully all the problems, and weigh the chief theories thereon. As a preparation for such an inquiry, we shall now take up, in this order, the chief problems of constructive philosophy, with especial reference to their present status. These are—*Evolution and Teleology, The One and the Many, The Self, The Problems of Ethics, The Status of Values, The Meaning of History, and the Problem of Knowledge.*

The theory of the evolution of living species by natural causes has wrought such a transformation in all departments of human thought that one can best begin a study of the live issues in philosophy to-day by a consideration of the bearings of the theory on philosophy.

The theory of evolution is as old as Greek philosophy, but it was not until the nineteenth century that the doctrine of biological evolution became the most deeply influential and far-reaching of all scientific conceptions. During the sixteenth, seventeenth, and eighteenth centuries, the concepts of mathematics and mechanics were dominant; but since 1850 these have gradually been made subordinate to the notion of evolution. This change is the result of the work of Lamarck, Darwin, Wallace, Huxley, and others. The labors of these investigators carried the concept of evolution over from the status of a speculation to its present status as a well-established scientific theory. They adduced a great mass of evidence which sustained both the *fact* and the *methods* of evolution. Up to their time the prevailing view was that species were unalterably fixed in character. This view had prevailed from the days of Plato who, in his epistemological language in the doctrine of Ideas, had hardened species into fixed and permanent types.

"All things flow," said Heraclitus. To-day the evolutionist again throws all things into the flux. Not even the truths of logic and mathematics are exempt from the influence of change, according to the thoroughgoing evolutionist. Evolution means change, but not blind and chartless change. It is change in describable and definable directions. The evolution of organic life means the descent of the more complex from the simple by the operation of causes which are similar to those observed in operation to-day. This type of describable and orderly change means increasing diversity *in* the parts and increasing interdependence *of* the parts.

Herbert Spencer describes the process of evolution in words that are quite ponderous but, notwithstanding this feature, they neatly express the state of the matter: "Evolution is an integration of matter and concomitant dissipation of motion; during which the matter passes from an indefinite, incoherent homogeneity to a definite, coherent heterogeneity; and during which the retained motion undergoes a parallel transformation."[1] In these few words are summed up for us a description of a process that has been going on for eons upon eons.

The evolutionist begins with the simpler phase of the evolving object. He makes no claim to be competent to deal with absolute beginnings. The substance in which life embodies itself invariably involves the colloids. The biological evolutionist starts out with protoplasmic colloids. The colloidal substances differ progressively in complexity both of structure and function. This diversification is at a minimum, not even apparent through the microscope, in some of the lowest forms. Socrates, in the *Phædo* and other of the Platonic dialogues, has given us a caricature of the notion of evolution as conceived by the early Greek philosophers. In this caricature is the view that the parts have been developed wholly independently of one another and later, by some *deus ex machina,* the aggregate of parts has been assembled in much the same way that a modern machine is assembled. From the modern evolutionary standpoint the organism develops, *as a whole,* into increasing diversity and interdependence of structure and function in its distinguishable but not separable organs. The higher, that is, the more complex, the organism, the greater the degree of interdependence in the parts. There is increasing interdependence of the parts of the living organism as life ascends the scale. We may cut a worm in two and, partly because of its annular structure, it develops into two worms. We may do the same thing to a magnetized bar of steel. Cut the bar at the indifference point and we find that we have two bars with their positives and their negatives and their indifference points. This is not true of man or, indeed, of any complex organism. We cannot cut man in two and have him develop as the

---

[1] H. Spencer, *First Principles,* Pt. II, Ch. XVII, ¶ 145.

worm and the magnetized bar. Thus, increasing differentiation of organs and their functions involves, at once, increasing coöperation and mutual dependence between the various organs, and increasing power of adaptation, by the organism, to the external conditions of its existence. The higher the organism, the greater degree of unity and interrelation between its parts and the greater plasticity of the whole.

The conception of evolution has been extended beyond the organic sphere, both below and above. Geologists hold the evidence to be indisputable that the earth is the result of evolution. No other hypothesis is adequate to explain all the observed facts. The glacial striations, order of the rock series, fossil remains, and other phenomena are best explained by the hypothesis that the earth has gone through vast evolutionary changes. Paleontology and biology reënforce one another. The remains of fossilized life in the geological strata correspond, roughly, with the biological scheme of evolution. To the astronomers also, the most plausible hypothesis to account for facts revealed by the telescope, applied mathematics, spectrum analysis, and sidereal photography is the view that the solar system is the result of evolution. The nebular hypothesis with its vortex movements in the cooling nebulæ has been supplanted by the planetesimal hypothesis. This hypothesis is only a more explicit recognition of the gathering of stellar dust around certain nuclei and their development into our present system.

Above the development of the organic life, the hypothesis of evolution is successfully applied. Consciousness itself is said to have evolved from simpler to more complex forms. Psychology explicitly builds on the conception that consciousness has evolved. Mind has evolved from simple sentience and blind reaction up to the richest, most highly organized, and culturally creative type of human mind. The evolution of mind has kept step, pace by pace, with the evolution of the nervous system from a simple ganglion up to the most complex human cerebrum. Man's own history is also an evolution. Humanity's whole cultural history, morals, language, social organization, science, art, religion, and philosophy itself, are the products of growth. It is a very interesting fact that, before the hypothesis of *biological* evolution was developed, Herder and Hegel had conceived, and at great length had attempted to carry out, the notion of an evolution of human culture, thought, social institutions, morals, which the philosophers and the scientists of the seventeenth and eighteenth centuries had been saying, with Hobbes, Locke, Rousseau, and others, were the result of invention, but are now agreed to be matters of growth. The old concepts of sudden causation, of divine creation and revelation of language, culture, and society, and of the origin of political society by deliberate human contract, were supplanted by Herder and Hegel, and the growth thought was introduced in their stead. Like Topsy in Uncle Tom's Cabin, there is a recognition that things have grown to be what they are, and that in order to understand fully what they are, and may become, we must know how they have come to be what they are. Philosophy elaborated this point of view and successfully applied it to man's whole cultural history before the biologists applied it to organic life.

Evidences for Organic Evolution

1. The fundamental similarities in the structures of skeletons and cells of all vertebrates are a witness to a certain type or degree of continuity of all vertebrates.

2. Embryology has indisputably established the fact that the embryo gives us a telescopic or epitomized recapitulation of the whole evolutionary process. The embryo of

all vertebrates recapitulates in its ontogenetic history all the stages of the phylogenetic series.

3. The existence of vestigial organs shows that they must have been at one time useful to the organic form. The most notorious instance of such an organ is the vermiform appendix, for which the biologists have struggled in vain to find a use.

4. The facts of geographical distribution of flora and fauna can be accounted for by evolution. The kinship of the flora and the fauna of Australia and Papua is taken to mean that they were once parts of one continent and that it was only afterwards that they were isolated.

5. The facts of paleontology are also a basis for this view. Huxley, for example, has given us a sketch of the stages through which the equine form has passed from Eohippus to the present horse. Huxley has reconstructed this series.

II. The Method of Evolution

The doctrine of evolution remained a philosophical speculation until the nineteenth century. Lamarck and Darwin, both of whom had a number of forerunners, were the most original in formulating theories of the *method of evolution.* The advocates of the fixed species view had challenged the biologists by asking them to say how evolution can take place.

Lamarck pointed to the facts of adaptation to environment, and to the effects of use, and argued that, just as organisms now develop new functions and thus modify their organs in response to the needs of the organism, so the process of striving and consequent modification of organs has been going on in all domains of life and the results of this process have been inherited. There has been a transmission of acquired characteristics. The giraffe got his long neck by reaching high for the succulent leaves of the trees and the tortoise got his horny back by striving to protect himself. The fish got his light ventral side as an adaptation to the upper air and his dark, mud-colored back as an adaptation to the bed of the stream. This double adaptation enables the fish to escape his enemy, for if he is nearer the surface of the water, by mounting upward he escapes his enemy because he has the color of the upper air, and if he chances to be nearer the bottom of the water, he escapes the enemy by dropping to the ground and is indistinguishable from the bed of the stream. Responsiveness to the wants or needs of the organism and inheritance of the results of successful response are thus, for Lamarck, the chief factors in evolution. There is, says Lamarck, an inherent tendency in living forms to expand and to enlarge their parts, up to a limit set by the living body.

Darwin and his fellow workers made an epoch making contribution to the subject. Darwin discovered, and supported by evidence, a reasonable method by which evolution takes place. Darwin took note of the fact that breeders selected the qualities which they wanted and they interbred those individuals that had these qualities and thus developed new species. They bred from those species that had the characteristics which they wished to perpetuate. The breeder presupposes the variations. What in nature takes the place of the breeder? This is Darwin's question. His answer is—*natural selection in the struggle for existence.* Because of the great fecundity of life, of the frequent variations that living forms undergo and because of the fact that living forms must struggle to survive, those types which develop characters that enable them to fit the environment, that is, to endure heat and cold, to conquer or escape their enemies, to get food and digest it, survive.

Mental and moral evolution are to be explained from

the same general standpoint. There are fortunate variations, in the shape of quantitatively varying mental power, memory, power of inference, and greater perceptual discrimination; all these are powerful instruments in the struggle for existence. Man's moral ideas and his religious practices are types of technic that are evolutionary in character. The group that hangs together the best wins the conflict. And moral and religious beliefs and practices are cohesive forces.

Since Darwin's day there has been much debate and investigation as to the relative importance of the various natural causes of organic transformation, such as—the true causes of variation, the degrees of variation, (whether minute or striking) the factors and methods of inheritance and transmission of organic characters, the effects of use and disuse, the respective potencies of germinal selection and selection by the environment, the powers of persistence by organic types in the face of changing environments, et cetera. But the beginner must not be misled by these debates into supposing that there is any doubt, on the part of competent biologists or psychologists, as to the truth of the general theory of evolution. In the sciences of life it has completely displaced the doctrine of a sudden and miraculous creation.

The Darwinian doctrine seems powerfully to support the view that all the changes that take place in this universe are really the consequences of mechanical motions. The mechanistic or materialistic metaphysics involves the denial of any directing principles in the world process. The defenders of teleology argue that the observed adaptation of organs to one another and of organisms as a whole to the environment could be explained only upon the assumption of a world-designer. Naturalistic selection explains these adaptations on mechanistic assumptions. Given original variations, all the rest follows. This is the point of view of natural selection. Given reproducing organisms, varying as they do because of the unstable character of the compounds of C. H, O, N, P, and S, the environment will do the rest. This selection hypothesis affords a very plausible explanation of the wastes, the failures, and the monstrosities of organic nature. The great optician Helmholtz once declared that if his laboratory mechanic should bring him an instrument so imperfectly constructed as the human eye, he would discharge him. Instances of lack of good adjustment, the cruel and wasteful processes of nature, the sufferings, the injustices and the stupidities of life, in which not even the righteous man seems to triumph, are explicable on this hypothesis. Yes, Bismarck, if the materialistic hypothesis is true, God is on the side of the strongest battalions and ultimately might makes right, and the good which Plato placed at the apex of the universe has been made to give place to ruthless might! God is, then, but a misleading name for the blind pushes and pulls of physical forces.

The advocate of teleology replies to these arguments as follows:

The mechanical theory does not account for the original organization of the universe, for the origin of life or the origin of consciousness and reason. The theory of evolution itself involves a kind of teleology which is more than the rubrics of mechanism take note of. We are here, and we are purposive beings with some capacity for the recreation of the natural environment. We are parts of nature —we are the products of nature. Thus the evolutionary process has produced beings that in part can control it. The human mind creates new conditions of existence. All our cultural ideals and all the institutions of society have been postulated, espoused, and made real by human teleological activity. These transcend the considerations of a merely mechanical struggle for existence.

Humanity has established a whole spiritual complex or set of conditions in the creation, out of the materials of nature, of civilization, and culture. In civilization "nurture" or education remakes "nature" or biological inheritance. This is the creation of a new environment. How different is this conception from the postulation of Herbert Spencer, for whom the moral complex is a matter of increasing the mere length and breadth of life, and of the passive adjustment of the organism's internal relations to the external relations in the physical environment? Not the prolongation of life only, not the mere uncontrolled outgo of our prime instincts, but the creation of a new Jerusalem in the way of cultural ideals seems to be the highest characteristics of a civilized human life.

The teleologist insists that the mechanist is incompetent to account for the origin of life, of consciousness, and of the spiritual set of conditions that the race has created and elaborated.

III. The Mechanical and the Teleological Aspects of Evolution

Our survey of the doctrine of evolution has convinced us that the old "watchmaker" theory of creation is dead and buried, so far as contemporary science is concerned. The question that now confronts us is this: is there any place, in the light of evolutionary theory, for a *finalistic, purposive,* or *teleological* interpretation of the world process? If this question must be answered in the negative, then materialism is the only rational philosophy and the critical and constructive arguments of the previous chapters have been in vain. There are three logically possible positions on the problem: (1) materialism or mechanism satisfactorily interprets the whole nature of the world process; (2) mechanism satisfactorily accounts for much, perhaps the greater part of the phenomena of nature, but at certain specific points it fails and we must have recourse to a purposive principle; (3) from the standpoint of philosophy, which is that of *totality,* that is of *an integral and all-inclusive view of things,* mechanism is a valid scientific program to be applied as far as possible in every field, but a mechanistic world view is quite inadequate to an all-sided interpretation of the world process.

Before we consider this problem it is necessary that we be as clear as possible as to what the mechanistic standpoint means. There is much confusion in present day discussions on this topic. Here, then, are several different points of view: (1) A mechanistic metaphysics is identical with materialism. Everything which exists and every change which takes place is the purely mechanical resultant of the movements of mass particles in space. (2) In scientific investigation, including biology, the mechanistic view is a canon or method of inquiry, a working hypothesis. As such it means (a) that the purpose of science is to determine the particular "go" or "how" of every thing or occurrence which it investigates; (b) all science is deterministic, therefore science cannot admit indeterminism in vital phenomena, since to do so would mean to admit that causes or conditions identical in character could have effects varying and hence unpredictable in character, which admission would bring scientific inquiry to a dead stop; (c) the aim of science is measurement or quantitative statement of its descriptive generalizations; to admit an indeterminable factor is to admit a nonquantitative factor.

Most biologists seem to take the mechanistic standpoint, and assuredly they are justified in using it as a working method as far as it will go. Pushed to the limit it means that there is a determinable and therefore unvarying one-to-one correspondence between every specific physico-chemical complex or configuration of molecules which is an organism and the sum of the manifestations of vitality by that organism. On the other hand, the *vitalists* (and their number includes some distinguished names in present biology, such as Prof. Hans Driesch, Prof. J. A. Thomson, J. S. Haldane, Pawlow, Prof. William Patten), maintain that the experimental facts cannot be accounted for, unless we suppose a nonmechanical agent, a *vital principle*, an organic individuality functioning in the organism; that the regulation of the life of the organism, repair of injured parts, reproduction and other vital phenomena, all presuppose a directive, nonmechanical agency. We have no concern with this quarrel among biologists except in so far as it bears on our more general problem. Mechanical explanation should be pushed as far as possible, for the aim of science is to determine, with the greatest possible degree of precision, the specific conditions under which things have taken place in nature. This is just what causal determination means, and even though it should turn out to be true that there is a one-to-one correspondence between physico-chemical and vital phenomena, including conscious ideas and purposes, this would not involve materialism, unless it could be shown that the physico-chemical series is the solely *real* series and the vital and conscious series merely *epiphenomenal*, that is, a useless phosphorescence thrown up here and there by mechanical motions. Such a possibility is very remote.

We might attempt to disprove the assumption of mechanistic metaphysics, as Prof. Hans Driesch [2] has done, by arguing that specific vital phenomena cannot be explained without recourse to a vital principle (which he calls an *entelechy* or *psychoid*); or we might proceed, in what seems to me a more effective fashion, to do as Bergson does when he adduces the parallel development of the eye of

---

[2] *The Science and Philosophy of the Organism*, Vols. I and II. See also his *Vitalismus als Geschichte und als Lehre.*

the Pecten and of the vertebrates, an identical organ fashioned by different means along divergent lines of evolution.[3] We might, with Bergson, point to the complicated and manifold correlation between organs and parts, to the fact that minute variations must persist and increase before they are useful in the struggle for existence, that adaptation of organisms to the conditions of existence takes place and increases along certain definite lines (orthogenesis), that there are useless variations (ornamentation and the æsthetic sense which are correlated), that instincts seem to be remarkable cases of unconscious purposiveness, and that, finally, it is only through supposing that organisms by integral effort, that is, by effort involving the organism as a whole, develop greater organization with more successful adaptation.[4] These are all important considerations.

As students of philosophy we should, however, look at the matter in a larger light. The subject we are considering is, like all basic philosophical problems, one of great difficulty and immense sweep. I prefer, therefore, in view of the introductory and fundamental character of this course of lectures, merely to call your attention summarily to the general principles involved, so that you may have points of view for further enquiry.

A mechanistic metaphysics of evolution falls short for the following reasons: (1) The theory of evolution is a general description of a universal historical process or temporal sequence which includes a multitude of diverse features. It assumes that the same kinds of forces that are now observed to operate have always operated in the world. Now *purposive activities* do operate and achieve things in our world. Humanly, a purpose means the conscious striving for an *end* or *value*, and the effectuation of a purpose

---

[3] H. Bergson, *Creative Evolution*, Chapter I.

[4] Bergson's *Creative Evolution* seems to me decidedly the most important recent work on the philosophy of evolution.

signifies putting in train the *means* or *mechanism* that will achieve the end. Human finalistic or teleological activity is activity directed either towards the attainment of new *values* (satisfaction of appetites, wealth, power, knowledge, justice, happiness, harmony, beauty) or the maintenance of values already attained. Thus in human life there need be no antagonism between mechanism and end. A mechanism devised for one end may indeed defeat other ends, as when an industrial process is run so exclusively for the owner's profit as to destroy the lives of the workers or injure the consumers of the product. But, normally, a mechanism is simply the most successful set of instruments for achieving an *end* or *value*.

In the life activities of organisms many teleological functions are performed without conscious prevision; for example, instinctive activities such as flight, repulsion, gregariousness, and sex, begin by being only vaguely conscious, and after having been satisfied become more fully conscious. Examples of adaptive activities that may continue to be unconscious are respiration, circulation, digestion, and even swallowing. While, then, a purposive activity in its higher form has its inception in prevision, and the whole process of fulfillment may be accompanied by consciousness, it cannot be gainsaid that a great many adaptive, end-realizing, value-producing activities are unaccompanied by consciousness. It is a fact, which no theorizing can explain away, that purposive, value-producing and value-sustaining activities are now effective on a large scale in nature and still more in human society. This being the case, no theory which explains the present state of nature and human life as being solely the product of blind and insensate mechanical movements, the product of brute accident, has any probability in its favor. A world in which purposive functioning is so large a factor cannot be a world which is the miraculous creation of blind chance.

If one were invited to suppose that the differences between the products of a Shakespeare and those of a navvy were fully accounted for in terms merely of undirected physicochemical processes, if he were not already a blindly prejudiced adherent of materialism, such an one would smile incredulously. To ask one to accept the above mechanistic position is, however, to ask him to accept only an infinitesimal fraction of what he is asked to swallow by the materialist. For the materialist or mechanistic philosopher invites us to believe that every achievement, every natural and cultural value of life in all its indefinitely complex and varying forms, is really nothing but the blind and necessary by-product of the mechanical interactions of mass particles.

(2) The universe of experience, as we know it, displays frequent creativeness, new discoveries and inventions, new creations in art, letters, and industry, new forms of social organization, original human individualities, even new forms of plant and animal life due either to the coöperation of the breeder with nature or to nature's unconscious fecundity. This present world of novelty and creativity in beings and values is, from the evolutionary standpoint, the descendant of a past extending through illimitable ages. The evolutionary story, in whatsoever chapter we may read, whether the evolution of solar systems, of the earth, of animal life, of consciousness or of human history, is the story of descent with *modification;* in other words, of qualitative novelties, different beings, the evolution towards and of richer individualities and values, the appearance of man and civilization, the growth of society, language, art, industry, religion, science, and personality. The struggle and the push forward of the vital impetus (Bergson's *L'élan vital*) never ceases to throb. Evolution is a creative process, a cumulative movement. *So far as we can see, its issue has been the fashioning of souls, of rational, self-determining, creative selves who continue the process by giving it a new*

turn, that of conscious coöperative activity in the realization and conservation of psychical values. Such is, broadly speaking, the continuity of direction and purpose which makes the evolutionary history of the world *not an endless, chartless drifting in the cosmic weather, but an evolution.*

If mechanistic metaphysics were true, this whole process would be inexplicable. For a purely mechanical process means only the external interaction of parts juxtaposed in space, a system of interchangeable parts; whereas the evolutionary conception of the world implies an organized and organizing unity of process by which the different phases and stages of the world history constitute a living whole. In a purely mechanical process there is no place for qualitative novelty, for discrete change, that is, change with a difference. The continuous process of evolution involves novelty, change, which brings forth differences; it involves individuality or organization of various qualities into a unity and the production of new types of individuality. A purely mechanical process would be reversible, a cyclical process. *The process of evolution is irreversible.* Even the history of the solar system or the earth's geological history is the description of an irreversible series of events; much more emphatically so, the history of organisms and the history of man. The maxim, "history repeats itself," is but the superficial fraction of a truth. We are justified in contending that the whole evolutionary process, when viewed as a totality and interpreted in the light of its results in individuality, in organization, in the creation and enhancement of vital and psychic values, is teleological, end-realizing, value-producing. Indeed the notion of a purposive and organizing system, such as we find at the highest level in a mind, or better, in a social life constituted by the interrelation of like-minded but different individuals, gives us the only adequate clue to the character of a continuous whole which develops or evolves in time.

From this standpoint the mechanistic way of thinking is valid as an analytic post-mortem description of the conditions and general features of particular phases of the evolutionary order. Mechanism uncovers the skeleton, but the living and evolving universe can only be fully understood and interpreted from the inner and appreciative standpoint of purposive selfhood. Mechanism lays bare the means by which new results *have been* achieved, but the forward movement of life and the universe, by which novel results *are being* produced, mechanism is inadequate to see and interpret. Reality is life and it lives forward, carrying with it whatever part of its past is really useful for its future creation. The mechanistic and teleological views of reality are both true, but teleology is the higher, more inclusive truth.

If reality in evolution be purposive what are we to make of all the wastes, failures, sufferings and cruelties which we find in nature and human history? Well we can see that much of the pain and discomfort, the dangers and obstacles in the natural order, are stimuli which incite organisms, and especially man, to a greater activity. A high civilization has never developed either in a tropical paradise or near the poles. The imminence of pain, want, and suffering, incite man to effort that, under proper social conditions, is joyful and successful. He makes discoveries and applications, organizes society, develops science, education, and for the enjoyment of his leisure, arts and letters. Yet there seems to be much undeserved and useless suffering. Because of the social solidarity of human beings, the innocent suffer for the guilty, the wise man for the fool, the saint for the sinner. Social redemption or improvement is a social process. Society is lifted up by its best and wisest who strive and often seem to suffer most. There is social progress through the enrichment of man's cultural heritage. So far as concerns the individual or the group, however, ethical justice would demand some sort of compensation for suffering and loss. Admitting that the imperfection of adjustment and the large-scale character of the process account for much of the failure, suffering, and apparent waste, as necessary incidents in a purposive, living and growing universe, it remains true that we cannot, in the light of our present knowledge, see the rationality or justice of all the defects of nature, taints of blood, of all the natural catastrophes and diseases and sufferings which nature visits on man and its other children. We are touching here on a large and difficult problem, one whose full discussion belongs to systematic metaphysics and the philosophy of religion, and I can but hint at the issues and principles involved.

It is not necessary to suppose that man, in his present stage, is the goal of evolution. Human life here can hardly be other than a transitional phase (though of value in itself) in the development of the supreme purpose and meaning of things. It is not necessary for us to be able to conceive the final goal in order to have the right to believe that the highest ends and values that we can conceive and follow are essential elements in the fulfillment of the universal meaning.

The wastes, sufferings, failures, and evils of the world process have suggested to philosophers, from Plato down to Bergson, that there is in the universe as a whole an obstacle not of its own creation or choosing, against which the supreme purpose or universal will to life and good must struggle. In Plato, Aristotle, and Bergson, this obstacle is a blind, unintelligent matter. In various religious systems it is the cosmical devil or principle of evil. In Hebrew and Christian theism, while the problem is not solved, the view held is that part of the evil in the world is due to man's capacity to sin, which capacity is involved in his freedom to develop into a self-determining being.

The possibility of moral evil is thus inherent in man's vocation to moral and spiritual self-education. The evils of nature are regarded as part of God's providential order, which incite man to activity and which, moreover, have no power to injure man's immortal spirit. The further discussion of these theories belongs to the philosophy of religion and systematic metaphysics and cannot be undertaken here.

References

Aristotelian Society Proceedings, 1917-18; "Symposium; Are Physical, Biological and Psychological Categories Irreducible?"

* BERGSON, HENRI, *Creative Evolution.*

DARWIN, *Origin of Species.*

* DE LAGE and GOLDSMITH, *The Theories of Evolution.*

DEWEY, JOHN, *The Influence of Darwin upon Philosophy,* Chapter I.

DRIESCH, HANS, *Science and Philosophy of the Organism.*

* *Encyclopædia Britannica* and *International Encyclopædia,* Articles on "Evolution."

* *Encyclopædia of Religion and Ethics,* Articles on "Evolution," and "Life and Death" (Biological).

HALDANE, J., *Mechanism, Life and Personality.*

* HERBERT, SYDNEY, *Principles of Evolution.*

HOBHOUSE, L. T., *Development and Purpose.*

HUXLEY, T. H., *Collected Essays.*

JENNINGS, H. S., "Doctrines Held as Vitalism," *American Naturalist,* 1913; "Heredity and Personality," *Science,* 1911.

LE DANTEC, F., *The Nature and Origin of Life.*

* LEIGHTON, J. A., *Man and the Cosmos,* Chapters XX, XXI, XXXVII and XXXVIII.

LOEB, J., *The Mechanistic Conception of Life.*

LOVEJOY, A. O., "The Meaning of Vitalism," *Science,* 1911; "The Import of Vitalism," *Science,* 1911.

MERZ, J. T., *History of European Thought in the Nineteenth Century,* Volume II, Chapter IX.

* MOORE, B., *The Origin and Nature of Life* (Home University Library).

MORGAN, L., *The Interpretation of Nature.*

OSBORN, H. F., *From the Greeks to Darwin.*
PATTEN, WM., *The Grand Strategy of Evolution.*
* PAULSEN, *Introduction to Philosophy,* Chapter II, pp. 150-232.
ROMANES, G. J., *Darwin and After Darwin,* Volume I.
SCHAFER, Inaugural Address, *Nature,* 1912.
SELLARS, R. W., *Evolutionary Naturalism.*
SEWARD, A. C., (Editor) *Darwin and Modern Science.*
THOMSON, J. ARTHUR, *The System of Animate Nature.*
* THOMSON and GEDDES, *Evolution* (Home University Library).
WARD, JAMES, *Naturalism and Agnosticism,* Volume I, Lectures 7-10.
WEISMANN, A., *The Evolution Theory* and *Essays Upon Heredity.*

CHAPTER XXIV

SINGULARISM AND PLURALISM [1]

(THE ONE AND THE MANY)

I. From Naïve Pluralism to Singularism

When we say cosmos, universe, or world, we imply that all things which exist and all events which occur are interconnected. There is a unity of some sort, and perhaps there are unities of many sorts. Yet this statement involves the recognition, not alone of the interconnection of things and events, but also of their manyness. There are many beings, there is a constant procession of events. What then is the relation of the manyness of things and the unity of the whole? What constitutes the togetherness of things? What kind or kinds of unity are there to be found? Does the universe in the last analysis consist of an aggregate or collection of discrete or discontinuous beings? Or, is the universe fundamentally a sort of block universe, all of a piece?

The Pluralist argues that the universe consists of a number of discrete beings, that is, that the universe is made up of beings which, with respect to their existence, are discrete and separate. The Singularist holds that there is only one real being. This *one* is the all-inclusive unity.

> The one remains, the many change and pass;
>
> . . . . .
>
> Life, like a dome of many-color'd glass,
> Stains the white radiance of Eternity. . . .
>
> —*Adonais,* Shelley.

---

[1] Singularism is frequently called "numerical monism"; inasmuch as "monism" has another widely employed meaning I prefer the terms singularism or unitarism.

This seems to be a very abstruse problem, and so it is. It seems, to the beginner in philosophy, very abstract and remote from life, but such is not the case. This problem bobs up everywhere when we come to think out the fundamental problems of science and social organization. Let me illustrate. The common conception of physical science is that matter is made up of indivisible units. Until recently the atoms were regarded as the ultimate units, but lately the atom has been broken up. The nature of these units is now regarded as made up of electrons, this being an improvement upon the old atomic conception. Now, whether it be the old atoms or the new electrons, in either case the assumption of the physicist is that the world is built up out of unchangeable elements. In biology also we find the same shifting from one unit to another as ultimate, but we also find here the assumption of something that is an irreducible element. When you have your unit, the question arises as to how these units are to be related. The physicist sees that a lot of entirely separate units will not constitute a cosmos, universe, or world. There must be something further which will account for the unity or interconnection of things, and it is to satisfy this fundamental motive that the physicist postulates the ether as the continuum, just as common sense postulates one continuous space-whole. The elements must have something to connect them. There must be some sort of ground for interaction. This same situation is evidenced in the life of the state. Does the state consist of entirely separate individuals? This was the old "laissez faire" doctrine, and even to us this assumption sounds good until there emerges a conflict between the individual's aim and that of the general good. We have here the same duality of unity and manyness. During the late war many a pacifist said: "I have no interest in the quarrels of Europe. I would rather be a live pacifist than a dead hero." What did we do with such a man as this? We either put him on the firing line, or in some way forced him to acknowledge the binding nature of the general good incorporated in the institutions and aims of the state. Extreme individualism leads to the total disintegration of society. Such individualism will not work. We have to learn that the state does not exist merely to feed us, to clothe us, and educate us, and in turn to ask nothing from us. The working theory of the Germans was that the state is divine, and that the individual should be completely absorbed in the state. In this Germanic theory we have an extreme application of the singularistic view of the state. The doctrine of the absolute supremacy of the state has been held by many political thinkers outside Germany. Indeed, not only political rebellions and revolutions, but the historic struggles of state and church, have turned on this question. Pluralism, on the other hand, in its emphasis on the rights of the individual, when it becomes extreme, develops into anarchism. It does not seem to have the element of togetherness which is indispensable to the formation and maintenance of the state as the necessary basis of social order.

How can we conceive rightly the relation of the particular constituents and the unity? This problem, as I am discussing it under the general title of the One and the Many, is but a generalization of the same problem in chemistry, physics, biology, ethics, philosophy of the state, and in all the other sciences. In religion our question is, what is the relation between God and man? Is God the all-inclusive being in whom literally we all live, move, and have our being? And do we exist only as parts of God? To this question Pantheism replies in the affirmative. All finite selves are only parts of the single being. Pantheism denies that we have separate or semi-independent existence. The only being that has reality is *natura naturans,* or *Active Nature,* which is God, as Spinoza puts it. This being the case, all reality is denied to *natura naturata,* or *Passive Nature.* The question emerges, are we separate, free, responsible beings? The answer of Spinoza and of all the thoroughgoing singularists or monists is "no!" Thus, the same problem appears in connection with the human will. Have we the power of self-determination? Can we in any way freely determine the courses of our actions and volitions?

Moral self-determination need not mean caprice. It means, however, that to some degree I determine my own destiny, that in some small way, I am the captain of my own ship. However, if I am to make a good voyage, there are certain conditions which I must acknowledge and obey. But moral freedom means that these given conditions are not the whole of the moral life. I am my own steersman. Necessitarianism says that man is like a pawn on a chess-board, or like a mote in the sunbeam; that his life is completely and inevitably determined by forces of which he is only the geometrical meeting point. Here again appears that fundamental contrast between the view of the Singularist and that of the Pluralist. But freedom seems to be inconsistent with absolute Singularism.

Let us consider briefly the motives which lead from Pluralism to Singularism. The naïve standpoint is pluralistic. This standpoint is natural to man. To us all the world appears as an aggregate or collection of many distinct beings. The primitive world view, as we have already seen, is through and through pluralistic. But the development of thought and the organization of society involve an increasing recognition of order and law in both natural and social phenomena. The growth of organization or order in social life tends always to be reflected in our interpretation of physical nature.[2] At first natural phenomena appeared to be capricious and wholly independent of any principle of organization. But as social and technical control increased, man began to find law and order in nature. It is at this point, where man has become conscious of the existence of some unifying principle in nature, that we find the early Greek philosophers. These men are singularists. Thales and the others felt that all finite forms of existence were modifications of the one all-inclusive substance. The wonderful suggestiveness of the Greek movement resides in the great diversity of types of unity which they suggested. They all agree in the assertion of the existence of unity.

Religion has also moved from Pluralism to Singularism. In its earliest stages it is generally a chaotic polytheism, and moves on until it becomes monotheistic. The highest form of monotheism is given us in such prophets as Isaiah. Such expressions as the following evidence this: "I am Jehovah; I form the light and make darkness; I make peace and create evil; there is none other beside me." Isaiah is in agreement with the early Greek philosophers. There is only one ultimate being.

Let us consider certain aspects in which the universe is one. Take, for instance, the perceptual order. In this order, space is an absolute continuum. It is impossible for us to imagine that there is no space between any two solar systems, or between any two electrons. We cannot think that space is bounded. There are no utmost limits to space. Neither can we conceive space to be so divided that there is no space between the parts. Mathematics has at last succeeded in defining linear and other continua in such a way as to make perfectly clear the meaning of our

---

[2] The great French movement in social psychology of the last generation, carried on by such men as Lévy-Brühl, Ribot, Dürkheim and others, has made its contribution at this very point.

inability so to conceive space. And, in the modern mathematical conception of the nature of the infinite, we have traveled a long way from the notions which regarded the infinite as the merely unlimited and also have traveled far from the Hamiltonian conception of the infinite as the mere negation of the finite. Space is not the only continuum. Time also appears to be a continuum. We cannot think of two successive events between which there is not time. It is quite true that experiential time comes for us, as James puts it, in drops, but the reason for this is the rhythmic character of our attention. Time does not so appear to us when we *think* time. We can only think time as continuous. In addition to space and time, we find a causal principle of unity. The causal postulate means that if the same kinds of antecedents occur, the same kinds of consequents or effects will follow. Causation appears to be a form of unity or order which is as fundamental as either space or time. We hold that there is a connection between the moving of the string on yonder window curtain and the planet Mars. We are told by the physicist that the fall of the minutest particle causes a tremor throughout the solar system. Tennyson has this form of unity in mind when he says:

> Flower in the crannied wall,
> I pluck you out of the crannies,
> Hold you here, root and all, in my hand.
> Little flower—but if I could understand
> What you are, root and all, and all in all,
> I should know what God and man is.

So the motives making for singularism are strong in all directions—in science, art, politics, and religion. The Singularist position has appealed to the speculative poets. Indeed, this attitude is an expression of the deepest motives of philosophical reflection. Philosophy is just this deep passion for the vision of the whole. The philosopher is convinced that this world of ours is not a junkshop world or a rummage sale universe. In some way or other this universe is really one orderly whole. Tennyson expresses this unity of the universe in his poem, *The Higher Pantheism:*

The Sun, the Moon, the Stars, the Sea, the Hills and the Plains—
Are not these, O Soul, the vision of Him who reigns?
Is not the Vision He? Tho' He be not that which He seems?
Dreams are true while they last, and do we not live in dreams?
Earth, these solid stars, this weight of body and limb,
Are they not sign and symbol of thy division from Him?

Glory about thee, without thee; and thou fulfillest thy doom,
Making Him broken gleams, and a stifled splendor and gloom.
Speak to Him thou for He hears, and Spirit with Spirit can meet—
Closer is He than breathing, and nearer than hands and feet.

Wordsworth in his *Lines composed a few miles above Tintern Abbey* thus voices his sense of a Universal Presence:

· And I have felt
A presence that disturbs me with the joy
Of elevated thoughts: a sense sublime
Of something far more deeply interfused,
Whose dwelling is the light of setting suns
And the round ocean and the living air,
And the blue sky, and in the mind of man,
A motion and a spirit, that impels
All thinking things, all objects of all thoughts,
And rolls through all things.

The doctrine of the universal soul or self, which includes and sustains all things finite and mortal as the being of their beings and life of their lives; the absolute and eternal spirit who is the undying and unchanging reality behind the illusory appearances of the many finite selves, is the most characteristic teaching of the Ancient Hindu religio-philosophical literature—the Upanishads. This doctrine, one of the classical forms of absolute singularism or numerical monism, is beautifully expressed in Emerson's little poem, *Brahma*:

> If the red slayer thinks he slays,
>   Or if the slain think he is slain,
> They know not well the subtle ways
>   I keep, and pass, and turn again.
>
> Far or forgot to me is near;
>   Shadow and sunlight are the same;
> The vanish'd gods to me appear;
>   And one to me are shame and fame.
>
> They reckon ill who leave me out;
>   When me they fly, I am the wings;
> I am the doubter and the doubt,
>   And I the hymn the Brahman sings.

The reader who will ponder well this little gem will find that it contains the gist of many pages of philosophical argumentation and explication. Spinoza's ethics is an elaboration of the same motif; Hegel's whole system is a subtle and labored endeavor to apply and deepen the meaning of the same fundamental intuition which consists in "seeing all things in God" (the latter expression is from Malebranche, a disciple of Descartes); Bradley and Royce essay, with somewhat different emphasis, the task of establishing the truth of the same insight in the light of modern logic and psychology.

What chiefly distinguishes our modern European philosopher-pantheists from their congeners of ancient India is the constant endeavor of the Europeans to find place and significance and value in the Eternal One for the various degrees of psychical and spiritual individuality and for the labors, sufferings and achievements of the historical life of humanity. Among them Hegel has made the bravest attempt of all; and Royce, with his reiterated emphasis on the volitional and purposive character of reality and his stressing of the significance, in and for the Eternal Individual, of the strivings, deeds, and emotions of the human self and the social order, finally developed, in his doctrine of God as the spirit of the beloved community, a standpoint which nearly succeeds in reconciling the belief in man's distinct individuality and freedom with eternalistic singularism. The course of modern speculation on this theme suggests the question whether the eternalistic singularists have not attempted an impossible task. Does not the initial assumption, that the temporal order, the entire realm of change, evolution, culture history, and individual development, is mere appearance of a timeless order, condemn philosophy and the reflective life to a denial of the meaningful reality of experience and human life and send philosophy on a flight into the inane from which, logically, it has no way of return and no means of finding a positive valuation for human life and experience?

There are two types of philosophical Singularism. First, is the Singularism of substance, Spinoza's doctrine. This is the view that there is one all-inclusive being, the absolute or one substance. True human freedom depends on our recognizing the illusory nature of our ordinary beliefs as to the separate or independent existence of finite being. True insight consists in understanding that we are nothing apart from God. Our true being consists in our membership in him. We are in the One. Substance is that which exists in itself and by itself, and the philosopher is the one who sees all things under the form of eternity. And in so far as we achieve genuine freedom, we live under the vision of things, *sub specie æternitatis*, "under the form of eternity." Bondage and error is the lot of all who are outside of this vision. We are all parts of the one substance, but these parts are not, however, of the same glory. There are degrees of reality in finite beings. The second, or Hegelian doctrine, is that the absolute is the one all-inclusive *spirit or individual.*

II. The Spinozistic Conception of the Absolute

The true or adequate view of reality, for Spinoza, consists in seeing all that is finite and temporal as the necessary expression of the infinite and eternal. This view Spinoza calls intuitive knowledge. The essence of every finite being is the striving to express its own being, but the true being of man consists in seeing himself as part of the One. In this way all finite evil and good vanish. Evil and good are functions of our failure to consider things *sub specie æternitatis.* Immortality is not a duration of our lives through endless time; the living in it is the vision of all things as seen in the light of eternal truth—of the Absolute. Passions and emotions belong to us as finite, but the idea of God enables us to detect and distinguish the higher from the lower elements in them. By this vision the negative elements of our experience are eliminated and this elimination is necessary for the bringing about of true and adequate ideas. True freedom consists *intellectually* in seeing ourselves and all things as necessary elements in the perfection of God. True freedom consists *emotionally* in what Spinoza calls *amor intellectualis dei.* This intellectual love of God is part of the infinite love wherewith God loves himself. (*Ethics* V, 36.) The finite, human self, with all its positive individuality disappears in an abstraction, and in this way Spinoza reproduces the principle of asceticism while rejecting it. So far as our life is penetrated and controlled by this insight of seeing all things in God, we have actually become God. It is only by means of this insight that man can actually partake in God's liberty. In so far as man is finite, he cannot achieve the liberty of God. In so far as man is finite, he is wholly determined by antecedents, and in so far as man is raised to the infinite, his individuality seems to vanish. All finite things as finite, are modes or modifications of this one infinite substance. Finite being is like a ripple on the surface of the ocean of being. This analogy, however, is defective for the reason that the finite self can become a conscious part of God.

How does Spinoza reach this conception of the One, the absolute substance, God? He starts out as a rationalistic mystic in a way that reminds us of the Stoic and of the Neoplatonist. He really sets out from an intuition. A pantheist is one who identifies God and the world. Now there are two types of pantheists. Spinoza is not a crude pantheist, that is, he does not regard God as the soul of the world. God is for Spinoza, not the soul of the world, but the only being that really is. God is the all-in-all, the all-one. Everything depends upon him and is determined necessarily so to follow from the divine nature. Things as such have no existence. The world of finite selves and other beings, for Spinoza, has no existence on its own account. It is only a manifestation of God seen from a finite point of view. God is *the only reality.* God is the *one substance.* Spinoza may well be called an acosmist or an acosmic pantheist, in that he denies to the world any independent reality except as a manifestation of God to the finite. It is no wonder that Novalis referred to him as the God-intoxicated man.

In contrast with his view, pancosmic pantheism regards God as nothing more than the all-pervading spirit of nature. For Spinoza, nature is taken up into God; for pancosmism, God is absorbed in nature.

In his method Spinoza is deductive and geometrical. He starts out, not with concrete fact, but with his *a priori* definition of substance. The definition which he gives of substance is somewhat as follows: "That which exists in itself and is conceived through itself; that is, which, in order to be conceived, does not need a prior conception of anything else." In other words, for Spinoza, substance is the self-existent being, and in this way the universe is truly one. There is nothing outside of God to either hinder or influence him. The human mind is a mode of the mind of God and the human body is a modification of his attribute of extension. All things exist in, and all events follow from, the divine nature by a necessity which is the same as the necessity which gives rise to the theorems of geometry. God is the universal, mathematical ground of all things. Nothing exists without him. All depends on and follows from his nature. Man is not free, save as he rises to this insight that he is a true part of the infinite substance. God is the necessary or absolute all-inclusive timeless cause and there is no cause aside from his perfect nature. God is the real being of nature—*natura naturans*—he is the active nature. God is the ceaselessly active ground of all events in the world; he is *not* a cosmical soul in the world—the world is in him. He alone is the eternal cause of the whole procession of nature.

God expresses himself to us in two parallel ways; to wit, thought and extension. Of thought we say that it is both intellect and will, but we must not attribute these to God as we do to ourselves. Our intellect is dependent on sensory stimuli for the materials of thought; our intellect works episodically and inaccurately, but God grasps all things in one timeless pulse of thought.

One conception made famous by Spinoza's extreme formulation of it is the meaning of definition. *Omnis determinatio est negatio,* that is, all definition is limitation or negation. To define anything is to deny the contradictory of the qualities involved in the definition and thus to limit the object defined. God is above all definition, and in this Spinoza agrees with the Neoplatonists and with the speculative mystics of the type of Bruno and Meister Eckhart. No positive statements can be made as to the nature of God or the One. Logically one can only say that He is not-finite, not-in-space, not-in-time, et cetera.

Spinoza really has two inconsistent views of the nature of substance. In the first place, substance is conceived as an indeterminate absolute without any definite nature, and secondly, he means by the absolute the totality of things regarded as a unity. Spinoza does not attempt to prove that there is only one substance. This is for him a rational intuition, the self-existent totality of being. All that is, is. But has he the right to further assume that all that is, is a single being or unity? It is [3] true that Spinoza attempts to deduce the many from the one; but the nature of the latter is assumed to be self-evident and, therefore, the doctrine that the many are but transitory and broken glimpses of the eternal and self-complete One is taken to be equally self-evident.

III. The Hegelian Conception of the Absolute

At bottom Hegel's point of view is that the Absolute is the all-inclusive unity of the Cosmical Spirit or Mind, and it is this point of view which he has so elaborately worked out as to make him the father of a distinctive school. His position is called *absolute idealism.* For Hegel the absolute or the all-inclusive unity is mind, spirit, *Geist.* For Bradley, the absolute is experience. For Royce, it is an absolute self or individual, the eternal knower and fulfiller of all finite purposes and meanings.

Hegel starts from the position that nothing can be real apart from consciousness or experience. We know nothing about anything apart from experience. Reality is

[3] I am indebted to E. Caird's article on Cartesianism in the *Encyclopædia Britannica,* 11th ed.

that which is present in experience. At this point Hegel shows, by his famous dialectic or argumentation, that all finite being is related or dependent. We cannot say anything about anything except by reference to something other than what we talk of. Thought is a process of othering.[4] Likeness, for instance, has no meaning apart from difference. Even a single object such as an orange is a relational whole of different or opposed qualities—for round is not sweet, yellow is not round, and juicy is not yellow, and so on. Cause and effect have no meaning apart from one another. Change and permanence, essence and accident, substance and attribute, force and its expression, imply one another. So too in the vital and human world. Life and death go together, humility and pride, the individual and the family, the family and the larger community of city and state, go together. The individual lives in and through the species, the species lives in and through the whole of living existence. Life and its physical environment imply one another. Inorganic and organic, mind and body, self and society, finite and infinite, God and the world, are interrelated in the whole, *which is an organic system.* Everything finite is related to something other than itself, and it is the unity of its opposite qualities. Anything can be the "same," that is, be itself only by reference to an "other," that is, not-itself. We can think of nothing that does not imply relations.

Kant had tried to solve this problem by saying that we know only appearances or phenomena. In our knowledge there are two factors—forms and sensations. Forms are the organizing or relating activities of the mind; sensations are the unorganized content which come to us from we know not where, and it is because of this dualism between the forms of thought and sensation that knowledge

[4] Bradley, Royce, and the Pragmatists share this view of thought.

for Kant is transcendentally ideal, while it is valid only empirically. We can have no knowledge of things-in-themselves.

Hegel's view is that a thing is what it appears to be. He holds that the Kantian distinction of phenomena and noumena is illogical. For Hegel everything is related. Reality for him is the systematic whole of interrelated qualities. It is not something remote or beyond our world. God is not something behind the stars. He is what he appears as being. Of Herbert Spencer's conception of God as infinite and eternal energy, Hegel would doubtless say, he does not go far enough. God is all that Spencer says, but he is also much more. God is thought and will organizing a spiritual world, as well as energy and life. Reality is to be interpreted in terms of experience. The completest manifestation of God is to be had in human life. This unity must also exist for itself, *für sich,* that is, it must be conscious, it must be spirit. Things are related. They constitute a unity, and they exist only for a self. Our experience is only a fragment. Our selfhood is finite. God is the absolute mind for whom the whole organized system of things exists.

The process of the world is the ever increasing manifestation and realization of absolute mind. In no finite mind does the thought of unity constitute the unity of the world, since the unity of the world is present to no finite mind. Therefore God is the absolute thought or mind, the absolute individual, and the measure of reality is individuality. The more any being is an organized totality, a coherent system of internal relations, the more individuality and reality it has. God is the absolute totality of relations.

The real is a living process, purposive and rational, an organized rational unity or spiritual system which is the absolute mind—God—in nature and in humanity, but realizing himself most fully in the spiritual life of the highest civilized humanity, through the forms of social organization, art, religion, and philosophy, in which God comes to the fullest consciousness of himself that is possible through finite beings. Thus reality is a spiritual process that ceaselessly realizes itself in the successive steps from unconscious nature to the most fully organized rational mind as achieved in civilized society—in civic community, the state, the work of art, the church, and, at the very summit, in philosophy's understanding of the whole process as the self-revelation and self-fulfillment of absolute mind. The Absolute is a spiritual system, a whole of interrelated, living, thinking, willing beings which exist as a whole in and for God—the unitary spirit of the whole. God is a spirit living in his own concrete differences, men and things. Mind is the true whole, but not any finite individual mind or system of minds, since these never constitute a perfect, self-sustaining, self-existing unity. The absolute mind—God—of which all finite minds and societies are parts, is the ultimate and true reality. All stages and forms of organization and all the works of culture—all organized social life, all art forms, all religion, and all science, are stages in the increasing apprehension and comprehension by the finite mind of the absolute mind, in and through which progressive apprehensions and comprehensions the absolute individual or cosmic mind comes to fuller self-expression in the temporal order. Of the whole unceasing process by which "the thoughts of men are widened with the process of the suns," God is the eternal ground.

The following are the chief points of contrast between the various leading forms of recent singularistic idealism or spiritualism. Whereas Spinoza's absolute substance is statically conceived and only by a pretty thoroughgoing inconsistency can be admitted to include individuality and purposiveness, Hegel's Absolute is conceived to be a dynamic and purposive totality of process, in which the various degrees of finite organization or systematic and rational wholeness embody the absolute precisely in the respective degrees to which they are organized wholes. Inorganic and organic nature, the minds of individuals, the objective mind, embodied in the organized social institutions of family, civil society and the political state, and absolute mind, which comes to more adequate conscious self-realization in the products of human art and in religious ideas and acts and which finally attains full consciousness of itself in philosophy—all these factors of the actual world are, in the order given, stages of increasing meaning and content in the ceaseless self-realization and self-incarnation of the absolute spirit or individual.[5]

Bradley explicitly denies that the absolute can be a self. It is an utterly harmonious experience and, therefore, it must be beyond the distinctions of self and other. It can have no objects beyond itself to know, no objectives for its will and hence no will or purpose. It includes truth, goodness, and beauty, but, in its ineffable perfection and harmony, it is beyond our human notions of goodness and truth, since for us these terms have meaning only through contrast with their opposites. What an experience can mean which no self owns or enjoys Bradley fails to explain.

Royce explicitly holds the absolute to be the self of selves and the eternal fulfillment of all purposes and meanings.

W. E. Hocking has developed a view somewhat like Royce's.

---

5 My own interpretation of Hegel is that he conceived God to be the *superpersonal* ground of the community of selves.

IV. Further Implications of Singularism

The singularist argues that there is an analogy between the relation of the various subsystems of ideas in a human mind to that mind as a whole, and the relation of all finite minds as constituting the system of the absolute mind to the absolute, that is, the human mind is the organization of a given body of subsystems of ideas, while the absolute mind is the organization of all the minds as such. From one point of view reality may be conceived of as only the one all-inclusive mind. The world is an absolute in which there are already cures for every disease and the solution of all problems.

The analogy between the structure of mind in man and in the Absolute has been carefully worked out by Bosanquet.

Spinoza at times appears to regard the notion of reality as this static unity, but yet he has to find a place for change and all the mutations of the temporal in his absolute. This problem is a difficult one for any person who takes such a point of view, and it is interesting to see how Spinoza meets the problem. In the first twenty-seven propositions of his *Ethics,* he discusses this bare abstract unity, and he then makes the suggestion that we now talk as the common man does and thus he begins to talk of finite things. This is the arbitrary way in which he, and not he alone, makes the transition from the infinite to the finite, from the eternal to the temporal. It is very difficult for one both to eat his cake and keep it. So it is difficult to keep this abstract unity, and also to conserve change. To recognize that there is any meaning or any significance in this world of time and change, is to put a severe strain upon the timeless unity. Our lives and those of others are involved in time. Life is a process of getting up, getting dressed, getting to work, getting something to eat, getting to sleep—in short, it is one thing after another.

But the absolute is an all-inclusive, unchanging principle. But what is the relation of these two to each other?

In Hegel's system the chief weight falls upon the evolutionary or process conception of reality. The universe is a dynamic and developing order. Hegel sometimes speaks as if God, or the absolute idea, were the subject of development, as if the dialectic evolution of the universe were the evolution of God himself. And, in one sense, this must be so in such a system. By far the greater part of Hegel's work consisted in tracing the stages in the evolution of reality. On the other hand, Hegel seems to hold that the entire process of cosmical evolution is the logical or necessary unfolding of an eternal order. From the latter point of view, all change and development must be internal to the absolute idea. Change takes place in it; it does not change, as such, but it eternally fulfills itself through change. All the biographies of individuals and all the histories of living forms and of worlds are necessary expressions of the timeless order of the whole. (*Cf.* Ch. XXVIII.) Thus the whole content of the temporal world is the ceaseless process of self-manifestation on the part of the timeless absolute. How a timeless order can realize itself in time, without either ceasing to be timeless or depriving the changes and acts of the realm of time of any real meaning, neither Hegel nor any of his disciples has ever made clear. Certainly an energizing life or will, or even a total experience, which neither experiences nor initiates change seems an unmeaning conception. A timeless consciousness or self is a senseless monster. If there be a single life or will that pulsates through the whole universe it must do deeds and suffer changes in time.

Royce is emphatic in his insistence on the significance of the temporal. He calls his position absolute pragmatism. God is the complete fulfillment of all the meanings of our ideas. Ideas are plans of action. They are not reports of the structure of things. Ideas are not cognitive functions so much as practical guides. An idea has always an aim, it is purposive, it is something which requires its own fulfillment. The absolute is the final fulfillment of all our ideas. The absolute is the inclusive will or purpose. For the absolute monistic idealist, our temporal experiences are elements *in* an unchanging whole, and our errors, sins, and failures, are transmuted into the perfection of the absolute. All of our sufferings and imperfections contribute to the harmoniousness of the whole. The whole is a perfectly harmonious and blissful unity. In the whole the good is eternally achieved.

Let us say a few words of the moral and religious implications of this theory. These implications are optimistic, deterministic, quietistic, and mystical. Singularism is essentially deterministic. The only freedom for the individual consists simply in a clear-sighted recognition by the individual of the fact that he, like all else, is a necessary element in this perfect whole and that his whole function is submission to this absolute. Job expressed this attitude when he said: "Though he slay me, yet will I trust in him." Every deed, every fate of each finite being, is as it should be and it could not be otherwise. The lout, the imbecile, the fool, the debauchee, the saint, yes, and even the wise man—all have their lives as determined elements in the absolute whole. The only freedom is the willing recognition of the dependence of all things as parts of the absolute. The second attitude or rather, implication, of this viewpoint is that all is well with the world, God is on his throne, let no man worry. This is the optimistic implication of Singularism.

> God's in His Heaven,
> All's right with the world.

In connection with this implication we have the fact that the goal of absolutism is, from the religious point of view, quietistic in much the same way as is that of Neoplatonism. With singularism of all forms there goes a certain type of mysticism. There is the *unio mystica,* an experience in which we feel the consummation of our being and this consummation expresses itself emotionally in what Spinoza called the intellectual love of God. The ultimate good to the wise is the insight that all finite beings have their true measure of being in the infinite. This quietistic attitude received its classical formulation in the Leibnitzian hypothesis—in the statement that this world is the best of all possible worlds. For the most adequate caricature of this position read Voltaire's *Candide.*

V. Criticism of Singularism

1. Some singularists, for example, Calkins and Royce, speak of the absolute as a self, as a person. Miss Calkins calls the doctrine of Royce and herself, "monistic personal idealism." She interprets Hegel as holding the same doctrine. The Singularist talks about the thought and will of the absolute. Our conception of a self is always of a being who is a self *in relation* to other selves. Genetic psychology affords us abundant ground for this. The materials out of which the notion of selfhood is formed are the original data of our personalities, yet selfhood develops only in social relations. If there is no other being distinct from the absolute, then how can the absolute be a self? Fichte expresses this social dialectic in these words: *kein Mensch ohne Menschen* ("No man without men"). Bradley says that the absolute is an absolute experience. Hegel calls it *Geist, spirit,* or *absolute idea,* and in this I believe they were more consistent than Royce. We have no justifica-

tion for calling the absolute a self, unless it lives in social interaction with other selves. In Royce's later view the absolute is the spirit of the perfected society—the *beloved community.*

As to the Bradleyan conception, I can here only say that I know nothing of experience unless it be experience by a self. Experience, that is, absolute experience in the Bradleyan sense, is a mere psychological abstraction. These men also say that the absolute is timelessly perfect, and that as a unity it is beyond both time and change. How can there be purpose in such a unity? Purpose is an aim, a goal, that is postulated, and if there is really no change and no time, then there is no such thing as cosmical purpose. Bradley agrees with this and says that, from the point of view of a timeless absolute, there is no place for development, no progress or evolution in *the sum of things;* these are mere illusions. For the absolute there is *no change.* The absolute may contain histories without number, but it can have no history. Therefore all the changes and histories which are included in the absolute must, in sum, cancel one another as factors in the harmonious equipoise of the timelessly perfect experience.

2. I think that I exist as a fragment, as a unique being, and I think of you as existing likewise. You feel things and no one else feels your feelings as you feel them. Each believes himself to be an individual self. What kind of existence can you and I have from the point of view of the absolute? My existence, as I feel it, is illusory, erroneous, from the absolute's point of view. How does the absolute know me as a minute constituent in its constitution? This is surely a very different type of experience from the way in which I know myself. If the absolute is really the absolute knower, I must exist only as the absolute knows me and then I do not exist as I know myself.

This is one way of showing the inadequacy of finite knowledge. It seems to cut the very ground from under us.

3. We have already seen that there is no freedom on the part of the human self, save as an absolutely determined part of the whole. Practically, this is a useless conception. It cannot be made applicable in courts or in any of our social institutions. Indeed social practice would be impossible if this assumption were true. As a working point of view, we must assume individual freedom, and we have already found that in the long run the demand is honored by the race. Singularism, therefore, does not seem to agree with our practical consciousness of freedom and responsibility.

4. All sin, vice, suffering, and other evils, are viewed by Singularism as being contributory to the universe as a whole. Sin is sin only from the finite point of view, but, if viewed under the form of eternity, it is seen to be contributory to the perfection of the whole. All is right in this world, all is for the best, let us therefore find, in all life's ups and downs, a blissful contemplation of the absolute.

VI. Pluralism

In its extremest form, *logical atomism,* this is the doctrine that there are many separate and mutually independent beings which, taken in the aggregate, make up the world. Pluralism denies that the world is a complete unity, systematic whole, or order. In strict logic, the pluralist must deny that there is a universe at all. Our so-called universe is a *multiverse.* It is a collection, consisting of an indefinite number, or at least a very great though definite number, of entities or beings having all sorts, as well as no sorts, of relations to one another. Indeed, from the standpoint of radical pluralism, the world is only a collection for and in the mind of the collector. In itself it is more or less a heap, which the "high brow" collectors, called scientists and philosophers, are constantly trying to sort out and classify into some sort of order like a museum or a library. It serves the economy of thought to have one subject for many predicates. "World," "universe" or "cosmos" is the most economical subject of thought, but it is only a *grammatical, not a real, subject.* Since its various predicates may have no relations to one another, they do not really make up one world, and the assumption that they do is due to substituting a mere grammatical subject for the aggregate of predicates. We may say, for instance, that the "world" consists of *minds, universals, or laws, physical and logical, physical things,* et cetera. But, in reality, *the world consists of nothing.* We ought rather to say that *there are* minds, universals, physical things. Thus, the universe, as a subject of discourse and reasoning is a mere abstract term that stands for nothing real. The atomistic pluralist is a thoroughgoing nominalist, when he is consistent. He has considerable difficulty in explaining why and how men come to talk and think of a universe at all.[6]

From the pluralistic standpoint *entities* (a convenient term to cover everything which exists, including true propositions which are said to *subsist,* whereas particular things *exist*) may or may not be interdependent. There are all sorts of orders and disorders in our miscalled "uni-

---

[6] Among the great philosophers of history I have not been able to find a simon pure pluralist. Perhaps David Hume is the nearest approach to one; but even he thought that the world gave the impression of being constituted and ordered by a designing intelligence. Atomistic materialism is the most consistent form of pluralism; but even here *space,* the void in which the atoms move, is a continuum. The new realists of to-day are the most vigorous of pluralists; but even Bertrand Russell, though he calls his philosophy logical atomism, speaks of union with the UNIVERSE as being the goal of philosophy, and he finds his pluriverse or atomistic collection of minds, universals, and sense data to be the product of the blind forces of matter. This is surely a unitary conception.

verse." Some entities are in some relations, and some are in no relations, except the relation of being in no relation. There are all sorts, and grades, of connection. *Same, different, like, unlike, on, under, above, below, equal, greater, less, before, after, simultaneous, part, whole, in, outside, with, and, if, but, never, always* (the reader can continue the enumeration for himself)—these terms express familiar relations. For example, a color and a typewriter are "on" the table in different senses. The color red and the virtue of temperance seem to be in no relation. The pluralist then admits some order and some chaos.

The neorealistic pluralist of to-day holds that many of the kinds of things and relations in the world might be absent, without the natures of the others being changed thereby. In particular, mind and its relation to other entities are such that they might be taken out and put back into the world without making any difference to the natures of many other things. Imagine, on the table, a heap consisting of marbles, apples, shoes, and onions. Now add a mind perceiving the heap. The apples and onions may be removed without affecting the nature of the shoes or marbles. The mind may be removed without affecting the natures of any of them, just as its presence made no change in them. But is this true? Would not finer perception detect, perhaps, a subtle change in onion, apple, marble, and shoes, due to their compresence? Certainly the mind is affected by their compresence. May it not, in turn, affect them? *The strength of the realist's argument here seems to depend on the assumption that the mind is a mere colorless and inert knower.* Against this the objective idealist argues that mind is a name for the *active awareness* of the characters and relations of the things which make up the world. If one suppose all mind abstracted from the world one could not then say what the remainder would be like, or even what it would *not be like.* Even the heap on the table is a rudimentary kind of whole for a mind. Whenever we think through the fact that this is a world, even in the sense of being a collection of different kinds of entities, we seem compelled to admit that it has a structure or texture which is nearest of kin to the organized texture of mind. For, the better the world becomes known, the more fully it reveals itself as an intelligible system or order of related qualities and powers, and as sustaining and expressing the kind of organization which mind builds up and, in building up, realizes its own nature.

Personalistic Pluralism is one of the vigorous and influential movements in Anglo-American philosophy to-day. It is not a radical pluralism, since it almost invariably argues for the existence of God as the Supreme Person or Spirit who is the ground and goal of the lives of finite persons or spirits. Hence the whole standpoint may be called a *pluralistic theism.* The advocates of this type of pluralism who also deny the existence of material entities are called *personal idealists* or *mentalists* or *panpsychists.* The latter doctrine, of course, harks back to Leibnitz. The selves or spirits, which alone exist, are like his *monads,* except that all personal idealists to-day admit their interaction. Thus, personal idealism stands in contrast, both to a materialistic atomism or pluralism and to a dualistic pluralism. From the last standpoint there exist a plurality of entities of two kinds—material and spiritual.

Personalistic pluralists deny the singularistic contention that finite persons exist only as constituent parts of the one absolute spirit. They contend that this doctrine, by denying the very nature of a person, which is to possess a private and unsharable experience, ends by denying that the absolute can be a personality or spirit. There is nothing in our normal and sane experience which entitles us to say that one person can be literally contained in another person. Only in diseased selves do we find anything of this sort, and the partial selves of a disordered self are not true selves. Hence, the pluralistic personalist insists that monistic or singularistic personal idealism is a contradiction in terms. One self simply cannot be *part* of another self. But the pluralistic personalist insists, with equal emphasis, that it belongs to the very essence of personality to exist only in social relationships with other persons. Therefore, for him, *ultimate reality,* or reality at its highest level (and, in the case of the personal idealists, *all* reality) *consists of a society or community of selves* living incessantly in communion with one another. Accepting, in a broad sense, the reality of the temporal process of evolution, which develops in its various stages, from the lowest organisms up to man, and presumably higher, as a *creative process,* in which there appear, at critical intervals, significant new levels of organization, meaning and value; the pluralists argue that, as this process reaches higher and higher levels of achievement, it becomes at once more personal and more social. For individual personality and community are two complementary aspects of the same reality. In humanity, social development has been at once the condition and the result of increasing moralization and increasing intellectualization of life. The evolution of man, as a cultural being, has been a social evolution, in which language, the arts, and sciences, religion and philosophy have appeared, as forms of spiritual achievements and the conditions of higher achievement.

Since the selves or monads, who are the immediate creators and bearers of the whole process of spiritual evolution, develop by interaction and coöperation, and in the direction of fuller personality, the life of the community of persons implies the reality of a Perfect Self or Person, who is the Source of the whole system, the Ground of its continuous movement towards fuller personal and communal life, and the eternally realized Ideal or goal of the life of spirits.

Since the fuller the personality of a finite member of the cosmic society, the more self-determination or rational freedom and responsibility he exercises, finite selves are free to err and sin. God has not willed a world of mere mechanism, but a society of spirits who can willingly coöperate with him, can oppose him within limits, can seek and find harmonious life with him as the great Other Self, the perfect comrade. The possibility and the actuality of evil are due to the fact that finite selves develop into freedom by a life of experiment and choice. God is not limited from without. Nor does he, at some instant or stage in time, limit himself. It is his will to create *creators,* free moral agents who can grow into wisdom and conscious coöperation with Him. The evil in the world is incidental to the development of selves. The goal towards which the whole creation moves, through its striving and suffering, is a *community* of ethical and rational spirits. Selves are generated in time, but they must be immortal, since they alone are the bearers and achievers of *Values.* Values exist only in persons, therefore persons must be immortal. Thus, the plural reality of the community of persons has its ground and its goal in God. Personalistic pluralism of this type ends in theism.

This view is persuasively presented in James Ward's *The Realm of Ends.* W. R. Sorley, in his *Moral Values and the Idea of God,* presents a similar conclusion from the special angle of a study of values. A. Seth Pringle-Pattison, in his beautifully written book, *The Idea of God in the Light of Recent Philosophy,* tries to balance more evenly than Ward the respective interests of singularism and pluralism. He dissents from Ward's view that physical nature can be regarded as an assemblage of finite spirits or monads. He also criticizes the theory of Ward that there is contingency or chance in the universe and that the laws of nature can be regarded as the expression of habits or automatisms acquired by the psychical monads. Pringle-Pattison holds that there is a real material order, which is the substructure for the life of personality. Persons are not transitory expressions or modifications of the Absolute. But God is immanent in human life and in nature. God is a superpersonal reality, the absolute being who is the ground of all things. He lives by imparting Himself to men. His essence is creative and self-imparting Love. There is purposive growth in the universe, since it exists to realize the good through the fruition of personality. But God does not grow. *Incarnation* is His eternal Will, His everlasting purpose, since He is self-imparting Love; "the ultimate conception of God is not that of a preëxistent Creator but, as it is for religion, that of the eternal Redeemer of the world" (The Idea of God, p. 412). "The universe is in no sense a finished *fact;* it is an *act,* a continuous life or process which (to speak in terms of time) is perpetually being accomplished" (*Ibid.,* p. 413). Pringle-Pattison's book is a fine interpretation of Christian theistic faith. Mention should be made of the school of theistic personalism developed in America by B. P. Bowne.

G. H. Howison, in his *Limits of Evolution,* argues that ultimate reality must be a society of persons, since the recognition by one person of his own selfhood implies the like recognition of other selves. And God, the perfect Person, must exist as the Supreme Instance and Exemplar of the ideal of personality. Logically, the single ethical individual implies a society, and the society implies a perfect Individual. While He is the eternally real instance of perfect selfhood, God is not the creator; all other selves are eternal.

H. Rashdall emphasizes the impenetrability, or self-inclosedness, of all persons. Thus far, he is an out-and-out pluralist. But he argues, in Berkeleyan fashion that, since nothing exists except in and for a mind, and since the world of selves is a whole or system, God must exist as the ground of the whole system. Since selves are self-determining, and there is evil, and God cannot be the author of evil, He is finite. He limits himself in order that moral agents may enjoy individual responsibility. The absolute reality is the society or community, consisting of God and other spirits. God is the creator. If, as he holds, selves are mutually exclusive centers of consciousness, it is difficult to see how Rashdall can avoid the inference that God is just a somewhat superior personality, but not essentially different from a man.

A radically *finitistic* form of pluralism is to be found in the writings of William James (especially in his *A Pluralistic Universe*) and F. C. S. Schiller, the English pragmatist, or "humanist" as he prefers to call himself (see, especially, his *Riddles of the Sphinx,* second edition). Here we have the picture of God, not, indeed, as a being who is shut out from the human self; for James thinks that, through his subsconscious life, man is probably in immediate contact with God; but the picture of God as a finite superhuman agent working for good, and helping man in the struggle against brute accident and evil. God is hindered by some mysterious force outside Himself. He needs man's aid, as man needs His aid. We have the right to believe, that, in the long run, God and man will win out in this great moral epic, of which the scene is the universe, or, rather, the *multiverse.* Complete harmony and a real *universe* may ensue in time. Schiller thinks that, when the blissful triumph does come, time will pass into eternity. H. G. Wells, in *God the Invisible King,* argues, in similar fashion, that there are two supernatural Beings—the Veiled Being who is responsible for the universe with all its badness, and God, our great Companion and Helper, who is finite. The doctrine traces descent, through John Stuart Mill, to the Gnostics and the ancient Persian dualism. It seems to find favor with some pragmatically minded theologians, who seem anxious to make God so good a democrat that they deprive Him of all monarchical or even aristocratic qualities. To my mind, it empties religion of all meaning. *Adoration* is as essential a feature of religion as fellowship. As I understand religion, in it man seeks communion with One whom he can worship.

The argument for a finite God runs as follows:

The postulate of moral responsibility and the existence of the evil in the world, in the shape of imperfection, failure, waste, undeserved suffering, injustice, cruelty, the "whole burden and weary weight of this unintelligible world"—all these considerations, say our "finitists," are best met by the doctrine that, while there is a unifying power and will and intelligence in the world, it is a finite, superhuman spirit. In other words, God, or the highest being, is not the absolute self or all-dominating, all-inclusive unifier but the permanent president of a democracy of selves, working with his more or less unruly constituents, and amidst external hindrances, to make the world a more orderly, shipshape or harmonious place; in other words, to turn the multiverse into as much of a universe as possible. This theory escapes the problem of evil, that is, of squaring the evil in the world with the goodness and power of God, by accepting a limited God. Its moral world is —*God and Company with assets and liabilities limited.* It seems to find an empirical basis in the feeling of privacy and uniqueness which belongs to selfhood. Nevertheless, it is a logically defective position; and, moreover, fails to solve the moral difficulties which are among the chief motives for taking it up.

For: (1) If we are to accept pluralism, and thus deny

that there is a universe at all, there are no cogent grounds for interpreting our multiverse idealistically or even theistically. No doubt the man who craves companionship with, and aid from, the superordinary, may, if he chooses, believe in superior, spiritual beings, and in *one* who is the most superior of all; but, logically, in such case the hindrances and contingencies to which such a being would be subject might well, in relation to the whole mess of pluralistic reality, be but little less than those to which man, in his naked aloneness, would be subject. Therefore the aid and comfort which such a finite God would render to the soul of man would probably be slight. God and man might lean on one another during the cyclones of the cosmic weather, without either affording the other much support. What the soul of man seeks, when in distress of weather, is a port that is *absolutely a port, a sure refuge.* The only cogent and dependable form of idealism or theism is monistic or cosmical; the unity of the universe as grounded in the all-sustaining mind or will-reason. If selves are separate and independent entities, who may "go it alone," there is no good reason why things other than selves should not be equally so. Personalistic pluralism leaves us just where we were, in the naïve position that the world is only a miscellaneous collection of things. (2) The doctrine that persons are really "windowless monads," separate self-inclosed entities, does not square with the facts of social life and intercourse, nor with the psychology of the development and disassociation of selves. (3) Personalistic pluralism leaves us with an unreconciled ethical and cosmological dualism on our hands. Its moral world really is God and Company, *with limited assets and unlimited liabilities.* In trying to square the reality of evil with the reality of superhuman, but limited, good, it makes evil eternal or coëval with good and independent of it. If evil be a metaphysical surd, an eternal, cosmical principle, by what right does the personal idealist assume that its power can and will surely be permanently reduced by the synergistic efforts of God and man? If the good be hindered and thwarted by an opposite principle, independent of itself, then how can we reasonably believe that the world whole will become better as it becomes more of a whole? How do we know that it is becoming more of a whole? If evil be outside the reach of the spiritual world of God or good, it must remain an irremovable obstacle. If it be not outside, then the possibility of evil, and, indeed, its ever recurring actuality, is a condition of the good. The real and trustworthy possibility of our human world becoming better presupposes that the structure or order of the universe is permanently good, that is, better than we sometimes find our empirical human world to be. And our main business is to discover this truth and act upon it. There is very slight hope that we human beings can remake the universe to suit our desires. I feel with Thomas Carlyle who, when it was reported to him that Margaret Fuller, the Transcendentalist, said she accepted the universe, commented, "Egad! she'd better." It is even doubtful whether we would make a very good job of the remaking, if it were put in our hands. But there is good hope that, if we can discover something of the real and eternal meaning of the whole spectacle and business, we may remake human life in the likeness thereof. It seems to me that some of the motives of personalistic pluralism, and connected forms of so-called *humanism* and *pragmatism* are the consequences of an unhealthy preoccupation with the all-too-human, with the small change and parochialism, which lays undue stress on the accidents, freaks and ephemeralities of human life, and fusses over these things with exaggerated emphasis. Instead we should stay ourselves by keeping company with the universal and stable and orderly in nature and the historical world.[7]

Indeed, personalistic pluralism is in a state of unstable equilibrium. It must either go over to absolutism in some form, or admit that its God is neither the creator nor governor of things, but only a somewhat superhuman product, like man, of the anarchical flux of reality. If reality be evolving, by chance, out of the primordial and indeterminate vortex, taking on habits of more regular behavior and getting personalized, by chance, too; no doubt the whole process is very interesting. But one does not care to worship even a superhuman product of the vortical flux.

In sum, personalistic pluralism faces this dilemma—*either God is not continuously immanent in both Nature and Man,* in which case he is either a finite part of the world-whole or He is an absentee landlord who intervenes but occasionally (a conception repugnant to scientific thinking); *or God is immanent in both Nature and Man,* in which case He is not a person alongside other finite persons. If one choose the latter horn of the dilemma, *God must be the living and absolute Spirit of Totality,* energizing in various degrees of fullness in the successive planes of empirical

---

[7] I have not discussed above the peculiar type of personalistic pluralism developed by Mr. J. M. E. McTaggart in his *Studies in Hegelian Cosmology* and *Some Dogmas of Religion.* Mr. McTaggart thinks reality is an eternal system or society of selves, without any God or conscious unity and ground. His view seems to have two fatal defects—(1) It is inconsistent with the facts of biological and psychological development. Human selves clearly seem to have originated and to have developmental histories. It makes the whole realm of time and history an illusion. It is, of course, a form of the doctrine of reincarnation. Like all attempts at a consistent doctrine of the eternity and reincarnation of the human soul, it reduces the significance of the present temporal order to practical nothingness. (2) I do not see how there can be any real and abiding principle or ground of unity for a society of selves, no member of which is the conscious or active ground of the social whole. As some one has wittily said, the unity of the cosmos in this system is like the unity of a college the members of which are on a perpetual vacation.

reality, from the cosmic star-dust up to man and higher finite beings than man. *If He be not the sovereign spirit of the whole universe, He is only a conditioned part thereof.* He cannot be both.

Leibnitz's view is a pluralism with a singularistic basis, and it is a form of pluralism that is most profoundly original. The significant thing for us here is that the world is regarded as a society of selves, and these members constitute the society because of a preëstablished harmony or unity. The members of the society have originated from God. God brings self-determining individuals into existence and these develop into a fuller selfhood. The universe is therefore a developing one and all individuals, within limits set by the supreme monad, are self-determining. Leibnitz thus has a creative ground of the existence of the selves.[8] This view has certain defects. First, the Leibnitzian conception of evolution is not that of to-day. Evolution for Leibnitz is the mere *unfolding* of what is already implicit in the germ. Our conception to-day is epigenetic. Leibnitz's conception is the old Chinese box theory of evolution. The biologist of to-day argues, on the basis of experimental findings, that the organisms and selves are not completely self-inclosed; they interact and thus they are modified.

The second point of weakness in the Leibnitzian conception is his failure to make an organic connection between the unity of experience and its manyness. With these two aspects corrected, we can to-day accept the theory of Leibnitz.

VII. A Synthesis of Singularism and Pluralism

I regard the world of selves as generated in time by the creative activity of the world ground, and I further

[8] See, further, Chapter XVIII, 2.

regard this process of generation as being without either beginning or end. The development of individuals in the time-process consists in their education into richer individuality. The goal of the process is the attainment of the fullest possible personality.

Reality I conceive to include a process and evolution in time, and the goal of this process is the realization of selfhood in society. Inasmuch as there must be a source for the energy and the individuality of individuals, and inasmuch as evolution takes specific direction, that is, moves towards certain values, I regard God as at once the immanent ground of the process and the conserver of its values. The world is a dependent reality, and in it selves have a relatively higher degree of independence than do lower beings. There are thus stages and degrees of individuality, freedom, and independence, evolved in the process of evolution. The human self is free and responsible within limits and the human self is clearly the product of the whole process, since it is an integral part thereof.

The motives and facts that are involved in Singularism and Pluralism might be reconciled in the following way. Let me say here, however, as an indirect mode of stating the reconciling position, that there are two objections to extreme Singularism. These objections are: (1) That Singularism does not give a satisfactory interpretation of the human self. The invariable tendency of extreme Singularism is to deprive human individuality of its place and worth in reality. It tends to derealize the human self by reducing it to a mere appearance of an ineffable absolute; personality becomes but a momentary and insignificant expression of the timeless Absolute. It is not unjust to say, if extreme Singularism is true, then our individuality, our freedom, our responsibility, our meaning, and our worth, are only egotistical allusions. This may be true. Perhaps we are not any more significant than

The flies of latter spring,
That lay their eggs, and sting and sing,
And weave their petty cells and die.

It is strange, however, that our life should have such a sharp tang, if this be all there is to life. It is equally strange that life should appear to exist in the only way in which it immediately appears to exist, that is, as the life of distinct and separate individuals. What we actually experience is individualized striving, suffering, hoping, dreaming, achieving, and even hoping when achievement falls short. Before we abandon our common sense conviction as to the reality of our individuality, we shall claim the right to be shown why we should give up this conviction. (2) The second objection is that abstract Singularism regards the absolute as timeless and static. Hegel insists that reality is a process. Royce also repeatedly lays great emphasis upon the purposive and volitional character of selfhood. Bosanquet also insists on the significance, for reality, of natural evolution and cultural development. But the process, as regarded by these men, seems to be more a function of logical implication than of actual causal sequences. Royce goes so far in his latest work as to conceive God as the spirit of the beloved community, and here he really abandons the timeless absolute. But perhaps all that the great idealists mean is that there is an enduring order of meanings and values that persists in and realizes itself in the time process. If so, I agree with them. What conception can we form of a reality in which there is no temporal movement? Evolution as a natural process antecedent to human history; history, which is but the story of the evolution of human culture as this has veered in its ups and downs; and the whole innumerable series of developing individuals—these are all temporal processes and they cannot be reduced to something which is not temporal. With what special acuteness does the average student realize a few days before the finals what a relentless master time is? It is only when care free that we forget time. *Dem Glücklichen schlägt keine Stunde.*

Our world is a temporal world, and, for my part, I can accept no philosophy which begins with a mystical flight from the temporal world. On the other hand, the numerical Monist or Singularist urges against the Pluralist that the universe is one, that there is a unity of structure, or, as Royce expresses it, there is a unity in the types of order in the world. No doubt all things are related in some fashion. Coexistence in space is one form of relation, but this is not necessarily a very significant or relevant type of relation. Culture relations, such as are ours by virtue of our life in the university, are more significant than our mere spatial relations on the campus. All events are temporally related; this also may or may not be a very significant type of relation. Singularism is right in insisting upon the existence of some sort of relation, but it errs in assuming that all forms of relations may be ultimately reduced to the whole-part type. I agree with the Singularists that there is some sort of unity or continuity in the world, but I do not agree that all the different types of empirical relations can be merged so as to make everything a part of one substance or cosmic self. There is a unity of the solar system; there is a unity of a fine machine, for example, a watch; there is a unity of a living organism; and finally, there is a unity of a society of like-minded beings. The differences between these unities are much more significant than the likenesses, and I see no way of discovering some common denominator which will effect a reduction of these unities to one. The tendency of the Singularist has been to reduce all forms of unity to that of the abstract unity of the universe, and then, subsequent to this reduction, he emotionally glosses over this type of unity with religious predicates. He baptizes this abstract unity with the most acute form of emotional experience.

Is it not more reasonable to suppose something of the following order, namely, rather than reduce all kinds of unities to one type, let us conceive a world ground which is not identical with any or all of these special types of unity? Such an assumption would enable us to take full cognizance of all the facts of Singularism and Pluralism. God, the world ground, is the ultimate source of whatever type of unity there is in any of these various systems. God in his own interior being is richer than the sum of the unities that we find in the universe. There is a world of partly independent, responsible individuals. This world is not eternally complete, and God shares in its growth. God is not an absentee Deity dwelling apart from the grime of this universe. He is the energizing good, and at this point our view is at one with Plato's. God is not a One in which all individuals are swallowed up and disappear.

The problem of the one and the many involves the place and the status of individuality in the world. The Singularist is the extreme realist. For him the particular is absorbed in the unity. The extreme Pluralist dissolves all unity; thus he is a revised edition of the extreme nominalist of former days. For him there are no universals and no general types of relations in the objective world. The mediating position is that we make the relations by reflecting on the data of experience and generalizing upon the basis of the results of reflection, but this generalization rests upon the real order that is in the world.

Objective social idealism is the only form of Singularism that can be worked out into a consistent and comprehensible theory. For Idealism presents the only clear and plausible conception of *how* the elements of the real world can constitute a unitary or systematic whole of being, and yet each be a contributing member. Materialism cannot do this; for, if the whole be made up of atomic units, these must be wholly external to one another, and no clear conception can be given, as to how they can be interdependent parts of one whole. If the atoms are deformations or centers of tension in an ether (the *continuous fluid*), then either they are not really atoms, that is, not discrete and indivisible units, or the ether is not really continuous. The same objection will hold if the units are called electrons. Dualism is open to the same criticism in its conception of matter; and, besides, it does not explain how body and mind can be interacting elements in reality, if they are not interdependent. Psychophysical parallelism leaves us with two unsolved problems on our hands: (1) *why* two so absolutely opposed entities as body and mind should be completely parallel, and (2) *how* a succession of bodily states and mental states can be parallel.

According to the Idealistic type of Singularism, the position and relations of every particular member in the whole system of reality to the whole, is analogous to the position and relations of any special mental system or complex of ideas, feelings, and impulses in an individual mind to that mind as a whole. Let us take the mind of a great and comprehensive genius, Plato, Dante, Shakespeare, Goethe, or a great scholar like the late Lord Acton or Josiah Royce, or a great statesman, such as William Pitt or Abraham Lincoln. The man, we say, was many-sided; that means that he had a great variety of mental complexes or systems, each organized by and permeated or transformed by a central and controlling idea or purpose. We say that he was a great individuality or personality, not a collection of systems; that means that all the varied complexes in his mind were organized into a central unity. But, if the highest members in the world system are selves or persons, I cannot see by what right one contends that these members have no more power self-determination in the whole than any special complex of ideas in my mind has in that mind.

No doubt, especially when an individual is obsessed by fixed ideas, in the case of diseased personality or lunacy, the special complex of ideas may run the entire self. But this would be a very poor sort of case to argue from. In the normal mind, the whole self grows and functions by complementary processes of unification and comprehension.

Moreover, if the whole of reality be a living system it must include real development, evolution, growth or progress in its members. It cannot be a unity which simply marks time or revolves eternally in a circle. Therefore, it seems to me, the best analogy, for the nature of the unity and continuity of the universe, is that of a society of selves, animated and guided by a central unity of ideal and purpose, which unity, from the standpoint of religion, would be the sustaining ground of the whole society. A society of persons, in which each member's will reflects, however imperfectly and intermittently, the spirit, ideal, aim or principle, of the whole society is a richer, completer, and relatively more self-dependent or substantial unity than the unity of any individual mind. A mental organization is a living and self-determining and progressive whole or unity, in a sense in which no other whole is. The principle of the whole pervades and lives in every one of the parts and every member lives by embodying the principle of the whole. But, in a social whole, these complementary truths are more fully exemplified than in an individual mind. For the mind of society both makes, and is remade by, the minds of its individual members. But even the leaders and renovators of society achieve their work, not by destroying, but by interpreting and fulfilling the intent of the social will. Historically, religion is the incarnation of the ideal of the social will. God, in the highest and most progressive forms of religion, is not the single ego which swallows up the cosmos. In *every form of spiritual religion, other than those aberrant forms of mysticism in which the defeated soul flees from the world, God is the supreme social self.*

In brief, our standpoint is an objective social idealism: God is the transcendent ground of the community of selves, not the merely immanent and impersonal spirit of the community. But I cannot understand how, in a spiritual universe, or even in a merely vital universe, there can be growth or change in individual members that does not affect the spirit of the whole. St. Paul's words, "If one member suffer, all the members suffer with it, and if one member rejoice, all the members rejoice with it," seem to me profoundly true of the universe.

Before bringing to a close this grand tour in which we have touched only the high spots and have seen only a few of the most important sights, let me give a few words as to the moral and religious implications of pluralism. The standpoint of Pluralism is *melioristic.* The world may become better. It is not absolute optimism, the viewpoint that all is well with the world, nor is it absolute pessimism, the view that the world is irretrievably bad. From our standpoint also we must admit that there are evil, sin and suffering here. These really take place, but they can be regarded as the conditions for the development of free personalities. They are a part of the process of education. But the superlative character of the good renders all this suffering excusable. One very interesting question emerges at this point. Does the very ubiquity of evil, sin and suffering, suggest the question as to whether there is not some obtrusive element which forces us to admit a dualistic strain in the structure of the universe? Bergson's suggestion at this point is that such is the case. The *Life force* ever strives upward, *matter* ever pulls downward. (Plato recognizes a similar situation.)

References

* Avey, A. E., *Readings in Philosophy,* Chapter XX.

* Bowne, B. P., *Personalism, Philosophy of Theism,* and *Metaphysics.*

Bradley, *Appearance and Reality,* especially Chapters XIV, XV, XVI.

Bosanquet, B., *The Principle of Individuality and Value,* especially Lectures VI, VII, IX, and X.

* Calkins, M. W., *The Persistent Problems of Philosophy,* Chapters IV, VIII, X, XI.

Hegel, *Logic,* and *Philosophy of Mind* (translated by Wallace).

* Howison, G. H., *The Limits of Evolution.*

Hügel, F. von, *Eternal Life.*

* James, William, *A Pluralistic Universe,* and *Some Problems of Philosophy.*

Joachim, H. H., *The Ethics of Spinoza.*

* Leighton, J. A., *Man and the Cosmos,* Chapters XII-XVII and XXXV-XXXIX.

McTaggart, J. M. E., *Studies in Hegelian Cosmology, and Some Dogmas of Religion.*

Pringle-Pattison, A. Seth, *The Idea of God.*

Richardson, C. A., *Spiritual Pluralism and Recent Philosophy.*

* Royce, *The World and the Individual,* Vol. I, Lectures VIII, IX, and X, Vol. II, from Lecture VI.

For Royce's later view, *The Problem of Christianity.*

Royce and Others, *The Conception of God.*

* Schiller, F. C. S., *Riddles of the Sphinx,* Chapter X.

Sorley, W. R., *Moral Values and the Idea of God.*

* Spinoza, *Ethics* (translated by White, or Elwes, especially Books I and V.

* Taylor, A. E., *Elements of Metaphysics,* Book II, Chapter III, and article *Theism,* in *Encyclopædia of Religion and Ethics,* XII.

Varisco, B., *The Great Problems.*

* Ward, James, *The Realm of Ends.*

CHAPTER XXV

THE SELF

I. The Nature of the Self

The problem of the nature and place of the self is of quite central importance in modern philosophy. In this respect there is a decided contrast between ancient and modern philosophy. It is true that the doctrine of the soul plays a very important part in the philosophy of Plato, and that Aristotle's conception of the real as entelechy or individual is derived from the notion of the soul. But in Greek philosophy we miss the acute sense of the subjectivity, the privacy, and uniqueness of the self, the feeling of the poignancy of experience as personal and, consequently, that consciousness of the existence and difficulty of such problems as how the self knows the external world or how one self knows another. *The note of subjectivity, the feeling of and for personality,* pervades the greater part of modern philosophy and literature, and is chiefly the result of the Christian emphasis on the seriousness and worth of the soul, or the inwardness of the true life, reacting upon peoples whose whole civilization, as perhaps their original native bent, has tended to foster a keen sense of individuality. Thus at the very outset of modern philosophy we find Descartes, amidst universal doubt, clearly conscious of his existence as a thinking being.[1] Locke believes in a soul substance, although he

[1] He says, "I can doubt the existence of everything else of which I have an idea, but I cannot doubt that I exist as a thinking

admits it is only a hypothesis and that we cannot know the *nature* of this substance. But he is certain that we have empirical consciousness of our own personal identity. Berkeley is equally certain that we can have a *notion* or intuitive consciousness of the self as the unitary spirit which thinks, perceives, and wills. Kant makes the synthetic or organizing activity of the self (or ego) the agency by which the disjointed sequences of our sensations are formed into knowledge of nature as a rational whole or ordered world. According to Kant, we do not perceive the true self, but the "I think" accompanies all knowledge, and we may become conscious of it when we will. The self, as the organizing principle of knowledge in Kant's system is universal—the same in all men, since it is simply the power of intellectual synthesis. But the self is individualized in the fulfillment of one's moral vocation. The self as purely moral will, subjecting itself to the commands of duty, is the real individual. Kant's disciple, Fichte, builds his whole metaphysical system of ethical or spiritual idealism on the intuition of free self-activity in the individual's moral will. The existence of other selves and a world of nature are deduced as necessary to the fulfillment of one's moral vocation. Hegel makes selfhood or spirit the key to the structure and meaning of the world, although it is doubtful whether he regarded the absolute as a self-conscious individual. More recent idealists, such as Bradley and Royce, make the self or individual center of experience the clue to the nature of reality. Royce especially emphasizes the volitional character of the self.

One great iconoclast, David Hume, challenged the

---

being; for doubting is thinking (cogito, ergo sum)." Herein Descartes repeats the thought of St. Augustine (+ 430), the most influential thinker of the Christian middle ages. The latter's start from the luminous self-certainty of his own existence as a conscious being is an expression of the central place which the Christian religion gave to the human soul or spiritual personality.

grounds of belief in a single or unitary and permanent self in a classical passage, in which he asserted that he could find no self when he looked within himself, only particular impressions, ideas, and feelings in perpetual flux and movement.[2] The modern phenomenalistic idealists, such as Mach and Pearson, take the same position. As for psychology, William James argued that the only self which psychology knows or needs is the momentary "unity of the passing thought."[3] Nearly all psychologists would agree with him. Some, such as M. W. Calkins, contend that we have an immediate feeling of selfhood, and therefore the self is the most real thing we know.

But the self which I feel immediately is not identical with the self which is held, by the man in the street and by many philosophers, to exist as a substantial reality. For (1) in the first place, when I am self-conscious, that aspect of myself which is conscious cannot be identical with the aspect of my supposed self concerning which I am conscious. The contents or data of self-consciousness are ever fluctuating, though not so much as the data of our consciousness of the world. (2) At any moment I may, it is true, be conscious of the unity of my thought, but what I mean, when I say that I believe in the self as a single and enduring reality, is that there is a permanent, intelligent, and purposive principle of action which is my real self. (3) What I regard as the center or core of my selfhood varies from time to time and is largely dependent on the influence of my social, and even my physical, environment. I am a quite different person, cold or warm, hungry or satiated, happy or miserable, successful or failing, popular or disliked, wealthy or poor, playing or working. As my bodily condition alters so my conscious and active selfhood alters, and my bodily condition depends in

[2] Hume, *Treatise of Human Nature*, Bk. 1, part 4, Sects. 5, 6.
[3] James, *Principles of Psychology*, Vol. I, Chapter 10.

large part on the physical environment. As my social atmosphere alters, my self suffers alteration too. If the self be not wholly a product of physical and social influences, it is, at least, notoriously subject to alterations at the hand of these factors. (4) The actual self is clearly a changing complex of experiences—of perceptions, wants, feelings (emotions and sentiments), strivings, purposes, ideas, satisfactions, and dissatisfactions. The complexity and instability of the actual self is signally evidenced by the many striking cases, which have been written up in recent years, of multiple personalities. Two or more different "persons" or characters may control the same living body in successive periods, longer or shorter, or in alternating periods. Even different characters or complexes of feelings and strivings may struggle simultaneously for the control of the body. A "personality" may disintegrate. An individual may suffer loss of his normal or average selfhood and become quite different; he may permanently recover his former selfhood or he may oscillate back and forth between the old and the new. Logically, we should not even speak of "he" or "she" in such cases, for "he" cannot recover himself from a state that was not "he" at all. (5) We are discussing the consciousness or experience of selfhood, but, as a matter of fact, at any moment, by far the greater part of one's personality as it is believed to exist, by one's self, one's friends and associates, is not *in* consciousness at all. At the present passing moment, all that is in my consciousness clearly is what I am writing and, more dimly, the skill and tools with which I am doing the writing. All my other accomplishments and defects are out of consciousness. Where are these? Is my selfhood chiefly an unconscious substance or enduring complex of physical powers or dispositions, or is it a mass of brain paths or engramms in the central nervous system?

Much fresh light has been shed on the nature of the self

by recent investigations of the disorders of personality; such as, lapse of the consciousness of personal identity, the struggle between alternating and conflicting characters for control of the organism, mental obsessions and conflicts which may result in nervous and mental breakdown, and, finally, in the field of psychical research, so-called (telepathy, telæsthesis, telekinesis, and communications from the dead). The last field is large and confusing, and, it seems to me, no definite results have been reached in it, except that it is a fruitful area for fraud, self-illusion, charlatanry and superstition.

I have space here only to summarize the results of the recent work on disorders of personality.[4] The data show: (1) That the empirical self is an imperfect and growing organization or synthesis of many complexes or clusters of impulsions, cravings, memories, ideas, and aims. Every self is very complex. Every main set of ideas, interests, and habits may be regarded as a specific complex; and the whole self is the sum or combination of these specific complexes. Disintegration or disorganization results from the persistent conflict of these constituent complexes or clusters. Progressive organization results from their successful synthesis under the control of a life plan or harmonious system of purposes. The achievement of this synthesis is often blocked by the hidden conflict (that is, hidden from clear consciousness) between individually acknowledged, and socially accepted, purposes and standards of conduct, and subconsciously working cravings that are thwarted by the acknowledged standards. Thwarted sexual impulsions are the most frequently occurring of these cravings, but other blocked cravings, such as ambi-

[4] The best books in this field are probably, Morton Prince, *The Dissociation of a Personality,* and *The Unconscious;* Sidis and Goodheart, *Multiple Personality;* Sigmund Freud, *The Mechanism and Interpretation of Dreams* and *The Psychopathology of Every-Day Life;* C. G. Jung, *Psychology of the Unconscious.*

tion or creative impulse, may have the same effect. (2) The unconscious parts of man's affective and appetitive life—his not consciously acknowledged instincts, impulses, desires, old habits, forgotten conflicts, fears, and longings—play a large part in determining the total character and bent of his personality. The study of disorders of personality emphasizes what is often overlooked in the study of normal selfhood, namely, that, interwoven with our clearly conscious life, is a great mass of unconscious psychical dispositions, or impulsions. Some of these are the unchanged natural heritage of man from his biological ancestry. Others are the results of social perversion. Still others are the acquired or achieved results of normal and beneficent activity and training in the past. A vigorous, healthy, and progressing personality is possible only through the *integration* of all man's psychical dispositions or soul elements. To achieve this integration is the most difficult and important task of human life. All economic and social institutions, including education, religion, and art, should be directed to this end. The economic order, and even moral customs, and education, instead of ministering to this supreme end of human life and the evolutionary process, may actually thwart and distort it in many selves. "Is not the body more than raiment, and the life more than meat?" "What shall a man give in exchange for his soul?"

All parts away for the progress of souls,
All religion, all solid things, arts, governments—all that was or is apparent upon this globe or any globe, falls into niches and corners before the procession of souls along the grand roads of the universe.
Of the progress of the souls of men and women along the grand roads of the universe, all other progress is the needed emblem and sustenance. (Song of the Open Road.)

I swear I begin to see the meaning of these things,
It is not the earth, it is not America who is so great,
It is I who am great or to be great, it is You up there, or any one,
It is to walk rapidly through civilizations, governments, theories
Through poems, pageants, shows, to form individuals.
Underneath all, individuals,
I swear nothing is good to me now that ignores individuals,
The American compact is altogether with individuals,
The only government is that which makes minute of individuals,
The whole theory of the universe is directed unerringly to one single individual—namely to You. (By Blue Ontario's Shore.)

"And I will not make a poem, or the least part of a poem but has reference to the soul,
Because having looked at the objects of the universe, I find there is no one nor any particle of one but has reference to the soul." (Starting from Paumonok.)

I might have culled, from *Leaves of Grass,* dozens of such passages. For the dominant and ever recurrent theme of Walt Whitman, the bard of democratic individuality and comradeship, is that the whole meaning and purport of the cosmical and the social process is the unending progress of the self or soul. If he is wrong there is no meaning in the universe, and it is but an insane jest. Certainly human beings are fools and blind, in so far as they do not straightway make all institutions, customs, and laws subservient to the universal perfecting and fruition of human individuality, of selfhood throughout the round world. As Keats said, this world is a "vale of soul-making."

The self is not simple or unchanging. Plato's doctrine of the soul will not hold in the face of the facts. The self, whatever it may be, is certainly largely the product of its surroundings, unstable and dependent. And yet we do inexpugnably feel in our best moments the reality of our individualities. We feel ourselves to be responsible agents, and society treats us as such, in education, social, and business intercourse and law. We feel ourselves to have enduring natures which are expressed in the purposes which we pursue and cling to, even amidst seeming shipwreck of all our hopes and plans. The stronger among us persist in being true to ourselves, in pursuing our chosen aims and ambitions, in serving our elected ideals of life. And society, almost by instinct, recognizes and respects, even worships, the strong and self-reliant individual. It turns to him in its days of perplexity and distress. The history of human progress is chiefly the story of the creative beginnings made by great individuals in all directions. Knowledge, discovery, invention, industry, politics, education, art, and even religion, are modified, reconstructed, added to, propelled by the creative, exploring, and organizing individuals.

Must we conclude that selfhood is complex and yet a unity, ever changing and yet permanent, passively moulded and yet truly self-creative and creative of other existences and values, a partially unorganized mass of cravings and experiences and yet an active organizing principle, the creature of its environment and yet the recreator of environments, the product of the universe, and yet the best clue to the meaning and purpose of the universal order? Yes, I think we must answer these paradoxical queries in the affirmative.

The self is subject and object. It feels itself to be "I," and yet the "I" is vastly more than the self at any instant feels itself to be. "I" and "thou" have meaning only because there is a feeling of selfhood, but this immediate sense of selfhood is but the starting point upon which is built the notion of *selfhood or individuality*. The latter is a *construction of thought,* but we have the best right in the world to believe that it is a valid construction.

For, (1) the critic, who sets out to refute the legitimacy of a belief in individuality, contradicts himself both in setting out at all and in every step he takes. He assumes the existence of other selves and himself and then proceeds, in terms of "I" and "you" and "they," to refute the reality of the self. (2) The self is indeed complex and growing. For selfhood or individuality is the progressive organization of the native capacities of a conscious organism into a more harmonious and richer unity of experience and deed. *The actual self is a self-organizing principle.* The materials of individuality are the inborn impulses of the organism. The patterns for the work to be done are the social types of conduct, thought, sentiment, character, and trained capacity, which have been worked out by other socially creative selves in the history of human culture. The ultimate agent in the process of self-development or creation is the attentively selective, valuing, purposing, organizing mind of the individual. The more truly the natural self becomes a spiritual individual or personality, the more socialized and rational, the more self-dependent and creative it becomes. Thus the individual grows more and more into a self-determining, self-initiating unity. He ceases to be the mere creature of his environment, and becomes in some part the transformer, the renewer and recreator of the physical and social environments. Instinctive cravings and imperious desires become transformed into dynamic factors in the organized and harmonious life of the whole self. The nature of the self is thus revealed as it is "realized" or "actualized" in the fundamental and increasingly systematic development of its active attitudes, its valuations, choices, persistent purposes and deeds. The self is thus not a mere "phenomenal" flux or stream of passively determined feelings and ideas. It is not, on the other hand, an unchanging "substance" or entity unaffected by its aims, history, and environment. *Selfhood or individuality has many degrees.* It is a complex, dynamic process always having some degree of unity in thought, feeling, and purpose; and is capable of developing more unity and harmony under appropriate conditions.

(3) The self is the product of the universe and the best clue to the nature of the whole. For the notions of *substance or permanence through change*, of *unity in multiplicity*, *of organization* or *systematic relation in a whole*, of *uniformity*, *intelligibility*, *coherence*, of a *purposive order* and of *individuality*—in short, all the fundamental notions, which man employs in the work of understanding and controlling nature, and so harmonizing himself with nature, by intelligent apprehension and rational mastery, are derived from the life of human society. Selfhood has as its original datum, its core, the inborn capacities and the dynamic principle of mental organization. But the full selfhood of the rational individual arises only in a highly developed social order. Every principle and instrument of thought which man employs in interpreting the world is a product of social experience. *Uniformity, law, order, finality*—these are social categories. This does not mean that nature as an intelligible order is created out of nothing by social effort. It does carry the implication that, since the intellectual tools by which man succeeds in understanding and controlling nature are of social origin, there must be a fundamental correspondence, or harmony, or organic interdependence of structure between nature and human nature. Kant said "the understanding makes nature." I would say "the social understanding and will make nature, because society is the highest product and value achieved in nature."

(4) The pathological disintegration of actual selves does not mean the absolute disintegration of the self. In all these cases there is still a unity of selfhood. It is obscured and thwarted by nervous disintegration. The various selves or "persons" in such cases are not true selves or persons. They are relatively isolated clusters of impulses and ideas

in an individual who has not achieved the integration of a full selfhood. Actual selfhood has all manner of degrees of organization of the congenital impulses to action.

(5) A considerable part of the life of selfhood *is* at any moment unconscious. Individuality includes much more than is in consciousness. It is an organized whole of many capacities. The questions involved in the relation of the conscious, the subconscious and the unconscious in mental life are too complex to be discussed here. I must leave this matter with the warning that the admission of an unconscious psychical life by no means commits one to the recognition of a distinct subconscious self. The latter is a bit of mythology.

Since we have already found grounds for rejecting materialism, we hold that the self is not identical with the nervous system. The mental self is, we have seen, intimately bound up with the central nervous system. The latter is the instrument by means of which the self affects and is affected by the world. The mind is a power or system of powers, of memory, inhibition, selection, generalization, valuation, and choice, by which the nervous responses are organized and made subservient to the enrichment, intensification, harmonization, and conservation of the conscious life of the organism.

We will now review briefly the chief theories of the *self*. These are five in number: (1) *Animism or the doctrine of a soul-substance, entirely different and separable from the body, but interacting with it.* This conception of the soul developed out of the early conception of the soul as a finer body. It is the form in which the notion of the *immateriality of the soul* emerges, particularly in Hebrew and Greek thought in the days of their maturity. In their immature phases both Hebrew and Greek thought conceived the soul to be simply the *vital principle,* which animates and directs the body; in this respect Greek and Hebrew thought did not differ from that of early thought among other peoples. In Plato, who seems to have been the first thinker to conceive the soul as an absolutely immaterial principle, we find the beginnings of the *tripartite* conception of man. The *Psyche* or *soul* is the principle of the physical life, the *Nous, reason* or *spirit,* is the seat of the moral and intellectual life and, thus, the organ of the *ideas;* thus, in Plato, man is regarded as being composed of a union of *body, soul* and *reason* or *spirit.* St. Paul, like Plato, conceives man to be composed of body, soul, and spirit. This tripartite conception became the orthodox Christian conception. This *Triadism,* or *Trialism,* as it is sometimes called, is to be found, confusedly intermingled wih Dualism, running through the history of Christian thought. Descartes abandons it, by eliminating the soul as the principle of natural life. He regards the living body as a machine and identifies the soul with the rational and spiritual principle. Locke and Kant follow him in this respect. The doctrine of Animism has had vigorous defenders in recent times.[5] The doctrine of *Vitalism* in biology is closely akin to, indeed is a form of, the two substances or animistic theory.

The difficulties in the way of accepting this theory have already been discussed. The chief are these—the soul is neither unchangeable nor independent of the body; animism finds it very hard to state how soul and body can interact if they are diametrically opposite in character; and, finally, if the soul be affirmed to be independent and unchangeable, no intelligible notion can be framed as to the relation between this mysterious substance and the actual self of experience.

The doctrine of *Triadism* carries us beyond dualism to a

---

[5] Prominent among these is Dr. William MacDougall in his *Body and Mind.* Among biological vitalists may be mentioned Professors Hans Driesch, Henri Bergson, J. A. Thomson, and J. S. Haldane.

conception of levels or stages of being that transcends dualism. This conception has already been outlined in Chapter XIX. (See also paragraph 5 below.)

2. *Materialism* affirms that the soul is simply a by-product of the body. Therefore the real or efficient self is the bodily self. We need not repeat the results of the critical examination of this theory already made in Chapter XVI.

3. *Spiritualism* or *idealism* affirms that only psychical or conscious selves are realities. It would be less misleading, in view of the several meanings which the term idealism has borne, to call this view *psychism* or *mentalism*. It fails to explain why bodies should appear to exist and to behave in a manner different from minds, if all bodies are nothing other than thoughts or volitions of minds. It must hold that, when an apparent body either helps or hinders the working of a mind, it is never anything but a case of one thought or volition helping or hindering another thought or volition.

4. *Psychophysical parallelism.* This doctrine has already been stated and examined in Chapter XIX.

5. *The self is a psychophysical individuality, potentially rational and spiritual.* It consists of an organic union of several levels or stages of being—*physical, vital, and sentient, and rational* or *spiritual.* Body is a genuine and essential condition of individuality or selfhood. I am unable to conceive a spiritual individual existing without bodily form or powers. I have never found, in the history of thought, a coherent and intelligible conception of this sort. I venture to say that no such conception can be framed by a human being. On the other hand, the facts seem to me to negative the assumption that living and sentient bodies do not differ in character from nonliving bodies. Furthermore, the facts of human nature, as manifested in the products of culture and in the social

order, seem to me equally to sustain the view that there is, in man, a third power—*one which, with regard to the chief phases and results of its operations, may be called reason, creative imagination,* and *moral consciousness.* This power is *one,* although its manifestations are diverse. Like the other powers of the self it may be thwarted or perverted. It does not exist in like degree in all selves. But it is, none the less, *a dynamic reality.* No one of these powers, which, in organic and harmonious interplay, make up the self, is absolutely independent of the other two. Sentient life involves a specific type of material organization. The functioning of the reason or spirit involves, and is built up on, the sentient powers of the self. The body is a dynamic organization. The sentient soul, through perception and feeling, supplies basic data of the relations between the self and its world. The rational and spiritual principle, starting from these data, interprets, evaluates, selects, devises, and wills. The spiritual principle is the *idea,* in the Platonic sense, of the body, or in Aristotle's terms it is the *entelechy* or end-realizing power. The meaning and value of the bodily and sentient life is realized, by being concentered, evaluated and redirected, in the rational life of the higher selfhood. Thus the soul is never mere soul nor the body mere body. Taking the word soul as the popular equivalent for the sentient and the rational principles together, we may say that states of soul plus states of body produce other states of body plus other states of soul. Negatively put, a state of either soul or body is never the product merely of another state of soul or body. The interaction is a multiplex process within one organic individuality. It is that of reciprocating elements in one living system.

In regard to the mental self, there is another matter of controversy to be considered. Which is more fundamental in the soul or mind, *intellect* or *will, thought* or *feeling and conation?* The *intellectualists* make intellect fundamental and the *voluntarists* make conation of prime importance. Descartes, Spinoza, and Hegel would be classed as intellectualists; Kant, Fichte, and Schopenhauer, as voluntarists. Voluntarism has been much in fashion lately largely due to the influence of biology. The whole controversy is a mistaken one. In man feeling, striving, and thinking are equally congenital and fundamental. One can understand why an irrationalistic pessimist like Schopenhauer should tie up to an extreme voluntarism because it supported his ethical twist, but it is difficult to understand why one who, without prejudice, studies carefully the facts of human nature should not see that, while man's impulses and instincts are indeed ineradicable and often imperious in their clamancy, they are the impulses, the conations, of a being who is conscious of his surroundings and who frames images and concepts of his world and acts by their guidance. Intellect is itself a kind of conation; but, on the other hand, distinctively human volition is voluntary action incited and guided by, and culminating in, knowledge.

Probably the one-sided voluntarism of the present time is the consequence of the undue emphasis on man's biological inheritance and the resulting failure to distinguish between the character of instinct, impulse, emotion, the will-to-live and the will-to-power in man and in the animal world. Even the will-to-live and the will-to-power in their most ruthless, dangerous, and ethically inhuman forms in human society are incited by ideas and guided to their accomplishment by thought.

II. Freedom and The Self

I close with a few words on the relation between the concept of selfhood and freedom. Freedom of the will properly means freedom of the self, and this in turn, means *self-determination.* The freedom that is implied in our conception of individuality is not that of unmotived or capricious and irrational choice. Such a freedom, if possible, would have no moral worth for man. On the other hand, the nature of the self, as a being that grows in rational and moral self-determination, implies that the self is not absolutely predetermined by its antecedent history. If the self be not the purely passive product of circumstances, it must have the capacity to free itself from the clutch of circumstance to the extent to which such freedom is involved in the fulfillment of its own rational nature. What the self wills at any moment is determinate, for it is the joint resultant of circumstances and that degree and manner of self-expression of individuality of which the self is, at that particular moment, capable.

But it does not follow that, in similar circumstances, in a future crisis, the self *must* choose as it did before. New and deeper or more rational aspects of the self's individuality may come into play. The truth is, it appears to me, that in the moral life of man exactly the same situation never does twice occur. For at least the self is not the same as it was, and in the infinite complexity of human life, the conditions subject to which choices and volitions are made must also be consequently varying in some degree.

The chief arguments advanced for *determinism,* by which I understand the view that human volitions are, like all the processes in the universe, the unequivocal resultants of antecedent conditions, are as follows:

1. The universality of causation. Human action, it is said cannot be an exception to the rule that every event is the perfectly determinate result of equally determinate antecedents. To this argument the advocate of rational freedom replies that the final determining factor in voluntary or chosen action is just the conscious self itself,

which weighs, evaluates, and chooses between possible actions in the light of an ideal standard.

2. The actual continuity of character and conduct. The determinist points out that the better we know a person the more certainly can we predict how that person will act in given conditions. The individuality of a person is a determinate quantum, a so-much. Moreover, he insists that our whole work of moral and intellectual education aims at building up a definite character, the type of character demanded by the structure and aims of the social order. He insists that the very notion of responsibility implies that the rational human individual is a being that can be counted on to act in specific ways corresponding to specific situations. He explains the functions of rewards and punishments, praise and blame, to be to produce the type of character that the educator, the parent, the judge, as the agents of the social group, or the group itself through its approvals and disapprovals, demands.

To these arguments the advocate of freedom replies as follows: He does not contest the fact of continuity in character and conduct; but holds that the highest degree of continuity exists just where the self is most truly a rational, self-determining individual, who has an *ideal* which he follows and who judges his own conduct in the light of that ideal. He argues that the aim of all social approval and disapproval, of all rewards and punishments, of all social inhibitions and incitements to the self, should be educative. But he holds that true education is education into responsible self-determination, that the highest aim of society should be to give opportunity for human beings to become more rational individuals, responsible to their own ideals. He holds that the highest type of society is that one which contains the largest proportion of persons who do not passively accept the current fashions in conduct and thought but who, actively and in the light of reflection, determine for themselves the right course of conduct. He insists that, in the case of punishment through the law, the offender should be treated as a responsible being who accepts the guilt as his own, and who thus can actively participate in his own moral renovation. He argues that the individual is not to be treated by society as an animal capable of being trained to do its tricks. He argues that the highest type of human being is precisely one who feels keenly his own responsibilities as a self-determining agent. He argues further that the possibility of *self-initiated change* is a necessary postulate of the moral life.

It is evident that the real question at issue is this—has the normal self to any degree the power of *rational self-determination* or is it the plastic creature of circumstances? If the self be the sort of reality whose characteristics I have sketched, this question may be answered in terms of the first alternative.

The meaning of this view may, perhaps, be illustrated by considering the place of the conscious self in relation to the neural activities. The cerebral cortex is a very intricate system of nerve cells and connecting paths (neurones and dendrites). Because of its original plasticity new connections are constantly being made in it in the process of the education of the individual. The *sensory and the motor segments of the nervous system constitute, respectively, specific sets of native ways of perceiving and responding to stimuli.* Thus, the organism has native ways of reacting, both directly to stimuli that originate in the external environment, and indirectly, through the responses motivated by the inborn and persistent needs of the organism. In purely reflex action the organism responds, fatally, to peripheral stimuli, that is to stimuli arising from the impact of physical and extra-organic energies, in fashions that have been determined by the ancestral struggle for existence of the species. In centrally initiated action of the purely impulsive or nondeliberative type, the organism's activity is determined by the inherited character of its needs or appetites—for food, drink, warmth, sex, shelter, companionship, play, constructiveness, æsthetic feeling, intellectual satisfaction, social recognition, power—which are the resultants of biological and social evolution. The function of thought is to revalue and organize these varied and often conflicting native impulsions into a harmonious, going concern under the guidance, first, of social patterns of conduct, and, finally, of a life plan or system of purposes affirmed by the individual. Without the intervention of reflective consciousness, without deliberation and choice, the human organism would respond in specific and complex ways, determined in part by the character of the external stimuli and in part by the character of its own native bodily organization and needs. The reactions of a wholly untrained and unthinking organism would be simply the results of the blind composition of inherited action-patterns with external stimuli. The native ways of reacting to external stimuli and organic cravings with sensory experiences and movements are complex and modifiable. It is the *plasticity* of its action-patterns that makes the human organism educable and free. They may be tied up together in a variety of ways. The tying up is done in the brain.

What new factors do conscious experience, deliberation, valuation, and choice introduce into the organism's reactions; in other words, what is the function of the conscious self? It delays responses. It builds up, in its system of ideas and purposes, a selective mechanism which shifts the emphasis, by attention and choice, on what shall be perceived and done. It generalizes from the perceptual and memory materials which constitute "experience." It weighs and evaluates the results of possible actions. It forms, in short, a moving system of selective interests or aims, which originate in its own affectively colored judgments of value, as to what is most worth noting, remembering, seeking to avoid, to attain, and to retain in its experiences. Delayed response is the condition of deliberation and choice.[6] But the latter involves, further, a "throwing of the switches" in the cortex, a "loading of the dice," *motivated by the organization of interests, the systematization of values in perception and action, which is performed by conscious selfhood; which indeed constitutes the very essence of selfhood.* For, at its highest level, conscious individuality is an organization of attitudes or dispositions to act, to know and to feel, guided by reflection upon the values yielded by the various types of sensory and motor reactions which it has had in the past and may have in the present and future physical and social environments.

In brief, the human self is *educable;* and true education consists in the gradual development, through the training of its plastic innate powers, by bringing to bear on them the race's store of wisdom, to the point where the self, having developed an ideal and scheme of life, can direct thoughtfully its own impulsions. The goal of education is the achievement of the power of harmonious, well-balanced and effective self-direction, or individuality, as a member of human society.

Rational freedom is nothing more than the actualization of the capacity to interpret, evaluate, and thus organize into an ideal or coherent system of purposes or values, the

---

[6] The brain seems to function chiefly as a blocking or inhibiting and coördinating mechanism. Reflexes and impulsions, the organism's prime movers, may be inhibited sufficiently long, in their passage through the brain, to enable new connections to be made. Inhibition and the neural plasticity which admits of the formation of fresh coördinations between appetitions and acts are the physiological conditions of purposive choice and volition. Impairment of these functions results in the disintegration of the voluntary life and the fatal rule of reflex and habit automatisms.

experiences which the organism has and takes note of. But we must not forget that, at the center of these volitional experiences, are the individual's own experience of its *ideal strivings* and *valuations,* its demands for the fruition of its yearnings for inner harmony and inner growth, for social harmony and social progress, for comradeship and justice, for the progress of great human causes; in short, for "more life and fuller" of the sort that one means when one thinks of the fellowship of noble minds, endowed with sympathy for humankind and enkindled with the passion for the increase and spread of truth, beauty, justice, and comradeship, participation in and service of which lift society and the individual out of the mire of sensualism, of selfishness, of a hardened and exclusive egoism, out of that static egohood which is the death of the soul.

It is the mission of philosophy to judge the possibilities of man in the light of the highest that man has lived and striven for. The philosopher who does not think nobly of the soul is no genuine philosopher. For, in a complex and changing world, an interpretation of its central factor which would read the meaning and destiny of the whole life of the spirit in man in the light of an arithmetical average is untrue to the meaning of the whole. Not the so-called "divine average" but the highest and rarest and most excellent that has been lived by men is the key to the meaning of spiritual individuality, of selfhood or personality in man.

References

* Avey, A. E., *Readings in Philosophy,* Chapter XXII.

Bergson, H., *Matter and Memory,* and *Time and Free Will.*

Bosanquet, B., *The Principle of Individuality and Value,* pp. 68-77 and the whole of Lecture IX.

Bradley, F. H., *Appearance and Reality,* Chapters IX, X.

* CALKINS, *Persistent Problems of Philosophy*, Chapter XI, B. II, *Personal Idealism*, also Calkins, *A First Book in Psychology*.

* HOWISON, GEORGE H., *The Limits of Evolution*.

* HUME, *Treatise of Human Nature*, Book 1, pt. 4.

* JAMES, WM., *A Pluralistic Universe*, *passim*, and *Will to Believe* (*The Dilemma of Determinism*).

LAIRD, J., *Problems of the Self*.

* LEIGHTON, J. A., *Man and the Cosmos*, Chapters XXII-XXXIV.

* MCDOUGALL, *Body and Mind*.

MCTAGGART, J. M. E., Art., Personality in *Encyclopædia of Religion and Ethics*, and *Studies in Hegelian Cosmology*.

* PALMER, G. H., *The Problem of Freedom*.

PARKER, DEWITT H., *The Self and Nature*.

* PRINCE, MORTON, *The Dissociation of a Personality*.

* RASHDALL, HASTINGS, *Personality, Human and Divine*; in *Personal Idealism*.

ROYCE, J., see index under Individuality in *The World and the Individual*, and *The Problem of Christianity*.

SHERRINGTON, C. S., *The Integrative Action of the Central Nervous System*.

WARD, J., *The Realm of Ends*, see under the Individual in Index, also Art., Psychology in the *Britannica*, 11th ed., and *Psychological Principles*.

CHAPTER XXVI

ETHICS AND SOCIAL PHILOSOPHY

The central problem of ethics is the determination of a standard of the *good* or a rationally definable criterion of intrinsic *values,* a standard for voluntary conduct. Is there any common measure for those ends that are intrinsically good or have value in themselves for the human agent? If so, what is it? Is it a maximum of agreeable feeling? Or obedience to rules of reason? Or is it something richer, more complex and concrete than either pleasurable feeling or the service of reason? The Hedonist holds that the ethical standard is the maximum of agreeable feeling for the individual agent and his fellows. The Rationalist holds that right consists in the subordination of feeling to reason. The Energist or Self-Realizationist holds that the standard of value is the organization and actuation of the fundamental interests of the self as a rational and social agent.

The controversy over the concept of the "highest good" has been spun out at inordinate length, and with unnecessary abstruseness, in treatises on ethics. Making a distinction between *momentary sensuous pleasures* and *happiness* as the relatively continuous feeling which comes from the satisfaction of the deepest interests of human nature, we may say that happiness is the affective index of genuine self-realization by the socialized individual or person. Therefore we may say that the *highest good* may be called either *happiness, well being* or the *development and activity of the true self or personality.* By saying this, we have stated succinctly, but not solved the ethical problem. For the crucial questions are these—what are the elements of true happiness or personal well-being, and under what natural and social conditions may the good life be lived?

The most urgent practical problem of ethics is this—how are the impulses and needs of human individuality to be harmonized with the existing institutions, customs, and beliefs whose function is to maintain social order as the condition of individual well being? Is it possible to formulate a *principle or set of principles,* by which the various interests of human beings in society can be so ordered as to take their places in a consistent and workable system of practical judgments with respect to their several values for promoting human well-being. It is admitted, by all ethicists, that human well-being is the supreme end of individual conduct and social order. But where laymen, as well as ethical thinkers, differ are on the questions—(1) In what does well-being chiefly consist, or on what principles are choices to be made between interests, each of which may be, in itself, conducive to well-being, but all of which cannot be satisfied in equal measure or sometimes cannot be satisfied simultaneously at all in the given circumstances? and (2) How can social life be best ordered and conducted so as to insure the maximum satisfaction of the genuine human interests? For example, which are to be preferred and to what extent, relative to one another—physical health and recreation, social enjoyment, æsthetic cultivation, intellectual development, public influence, and public interests? Should the individual, in directing his own life, aim at surpassing excellence or efficiency in a limited field of endeavor and sacrifice everything else to this, or should he aim at the all round cultivation and exercise of his powers? Is the epitaph said to appear on a tombstone, "Here lies one who was born a man and died a grocer!" the memorial of a human failure? Should a man devote himself primarily to the care of his family, and neglect or subordinate public service or the cultivation of æsthetic or intellectual capacities, in order to lay up economic wealth for his family? How far, and in what circumstances may or should the well-being or life of the individual or smaller groups, such as the family or the community, be sacrificed to the welfare of larger social groups, such as the nation or the church? How far should the welfare of the members of the present generation be sacrificed to the welfare of the generations to come? How far should the means for the achievement of cultural goods of exceptionally high quality, appreciated and used by a comparatively few members of society, be sacrificed to the distribution of creature comforts to the masses? In short, what things are really good for men to seek, and what are their respective degrees of preferability?

I may here remind the reader of a distinction to which attention has several times been called in the present work. I refer to the distinction between *instrumental* or *mediate*, and *intrinsic* or *immediate values*. Ethics is concerned primarily with immediate or intrinsic values. It asks what things or interests of man are good on their own account, or for their own sakes, as constituting worthful elements in a worthy human life. Such sciences as engineering, medicine, and economics, are concerned with instrumental values, that is, with things that have value as means for the support and conduct of social life in such ways that man will thereby be enabled to seek and realize the intrinsic values. Machinery, physical health, and economic wealth are instruments, not ends or values in themselves. They are ministrants to human welfare. Hence, ethics is concerned with these values and the processes by which they are attained, only in so far as such concern is necessary to determine their bearing on the intrinsic values of human well-being.

There is no doubt that all human valuations have their roots in *feelings*. Things have positive value in so far as they satisfy *interests* or *desires*, and negative value in so far as they thwart the satisfaction of interests. Anything has value that satisfies or promises to satisfy an interest of a self. A satisfaction is an agreeable feeling—agreeable because it *agrees* with some tendency, interest or desire of the self. But men reflect upon, compare, and weigh their immediate feelings of value. It is only in so far as they do this that they make *judgments of value*. Thought or reason is able to take an objective, impartial, or impersonal, and social standpoint in regard to values. Moral ideas and ideals, and the science of ethics, which is the systematic attempt to organize moral ideas, are the results of the exercise of the power of reflective judgment upon the immediate feelings of value. The individual's feelings of values are first licked into some sort of coherent shape by the discipline of the social code, in the midst of which he is reared and lives. Then, when he comes to reflective maturity, he critically examines this code, to see if it is consistent with the ideals of value, which he may have acquired by independent reflection, or from some other source in literature, history, or science, or perhaps, from a combination of all these sources. The science of ethics is always the reflective enterprise of critically examining social codes of conduct. If mankind had a perfect social code, or did not need one, there would be no occasion for ethical inquiry. Since men must live in society, they must have codes of social conduct. Since society is complex and dynamic, since it is, in advancing civilizations, always in movement, no merely traditional or customary code of society is adequate to meet the new occasions which demand new duties and new formulations of values, and the scientific study of Ethics is not only necessary but is of the utmost practical value. It is simply the systematic and persistent application of thought or reason to the problem of social values. In a completely static society the ethical problem never arises. But no civilized society is ever completely static. For man is a restless being and, even in ages that are conservative or static, there is always the problem of applying accepted social principles of valuation to changing situations. In ages like our own, in which civilization is in flux, the very foundations of the principles of socal valuation must be reëxamined, in the light of history, social psychology, natural science, and philosophy. There is no more urgent need of the present than the reformulation of a system of social values. *Conscience,* the popular name for the moral consciousness or faculty of moral judgment in the individual, is, in varying degrees, the composite resultant of the social code in which the individual is nurtured and his own reflective consideration of this code.

Many moralists, including the Stoics, the medieval Christian philosophers, Kant, Bishop Butler, and James Martineau, have held that mankind has, in *conscience,* a power of unerring moral judgment, which, if used and obeyed will always tell men what is right and wrong, good and bad. Kant holds that conscience does not err, but we err by not hearkening to our consciences. Bishop Butler said that, when we sit down in a calm hour, we can know what is right. He said that, if conscience had might, as it has right, it would rule the world. This doctrine of an innate and unerring faculty of moral judgment is called *intuitionism.* Intuitionists do not assert that reflection is unnecessary. They recognize that the application of the power of moral judgment to specific cases requires reflection. What they hold is that we have the power, if we will use it. The intuitionist doctrine is the source of the doctrine of the

Natural Rights of man. It is *ethical and political rationalism,* since it deduces, from the deliverances of conscience, the fundamental principles of social conduct—the *rights* and *duties* of men in society. It stresses the absolute bindingness of moral obligations, and deduces from these the system of laws and political relationships. Intuitionism has played a noble rôle in the social and political development of European and American society. The intuitionist insists on the *absolute authority* of duty, right, obligations. As to the source of this authority, we find differences of opinion among intuitionists. The *theological intuitionists* regard conscience, or the moral sense, as the voice of God in the human soul. The Stoics and Kant regard conscience as the supreme and sole authentic utterance of God in the spirit of man. More orthodox Christian intuitionists find two sources of moral authority—the conscience of the individual and the voice of a special divine revelation speaking in Jesus Christ. These two sources are believed to be in harmony; but many would say that the specific revelation adds, to the rational utterances of the natural conscience, the supernatural goods of love and grace and the assurance of immortality.

The fundamental difficulty with intuitionism, if taken on all fours as a complete theory of the origin of our moral judgments, is that it does not harmonize with the facts of man's moral history. Humankind has not agreed in the past, nor does it agree now, as to what deeds and motives are right and wrong, good and bad. With respect to the relations of the sexes, property, human life, social and political rights and obligations, and other matters, there is a bewildering diversity and disagreement as to what is right and wrong, good and bad. As Kipling puts the case—

> The wildest dreams of Kew are the facts of Khatmandu,
> And the crimes of Clapham are chaste in Martaban.

Conscientious persons, even those nurtured in the same

culture, but in different strata and with different affiliations—for example, the labor unionist and the financial magnate—may honestly disagree in regards to the ethics of industry, the ethics of art, or the ethics of marriage. Even those who agree that the Christian revelation is the supreme authority for conscience by no means agree in their moral judgments. Roman Catholics, Greek Catholics, and Protestants disagree in regard to many moral questions. Even Protestants disagree with one another. Nor do we find complete agreement even among Roman Catholics. The agreement approaches completeness in the degree in which there has been similarity of social nurture; although even here some allowance must be made for inborn, individual differences. This allowance must be increased as the social and cultural order becomes more complex and gives nurture and free scope for the development of individual personalities. The fact seems to be that, as W. K. Clifford put it, in simpler types of society the individual conscience is the echo of "the tribal self." Even in complex and advanced cultures, human consciences, as complexes of moral judgments, are made, for many individuals almost entirely, and for all individuals in large measure, by the whole cultural complex of social conditions in which the individual lives. The most enlightened and conscientious of us have to be on guard against two moral dangers—(1) The danger of being satisfied with the commonplace morality of our class, group, or clique. (2) The danger of moral priggishness or fanaticism; of setting up our own private feelings and individual prejudices as the measures of right and wrong. The moral life requires incessant thoughtfulness and open mindedness, no less than courage and loyalty to the best.

Intuitionism has this element of truth—in the last analysis, the enlightened individual, in a free and complex society, must decide the problems of moral value, of right and duty, of good and bad, by a reflective or conscientious choice. But as a theory of the origin of all human ideas of right and wrong it is erroneous. Opposed to intuitionism is the *teleological* theory of morality—so called because it traces the origin, as well as the authority of moral ideas to human beliefs in regard to their ends or purposes. The teleologist holds that right conduct is that which is believed to promote some social value, some individual well-being, or, more often both, since society and the individual are interdependent. The *teleologist* maintains that the specific judgments of conscience are the results of the influence of the social environment working through example and instruction, and by suggestion, reward and punishment, on the individual mind. The teleologist holds that the specific types of moral action which a type of society teaches and enforces are those which have been hit upon, either by a dominant class, or by the collective wisdom of a group, as conditions of the group welfare. Take, for example, the institution of private property; the intuitionist holds that conscience tells us, if we but listen to it, that the social rights and obligations appertaining to private property are founded in the nature of things. Private property is for him a *natural right.* The teleologist argues that the justification of private property is to be found in its value *as an instrument* for promoting human happiness. Therefore, if, owing to changes in the economic field of production and distribution, the existing forms of this institution hinder, rather than promote, general human well-being, the institution must be modified. The ultra-conservative thus appeals to intuition and the past; the teleologist replies that new occasions give rise to new duties and that, if the property laws of the forefathers no longer promote general well-being, they have lost their justification.

The intuitionist might reply that conscience only gives authoritative deliverances in regard to fundamental ethical principles—such as the inherent worth and dignity of personality, the social relations of justice, coöperation, and love. The application of these principles would be left to be determined by experience and on grounds of expediency. In this way intuitionism and teleology in ethics might be reconciled. Let us admit that the human conscience is moulded by its social environment. Nevertheless, is it not the case that, when the normal individual comes to maturity, he can, by reflection, arrive at certain universally valid, ethical principles, although he may be much in doubt as to how precisely these principles can be best applied in the existing circumstances? If there are universally valid ethical *principles* or *values*, if there is a final *good* for man, then the fundamental problem of the *metaphysics of ethics* is this—what status have human values in the universe as a whole? This question is discussed in the next chapter.

It cannot be doubted that social custom, established usage, is the main factor in determining the moral judgments, as well as the legal enactments, that pass current in human society. But when, as notably in the present hour, the customary or institutional modes of procedure and judgment upon such matters as private property, marriage, and the power of the state over the individual, seem to be breaking down, in the face of economic conditions brought to pass by the industrial revolution, it is necessary to reëxamine the entire foundations of our inherited standards of judgments. This means to seek a *philosophy* or thought-out doctrine of the right relations between individuals as members of society.

Moral conduct is conduct that has social reference, so that ethics and social philosophy cannot be sharply distinguished.

Social and political philosophy, in distinction from sociology and politics, which are sciences descriptive of actual social and political institutions in the present and in history, is concerned with the ethical ends or values that are involved in social institutions and activities. It studies the facts of social and political life from the standpoint of a systematic doctrine of the ethical values or ends that should be realized by social institutions, by family, school, industry, the state. Social philosophy is thus really applied ethics—the system of moral valuations applied to the judgment of existing institutions, such as school organization, economic organization, and political organization, in the light of the intrinsic human values or human interests which these organizations exist to further. Thus, ethics is inseparable from social philosophy, as Plato and Aristotle long ago soundly taught. Ethics is the philosophical doctrine of human values, of the various inherently worthful interests or ends which mankind has the right and duty to aim to attain and conserve.

The investigation of the problems of ethics and social philosophy involves psychology, since their subject matter is man as a feeling, thinking, and striving agent. A sound ethical and social doctrine of ends and values can be built up only upon an adequate psychology—one which makes a careful inventory of man's original nature, his inheritance of instincts, impulses, and more general capacities, such as reason or intelligence. But man's original nature is profoundly modified by his social nurture, including the social and spiritual patterns and ideals of conduct which are held up to him for admiration and imitation in his plastic period of youth. A sound theory of ethical and social values can be formulated only when the various cultural or spiritual-historical strains which shape and stimulate the individual in society have been examined and evaluated.

Ethics and social philosophy must, therefore, be based on an extensive and intensive appreciation of the historical development of the whole spiritual heritage of man.

There are two sharply contrasted social philosophies—*individualism* and *collectivism.* We might consider these as political doctrines; from the individualistic standpoint the true end of government is to insure the maxim liberty of action to the individual that is consistent with the maintenance of social order; the only justification for interference with individual liberty is the protection of other individuals in the exercise of their liberties. *Collectivism* is the theory that the true function of government is to subordinate individual liberty to the maintenance and progress of the nation or society as a whole. But at the present time it is not in the realm of politics, except as a handmaid of economics, that this opposition is acute. We may admit that government exists to promote liberty with order; that is, liberty for the individual in so far as this is compatible with a like liberty for all other individuals.

The acute opposition to-day is between *economic individualism and economic collectivism.* For our economic order is so collectivistic in character, so completely enmeshed is the average individual in the toils of industry organized on a large scale, that political, intellectual, and religious liberty are more or less mocking delusions if the economic order does not permit the individual to live decently. Our present economic order is increasingly collectivistic in organization while individualistic in control, in the sense that private groups, which governments either do not control or at best control rather badly, dominate the policies of industry. To a large extent, privately organized group interests control our law-making. When an employer or a group thereof have a controversy with union labor the public usually stands helplessly looking on, and, when it is settled, pays the bills.

Must we then have greater public control in the interests of fuller economic freedom and opportunity? If so, must we go much farther in the direction of state socialism or of that modified form thereof called guild socialism? It is impossible to do more than raise such questions here, in order to show the ethical principles involved. There can be no just and permanent solutions of these and related problems, unless the solutions are based on ethical principles. Justice must guide expediency.

What then is justice in the economic relationships of man? This again is a large and complicated question which there is not room to discuss here. I must be brief and dogmatic. The fundamental problem of social ethics is the problem of justice. *Ethical justice* implies that *every* individual (not one fourth or even nine tenths of them) shall have a fair opportunity to an education that will enable him to develop his powers; and the opportunity for a means of livelihood that will enable him, while doing his bit for the economic and cultural life of society, to lead a decent life as a member of a family, a citizen, and through all the relations of a human person.

There are three principal ways by which a nearer approach to equality of opportunity among human beings may be sought: 1. By the continuance of the present system of private enterprise, with the extension of public control through regulation and taxation; particularly, by the graduated income and inheritance taxes and the excess profits tax. This method might even go the length of fixing maximal rates of profits in various enterprises, the surplus to be used for the common good in public works, education, et cetera. This general procedure might be accompanied by an extension of free coöperation in industry and trade. It would imply a much more ungrudging recognition of labor unions.

2. State socialism. This means public ownership, and either public operation or private operation under lease, of the chief industries. It could not be applied to small trades or agriculture.

3. Guild socialism. The ownership and operation of the chief industries by the workers, the state to serve only as

the arbiter to regulate the rates of reward and thus determine the prices of the products in the interests of the consumers.

It would require too much space to discuss the ethical aspects of these three plans. Their operative practicability involves many technical questions; but, in the last analysis, the feasibility of any social scheme depends on *human motivation* and, therefore, comes down to problems in the psychology and ethics of conduct. Human nature includes certain inexpugnable impulses or "propulsions," as older writers called them. Chief among these impulses are the sex impulse, the possessive impulse, the craving for power and social recognition, the constructive impulse, or the impulse of workmanship. These impulses are plastic and can be turned in various directions under the influence of the social environment. Social institutions are the moulds which shape the natural impulses. The mature individual becomes a creature of habit through the set which his native impulses have been given during the years of training. No economic or other social system will work which thwarts a strong and ineradicable human impulse. The best system will be one which gives most scope for the harmonious development of man's basic impulses. Any proposed economic change must reckon with the sex and family impulses, with the possessive impulse, with the impulse of craftsmanship, and with the striking differences in the impulses towards power and social influence that human beings have. It must also reckon with the native inequalities among human beings, with respect to their physical, intellectual, emotional, and practical capacities. In the light of these considerations it seems to the writer probable that the continuance and extension of the present plan of public control of the industrial system is most in accord with the psychology of conduct, and that its ethical injustices are to a large extent remediable. It is doubtless impossible, by public action, ever to remove all causes of social injustice, but it is probably possible to insure a larger measure of equalization of opportunity. This is all that can be humanly expected. Minimal wage scales with moderate working hours and a better provision for education and recreation would go far in the direction of equalization of opportunity.

References

Ethics

* *Introductory Works* by Drake, Fite, MacKenzie, Seth and Wright.

Alexander, S., *Moral Order and Progress.*

Dewey and Tufts, *Ethics.*

* Everett, W. G., *Moral Values.*

Green, T. H., *Prolegomena to Ethics.*

Hobhouse, L. T., *Morals in Evolution,* and *The Rational Good.*

* Mill, J. S., *Utilitarianism.*

Moore, G. E., *Principia Ethica.*

* Paulsen, F., *Ethics.*

Rashdall, Hastings, *The Theory of Good and Evil.*

Rogers, A. K., *The Theory of Ethics.*

Social Philosophy

Bosanquet, B., *The Philosophical Theory of the State.*

Dewey, J., *Human Nature and Conduct.*

Hegel, *Philosophy of Right.*

Hobhouse, L. T., *Justice.*

MacIver, R. M., *Community.*

MacKenzie, *Outlines of Social Philosophy.*

McDougall, *Social Psychology.*

Mill, J. S., *On Liberty.*

Santayana, G., *Reason in Society.*

Wallas, Graham, *The Great Society.*

CHAPTER XXVII

THE STATUS OF VALUES

Since man is not a colorless and passive knower, who might reflect the characteristics of his surroundings as a good mirror reflects things, or as a glassy water surface reflects its bank, but a knower who *feels and acts,* he judges the objects he knows to have various degrees and kinds of *worth* and *unworth;* and he strives to so alter or maintain the interaction of his surroundings and himself as to remove the experiences that have unworth for him, and to maintain and increase these experiences that have worth.

Knowing is a human affair. The objects of knowledge may be *physical things,* complexes of sense qualities, that is, groupings of the qualities apprehended through man's perceptive mechanism; or *relations* between physical objects and events, that is, laws of nature generalized by the mind from the analysis and comparison of sense perceptions; or *selves and their actual relations* to the physical order and to one another; or, finally, the objects of knowledge may be the *appreciations* or valuations with which man stamps the objects known, and the aims and ideals by which he determines his active relations to physical nature and to other selves.

There are some things in the world of my daily round of experiences that have little or no plus or minus value for me. To meet and apprehend them has little or no bearing on my weal or woe. Such are most of the buildings and many of the people I pass in the streets. Ordinarily, I ignore them. I am scarcely aware of their existence. On the other hand, the buildings in which I live and work, the members of my family, and my professional associates, and even the weather, have worth for me. I apprehend them with interest and I react to them with approval and disapproval. I exercise preferences in regard to the actual and possible objects of experience.

In short, man appreciates, enjoys, loves, admires, and therefore seeks, or he dislikes, fears, hates, and therefore avoids certain objects and situations. *Valuation* is the most persistent and characteristic attitude in human nature. Man seeks to acquire and retain knowledge, power, wealth, comfort, fame, love, and friendship, because he values these things as experiences. The systematic study of the main types of human valuation and the relations between them is an important part of philosophy. As we shall see, in Chapter XXXI, ethics, æsthetics, and the philosophy of religion, are *sciences of human values* or *axiological sciences.* The word "axiology" means science of values. It is derived from the Greek ἄξιος (worth) and λόγος (reason). All these divisions of philosophy are concerned primarily with the central fact that man, in the various aspects of his cognitive and active relations to his world, is a being guided by *selective preferences* or *interests.* These preferences, in the last analysis, are derived from *feelings,* from the emotions and sentiments which constitute the affective complex which is the self considered as a center of feeling and source of valuation, choice, and volition.

Here we are concerned only with making distinctions and definitions with sufficient sharpness to see what is the problem of the status of human values in reality. And, first, we note that there is an important distinction in human values between *instrumental* or *mediate values* and *intrinsic* or *immediate values.* Wealth, position, manual skill, tools, knowledge of foreign languages, are usually means to ends. My pen, for instance, has only an instrumental value. It mediates my getting my thoughts on paper, and this achievement, in turn, is a means to getting them noticed and accepted by my fellows. On the other hand, to love and be loved, to have friends, to be esteemed by one's fellows, are values in themselves. These latter are *intrinsic values.* To live in these experiences is to enjoy *immediate* values. Even to *know* the facts and laws of nature, historical facts and relations, or philosophical principles, has, for some people, intrinsic value. One may take satisfaction in knowing things, regardless of whether anyone else knows that one knows, or esteems or rewards one for knowing, regardless of whether knowing makes one healthier or wealthier, or physically more comfortable. One values knowledge for its own sake, because one feels that an essential demand of one's life is being satisfied by knowing. Moreover, certain kinds of knowledge give æsthetic satisfaction. We speak rightly of the *beauty* of a piece of deductive reasoning, the *grandeur* or *sublimity* of a scientific principle, such as that of gravitation or evolution. Æsthetic experiences gained through poetry, the drama, fine prose, music, painting, or the enjoyment of nature, are to many people intrinsically worthful. "Beauty is its own excuse for being."

While many persons have no joy in knowledge for its own sake and, hence, knowledge has for them no immediate worth; or, have no keen joy in beauty for its own sake which, hence, for them has no immediate worth, there is one type of values which is universal in its appeal. The individual who has no preferences in this type is an idiot or a monster. This type consists of the fundamental valuations or preferences of human persons as individuals and as social beings. Every normal human being desires the companionship, esteem, friendship or love of some other human beings. Every human being who has any self-respect desires the respect of others. Every human being desires to satisfy the fundamental interests of his being, desires to feel and act in the ways that express and realize what he esteems his true selfhood. Now, ethics is the scientific or systematic study of these fundamental types of human value and of the principles of social organization by which the achievement and permanence of these values are furthered. Honesty, integrity, justice, fair-mindedness, active sympathy, conscientiousness, kindness, the spirit of service—these terms connote qualities of selves which constitute fundamental ethical values; because they are not merely indispensable means to the maintenance of a social order in which selves can be truly selves, but, moreover, they are intrinsically worthful qualities of human nature. If "love is the fulfilling of the law," that is because love is taken to include all the other qualities in the presence of which man's higher selfhood can come to its full expression.

And all the movements which have aimed at social justice, at the bettering of the economic, industrial, educational, and political conditions of man's social life, are to be judged by their serviceableness in promoting the realization of the fundamental human values. *It follows that all intrinsic values are located in the conscious lives of selves or persons.* It is nonsense to talk about values that no self feels or seeks, about preferences that no self prefers. *The status of values in the universe of reality is the status of selves.* For selves alone feel, enjoy, suffer, strive for, and win values. If selves, with all their strivings, sufferings, and enjoyments, with all their poignant feelings and unremitting efforts, are but evanescent spume cast up by the waves of the blind and chartless ocean of being, then certainly love and justice, integrity and loyalty, and the other ethical qualities which lend dignity and worth to human life are equally transient. The world is not just and not rational, much less kind, if the whole sequence of human life, in which alone, so far as we know experimentally, justice, reasonableness, kindness, are to be found in finite and imperfect but ever present and ever growing forms of realization, is doomed to extinction. Indeed, if the life of selfhood, the life which is now throbbing in humanity, does not endure and grow permanently the very norms of thought, the logical values themselves, are homeless in the universe and there is no universe, only a hideous bedlam.

Science and logic postulate the rationality, in a broad sense the justice, of the universal order. Science and logic presuppose the validity of the fundamental intellectual values, presuppose the obligation to observe carefully, to think clearly, disinterestedly, and persistently about whatever subject matter we may be concerned with. In the last analysis science, logic, and ethics rest upon the same postulate—the rationality and justice of things, the permanence of fundamental values in the order of reality. But to talk about reason, much less justice and love ruling the universe, if all selves or souls are ephemeral phenomena, is, I repeat, to talk nonsense. To talk of eternal values which rule serenely in a timeless world of being, if the life of humanity does not endure somehow as an essential and worthful constituent in the universe of reality, is to talk "transcendental moonshine."

Science, a better social order, a freer, fuller life for human personality, beauty, philosophy itself, are all vain dreams which man conjures up to hide from his gaze the reeking shambles of reality which he fears to face, unless the fundamental human values endure through the permanence of rational and ethical spirit.

The last and deepest problem of philosophy which is, I remind you, the reflective study of life and experience in their wholeness, is the problem of religion. And religion, as I have already pointed out, is always at its best an affirmative answer to the final question of humanity—do our highest values endure and if so, under what conditions?

The true meaning of postulating a God, the animating principle of faith in God and the higher order of which he is the guardian and sustainer, is this affirmative response to the cry of mankind for the assurance or promise of the *permanence of the life of most worth.* Religion is the yea-sayer to all the higher values. If it denies some values dear to the hearts of some persons, if it calls to renunciation and sacrifice of the lower self, it does this in the interest of higher values.

As to the questions, how fundamental values come to appear in the life of humanity, and whence they derive their authority, three chief answers have been given—1. Dualistic Supernaturalism, 2. Agnostic Relativism or Subjectivistic Humanism, 3. Teleological Idealism.

1. The dualistic supernaturalist avers that the source and authority of all supreme values is the descent into human life, at special times and at special crises, of heaven-sent messengers authenticated with supernatural power. The "Thus saith the Lord" has its seal in miracle working and mystery mongering. Jahweh thunders from Mount Sinai. God speaks through a divine revealer and validates his utterances with physical portents, or he leaves, through the divinely appointed succession of a hierarchical order, continuous special authorities in an ecclesia or church.

2. The agnostic relativist points to the fact that the language and the very contents and meanings of the speech of revealers are conditioned, indeed, determined by the whole social culture of their times. He points, with the eye of the critical historian, to the way in which fundamental values have changed and evolved under the influences of industrial, political, and scientific changes. He points out, for example, that the values authorized by Mosaic religion differed from those of later Hebrew prophetism; the latter from those of primitive Christianity. He triumphantly shows, by historical analysis, that the

social values of the primitive Christian community differed greatly from those of a present day Christian state. He shows that the change is due to a mass of economic, political, and intellectual changes. Finally, he calls attention to the significant fact that dualistic supernaturalism rests upon a cosmology that is inconsistent with modern science. The latter has built up, step by step, a conception of the infinite extent, complexity, duration, and orderly character of a world in which there is no place for the eruption now and then of miraculous portents.

The agnostic relativist concludes that the human values are the products solely of the social workmanship of man, a creature weak and ephemeral but gifted with an indomitable will and a strange capacity for planting and training up, amidst the savage wastes of the blind forces which alone operate in nature, a cultivated plot of the finer humanity. Man, he says, is engaged in an incessant struggle with the savage and relentless forces of nature. He will ultimately go down to defeat and extinction, but in the meantime the only life of effort that gives at least a transitory, though pathetic, gleam of grace and sweetness to life, is ceaseless endeavor to improve his little garden of the spirit, to tend and nurture in it the fruits and flowers of honesty, integrity, loyalty, justice, truthfulness, comradeship, and sympathy. These values are all doomed to ultimate extinction but, in the meantime, let us nobly strive and nobly help one another.

The agnostic relativist fails to solve one riddle. How, if nature or reality be as he conceives it, could it ever have given birth to man, its insurgent son? If man, too, be but the blind offspring of savage and insensate forces, surely it makes an even greater draft on one's credulity to say that from the blind welter of mass particles in endless, whirling motion there could have sprung the tendernesses, the heroisms, the noble friendships, the undying devotions to human kind, the willing self-sacrifices for those illusions of great causes and high enterprises, which the better part of mankind displays? How could even such illusions as justice, integrity, sympathy, love, loyalty, and self-sacrifice have come into being? Agnostic relativism, which holds that values have no status except in the better members of the living generation, hence is a *subjectivism,* in which the present living generation of the race, not the individual self, is regarded as the subject who creates values out of nothing. This view is, of course, materialism, and the single criticism in which all criticisms of materialism concenter is that it makes all human values illusions, mysteriously and episodically engendered by the operation of blind physical forces.

3. Teleological or Axiological Idealism. This view accepts the criticisms of dualistic supernaturalism and holds, too, that values are wrought out by man in history and, hence, are subject to fluctuation, to change and evolution, as man's social life develops from simpler to more complex forms, as his tools for intellectual analysis and economic and social organization improve. But the teleological idealist holds that the persistence and evolution of values, the change which involves continuity of growth in the process of discovering values and means to realize them, logically implies that human values, and the selves which realize and enjoy them, are not mere ephemeral by-products of nature. Man is a true and effective part of reality. He is a legitimate offspring of the universe. He must be heir then to a part of the universal heritage. The values he creates he does not create out of nothing. Values are not vain imaginings. It is the same being who perceives and knows who likewise values, prefers, chooses, and acts. It is the same homogeneous world in which he grows in knowledge and power, and in the consciousness of values, and the ability to realize them. Man and his valuations

are somehow at home in the universe. Man is quite as able to cash in on his preferences, his valuations, as he is on his knowledge or his industrial activity. The universe which, in part, we know, is a universe which answers questions that are rightly put and to which answers are persistently sought. It is the same teleological order which sustains and honors human values. Values are neither mysterious visitants from an alien sphere nor phantoms of human imagination. Values are the ways in which the ruling purport, the ineluctable life and feeling of the universe, are expressed in a multitude of finite centers of feeling and action—in the life of humanity.

In almost all the great historic systems of philosophy, the author's concept of value determines the character of his fundamental standpoint.[1] The ideas that play the chief part in Plato's interpretation of reality are ideas of values —logical relations, beauty, justice, wisdom; and the supreme and ruling idea is the good. The same is true with regard to Aristotle. God, the pure form, is the ground of all forms, and the finite forms or entelechies are the ordering principles in nature. The highest value for Aristotle is the æsthetic-intellectual concept of the pure self-activity of reason. Plotinus' conception of reality is controlled by the ideal of mystic union of the finite selfhood with the absolute spirit. Despite his show of geometrical demonstration, Spinoza's world view is determined chiefly by his vision of finite selfhood as finding its fulfillment and euthanasia in a blessed absorption in the divine substance. For Leibnitz the supreme values are the infinitely diversified individuality of the monads and the continuity and organization of the universe into a harmonious whole.

---

[1] Even in systems of materialism it is the apparent clearness, simplicity, self-evidence, and cogency of the principles that determines the standpoint taken.

Kant's system is controlled by his concept of the moral dignity and freedom of the human personality; of the tremendous seriousness and infinite significance of man's moral vocation. The same motives determined the fundamental outlines of Fichte's philosophy. For Hegel the supreme value is the spectacle of the self-realizing march of Spirit through history, having as its goal the harmonious organization of finite selfhood into conscious union with the infinite idea. For Schopenhauer the peace which comes from the cessation of all desire and the ending of all inner discord is the highest value.

For Berkeley the vision of God, the great other spirit, is the highest value. For Hobbes, Locke, Hume, and Mill the highest value lies in the reconciliation of the social and political freedom of the individual with the needs of a social order and authority. How to ensure to the human individual the liberty to develop and lead his own life as a member of the social order, without which the development and exercise of individuality is impossible—such has been the dominant problem of English philosophy from Hobbes to John Stuart Mill. Mill expressly states that he was led to his logical investigations in order to lay secure foundations for a science of society.

It is in this British feeling for the worth and rights of human individuality that we find the keynote of William James' philosophy. For the school of objective idealism (Bradley, Bosanquet, and others), the supreme criterion of value is the harmonious organization of experience into a systematic whole, the fusion or union of all aspects of experience into a living totality, in which all differences are unified, all conflicts are healed, all discords are harmonized. In this harmonious totality the contrast between reflective thinking and its objects passes away into a perfect intuition or state of feeling in which knower and known are wholly one; the conflict between the "is" and the "ought-to-be," between desired ideal and achieved fact, is laid at rest. In it all pain and discord are contributing elements in the harmonious feeling which pervades the whole. The whole is the all-inclusive individual experience in which all imperfect individuals are elements. Thus the highest value is the highest reality. The same standard obtains for truth as for other aspects of value. For the measure of truth in any system of judgments is the internal coherence of the system.

Royce's conception of value does not greatly differ from the one just stated. Absolute reality is the fulfillment of all values, for it is the complete fulfillment of the meaning of all finite ideas, the complete satisfaction of all finite purposes.

The chief objections raised to the idealistic theory of value are: (1) in its eagerness to identify the absolute value of harmony, internal coherence, perfection of organization in experience, with reality, it overlooks the fact that, for human beings, value is an ideal aim only gradually and partially achieved in time, and thus it seems to deprive the human process of striving for and achieving harmonious organization, the whole temporal life of effort and progress towards higher values, of any final value. For, identifying absolute value and absolute reality, this doctrine assumes the timeless reality of the ideal values; (2) consequently, it is objected, eternalistic idealism cannot find any lasting significance in the deeds and experiences of the imperfect and striving human individual.

The pragmatists and personal idealists have, while admitting that the ideal of value is harmonious experience or harmony of life and feeling, protested against the assumption that all value is eternally or timelessly real. This protest, on behalf of the human person's life as a process in time, is the chief motive of the tendency known as *temporalism,* which insists that all reality must traffic in time, that value must inhere in the temporal activities of selves and the historical order, if there be any value in reality.

Windelband, Rickert, and other representatives of the Philosophy of Values in Germany, have insisted that the validity of the norms of logical thinking, the very basic principles of knowledge, no less than the acceptance of moral ideals and canons of æsthetic judgment, rest on the *act of the thinker* in accepting the conditions under which alone the purpose and will to know the truth, to will the good, and to accept the beautiful, can be fulfilled. In other words, if you seek truth you ought to and must accept the rules of the thinking game, just as if you seek the good you must accept the norms of goodness. This attitude of the self in acknowledging the values of truth, goodness, and beauty is an act of faith in universal purposes which rule the time order.

From our standpoint the only sense in which we can speak of eternal values is that there are universal purposes and meanings which maintain themselves and prevail in the temporal flux. In other words the eternity of values means their active perduration through the endless process of change and evolution and their continuing victory, won in part through the service by human selves of the universal purpose or universal value.

This standpoint I call *teleological idealism.* It accepts, as the *ideal* or *criterion of value,* the harmonious organization of experience in persons. It finds such harmony fulfilled in the development of truth through increasing coherence, in the development of the good through the organization of human interests, in the development of feeling through the fulfillment of æsthetic ideals and personal affections. But it does not admit that the ideal of value is in all its fulness timelessly fulfilled in the shape of a completed reality. It does not admit that the present order of facts is transparently and completely the fulfillment or expression of value. It finds that the conflict between actual existence and ideals, between finite fact and value, is real and it is led to suppose that only through continuous activity by selves can this conflict be overcome.

Thus teleological idealism admits the necessity of postulating a ruling principle or ground of values in the universe. It can believe in progress and admit retrogression in the values of life. It knows no absolute but the absolute need that man, if he is to be true to his vocation as a spiritual agent, shall loyally cleave to the service of the ideal values, to steadfast service of truth, integrity, justice, fellowship, the furtherance of beauty and harmony in the world of society and in the inner man. For we know only in part and prophesy in part and we prophesy in faith according to the measure and urgency of our spiritual needs and cravings.

Teleological idealism does not deny that in special individuals, and at significant junctures in man's history, old values are transformed and new ones created. In fact teleological idealism sees in the religious genius, the moral genius, the artistic and scientific geniuses, in the creative poet, musician, artist, discoverer, organizer and protagonist of higher ideals, special organs through which the common life of man is transformed by the breaking forth, into a new power of creative utterance, of the universal spiritual order, the ever energizing cosmic meaning of life.

The problem of the status of value in the universe is the problem of the status of humanity or selfhood. The idea of God is that of a supreme reality or spiritual order, in and through which human personality and its values are sustained. God is the cosmical ground of values, the ground of human personality, the overself which is the source and goal of all selfhood.

The evil is that which thwarts values, which impedes and destroys them. I cannot here enter upon a consideration of the problem of evil. Let me point out that, from the present standpoint, namely that God means the supreme principle or ground of Values and of personality, the question of the origin of evil ceases to be a question of vital interest. The world is as it is, no matter what were the conditions of its origin. There is no point in crying over the irrevocable past. It could not have been otherwise, either from the point of view of materialism or of teleological idealism. The apparent wastefulness and cruelty of the natural order is to be faced as a fact. These things can be, and are being controlled. Man's inhumanity to man is capable of being remedied. Nature's inhumanity to man has been in part overcome and may be still more successfully lessened, when man's social capacities are better organized and more fully brought into play. From our standpoint we are to regard the defects of nature and the defects of man as challenges to concerted human effort, by which the human values already caught sight of and acknowledged shall be enhanced and conserved and, in the process, new and richer human values shall be engendered.

Teleological idealism does not imply that there are no forces in the universe hostile to the achievement or conservation of values. It does mean that humanity and its values, being essential features of a universe, which, thus far, is humanistic in character, may endure and win the victory. Thus it is a *rational faith* in human values; *rational,* because values and selves are the offspring of the very universe in which reason lives and works, *faith,* because admittedly we can see but a little way and that not very clearly, along the pathway of humanity in its course through time.

In conclusion it may not be amiss to note the bearing of this position on the traditional arguments for the existence of God. The ontological argument—the idea of God is the idea of a perfect being; the idea of a perfect being involves the existence of such a being; therefore God exists —is nothing more than the putting into the form of a syllogism of the *postulate* of a supreme principle or ground of values—the perfect being. The cosmological argument —that the existence of the world implies the existence of a unitary cause—has no religious value, except in so far as it is assumed that the world is good and, therefore, its values must have a single source. The physicoteleological argument or argument from the evidence of design or purpose in the structure and process of nature is but a clumsy and roundabout way of stating the fundamental postulate of life, morality, science, and religion, namely that values are operative and controlling principles in the universal order.

References

* Avey, A. E., *Readings in Philosophy,* Chapter XXVI.

Bosanquet, *The Value and Destiny of the Individual.*

* Höffding, *The Problems of Philosophy.*

* Huxley, T. H., *Evolution and Ethics.*

* James, *The Will to Believe,* and *A Pluralistic Universe.*

Leighton, J. A., *Man and the Cosmos,* Chapters XXVIII, XXIX, XXX, XXXV, XXXVII, and XXXVIII.

* Mill, J. S., *Three Essays on Religion.*

Münsterberg, *The Eternal Values.*

Nietzsche, F., *Works,* translated by A. Tille, especially *Thus Spake Zarathustra, Beyond Good and Evil,* and *Genealogy of Morals.*

Rickert, H., *Vom System der Werte, Logos,* Bd. IV, 1913, pp. 295-327.

* Russell, B., *The Free Man's Worship,* in *Mysticism and Logic.*

Windelband, W., *Einleitung in die Philosophie,* Pt. II, and *History of Philosophy,* pp. 518-528 and pp. 648-659.

Works on Metaphysics and the Philosophy of Religion previously cited.

CHAPTER XXVIII

THE PHILOSOPHY OF HISTORY

I. A Sketch of Some Leading Philosophies of History

The philosophy of history must be distinguished from the philosophical study of history. The latter consists of reflection upon and generalization from the study, either of special periods of history, or in its widest form, of universal history. Excellent examples of philosophical historians are Ranke, Taine, Lecky, and Burckhardt. The philosophy of history is the quest for a determination of the right standpoint from which to view the whole activity of man as an historical and social being. What does the life of man, as an historical being, mean? What ends or values does the historical life aim at and achieve? What is the worth, the purpose, the promise of man's life in time on the earth? Is human history, as the successive generations run their courses, a meaningless and futile tale? Or does man lay foundations, build up values, partially see and achieve ends that are inherently worthful, however fragmentary and imperfect their fulfillment at any given time may be? Does the historical life of man imply the further progress and fruition of human values? Are justice, rationality, liberty, humanity, the achievement of fuller individuality and a finer social order, mere dreams and illusions of a being who is inexorably and unconsciously driven on by physical and economic forces alone? Or does history show, on large scale patterns, the working out of ethical and rational ends? To raise such questions is to indicate that the philosophy of history is the application of metaphysics and ethics to the whole spectacle of man's temporal life. On the other hand, metaphysics and ethics are enriched, given content, endowed with body and blood, only by bringing their categories down into, and putting them to work in, the concrete life of man. Metaphysics and ethics must draw from the contemplation, on a wide scale and in sympathetic manner, of the march of man and civilization through time, fruitful suggestions, materials, and points of view.

The germs of a philosophy of history are to be found in the writings of Hebrew prophecy (in Isaiah, Amos, Jeremiah, Ezekiel, and others) in which the course of nations is for the first time conceived and depicted as controlled by the one divine, governing purpose. Jehovah is the ruler of all the nations and he judges them and determines their fates in accordance with the eternal principles of social righteousness and mercy, which are the expression in human society of his holy will. Special privileges entail special obligations and Jehovah judges and allots to Israel its historical destiny in accordance with the measure of its loyalty to the laws of social justice and loving kindness, which he enunciates through the mouths of his prophets. In this connection see especially Isaiah 40:12 ff., 42:5 ff., 45:21-23, Amos 9:7, and the whole treatment of the relations of the various peoples in Isaiah, Amos, Micah, and Jonah. Israel and Judah must not look for special favors at the hands of Jehovah. He is not their God alone, but the God of the whole earth, and, indeed, of the whole universe.

This prophetic conception of the moral order of history, that is, of the course of historical change as the working out of cosmically effective principles of social or ethical value, was their solution of the ethico-religious problem which confronted a group of great thinkers who started from the fundamental postulate of an ethical and social religion. Jehovah was believed to stand in a peculiar relation to the people to whom he had made known his true character and who had accepted him by an act of will (the covenant relationship). Now political disaster, conquest, and suffering confront the chosen people. If Jehovah be, indeed, the ethical will who rules the world, these disasters must be the consequence of Israel's disloyalty. The prophets have no difficulty in pointing to the social corruption, the luxury, sensuous indulgence, dishonesty, and oppression, that are rife in a luxurious state, as the sins of disloyalty, the continuance in which brings disaster because the Judge of all the earth is holy. This *new* view of the nation's relation to Jehovah carries with it the ethical universalism which sees in the vicissitudes of all the nations the work of Jehovah's will. Assyria is for the time the rod of his anger. Cyrus, the Persian, is his instrument.

The prophetic doctrine of a providential moral order, ruling the course of history and having its consummation in the full establishment of the Kingdom of God, is taken over and further developed, in the light of the belief in Christ as the fulfiller of the prophetic teaching, by the fathers of the Christian Church. It furnishes the means by which the civilization of Greece and Rome are set in their relations to the Hebrew-Christian process of revelation and redemption. St. Paul and the author of the Epistle to the Hebrews philosophize on the relation of Hebraism and Gentilism to Christianity. See, in this connection, St. Paul's Epistles to the Romans, and Galatians, Chapters 3 and 5, and Hebrews, especially Chapter 11.

Justin Martyr, Irenæus, Tertullian, and especially Augustine, carry on the work of setting the history of the world in the framework of the Christian religion as the final revelation of God's purpose. Augustine, in his *City of God,* formulates, in comprehensive fashion, for medieval Christianity the whole providential order of history. The goal of history is the parousia or second coming of Christ, which will mean the complete establishment of the Kingdom of God on earth. The Christian eschatology or doctrine of last things thus supplies the *norm* for the judgment of historical progress.

The Manicheans and Gnostics, heretical sects in the early Christian centuries, conceived the historical process in thoroughly dualistic fashion as a battle of the gods, a conflict between the cosmic powers of good and evil, light and darkness, spirit and flesh. This dualistic interpretation of history has its roots in the dualism of the Persian religion and in the metaphysical and ethical dualism of spirit and matter which is so prominent a feature of the later Greek and Hellenistic-Roman speculation, especially in the Neoplatonic school. Augustine was profoundly influenced by it. Augustine, in his *City of God,* maintains that the course of history is regulated by the will of God, according to a predetermined plan. Nevertheless, man is free, and, by the sin of Adam, the unity of the race was broken into two societies—the city of evil or selfwill and the city of God, ruled by love. The race, like the individual, passes through three periods in its education—youth, manhood, and mature age. The end of history will be the establishment of a new earth, the triumph of the city of God when the number of the elect is completed. Bossuet, the great French preacher, in the seventeenth century develops a similar theory of history.

The great philosophers of the seventeenth and eighteenth centuries were not interested in history, with the exception of that universal genius, Leibnitz, who in this respect, as in others, is beyond his time. For Hobbes, Descartes, and Spinoza, and their followers, the norms of all knowledge are mathematics and mechanics, the mathematics of the physical order. For Locke and Hume the chief interest lay in the psychological and epistemological analysis of knowledge. For them, too, mathematics was the highest and exactest kind of knowledge, since it dealt only with the relations between ideas. The notion of the gradual growth of evolution of human institutions was foreign to their thinking. Everything social and human was conceived to be a deliberate invention of reason or the result of a voluntary convention or conscious contract. This attitude is not entirely true of Hume, who, in his *Natural History of Religions,* did employ the historical method.

The first thinkers to formulate a doctrine of historical progress were Turgot (in 1750) and Condorcet (in 1793). Turgot conceives history as the life of humanity progressing towards perfection, by the gradual elevation of man's whole nature—of his intelligence, feelings, economic lot, and social order. Mental or spiritual progress is the mainspring of history. He does not think that progress moves at a uniform pace or at the same rate in all directions. Condorcet believes in the perfectibility of man through continuous progress. He holds the next steps to be the establishment of equality between nations and individuals.

J. J. Rousseau (1712-1778) challenged the whole civilization of his time. He held (1) that human nature was originally or naturally good; (2) that it had been corrupted, and misery, vice, and crime introduced into society, by political and economic inequality; (3) that the whole history of civilization had been a career of illusion, suffering, and crime, resulting from the oppression of the poor and weak by the strong and unscrupulous; (4) therefore, social authority and order must be based on a free contract in which the social or general will shall be determined by majority rule. The end of social order is the free and spontaneous development of individuality, subject to the good of all as determined by the general will. Rousseau has had a widespread and deep influence on social and political thought, in England and America, as well as in France. He deeply influenced Kant and Fichte, but the general course of German political thought since Hegel has been quite different. In a land in which, until the great crash came in the autumn of 1918, bureaucratic class rule and the divine rights of kings and yunkers, seemed to become ever more firmly seated in the saddle, Rousseau, the gospeller of democracy and equality of opportunity, soon went out of fashion; indeed, never was in fashion.

Kant in his *Ideas Towards a Universal History* did not break away from the prevailing type of unhistorical rationalism. He did, however, formulate the idea of progress toward rationality; as did also Lessing (1729-1781), who conceived the historical process of humanity to be a gradual progress in God's education of the race up to the goal, which is full recognition of the religion of the spirit and love, first enunciated in the Gospel of St. John. Herder (1744-1803) in his *Ideas for the Philosophy of the History of Mankind* has a much broader conception. He attempts to bring the whole course of man's development in time under the conception of a law of progress, whose goal is the rule of reason and love in human society. Herder takes account of the influence of geographical and climatic conditions in the historical developments of peoples, and also gives a place to the operation of the more or less unconscious *spirit* or *soul of a people.* The goal of history is the fulfillment of the ideal of humanity; that is, the harmonious development of all the capacities of man into rationality, æsthetic harmony, social freedom, and love. This was the ideal of Goethe and Schiller, too. Fichte and Hegel agree with Lessing and Herder in conceiving the course of history to be the progressive realization in human society of rational freedom and love. The goal of man's earthly life, says Fichte, is that humanity, in all its relationships, shall direct its life with freedom and in accordance with reason. Fichte, too, regards the Johannine Gospel as the first clear enunciation of the spiritual end and meaning of history. Reason, he says, works first unconsciously as instinct, then externally as the authority of custom and law, and finally, inwardly in the complete insight of conscious and rational freedom. Fichte's doctrine is a metaphysics of history read in terms of his theory of ethical values.

Hegel's *Philosophy of History* is the most elaborately worked out metaphysics of history produced by the school of absolute idealism. In a broad sense, Hegel's whole philosophy is historical, an evolutionary idealism. The dialectic process or development of the full truth and meanings of things through the "might of the negative"; that is, the impulse resident in every finite thing and event to pass over into its opposite, and for the opposites to be absorbed into a higher unity in which opposition again breaks forth, this *logic of passion,* is exemplified on the grand scale in the history of human culture. The whole story of humanity is the development of spirit to fully conscious and rational freedom, through the incessant breaking forth, and reconciliation on a higher level, of the oppositions inherent in the movement of spirit through the finite forms of reality. Art, politics, and religion, all pass through this dialectic growth, and Hegel threads the whole history of the religious and political institutions of the world on his dialectic framework. The meaning of human history is the progressive realization of the consciousness of rational freedom on the part of man. Rational freedom is attained when there is a recognition of the complete harmony of the will of the individual with the universal will embodied in the state. It is identical with true morality, for this consists precisely in the conscious and complete acceptance by the individual self of the rights and duties which are prescribed to him by the whole spirit of the state. So freedom is fully realized where custom, law, and morality are wholly harmonious. It is in the state that the individual life, family life, and the life of civil society, find their fulfillment. History, therefore, begins and ends with the state.

The dialectic of history is the struggle of the succession of state ideas. "The state is the march of God in history." "The state is the Divine Idea as it exists on earth." In it are found the union of morality and religion. God is the absolute reason who governs the world. God is the world-spirit who realizes his idea or purpose in time. In each successive great epoch of history, one state represents the aspect of the divine idea which is then being realized. The struggle between states is the struggle between stages of the idea.

The victorious state represents a higher phase of the divine idea than the conquered state. For example, in the ancient oriental empires of China and India but *one man is free*—the ruler—and he is capricious and despotic. The subjects do not *know* that they are free subjects and therefore are only unconscious subjects. The religions of the Orient, especially Brahmanism, make the infinite all and man, the finite individual, nothing. Thus they correspond with the despotic state idea. Greece conquers the oriental world because Greece, particularly Athens, represents a higher stage in the consciousness of freedom and individuality. *Some men,* that is the citizens, *are free.* Greece gives free play to individuality, and her religion is the religion of the finite, of free and beautiful individualities who express the Greek ideal of humanity. But Greece succumbs because she does not attain the full consciousness of the identity of man as man with the universal, of the finite with the Infinite, of the identity of the individual spirit with the spirit of the social order. In order that this consciousness of the universality of freedom may be achieved, it must appear in the form of *abstract universality,* the abstract power of the universal state. This is the Roman Empire. Christianity infuses into the Roman world the consciousness of the identity of the divine and the human, the infinite and the finite, in its doctrine of the God-Man. Politically, this consciousness is realized in the modern Germanic world, in which all men are free as rational beings who find the substance of their wills in the complete but free and rational identification of their subjective or personal wills with the universal will embodied in the organization of the state, in which they coöperate as rational members. Thus the goal of history is reached. What remains to be achieved in future time, Hegel does not indicate.

The great personalities, world historical individuals, statesmen, conquerors, and rulers are the chief organs of the universal will, instruments of the idea, of the world spirit. They pursue their own aims, but *Reason* in its cunning uses them as its tools to further its unhasting and unresting movement.

Hegel's conception of history thus differs from the traditional Christian conception in that his providence is a world purpose or a world idea that is the *wholly immanent* driving force that operates according to the dialectic or logic of history, using the passions and wills of men, the vicissitudes of empires and rulers, to achieve full consciousness of itself, by *an immanent necessity* that admits nothing contingent, nothing that can arrest its resistless progress. Hence, the course of history is the majestic progress of the true and the good in and through all the error and the sin, the passion and pathos, the tragedy and comedy of man's political and social life. The Christian view, on the other hand, regards man as a free and responsible agent who may contravene, although he cannot finally thwart, God's purposes in history.

Hegel's *Philosophy of History* is a combination of philosophical history, in which the facts are often badly distorted to fit his scheme, and metaphysics of history. For Hegel history is the resistless and inevitable march of the absolute idea through time, until it becomes fully conscious of itself in the culture of the modern Germanic world and discovers, in the Hegelian philosophy, what it has all meant. This victorious march of the absolute through time is the metaphysical ground of all culture. It is the progressive realization by the human spirit of its identity with the absolute spirit, which consciousness of itself through the human spirit by the absolute spirit is the full and true meaning of freedom. Karl Marx, the author of *Das Kapital,* the socialistic Bible, stood the Hegelian philosophy on its head when he proclaimed that the march of the absolute through time is the march of economic necessity, and every culture factor, every ideological motive in history, is but a sublimation of economic forces. Marx, in a one-sided fashion, thus called attention to a very important consideration neglected by Hegel, namely the influence of economic factors in determining the course of man's historical evolution. The economic or materialistic interpretation of history has become almost a commonplace since then; but to assert that economic motives are the only ones that rule in history is to take a distorted view of human nature.

Auguste Comte (1798-1857) regards historical progress as due primarily to intellectual causes. There are, he says, three stages in man's intellectual history. In the earliest or theological stage, man explains events by recourse to spirits (animism); in the second or metaphysical stage, explanation is given in terms of abstract metaphysical entities (for example, to explain the effects of opiates as due to a "dormific" capacity); in the third or positivistic stage, of which Comte was the herald, man concerns himself only with formulating the correlations between phenomena, to the end that he may establish social harmony and well-being. Comte formulated a polity for the positivistic society, his social ideal, in which altruism as the supreme motive and the detailed regulation of social life are to be the chief factors. The goal of history is the perfection of man in society, motivated by altruism and directed by positive science. Buckle, the English historian, was a pioneer in showing the influence of physical conditions in determining the course of history. He did not, however, deny the influence of mental causes.

Nearly all modern systems of sociology include theories of historical progress. Herbert Spencer, for instance, elaborates at great length the view that society has progressed, and is still progressing, from militarism with centralized organization towards *industrialism* with political decentralization. Some sociologists, such as Gumplowicz and Ratzenhofer, emphasize the struggles of races and groups for political domination as the chief cause of historical change. Much use has been made of the evolutionary doctrines of struggle for existence and survival of the fittest as ruling forces in historical changes.

Social psychologists or psychological sociologists, of whom there are many to-day, following Wundt, emphasize the central place of psychical forces, feelings, and volitions, in historical change. Wundt holds that the philosophy of history is applied psychology. There are social psychological laws or principles which are illustrated by the facts of history. The sociologists in general hold that there are laws of historical change. Thus they are determinists. But many of them would agree with Wundt that the laws of historical causality are psychological and thus differ from physical laws. In a physical process there is quantitative equivalence between cause and effect. This is not the case in the psychical sphere. Here the effects differ quantitatively as well as qualitatively from the causes (Wundt's Law of the Increase of Psychical Energy).

A considerable and influential number of writers on the logic of history, chief among whom may be mentioned Dilthey, Windelband, Rickert, Simmel, Troeltsch, and Croce, deny that there are historical laws even remotely analogous to physical laws. They hold the function of history to be the description and interpretation of unique, nonrepeatable occurrences. The subject matter of history is the irreversible series of unique nonrepeatable events that constitute the historical development of human culture. History does not repeat itself and the historian deals with individualities, chiefly the individualities of culture groups, epochs, and movements. The historian employs general concepts and makes generalizations. But these are *teleological concepts* or *concepts of value.* In the selection and interpretation of historical occurrences, it is not merely legitimate but inevitable that the unique members of historical series of events should be related or connected into a systematic interpretation, and this relating takes place in terms of *values* or *teleological principles* of action. For historical events are the expression of the clashing and coöperating wills of men.

II. Problems of the Philosophy of History

I will now briefly indicate the problems of the philosophy of history. This discipline has no concern with the determination of the facts of history or their empirical relationships. That is the province of the historian. The consideration of the logical processes or methods and principles of historical investigation and interpretation, and comparison of them with the methods and principles of natural science constitute the *Logic of History*, an important division of logical inquiry. Inasmuch as the principles of logic have the closest connection with metaphysics, the logic of history is intimately associated with the *Metaphysics of History*. In the latter field, the chief questions are the following: First, the determination of the system of human values or standards of judgment, in the light of which philosophy can intelligently weigh the questions as to the fact and character of human progress, the growth of culture or civilization. The general problem of progress falls into several divisions—the problem of the nature and facts of moral progress, political progress, economic progress, intellectual progress, religious progress, and their interrelationships.

In the consideration of the problem of progress there are two chief factors to be taken into account; first, the original or biological nature of man. Is human nature modifiable through the inheritance of acquired characteristics? Man's inherited nature is an original datum for all theories of progress and practical efforts towards progress. The members of every living generation set out upon their social careers with about the same fixed capital of native impulses and powers. There is no evidence of any natural increase in the native capacities of men. Thus, as civilization grows more complex it increases the strain on the human organism. Unless the increased tension be relieved by improved cultural methods, civilization disintegrates. This has often happened; very likely it will happen again. The changes in the way of improvement and decline in the character of the social inheritance or cultural complexes, into which the generations are born and by which they are nurtured, is the second factor in estimating progress.[1]

[1] I use the term "culture" here, in a broad sense, to include all the products of human thought, imagination, invention, and organ-

The formulation of the system of values is the critical problem of ethics. Thus the philosophy of history must rest on ethics. On the other hand, the study of history furnishes material for ethics. There is here a logical circle. History is interpreted and judged in terms of a system of ethical values which, in turn, are derived from history. There is no escape from the circle. The philosopher must simply do his best to attain the fullest possible objectivity by the fairest, widest and most penetrating survey of the facts of cultural evolution. The questions —wherein does progress consist, and has it taken place or is it now going on—can be answered only in terms of a theory of human values. It is absurd to dispute about progress, if we do not know what we are talking about; and we do not know, until we have formulated a comprehensive and coherent philosophy of the true values and ends of human existence.

In the past those who have speculated on the meaning of history have usually judged the facts from the standpoint of a standard of valuation arbitrarily assumed or deduced from some theological or metaphysical belief in regard to the absolute or supreme values to be served or won by man. Now, a candid and searching examination of the types of judgment, the conceptions of the good, or the values to be pursued by civilized man, as these are revealed in man's social, political, and religious deeds and aspirations and are expressed in his literatures and philosophies, will show that there has been change, growth with improvement in certain directions, perhaps retrogression in others. The ideals of a Greek gentleman, as reflected in Plato and Aristotle, differ quite markedly from those

---

ization, that enter into, and are transmitted by, the stream of social life as it passes from generation to generation. Thus culture includes all physical discoveries and inventions, no less than art, science, morals, and religion.

of the best Hebrews of Isaiah's day or of a Greek Christian or a medieval Christian. The ideas or values of life for a medieval Christian are quite different from those of an eighteenth century philosopher and of a twentieth century American. The ideals and values of the latter differ from those of a good Chinaman or Burmese.

A doctrine of ethical and social values or norms of conduct and social organization, which shall be clear sighted and well-rounded, must be based on a critical and sympathetic examination of the principal ideals of life in their historical evolution. The doctrine of ethical values or goods is really a distillation or sublimation of the dynamic trend, the driving purport, of the history of man's inner or spiritual civilization. The attempt to construct such a system by abstract rationalizing or even psychologizing can only result in a distorted skeleton.

Ethics cannot be based simply on psychology. For the norms of conduct, which issue demands to the will of the individual and which shape his congenital tendencies, are the products of the evolution of social culture. These norms live and operate, without systematic self-consciousness, in the social atmosphere in which the individual lives. The task of ethics is, by historical and sociological analysis and philosophical construction, to disengage them from the mass of tradition and custom and to organize them into a coherent whole.

Only when this has been done have we a clear and self-conscious standpoint from which to judge the facts of history. Without a systematic theory of moral values educed, by constructive analysis, from the systematic study of the moral history of humanity, judgments in regard to the purport of history can be nothing better than the expression of inherited beliefs, personal prejudices, and subjective emotional reactions.

Inasmuch as the historically grounded and systematically organized doctrine of ethical value-judgments remains as yet largely unachieved for contemporary society, a society in transition, it cannot be said that we have the instruments ready at hand for formulating a philosophy of history. And yet, if man is to guide his further efforts towards a better social order and greater individual well-being in the clear daylight of an enlightened and instructed intelligence, a philosophy of history is much to be desired. Certainly the struggles and confusions of the present, the cataclysmic upheavals in the whole social and political fabric of western civilization, constitute an urgent call to scholars and philosophers to devote themselves to the task of clarifying and organizing human convictions on the true ends of human life, the true values to be aimed at and achieved by our social order. We must not go it blindly. We must seek with all our power, and with all the light available, to formulate an ethical philosophy of history. Statecraft, education, industrial society, stand in urgent need of just this guidance. In this sense philosophy is called upon to be an interpreter of history and a guide to the life of man in society. The need of a broader based, and more profoundly conceived, social ethics is clamant.

In the second place, assuming that we have attained a system of ethical values, a normative standpoint from which to estimate the relative worths of the various stages and factors of historical change; in other words, that we have arrived at clearly defined standards of progress and apply our standards to the factual order of history; a candid examination of the latter order up to the present moment will compel the admission that there is but scant evidence that mankind, taken as a whole, is surely moving towards one universal goal or end. The course of historical change is exceedingly complex and confusing. Certain peoples are stationary for long periods. Others, such as the extreme

Orient and the Occident, lived for many centuries without influencing one another. Now that the oriental and occidental civilizations are in closer contact, it is not clear what the issue of this meeting will be. Even Occidental civilization does not show steady progress in all directions. It halts and even retrogrades. Who would assert that the recent World War was not followed by profound ethical retrogression? The occidental man does not seem to have mastered the vast industrial mechanism which he has evoked from the forces of nature to do his bidding. The monster he has created threatens to engulf the finer spirit of life.

Moreover, were it clear that moral and humane progress goes on even through the welter of industrialism, commercialism and war, who are to enjoy the final fruits of the movement? Is it the lot of the living members of each generation simply to toil and suffer and achieve somewhat, in order to hand on to the following generation a heritage of instruments and a nest of problems, with and at which that generation, in turn, will labor, to pass to the grave and be forgotten after a brief toil at an endless task; one which is never done, but continues and changes throughout the centuries and the æons without final goal, without enduring results in human values? Either humanity, as it toils in history, is engaged in an endless and goalless task and progress is a self-contradictory notion; or the goal is to be reached by some far off generation, and then all the preceding generations will have been mere hewers of wood and drawers of water to serve the welfare of the final happy one; or there is, in the lives of each generation, as it toils and suffers and aspires in the living present, an inherent value and then, since this value is only in part achieved by it, must we not postulate, if our ethical and humane values are to retain their validity and dignity, a continuous existence and progressive fulfillment of value for the life of man beyond the visible bournes of the present time and space? Does not the supremacy of ethical values imply the immortality of the generations?

Furthermore, while the individual lives a worthy life only in so far as he coöperates manfully in the social work of his own day and place as a member of the community, the nation, the group, in which his calling and election give him membership and, in the widest sense, in the work of humanity, *the individual life* which alone feels, thinks and wills, alone knows the bitterness of defeat, the joy of achievement, alone feels the sorrow and the happiness of the common human lot, is the actual agent and embodiment of ethical values. How, then, can ethical values endure and grow if individual souls are, in the final outcome, but dust and ashes thrown on the cosmical scrap-heap by the winds and tides of the blind cosmical weather?

Thus, the final issues raised by ethics and the philosophy of history are the issues that lie, and have always lain, at the heart of man's whole practical and affective life. These are the issues out of which arise the cry for a religious world view, and assuring answers to which the genius of religion aims and has always aimed to give. For religion, at its best, is the consecration of the highest human values; it is the affirmation in faith and deed that these values are integral constituents in, or essential qualities of, the universal and enduring order; that the higher meanings and purposes of the human spirit are blood kin to the supreme meaning and purpose of reality.

An interesting and important application of these problems arises in connection with the ethics of the state, the most comprehensive and powerful form of social organization. What ends does and should the state exist to serve? Is there discernible, in the light of ethical values, any line of political progress in history? Should the state be ordered so as to promote primarily the universal self-realization of the mass of mankind, to enable all individuals to attain and enjoy a fair measure of physical and mental well-being? If so, what is a fair measure of well-being? Should the means to develop and exercise exceptional abilities and achieve distinguished results be denied the comparatively few in the interest of a moderate average of well-being for all? Or are both aims possible of realization? In short, can the democratic and the aristocratic ideals of social order be reconciled? If so, how? Which is more nearly in accord with the highest ethical values, well-being and enjoyment made cheap and accessible to everyone, or a political and industrial organization that aims primarily at producing the highest results in art, science, literature? Or can these two ideals be realized simultaneously in the same social order? To seek an answer to these questions is to formulate a system of ethical values by which history and the present social and political orders are judged.

Or are, perhaps, the Buddhist, the Neoplatonist, the quietist, the contemplative mystic, right in holding that the only permanent peace, the only lasting values, are to be attained by escaping from the roaring loom of time to the calm haven of unruffled contemplation and mystic union with the one changeless absolute in whose presence all the fretful stir unprofitable and the fever of this jarring world are seen to be illusion?

III. Causes and Criteria of Progress

Anyone who has considered carefully the historical spectacle will admit that all theories of historical evolution or progress that reduce the course of history to some simple formula of a necessary sequence, whether it be an idealistic determination like Hegel's, or Comte's law of the three stages, economic determinism like Marx, or one of the more recent and equally grandiose *sociological* theories, are false to the complexity and richness of the facts. Certain broad lines of *tendency* or *general direction* can be traced in the historical movement of man, but these lines are neither straight, nor regular spirals nor even regular zigzags. They are *wobbly*. The general tendencies are subject to arrest, diversion, and retroversion. It may be that, if one knew enough, one would see that the historical order is an absolutely predetermined sequence. But, then, no one knows enough to enable him to establish this. The only relatively constant factors in history are the primal needs and impulses of the natural man and the general character of his physical environment. But, as civilization advances, the fixity of the environmental conditions of life decreases through increased social control of nature. Man continues to be hungry and thirsty, to acquire and to construct things, to love and hate; to engender his kind, to seek the company of his fellows and to quarrel with them; but with more complicated instruments and in more numerous and effective ways, as his social heritage of invention, knowledge, and organization increases in complexity. Moreover, as man has evolved in civilization, he has acquired increased power of *self-determination* and *self-direction.* This principle of human evolution in itself seems to negative the assumption that a complete body of necessary laws of historical evolution could be framed.

I propose to outline, very briefly, a theory of the criteria of progress. Before doing so it may be well to summarize the chief forces that operate in history. These are: 1. *Physicogeographical forces*—climate, soil, contour, and fertility of the land, and facility of communication and transportation are powerful factors in moulding the character of a civilization. Consider the fact that the Nile valley and Mesopotamia are probably the earliest seats of a continuous, long enduring and highly developed civilization in the west, and that Chinese civilization grew up in river valleys. Consider the influence of the Mediterranean and of the

Temperate Zone in the Northern Hemisphere on the course of European civilization! But, as civilization advances in the technological control of nature, these physical factors become subordinated and cease to play the dominant rôle. Man has in part conquered the natural factors. He has discovered how to protect himself against inclement climates and to utilize apparently unfruitful soils and useless minerals.

2. *Economic forces.* The course of historical change is very largely a consequence of the struggle for food and creature comforts. "While the philosopher talks, hunger and love rule the world." The migrations and expansions of peoples are due largely to economic needs and lusts. This was true of the barbarian invasions and, in lesser degree, of the European expansion in America. So, too, the class struggles between masters and slaves, lords and serfs, exploiters and exploited, and, to-day, between capitalists and proletariat, are based in part on economic motives. I say *in part,* for I hold that, above the level of the lowest savage, the most powerful motive that impels men to social change is the *desire for self-determination.* Consequently, the economic motives are interwoven with other and more ideational factors.

3. *Idea-Forces. Ruling ideas* are those which dominate the members of a group or people in any age. As civilization develops, in mental and social complexity, ruling ideas become more powerful factors in social life. Consider the conception of a covenant relationship with the righteous ruler of the universe as the ruling idea of Jewish group solidarity, the supremacy of the spiritual order as the ruling idea in the Catholic middle ages, the ideas of liberty, equality and fraternity in the French revolution, and the power of such ideas as democracy, social justice, equality of opportunity to-day! Ideas are increasingly potent factors in social life, as society becomes more diversified and highly

organized in its activities and as education becomes more universal.

4. *Great Men.* One does not need to be an orthodox Carlylean to see that great men are potent historical forces, as military leaders and chiefs of marauding hordes and peoples, as rulers, legislators, and statesmen, as inventors, discoverers, prophets, reformers, artists, teachers. Often a social movement has been turned aside from its original aims by the dominating power of a leader. Napoleon I and the French Revolution are the classic instances here. Often a social movement fails to fulfill its pristine promise for lack of effective leadership. It has been argued that great men are creatures of their environment and, in opposition to this, that the great man moulds his social environment after his own will. Both views are false. The greatest man is limited and moulded by his environment; but, in turn, by taking the leadership and directing the forces in his environment, he may produce great changes and stamp society with the impress of his personality. It has been said by some that the influence of the leader is decreasing in modern industrial and literate democracy. This seems doubtful. It is now harder to maintain a position of leadership for long, but the facts seem to indicate that the opportunity for leadership has not decreased with the increase in the proportion of literate members of society, and in the complexity of its economic structure. In fact, the need for *experts* to lead and direct its complex social forces becomes greater than ever.

5. *The Cultural-Psychological Forces.* By these I mean the whole social heritage, which is constantly being added to in the movement of culture. This includes inventions and discoveries and changes in the industrial, economic, and political orders, spread of education and knowledge, changes in laws and rules of conduct, changes in ideals of conduct and religion, changes in art and letters. The

cultural-psychological forces include the effects of increased scientific control over nature, economic factors and the influence of great men in building up and reshaping the institutions and beliefs of society, as well as the vast and subtle changes wrought in the social texture by the constant and often silent reactions of the masses of human beings.

The statement of criteria of progress involves a definition of civilization. But civilization exists only in the civilizing process which is progress. Hence, a definition of progress is a definition of civilization.

More specifically, we may say that progress consists—(1) In the increasing *humanization of nature,* through improvement in man's technic in science and industry. Since material progress is the humanization of nature, it follows that any industrial system in which man is dehumanized, by being treated as a mere tool for turning out material products, vitiates the first principle of progress. Genuine progress is not possible, in so far as part of mankind is ruthlessly sacrificed in the process of turning out more material instruments of progress. Progress consists—(2) In the increasing *humanization of man.* By this I mean the enrichment of man in society, through the enhanced opportunity to exercise the distinctly human capacities for their own sakes—opportunity to satisfy *feeling,* in the relations of love and friendship, and the enjoyment of art and nature; opportunity to satisfy *thought,* in the study of literature, history, and science; opportunity to satisfy the *constructive and other active impulses,* either in his work or leisure hours. This humanizing process will produce a higher type of religion and philosophical attitude —an attitude of reverent and joyful contemplation of the universe as the expression of one divine life.

There are certain great and central moral conditions or elements of progress. There are (1) *Justice,* (2) *Liberty* and (3) *Opportunity.* These are really three aspects of one principle—*the humanization of man.* A few words of comment thereon and I am done.

1. *Justice.* The ideal end of justice, as it has become clarified in the historical process, through the work of legislators, ethicists, and religionists, the ideal end working from primitive custom, through Hebrew and Roman Law and the progress of Anglo-Saxon law and the growth of political freedom, is this—the progressive discovery and recognition of the right of every normal human being to be treated as a *self-determining individual, as a rational self,* free and responsible. Henley's words

> I am the master of my Fate,
> I am the Captain of my Soul

express the basic and elemental condition of the very being of selfhood or personality. Thus the dynamic principle in the evolution of the concept of justice is the emergence and universalization of the ideal of *moral personality.* The development of the idea of legal responsibility, as dependent upon voluntary choice or moral responsibility, and of equality before the law, and the doctrine of the natural or inalienable rights of man, are all expressions of this central principle. The recognition of the moral equality of all human beings, of the equal right of all human beings, as free and responsible agents, the right of every self to the opportunities to become and live as a rational self, is the moral essence of democracy.

2. *Liberty.* Progress in the recognition of individual liberty or freedom keeps step by step with justice. For justice and liberty are two aspects of the same ethical principle. Liberty is the sphere or scope of the exercise of individual freedom, of self-direction in society, in so far as such exercise is compatible with the exercise of a like freedom on the part of all the other members of society. In a primitive society a man's liberty of action

and thought is very circumscribed—is hedged about by customs of all descriptions. As civilized states developed, and law became formulated in general principles, and was made more responsive to the ideal demands of equity, liberty of action and speech increased. But it was not until very modern times that the right to freedom of speech and opinion in matters of scientific and religious belief was recognized. It is now, in principle at least, admitted in democratic states that intellectual or spiritual liberty, as well as political and religious liberty of association, is a logical sequence of justice.

One form of liberty has been circumscribed rather than furthered with some members of society, possibly, through the development of the large scale of industry—the liberty to earn a living. The enmeshment of the individual in the vast and intricate network of the modern industrial system often hinders him greatly in the exercise of economic self-determination or freedom. And spiritual liberty, too, is greatly hindered by economic serfdom. The next great step in social progress will be to establish a fuller measure of economic liberty. This is implied in the demand for fuller opportunity. For a fair measure of economic freedom is the necessary condition for the exercise of opportunity for self-development.

3. *Opportunity.* If the nature of progress be such as I have sketched, it follows that a fair opportunity to become and live as a full and free moral agent is the logical sequence of justice and liberty. For such opportunity is part and parcel of our supreme standard of progress, which may be summed up as follows: *Progress consists in the control of nature and the improvement of social institutions to the end that every human being shall enjoy a reasonable opportunity to enter into the use of the full cultural heritage of the race, and by using it, to develop and enjoy his own inherent capacities, so that thereby he*

may become, in the measure which these capacities admit, a rational, free, full, and harmonious personality.

On the other hand, the contention that equalization of opportunity implies absolute economic equality has no foundation in ethics, psychology, or biology. Ethically, the individual is entitled to so much opportunity as he can use. From the standpoint of biology and psychology there is an inherent and irrevocable basis of inequality. Human beings are not born either with equal, or even nearly equal, mental and physical capacities. On the other hand, there is at present no even fairly constant relation between the economic status, into which an individual is born, and his congenital abilities. Social progress will depend chiefly on the degree in which the economic life of society is so ordered that the individual shall have a full opportunity to develop and exercise his native abilities. To say that such is the case now is to be false to the facts. Here is the heart of the social problem. Social institutions should be organized so as to remove, as far as possible, the hindrances to the development of personality that are due to economic handicaps, thus leaving free play to the natural and uncontrollable source of individuality and inequality, the *reproductive* process, which is a *re-creative* process. The solid and lasting progress of man in the future, as in the past, will depend on the liberation and activation of free creative individuality, of dynamic personality. The average man will never get far beyond the satisfaction of his belly needs without superaverage persons to find the ways of progress and show them to him. If democracy be interpreted to mean that all human beings should be treated as equal, economically, intellectually, or as arbiters of good taste and knowledge and culture, then it becomes one of the most disastrous forms of sentimental moonshine, one of the silliest superstitions that have been foisted on human society. The real value, and limit, of Democracy lies in its usableness as an instrumentality by which, through a fair opportunity being vouchsafed to every self to find and show what is in him, a larger proportion of exceptional individuals rise above the common level, and, thus, *become potent factors in raising the average level of intelligence, efficiency, fair play, good taste, coöperation, and honest service. In short, democracy is a means to an end—the enrichment and harmonization of the physical and rational—or spiritual—values of life. The better achievement of this end by all will depend upon the nurture of a larger proportion of creators and leaders.*

References

AUGUSTINE, *The City of God.*

• AVEY, A. E., *Readings in Philosophy,* Chapter XXVII.

BAGEHOT, *Physics and Politics.*

BARTH, P., *Die Philosophie der Geschichte als Sociologie.*

BERNHEIM, *Lehrbuch der historischen Methode.*

BUCKLE, H. T., *History of Civilization in England,* Chapters I and II.

CARLYLE, THOMAS, *Heroes and Hero Worship,* and *Past and Present.*

COMTE, *Positive Philosophy,* translated by Martineau.

CROCE, BENEDETTO, *History: Its Theory and Practice.*

EUCKEN, *Life's Basis and Life's Ideal, The Problem of Human Life,* and Article, "Geschichtsphilosophie" in *Systematische Philosophie* (in series *Die Kultur der Gegenwart*).

FICHTE, J. G., *Characteristics of the Present Age,* and *Addresses to the German Nation.*

FLINT, R., *History of the Philosophy of History.*

GIDDINGS, F. H., *Principles of Sociology.*

GROTENFELT, ARVID, *Geschichtliche Wertmassstäbe in der Geschichtsphilosophie.*

HEGEL, *Philosophy of History.*

KIDD, B., *Principles of Western Civilization.*

LAMPRECHT, K., *What is History?*

LOTZE, *Microcosmus.*

MATTHEWS, SHAILER, *The Spiritual Interpretation of History.*

RICKERT, H., *Die Grenzen der naturwissenschaftlichen Begriffsbildung,* IIte Auflage, and Article, "Geschichtsphilosophie" in *Die Philosophie im Beginn des Zwanzigsten Jahrhunderts.*

ROBINSON, J. H., *The New History.*

ROUSSEAU, J. J., *Social Contract, Emile,* and *Discourse Concerning the Origins of Inequality.*

SIMMEL, G., *Die Probleme der Geschichtsphilosophie,* IIte Auflage.

SPENCER, H., *Principles of Sociology,* and *Principles of Ethics.*

TEGGART, F. J., *The Processes of History.*

TROELTSCH, ERNST, Article "Historiography" in *Encyclopædia of Religion and Ethics.*

WARD, L. F., *Dynamic Sociology.*

WINDELBAND, *History of Philosophy,* pp. 255-262 and pp. 648-659.

WOODBRIDGE, F. J. E., *The Purpose of History.*

XÉNOPOL, A. D., *Les principes fondementaux de l'histoire.*

CHAPTER XXIX

EPISTEMOLOGY

Theory of Knowledge

Epistemology (from the Greek *epistēmē,* knowledge or science, and *logos,* theory) is the technical name for systematic enquiries into the nature, conditions, and criteria of human knowledge in general. It is intimately connected with metaphysics, the theory of reality, and with logic, the theory of thought. Indeed it might be called the logic of metaphysics.

All the principal theories of knowledge have been already discussed. It is indeed impossible to discuss systematically theories of reality or the theories of the great philosophers without going into epistemological questions. In the historical introduction it was pointed out that the problem of knowledge was definitely raised and discussed by Plato and, indeed, we find more or less fragmentary theories of knowledge before Plato. It has occupied a foremost position in modern philosophy ever since Descartes and Locke. At this point we wish to get a summary view of the principal problems of knowledge and of the principal answers to these problems. It will be my aim systematically to gather together the discussions and the points of view as to the nature, structure, and function of knowledge that have been scattered through our previous discussions.

In modern epistemology there are three chief problems. These of course cannot be absolutely separated. No principal problem of knowledge can be thus isolated from the other chief problems. In philosophy our quest is for a unified conception of reality. One's standpoint on any one of these problems of knowledge will determine largely, if not entirely, his standpoint on the other problems. For emphasis, however, it is possible to distinguish between these problems. The three problems are the following:

1. What are the sources of knowledge—whence is our knowledge derived?

2. What is the place of knowledge in the world of being—what is the relation of cognition to reality?

3. What are the norms, the criteria, the standards of knowledge? (This problem will be the subject-matter of the next chapter. In the present chapter I shall consider the first and second problems.)

I. Problem of the Sources of Knowledge

From the beginning of modern philosophy down to the present time, one finds two antithetical views as to the sources of knowledge, namely, *empiricism* and *rationalism*.

Empiricism is predominantly a British tradition in philosophy. We find its beginnings in some of the nominalists of the Middle Ages and it then moves forward, with ever increasing momentum, through Francis Bacon, Hobbes, Locke, Hume, J. S. Mill, and others. The central thesis of this movement is that all knowledge is derived from sense experience. Locke, for example, while not an out and out empiricist, in that he admits that there are certain kinds of knowledge arrived at by reflection, says that there are two chief sources of knowledge, namely, ideas of sense and ideas of reflection. Hume, who is a thoroughgoing empiricist, has a different terminology from Locke. Hume calls Locke's "ideas of sense" "impressions," and uses the term "ideas" to designate copies or traces of sense impressions in the mind. All ideas are derived from sense impressions for Hume. These men, save to the extent that Locke is a rationalist, regard the mind as a sort of wax tablet or sheet of paper on which impressions are made. The mind is but a name for the records made by the sequences of impressions. Impressions are made on the mind and thus the mind is modified. We must be careful to note, however, that there is no substance-mind for Hume. For him, at least, mind is only the tied-up succession of impressions. Mind is only the processions of ideas and impressions.[1]

Where do these impressions come from? Hume's answer virtually is, "I don't know." "I feel," he says in effect, "only a constant succession of impressions and ideas." Nowhere can Hume find a substantial mind. As to the modes whereby these successions get tied together, Hume says that this is accomplished by means of such psychological laws as—*association by contiguity, resemblance,* and *succession.* It is by means of these laws that ideas get married. The fact that you have had two impressions contiguous and immediately succeeding one another leads an impression or idea similar to one to call up the other. Hume says that all our knowledge is built up in these ways from impressions which are connected up by means of these laws of association. We had better not say *we have* impressions and copies, since there is no self; it would be truer to say *there are* impressions and these mysteriously engender copies which get associated in a variety of ways.

The idea of causation, which was the central difficulty for Hume, and which Kant later generalized in such a way as to show that it is but one of the many types of synthetic *a priori* connections, is derived, says Hume, from

[1] William James has a better way of stating how ideas are connected. He calls the connection "the unity of the passing thought."

the repeated succession of our impressions. If it is noticed that A is always followed by B, there is soon formed the habit of expecting, of looking for B, whenever we see A. All we mean by causation is that there have been in a number of cases similar sequences of impressions. If, for example, A is followed by B and A_2 by B_2, and so on, then if we ever perceive A_n we shall of course expect, through the force of this habit, that B_n will follow. Causation is the name of a habit engendered by such a repetition of resembling sequences of impression. For the pure empiricist, the mind is either *wholly passive* or it is *nothing at all.* Knowledge consists of the repeated association, in various ways, of sense impressions and copies of sense impressions. We can, according to empiricism, account for images and concepts and for their modes of association, but we remain absolutely mute when we try to give an account of the source of the original perceptual knowledge.

The rationalist maintains that true knowledge is derived from thought itself, from the *activity of reason.* He believes that truth is a function of the power of thought to constitute a totality. The highest kind of knowledge consists in universally valid propositions that are consistent with one another. Sense experience does not give us propositions which are universally valid or mutually consistent. By the great philosophers of Greece and such modern philosophers as Descartes, Spinoza, Leibnitz, Kant, Hegel, and all the later idealists after Hegel, this claim of the inability of sense experience to give us coherent and universal judgments is reiterated. From sense perception, say the rationalists, we can get only a number of particular cases. The cases may, to be sure, be similar to one another, but we never get universally valid linkages of thought. Now, our sense experience is full of inconsistencies and discrepancies, and the rationalist maintains that, when we examine these inconsistencies and discrepancies in sense perception, we find them to be due to the imperfect activity of thought. Knowledge for the rationalist is more than a connection of experiences by passive repetition and association and by emotionally engendered beliefs. Reasoning is a process of actively relating and classifying our experiences, but this may be done so hastily that sufficient scrutiny is not exercised to avoid error. We may correct error under the guidance of certain innate or *a priori*, fundamental laws of thought. In this way the very principles that we employ in organizing our experiences have a different source from our sense impressions. Our intellectual structure is such that we cannot tolerate incoherences and contradictions in thought. Our rational nature demands consistency. Two contradictory propositions cannot be true simultaneously, and if one denies this he virtually denies the possibility of science. He negates the very nature of reason.

Our ordinary sense experience, as interpreted under the influence of tradition and feeling, gives us many contradictory propositions. Of these we say that they are misconstrued data, that the experiences cannot have been taken in their right relations. In order to think scientifically we are obliged to accept the validity and authority of the laws of thought. The first of these laws is called the *Principle of Identity*. It means that in any discussion that is to get anywhere we must stick to our definitions. Its objects must have certain *invariant characteristics* if thought is to continue. Another of these fundamental principles is called the *Law of Contradiction*—two contradictory propositions cannot both be true simultaneously. These principles, together with others which logic formulates, are the presuppositionless or ultimate bases of all valid thinking. In regard to all the other sciences, we find that they rest upon certain logical presuppositions. There is always some Atlas upon which the group of order series, which constitutes any particular science, rests. But at this point in the discussion of the theory of knowledge we come upon a unique situation. The primary presuppositions of knowledge are the logical principles which guide and control the mind in its entire quest for knowledge. They are justified by the fact that, by their use, experience gets more meaning, becomes more harmonious, more intelligible.

Another of these ultimate logical principles is that of the causal category or *Principle of Sufficient Ground.* Why does one always look for causal relations? We say that nothing can happen without a sufficient cause or ground. This attitude seems to be native to the mind. We are not satisfied with saying that things just happen. We look diligently for causes. Many of us are uneasy until we find out the how and the why of happenings. We distinguish between causal sequences and those that are not causal. Of the latter, the sequence of day and night may be taken as an illustration. The causal series differs from the noncausal in that the former is an irreversible series. We may agree with the empiricist that the specific aspects of any given causal sequence are, in all particular cases, dependent upon empirical data. But the empiricist fails to account for the native propensity of the mind insistently to demand the causal grounds of every event. *Thus the mind seems to have certain specific native ways of operation,* and in logic we study these ways. The whole subject matter of logic is the study of the structure of human reason. The empiricist is evidently right in saying that the data of knowledge are found in experience, and no reasonable rationalist will deny that postulate, but he insists that the data do not fashion the tools by which knowledge is made. Indeed, Kant emphatically asserted that there could be no knowledge without empirical data and became agnostic only at points where such empirical data are not present. Empiricism has a tendency to confine experience to what we perceive through the outer senses, but in doing so it overlooks the fact that we have a large framework of affectional, moral, social, and logical context; all of which belongs to experience in the full sense of the term.

The sound position may be called *rational empiricism* or *empirical rationalism.* In contrast with *a priori* rationalism, it stresses the dependence of all our knowledge on experience. In contrast with sensationalistic empiricism, it insists on the purposive activity of the mind in knowing and holds that the success of this activity implies a vital intercourse between the mind and reality. Such a point of view makes an organic synthesis of the valid claims of both rationalism and empiricism. From this standpoint we explicitly hold that the materials of knowledge come to us in experience, but the materials thus given are organized by the activity of reason into the texture of our sciences. This native capacity of the reason is not to be interpreted, as many interpret Plato and other historic rationalists, as being a body of categories which have come into existence independently of the creative or synthetic processes of experience. The universal principles of knowledge are the mind's fundamental ways of working as these develop in and through the organization of experience.

Sensationalistic empiricism is *nominalistic.* Concepts and universals, which are the chief tools of science, are from this standpoint nothing but signs or symbols, and it is impossible to determine with any degree of accuracy what the relation is that subsists between the symbols and the things symbolized. The thing signified or symbolized is not a matter of experience, consequently our concepts and universals are subjective formations; they are names for relations which arise in the mind between ideas. Hume, who is one of the most instructive figures in the history of philosophy because he worked out the logical consequences of empiricism, argued that the only kind of knowledge that has any certainty is mathematics. Now this certainty is due to the fact that mathematics deals only with relations between ideas. Such relations as these of identity, difference, magnitude, and degree have to do only with the comparison of ideas with one another. Yet Hume is constrained to say that even in mathematics the oftener we run over a proof the more certain do we become. Repetition of similar experiences is the test of truth. Thus empiricism is not just to the character of mathematics. Mathematics does not deal with existence theorems. It is not concerned with the existence of points, lines, circles, et cetera, in nature. Indeed it abstracts even from the relation of mathematical space to the space of perception. Pure mathematics deals with ideal constructions. Thus far Hume is correct, but the validity of a mathematical theorem is in no wise dependent on the frequency of our running over the proof. In the last generation the science of mathematics has been very largely reconstructed by the discovery and the elaboration of more rigorous methods of proof. Keen, critical minds, endowed with a passion for certitude, have discovered flaws even in Euclid. Minds, in the highest degree equipped with the rational structure of which I spoke above, have criticized and discovered flaws in certain mathematical demonstrations which had been supposed to be irrefutable. But these more rigorous methods of proof have not increased in rigor merely by being repeated many times by many persons.

There is another difficulty with the empirical attitude. Granted that mathematics deals, not with existence, but with relations of ideas connected by reason, we are justified in saying that mathematics is an invention. We must say that it is a product not of the senses but of the reason. But mathematics applies to the world in which we live. The triumph of the modern mechanical theory of nature is due to the faith its authors had that nature is a kind of crystallized mathematics. It is small wonder that Galileo and others called mathematics divine—"What we can measure we can know." Mathematics works. It works in its application to past experience, to present experience and further, to possible experience. The predictive power of mathematical science is great. Take this illustration. In 1843 two astronomers made a calculation, based upon the deviation of the *observed* path of the planet Uranus from the path it should describe in view of the relations, the relative points, and motions of the planets known by observation to exist. The path of Uranus as calculated from the observed relations of the recorded planets should have been of a certain character. The observed path, however, was aberrant. In view of this, what did the mathematical astronomers do? The astronomer said, "there must be an hitherto unobserved planet," and he calculated the locus of this planet. At Berlin the royal astronomer heeded the order of the astronomers in question and looked as he was told for the planet and lo, it was there. This is only one of the many cases of prediction. The most recent striking instance was the approximate agreement of the observations of the solar eclipse of 1919 with the calculations based on Einstein's theory of the deflection of light. The more science develops by so much the more do we have cases of this kind. Let me note as a curious fact that Hume, who says that the whole idea of causation is a mere result of habit, presupposes the very idea he seeks to explain, inasmuch as he is already seeking a cause for the origin of our belief in causation.

Our view is *realistic.* It is realistic in that it regards universals and other relations as facts that the mind discovers by the use of its fundamental ways of working. Reality has rational order, texture, coherence. It is not chaotic, and it is because of this doctrine as to the texture of reality that rationalistic realism finds a place for science, whereas for nominalism science is but a set of subjective symbols of an unknown reality. Science is objective in its application.

Kant, though he answered Hume, never freed himself completely from the influence of empiricism. He said that the materials of knowledge come into the mind as a chaotic manifold and that mind, through its synthetic organizing power, arranges this chaotic mass into the ordered whole which we call the world. The mind *puts* the relations into nature. This view is an inconsistent one, for, if mind puts the relations into nature, then the world is the fabrication of our own powers and we are not delivered from subjectivity.

Later idealists start from Kant's view that mind is an organizing principle, and they hold that the successful working of the mind in the world shows that the environment has an intelligible texture. This is what objective idealism teaches. It is not true that we know only ideas, as Berkeley argued. It is the fact that in science we are discovering the nature of mind and finding that it has a given structure, which has its correlate in nature, that gives efficacy to mind. Mind is an effective part of the world. In short, mind is at home in the world.

William James, who partially misunderstood rationalism, and was at the same time rightly dissatisfied with empiricism, called his view *radical empiricism*. It is pure mythology, he says, to argue that all that comes to the mind is mere unrelated data. We cannot put our finger on any disconnected item of experience. Every item is related. The minimum of experience at least involves the relating implied in the answer to such a question as, "what is that?" The mind starts out with its classificatory tentacles, its incipient universals. We are everlastingly propounding the question "what does this fact *mean?*"; and thus we start on the endless process of relating data. There is no such thing as an unrelated datum of sense. Psychologists are now agreed that there are no such things as pure sensations. James misunderstood rationalism, in so far as he thought that it is one of the cardinal doctrines of this view to suppose that mind comes down from above, as it were, and puts relations into the data in an external fashion. James, in his doctrine of a "pure experience" free from the distinctions and relations which thought makes, overlooked the fact that it is impossible for us to have mere sensations, although, in other passages, he recognizes that there are no *pure sensations.* He seems to have held that this so-called pure experience is the reality which thought distorts and disfigures. The truth is the mind is always active and all that comes to mind is related. The meaning of this is that our world has an intelligible, rational, texture or structure.

II. Knowledge and Reality

We have already discussed incidentally the place of knowing in reality. It now remains to gather up briefly these suggestions into a systematic view.

The simplest answer to the query, what is the relation of cognition to reality? is called *naïve* or *presentational realism.* This is the view of the common man (that horrible example), the person who has not thought of this problem. He is naïve; for him there is no distinction between mind and the object of mind. For him mind is at one with its object. The object known and the knowing process are numerically and qualitatively identical. The thing perceived is identical with the percept.

This position is untenable. No two of us in this classroom see this table before me in the same way. Your perception is a function of your position, of light, shade, of movements, and of infinite other variations. In fact your perception is a function of your sense organs, of your perceptors as these are determined by your mental habits and interests. From Zeno down the skeptics have been pointing out arguments that show the duality of the knowing mind and the known objects.

One remove from naïve is *representational realism.* The stock example of this point of view is John Locke. This view admits the validity of the criticism just made of naïve realism, and so this view starts from the existence of percepts, images, and mental conceptions, as being the sole immediate data of knowing, and says that we know only our ideas. Our ideas are representations, copies, symbols, of the real things.

It is quite true that representation does play a considerable part in our knowledge. In response to my request, you describe the State House. In doing so you call up images of the State House. Your idea is a kind of representation, replica, or copy; but how do we settle whether the description you give is a copy? We appeal to the fact. The fact confirms or rejects the copy. If we take, however, the copy view on all fours, we never get anything but ideas. Then how can we settle, how can we ever agree? Representational realism is only a halfway mansion; we cannot stay at this place. Any man that thinks must pack up his tent and move on to some more substantial city. One more remove is the position known as *phenomenalistic idealism.*[2] Ernst Mach, Karl Pearson, and, in part, Immanuel Kant are representatives of this position. These men assert that we do not know reality. We cannot

---

[2] Improperly so-called. It should be called *phenomenalistic psychologism or ideaism.* This is Hume's position.

tell to what extent, if indeed to any at all, our ideas truly represent reality. The really real things forever retreat up the spiral stairway of reality. We reach out our conceptual tentacles to make a seizure into reality, but we remain in the veil. Between us and reality there is a wall of partition which no thinking can ever penetrate. We do not know reality.

Herbert Spencer, too, teaches phenomenalism. He calls his position *transfigured realism.* In knowing reality, he says, we transfigure it; it becomes in the knowledge context something quite different from what it is outside the knowledge relation. The knowledge relation does not bring us into touch with reality as it is. Through our experiences of resistance we know *that* there is an external reality; *what* it is we know not, beyond the inference that it is something which resists our efforts. From this empirical fact, he concludes that the sense of effort is the key to the nature of reality, and that reality is an infinite and eternal energy from which all things proceed.

Let me briefly indicate two difficulties in this view: (1) Knowledge works in the world. In the only world with which we have anything to do, we find that knowledge does function effectively, and we further find that the increasing success of knowledge is due to the fact that we have analyzed and systematized our experiences. Errors are half truths. Illusions are experiences wrongly interpreted, set in the wrong relations, in the wrong context, and the distinction between the knowledge of phenomena and the knowledge of reality is only a distinction of degree. (2) Phenomenalistic idealism is inconsistent in the very distinction which serves as its starting point. How do we know that we know only phenomena, if we do not know the real? The lapidarist says of a certain specimen handed to him, "this is a sham diamond." Such pronouncement is impossible unless there be a knowledge of the real diamond. Phenomenalism assumes that there is a veil between us and reality. How do we know it is a veil if we have never been through the veil and looked upon the holy of holies? Our world of experience is the only world with which we have to deal. The phenomenalist makes a distinction which involves him in a contradiction. By what sources does he know that we do not know real things? There is no meaning in the distinction between the sham and the real, unless we know enough about the real to be able to compare it with the sham.

III. Critical Realism

Our solution of the above problem rests on the thesis that we know reality in part and are capable of knowing it more fully. It is also our contention that the progress of knowledge shows an increasing correspondence between mind or the knower and the world. There is a growth in the agreement between thought and things, and this evolution is manifested in the progress of pure science and in its successful applications. Many of our ideas do seem to consist of mental representations of actual past or possible future experiences. Considered as ideas, these representations vary in concreteness and pictorialness from images to the symbolic formulas of mathematics and logic. But these representative ideas contain truth, because the representative experiences that human beings have had stand for further experiences which may be had under definite and assignable conditions.

The standpoint of critical realism is that mind is a live focus of reality, that there is an active correspondence of mind and reality, in short, it is that mind is a true part of reality. Minds are centers in which the nature of reality becomes conscious of itself, and in this way, mind is seen to be something very different from the old soul principle which was shut off by unscalable walls from the world. Reality is not something impenetrably hidden behind a veil. Reality is what is or may be experienced, and what may be inferred from experience. The other side of the moon, the center of the earth and the polar ice cap of the Antarctic region are items of rational belief which we infer from our experiences.

By saying that there is ether or that there are electrons, what does one mean? I take it that we can only mean that these are logical constructions inferred from experiences. These constructions, however, are based on experience, and if there are electrons, then under certain assignable conditions they should be perceptible. Otherwise the electron theory is a useless hypothesis. Reality is experience as both actual and possible. Our minds and sense organs are genuine functioning parts of the real world. There is an active and effective correspondence between thought and reality and, since we make our concepts, our formulas and symbols of things, by thinking about sense data and since, furthermore, these formulas work in experience, it follows that reality has an orderly or structural character. In short, we agree with Hegel in saying that reality is rational.

What then shall we say of illusions and the so-called errors of the senses? In reality they are errors of judgment and not of the senses. The error is a function of the judgment which I make. The man in delirium tremens has a real experience, so also the one who sees ghosts, but it is only in his *interpretation* of his experience that he errs. He does not set his sensory data in their right relations. In epistemology one of the most hackneyed illustrations is the case of the straight stick that is bent in the water. In the water it looks bent, but we say it is *really* straight. The bentness of the stick is due to the different refractive powers of air and water.

The visual stick is really bent, but the tactual stick is not bent and further, the visual stick out of the water *is not* bent. Which is the real stick?

We live most of our time on land, and we have learned that the properties or qualities which are practically important for us are those an object has when close to us. So we agree to make certain sets of conditions define the standard for us and we all agree to that. The "real" stick is the result of the tacit agreement among us socially as to what aspects of the whole series of sensory qualities called "stick" are most important. Our standards of measurement are all of them postulates of the social will. They are a matter of social convention. So then, to return to the stick in the water, suppose that we were like seals, living in the water and were without hands, the type of important qualities would doubtless vary greatly from what it now is. Or suppose that we lived on the surface of a sphere and were unable to lift ourselves up. Here also we would have a very different set of standardized qualities and relations. It may be objected to this view that what we mean by a real thing is the thing as it exists independently of our percepts. To this I reply, yes and no! Independent of *my* perceiving it, yes! But no meaning can be attached to the idea of an object existing independently of *anybody's* perceiving it. The independent reality of an object is the reality of something that can be perceived under definite assignable conditions by some sort of percipient organism. Who cares about a real object which is apart from and indifferent to any percipient organism?

The real world is the world of social perceivables. It is the world of things which, under definite conditions, can, by anyone equipped with the proper mental and sensory equipment, be experienced. Some say that the real object is what God or the Absolute perceives—I don't know what he perceives.

When we take into account the specific characteristics of the percipient, his place, his relations to objects, his history, and interests, we can recognize that what he perceives is relative to him and yet real. Rational empiricism or, as it might be called, critical realism, is the view that we know reality, not uncritically, however. It is a fact that we do perceive, and it is further a fact that we can improve our perceptions by means of the organizing activity of thought. This circumstance indicates, it seems to me, that the world is in agreement with mind.

Many critics of objective or teleological idealism, as a metaphysical theory, shoot wide of the mark, because they insist on identifying all idealistic standpoints with either phenomenalistic "ideaism" or Berkeleyan idealism. Modern or teleological idealism from Hegel down to the present is realistic in its epistemology, as indeed so were Plato and Aristotle. It insists that the human mind knows reality, through experience, as the resultant of the active intercourse of the knower with his world. Knowing may be described, on the one hand, as the process by which the real world becomes conscious of itself in human minds; or, on the other hand, as the process by which minds transcend their merely "given" or biological individuality by becoming aware of the qualities-in-organic-relation which constitute the world. In short, the organization of experience is the organization of selfhood, through the increasing discovery of the nature of reality. The knower, in his perceptual reactions, apprehends in some degree and manner the actual qualities of the real. The knower in *thinking,* and thus organizing perceptual experience, is discovering the systematic and intelligible character of reality as an ordered whole of things-in-relation. The very realistic character and practical success of human knowledge indicate that reality is a purposive and intelligible order. To hold this is the essence of teleological idealism, which is thus a *metaphysical* theory of reality. Reality as a whole has a significant structure. But such a view is built on an essentially realistic conception of the function of knowing. We know reality in perception and thought, and we know reality thus because it is responsive to the aims and activities of minds and, therefore, is the expression of intelligence or reason.

References

ALEXANDER, S., *Space, Time and Deity,* Volume II, Book III, Chapters I to VIII.

* AVEY, A. E., *Readings in Philosophy,* Chapter XXIV.

BERKELEY, *Three Dialogues,* and *Principles of Human Knowledge.*

BOWNE, B. P., *Theory of Knowledge.*

BRADLEY, *Appearance and Reality,* Chapters XV and XXIX.

* DESCARTES, *Meditations.*

DRAKE, D., AND OTHERS, *Essays in Critical Realism.*

HEGEL, *Logic,* and *Phenomenology of Mind.*

HUME, *Enquiry Concerning Human Understanding,* Sections II to VII, and *Treatise, Of the Understanding,* Parts I and III.

* JAMES, *Essays in Radical Empiricism,* II, III and IV, and *Some Problems of Philosophy,* III and IV.

JOACHIM, H. H., *The Nature of Truth.*

KANT, *Prolegomena,* and *Critique of Pure Reason.*

LAIRD, JOHN, *A Study in Realism.*

LOCKE, *Essay Concerning Human Understanding.*

MILL, J. S., *Logic,* Book II, Chapters III and IV.

* PAULSEN, F., *Introduction to Philosophy,* Book II, Chapter II.

* RUSSELL, B., *The Problems of Philosophy,* especially Chapters VII and VIII, *Philosophical Essays,* and *Our Knowledge of the External World.*

SPAULDING, E. G., *The New Rationalism.*

The New Realism, Essays by Perry and others.

CHAPTER XXX

THE CRITERIA OF TRUTH

The third main problem of epistemology is the fundamental problem of logic. Inasmuch as philosophy is the application of logic to the systematic interpretation of the most general features of experience, we have been compelled to use the logical criteria of truth all along the line in this course. It now remains to state systematically what these criteria are and to examine them critically. There are three chief doctrines on this matter—(1) the Copy Theory, (2) the Pragmatic Theory, and (3) the Rationalistic Theory.

I. The Copy Theory of Truth

According to this theory ideas (including in the term "idea," images, concepts, and propositions) are true if they are good copies of realities. Some of them, that is, images, are pictures of realities. Some of them, abstract concepts and propositions, and in general the conventionalized formulas of mathematics and science, are linguistic symbols of realities.

It is not necessary to spend much time now examining this theory. A great many of our ideas, namely all those which refer to objects not present to sense, are either representatives or symbols of realities. But the test of the validity or truth of these ideas is whether they correspond with, and will lead us, under the appropriate conditions, to an adequate experimental acquaintance with, the things which they represent or symbolize. *The test of their truthfulness is their agreement with experience.* The knowledge about things which they appear to bear is true knowledge only in so far as they can be cashed in in direct experience by perceiving, handling, working with the things represented by them. If I have an idea of a certain office building and the distance to it, my idea is true if it will guide me there. If I have a scientific formula, it is true if it will enable me to solve a chemical or an engineering problem. But when it is maintained that all ideas are copies of realities, we answer that if there are two worlds, the mental world of ideas and the real world outside, which are shut out from direct contact with one another, then we are landed in phenomenalism; and finally, when we think this doctrine through to the end, in an inconsistent subjectivism and skepticism. For, unless we have direct acquaintance at some points with reality, we can never know whether we know anything truly and we can not explain why we should make any distinction at all between ideas and reality, between phenomena and things in themselves.

II. Pragmatism

Pragmatism is the name that has been made fashionable by William James and others for a theory of truth which is offered as a correction of the copy theory.

I think the novelty and importance of the pragmatic theory of truth has been overemphasized, probably because its progenitors, who were psychologists, were overjoyed at finding a way out of the subjective world of the copy theory into which the undue subjectivism of Locke, Descartes, Hume, and even Kant had kept them imprisoned so long. If they had kept company more faithfully with Plato, Aristotle, and Hegel, they would not have been immured in the prison house of subjectivism

The pragmatist insists, with justice, on the *purposive* or *instrumental character of ideas.* Ideas, he insists, are not internal copies of external realities, but working plans of action, devised and invented by man to remove pains and discomforts, escape dangers, promote his affectional and practical interests, maintain and enhance his own well being. The pragmatist is an evolutionist. He looks upon mind and all its products as biological instruments—like sharp fangs and strong jaws and swift feet, only much more powerful and supple weapons in the struggle for existence. Indeed, he admits that mind has the strange power of creating a cultural environment by which human life is lifted far above that of the brutes. Still he insists that reflective thinking would, in all probability, never have arisen, and certainly would never have thriven, if the affectional life of the *genus homo* had always been serene and blissful without alloy, if his desires had always been satisfied the instant they made themselves felt and if the satisfactions had never left him with a bad taste in the mouth, if promise had always led straight to fulfillment.

Because of discordances, discomforts, pains, because of discrepancies between belief and experience, expectation and fulfillment, thought arises and continues to work until the jarring discords are removed.

"Thought is the means by which the consciously effected evolution of reality goes forward" (Dewey). The only part of reality which we know and are concerned with is in evolution. "Reality is still in the making and awaits a part of its complexion from the future" (William James). In fact, for the pragmatist, *reality is just the process of experience itself* and experience is the result of the continuous and active commerce of man with his natural and social environment, in which commerce, *in sæcula sæculorum,* he remakes both environments and remakes them again and again, even though only in small degree. *Thus reality is the joint product of man's intelligent will and the environing nature.* There is no eternal nature of things which the mind has to copy or gaze at; or if there is, it is *ultra vires,* beyond the jurisdiction of the court of human intellect. The world that thought lives and works in is a humanistically colored world, a world that has engendered minds just as it has engendered stomachs and hands. But, of course, the pragmatist would not assert that the intellect has no larger or more varied uses than the stomach, although he would doubtless say that without a stomach the mind could not do much in this world.

But the pragmatist is not a materialist. For he holds that the mind is a very important kind of organic behavior. It is active and experimental. It not only reacts to stimuli in its own ways, but is a selective and successfully purposive agent. *Ideas are not inherently true. They are not eternal verities. They are made true, become true, by leading to all sorts of satisfactory results.* An idea of the way to a certain place to which you want to go becomes true by leading you there. An idea of a certain ethical or chemical process becomes true by leading to the promised land of results. An idea in education or social reconstruction is made true by being put to work and "delivering the goods." "The true, to put it very briefly, is only the expedient in the way of our thinking, just as the right is only the expedient in the way of our behaving."[1] If you can cash in on the amount indicated by the idea, in the currency that the idea promises, *the idea is made true.* Ideas are checks drawn on the bank of experience. If they are returned marked "no funds," they are false. If the money is counted out to you in the shape of concrete satisfactions, they are true. The satisfactions may be paid in terms of worldly success, honor,

---

[1] James, *Pragmatism*, p. 222.

fame, wealth, power; in terms of the gratification of personal affections, love, friendship, comradeship; in terms of social welfare, in terms of æsthetic gratifications, in terms of the mind's craving for intellectual satisfaction; even in terms of the soul's craving for a God to lean on and commune with.

The pragmatic method means "*the attitude of looking away from first things, principles, 'categories,' supposed necessities, and of looking towards last things, fruits, consequences, facts.*"[2] "*The true is the name of whatever proves itself to be good in the way of belief, and good, too, for definite assignable reasons.*"[3] "*True ideas are those that we can assimilate, validate, corroborate, and verify. False ideas are those that we cannot.*"[4] "Truth is *made* just as health, wealth, and strength are made, in the course of experience."[5] For thought to be true it must "agree" or correspond with reality. "To 'agree' in the widest sense with a reality *can only mean to be guided either straight up to it or into its surroundings, or to be put into such working touch with it as to handle either it or something connected with it* better than if we disagreed."[6] "The essential thing is the process of being guided. Any idea that helps us to deal, whether practically or intellectually, with either the reality or its belongings, * * * that *fits,* in fact, and adapts our life to the reality's whole setting, will agree sufficiently to meet the requirements. It will hold true of that reality."[7]

"This function of agreeable leading is what we mean by an idea's verification."[8]

Truth is made largely out of previous truths. "Men's beliefs at any time are so much experience *funded.* But

---

[2] *Ibid.*, pp. 54, 55.
[3] *Ibid.*, p. 76.
[4] *Ibid.*, p. 201.
[5] *Ibid.*, p. 218.
[6] *Ibid.*, pp. 212, 213.
[7] *Ibid.*, p. 213.
[8] *Ibid.*, p. 202.

the beliefs are themselves parts of the sum total of the world's experience, and become matter, therefore, for the next day's funding operations. So far as reality means experienceable reality, both it and the truths men gain about it are everlastingly in process of mutation—mutation towards a definite goal, it may be—but still mutation."[9] In short, reality is mutable and so is truth.

These quotations require no comment on my part. They are so clear as to be wholly self-explanatory. Any idea that is useful in enriching and harmonizing experience, in satisfying the interest of the individual or society, by performing that function as a *good instrument*, becomes thus far true. An idea that cannot be put to work is meaningless. An idea that will not yield satisfaction when put to work is false. The pragmatist can even find some uses for the absolute all-inclusive knower or experiencer of a Hegel, a Bradley, or a Royce, although James did not think that the moral and religious uses of the absolute counterbalanced its practical, moral, and scientific uselessness and so rejected it.[10]

Pragmatism is right in insisting on the instrumental value of ideas, on their purposive character, and in demanding that ideas should be put to work in life, in concrete experience. It is right in insisting that the fact that an idea works in experience and conduct is a test of its truth. Pragmatism accounts for the origin, utility and truth-value of many of our ideas. A good deal, perhaps the greater part, of knowledge arises and is validated precisely in the ways which the pragmatist describes. He propounds a sound although not novel method of testing the truth of ideas—the scientific method of taking ideas as hypothesis, deducing conclusions from them, and testing these deductions by putting them to work and finding they

---

[9] JAMES, *Pragmatism*, pp. 224, 225.

[10] *Ibid.*, pp. 291 ff., and *A Pluralistic Universe*, Lecture VIII.

lead to the promised concrete results in experience. If a concept, a judgment, a belief works well in practice, there must be something true in it.

James' own statement of pragmatism was too *individualistic.* Ideas may work well for individuals in terms of satisfaction, but their so working may be harmful to society in the long run. A conscienceless profiteer may make millions from the nation's patriotism in time of war and die rich, working untold injury to society. John Dewey emphasizes the social test of working and thus corrects James' view. And, of course, the social and long run satisfactions as tests, are logically compatible with the pragmatist position. But even the later pragmatists have not made it clear as to *how,* pragmatically, the conflicts between individuals, or between an individual and a social group, as to the respective claims for satisfaction of their interests, are to be adjudicated.

Pragmatism talks much about *good* fruits and *good* consequences, but it has failed hitherto to formulate any comprehensive theory of how relative goodnesses in fruits or consequences are to be judged. It seems to me that the pragmatist must admit that the ability of the stronger or of the majority to dragoon the recalcitrant individual or minority is the final social test. If expediency is to rule both in practice and in theory, I can see no other argument. Expediency thus becomes an euphonious name for brute power, analogous to the "survival of the fittest in the struggle for existence." Perhaps this *is* the ultimate test, but the choicest spirits of the race have not hitherto thought so and I for one cannot think so. I am unable to admit that the right is always on the side of the biggest battalions. Belgium may be blotted from the map but the wrong remains eternally a wrong. Hence I agree with Royce [11] that

---

[11] "The Problem of Truth in the Light of Recent Discussion" in *William James and other Essays.*

there are absolute truths in logic, mathematics, ethics, history, and experience; and the truths of logic, mathematics, and ethics imply that there is an absolute creative, rational will which is their ground and source. "Absolute" pragmatism is the only form of the doctrine that is in harmony with the nature of logical and ethical truth, as at once volitional or purposive and drawing its character and meaning and its inherent authority from the determinate structure of the absolute, rational and ethical will or purpose involved in the teleological or worthful and meaningful order of reality.

Pragmatism takes too narrow, too provincial a view of the criteria of truth. In the long run ideas work and yield good results because they are in harmony with the actual structure of reality. And there is useless—that is, useless from any present view of individual or social utilities—knowledge. The story is told of a great mathematician that, having worked out a new theorem, he said, "thank God, there is a truth that no one can make any use of." In higher mathematics, in history, archæology, and science, yes, even in perceptual experience, there are many things recognized as true that men have not found any use for beyond the satisfaction of knowing them, which means the satisfaction the mind has in being in conscious and loyal harmony with the intelligible order of reality. How are these propositions known to be true? Either because men cannot help perceiving them, as I cannot help perceiving the hideous and useless things that deface the landscape in my town, or because they express the intuitively recognized objective structure of the *rational will* in man, or because their truth follows by the laws of logical consistency from some other proposition, definition or axiom which expresses some fact of the objective rational order. It may be that use will be found for every truth ultimately. Let us hope so. If the world is rational and just, it must be so.

There are disagreeable truths which we must face. When my banker informs me that my account is already overdrawn and I have no money to put in, or I am wholly bankrupt, I have yet to find the person to whom the knowledge of the truth is agreeable. In the great war, we had to face as a nation discomforts, sacrifice, and death of many of our choicest sons in *loyalty to a cause.* The pragmatist says that what proves satisfactory, when the returns are all in, will be true. But, in the matter of moral principles, ofttimes the returns are never all in, in this world. How did one know that more satisfaction would ensue to anybody if one went to the war and sacrificed one's self for one's country or if one sent one's son? How did one know that one's family or even the third generation to come would be happier? One did not. One only knew that if it were clearly one's duty—one *ought* to go, one *ought* to send one's son. How did I know that by conscripting the youth of this land to fight in Europe the world will be made safe for democracy and this will be a better world? I did not know. I only hoped so. But in loyalty to the cause, I knew that we could not shirk the issue. I only knew that since we were convinced of the justice of our case, and that if a brutal militaristic autocracy triumphed the world would not be a fit place for our children and our children's children to live in, therefore, we ought to do whatever is necessary to defend that cause.

III. Rational Empiricism

Knowledge comes from several sources. What one perceives or feels, one perceives or feels just as brute fact. We may recognize, examine and analyze experience very rigorously but, finally, we get down to data that are not further analyzable. I see the light and feel the heat and cold, whether these be agreeable or disagreeable. I apprehend impacts and motions as brute facts. Any idea in regard to experimental facts is true only if it is in agreement with the determinate experience or experienceable facts. The facts may be unsatisfactory to you or me, but there they are.

I also intuitively recognize, by my reason, certain truths of logic and ethics. The elementary propositions and axioms or postulates of mathematics and logic, on careful reflection, appear to me true whether you or I care for them or not. *They express the intellect's native ways of working.* They reflect the rational structure of reality. The statement that two contradictory propositions cannot be true simultaneously and in the same situation appears to me self-evident. I cannot conceive a world in which it should be false. In such a world "true" and "false" would have no meaning, and it would not even be a world.

Thus there are ideas that are true because they are in agreement with the given or finite facts, and there are ideas that are true because they express the meanings of the mind's own reflective intuitions, of its own rational procedure in thinking about its world. So far as these truths go they are absolute. Further than this, some minds have a passionate hunger for putting truths together into a coherent whole, for organizing ideas into a system. This ideal of truth-seeking is the philosophical ideal. It is the harmonious organization of all separate truths into a coherent whole. James really admitted these criticisms when he said that we are *coerced* by the determinate order of fact and of intuitively recognized truths of abstract relationships, and when he said that intellectual consistency is the most imperious claimant of all for satisfaction. The fact is that our purposes and our interests do not always get or deserve satisfaction. Sometimes they are shattered into fragments and remade, by the *logic of events,* into larger purposes and meanings. Reality is in mutation, but there is a logic of events, *a determinate order of mutation.* The process of reality has a specific structure, and part of our truth consists in apprehending and symbolizing that structure *as it is.* Mind in us has a logical and ethical structure. Our images, concepts, theories, and assumptions change, to fit enlarged and finer apprehensions of the factual order and to meet the mutations in that order. But, through all the changes and chances in the mental life of ideas, through all the scrapping of old ones and the making of new ones to fit the facts, there run certain fundamental ways of thinking and acting; the elementary principles and postulates of knowledge and conduct. It would belong to a treatise on logic and epistemology to discuss these theoretical principles fully, but we may state the principal ones briefly—*the logical identity of objects of thought with themselves* or *the invariant character of these objects, the impossibility of admitting the truth of two contradictory propositions, the self-evidencing quality of the elementary propositions of logic and mathematics, the rationally evident character of our most universal and fundamental moral judgments, the demand of the mind for the organization of knowledge into a coherent whole which gives us the logically self-consistent systems of mathematics and which, in the form of the principle of sufficient reason or ground, appears in our insistent need in science to discover the relevancy of facts to one another, to classify facts and connect them in a system of causally related or reciprocally interdependent elements.* One could sum up this matter as follows—*the absolute postulates of knowledge are the logical identity of every object of thought with itself, and the harmonious organization or relevancy of all true judgments to one another in a systematic whole.* And there are ethical principles which are valid whether you and I obey them or not, whether we find that they satisfy our concrete interests or not. We may as individuals or social groups be loyal or disloyal to honesty, justice, love, fellowship, loyalty itself, but our actions do not make these qualities right if expedient, and wrong if inexpedient. If expediency be the highest good, there is no highest good. Plato was right in holding that there are values and relationships, principles of moral and rational order, that give meaning and status to, and that endure through, the temporal flux of human experience.

This generation has been permeated and captivated in its thinking by the thought of evolution, ceaseless flux and relativity in all things. Let me remind you that there is no meaning in evolution, or even in flux and relativity, unless there be an enduring teleological order of meanings, by reference to which we measure and judge the dates and relations and meanings and values of the tides and times of human circumstance and deed, and of physical circumstance as well.

The fullest criteria of truth are the coherence of ideas with experiences and the coherence of ideas, as interpretations of experiences, with one another. The ideal of knowledge is the harmonious organization of thinking and experience, in which thinking appears as the instrument for the organization or interpretation of experience, by which experience becomes conscious of its own meanings and by which its own enrichment and more harmonious fulfillment are furthered. This ideal, although never fully realized, is the animating motive of the thinker at his best.

Reality is a teleological and self-organizing system, and thinking is the chiefest instrument for the maintenance and enhancement of this system. The function of thought is both to discover the existing relations or relevancies of things to one another and to promote the increase of these relationships. Thinking is the chief instrument of organization in a purposively ordered world, a world controlled by a rational and ethical order, as I believe.

References

* AVEY, A. E., *Readings in Philosophy,* Chapter XXV.
* BAWDEN, H. H., *The Principles of Pragmatism.*

BRADLEY, F. H., *Appearance and Reality.*

* CARR, H. W., *The Problem of Truth.* (An excellent, brief discussion.)
* DEWEY, JOHN, *Studies in Logical Theory,* and the articles "Beliefs and Realities" and "The Experimental Theory of Knowledge" in *The Influence of Darwin on Philosophy.*

DEWEY AND OTHERS, *Creative Intelligence.*

HEGEL, *Logic,* translated by Wallace.

* JAMES, WILLIAM, *Pragmatism* (especially Lectures II, III, V, and VI) and *The Meaning of Truth.*

JOACHIM, H. H., *The Nature of Truth.*

MARVIN, W. T., *A First Book in Metaphysics.*

* MOORE, A. W., *Pragmatism and Its Critics.*
* ROYCE, JOSIAH, "The Problem of Truth" in *William James and Other Essays.*
* RUSSELL, BERTRAND, *The Problems of Philosophy,* Chapters X, XI, XII and XIII.

SCHILLER, F. C. S., *Humanism, Studies in Humanism,* and *Formal Logic.*

* SPAULDING, E. G., *The New Rationalism.*

STURT, H., AND OTHERS, *Personal Idealism.*

CHAPTER XXXI

OTHER PHILOSOPHICAL DISCIPLINES

THE SYSTEM OF PHILOSOPHY

The central and fundamental philosophical discipline, metaphysics, is the theory of the nature or structure and meaning of reality as a whole. While writers may show philosophical insights in various special fields and, to the extent of these insights, deserve the name philosophers, a system of thought can be properly called a philosophy only when its various aspects are built upon and articulated with a metaphysics or doctrine of reality. Metaphysics includes, as special divisions:—*cosmology* or philosophy of nature, whose chief problems are the nature or meaning of space, time, matter, motion, and evolution; *metapsychology,* or philosophy of selves and society; *epistemology,* or philosophy of knowledge; and *axiology,* or philosophy of values. These special divisions of metaphysics cannot, however, be pursued successfully in isolation from one another. The subject matter of the present work has consisted: (1) in tracing the emergence and development of the fundamental problems and theories of metaphysics, ethics, and the theory of knowledge; and the interrelationships of these subjects; and (2) in discussing the present status of these problems and theories. It now remains for us to consider briefly the respective fields, and relations to general philosophy or metaphysics, of the remaining philosophical disciplines. These are: logic, æsthetics, and the philosophy of religion. Before proceeding with this matter, it is desirable that an indication be given as to the relation between philosophy and psychology.

I. Psychology and Philosophy

There is no unanimity of opinion among the psychologists as to the proper field and methods of psychology. The point on which there is nearest approach to agreement is that psychology is *not* the science of the soul, that it has no concern with the question whether man is a soul or permanently unified self. It is also pretty generally agreed that psychology is as much an independent science as, say, chemistry, and therefore, like any other special science, is independent of philosophy. Still there must be some good reason, other than the slow development of the science itself, why psychology has remained so long in closer association with philosophy than the other sciences. Before we can discover this reason, we must essay a statement as to the province of psychology.

It used to be said that the business of psychology is to analyze, describe, and correlate the elementary constituents and processes of consciousness, to determine in detail the *structure of consciousness* in all its forms and stages. This, the standpoint of *structuralism,* was the classical standpoint until after the middle of the nineteenth century, when evolutionary biology began more and more to hold sway over men's thinking about human nature. Of course it had been already recognized that psychology is concerned, too, with the relation between consciousness and the nervous system, or, in general terms, between mind and body.

The rapid development of the evolution hypothesis led to a change of emphasis in psychology. Mental processes began to be viewed as instruments of adaptation to the environment, as tools for the more successful adjustment of the relationships between man and nature, and the individual man and society. This is the standpoint of *functionalism,* which does not deny all value to structural analysis of mind but makes such analysis subservient to the determination of the biological or life-serving functions of the mind. The mind in all its phases, whether clearly conscious, subconscious, and perhaps unconscious, consists of special types of functional adjustments of the organism. William James' great work, *The Principles of Psychology,* was the most influential in making this change of emphasis. Herbert Spencer's *Principles of Psychology* is written chiefly from the same standpoint. Lately a third standpoint has arisen—*behaviorism.* The ultraradical behaviorist denies that consciousness is a fruitful or even legitimate subject of study. He proposes to consider only the objective or physical side of behavior. The moderate behaviorist admits that the most important data for psychology are those obtained from the study of conscious thinking organisms, but he insists that psychology is primarily the science of human behavior. I am of the opinion that the psychologist cannot afford to neglect permanently any one of these standpoints. Psychology, as I understand it, has for its central domain the systematic investigation of the conscious and intelligent behavior of human individuals. To successfully carry on this work it cannot afford to leave out of account, either the purposive adaptation functions which the mind of the individual performs, or the structural analysis of mental complexes, such as perceptions, memories, images, judgments, conceptions, instincts, emotions, and sentiments, into their elementary features.

What, then, is the right relation between psychology and philosophy? Psychology is a special science, inasmuch as it studies the behavior of the conscious individual in relation to the physical order and the social order, without raising the metaphysical questions as to how one is to conceive, *ultimately*, the nature of the self in relation to the body and the relation of the psycho-physical individual or group of individuals to the world as a whole; in so far as it describes the process of thinking, without attempting to determine what are the final norms or criteria of knowledge; in so far as it describes the processes of volition, without attempting to determine the valid norms or standards of conduct; and in so far as it describes the processes of æsthetic feeling, without raising the question as to the place of beauty in reality. But when psychology does attempt to deal with the ultimate problems of the relation of mind and body, of self and world, of the criteria of truth and goodness and beauty in the universe, then it passes into philosophy; it passes into metaphysics, ethics, logic, epistemology, and æsthetics. Moreover, it is not easy for the psychologist to avoid raising the philosophical issues. Psychology is concerned with such questions as these—the nature of conscious life, with its chief aspects, namely: feeling, thought, and volition; the genesis of voluntary action from impulse, of emotion and sentiment from the primary affections of pleasure-pain and desire and aversion, and with the development of cognition from rudimentary perception up to the highest forms of imagination and conceptual generalization; with the nature of the subconscious, and the relations between the conscious and the subconscious; with the relations between the mind and the nervous system, and between the mind and the bodily processes as a whole; with the relations between the conscious organism as a whole and its social and physical environments. All these problems are of cardinal import for metaphysics and ethics and social philosophy. Indeed any attitude taken by a psychologist on any one of these problems involves, straightway, a definite attitude towards some fundamental problem of human conduct and belief—in short, towards some vital question in ethics and social philosophy, in religious belief and conduct, or in metaphysics (which is simply the final clearing house for all such questions). It is useless and confusing for a psychologist to waive aside the final practical, ethical, and metaphysical implications of his theories. Since psychology, if it have a definite field at all, is the science of human nature, and since philosophy is the attempt, by thorough and comprehensive reflection, to think out the place and meaning of human nature in the universe, psychology runs into philosophy more quickly and at more points than any other natural science. Biology, the science which is next of kin to psychology among the natural sciences, is likewise next to it in the closeness and frequency of its contacts with philosophy. But psychology, unlike biology, is more than a science of life in the raw. As the science of human nature, psychology is concerned with man as the creator, sustainer, and subject of culture—that is, with the whole broad stream of human civilization.

Inasmuch as the problems of philosophy all center in the questions as to the place of the self and society in the universe of reality, it is quite evident why psychology has always lived, and should continue to live, in intimate association with philosophy. It is not for the permanent good of either discipline that they should be kept asunder. Without philosophy psychology's work becomes a blind trafficking with physical instruments and physiological measurements. Without empirical psychological foundations philosophy becomes a dialectical exercise in spinning logical cobwebs.

II. Logic

Logic is the systematic investigation of the fundamental processes or methods by which thought arrives at truth, or the right methods of making judgments and inferences. Psychology likewise studies the processes of knowing, but from a different standpoint. Psychology is concerned to analyze and describe the cognitive processes simply as mental events which occur in individual minds along with other kinds of mental events. It is not the aim of psychology either to formulate the most general canons or norms of correct thinking or to formulate all the various methods by which these canons are applied in the actual work of science. But this is just what logic aims to do. It is true that logic studies actual processes of thinking and therefore makes use of psychology, but logic finds its material chiefly in the analysis of typical cases of correct thinking as exemplifying the norms of knowledge. Hence, fair samples of correct thinking in the practical affairs of life and in all the sciences furnish the materials of logic. It studies analytically such cases in order to determine the fundamental procedures, in judgment and inference, that are involved in them.

In short, whereas psychology studies thoughts as natural events that occur, along with other events, in the minds or heads of individual agents, logic studies thought as that function of mind which is objective and universal, or, in other words, as the instrument by which truth is discovered and apprehended. By *truth* is meant *propositions that are objectively valid or valid for all normal thinking beings under similar conditions of experience.* Thus, while all sorts of thoughts or ideas, normal and abnormal, sane and insane, are grists for the psychological mill, the logician is interested only in thought as the normal and normative function, by the exercise of which objective, universal, and mutually consistent propositions are found or grasped. By *objective truth* is meant, in logic and science, propositions that are valid independent of the accidents, whims, idiosyncrasies, of particular selves; by the *universality of truth* is meant the same thing; that is, that a proposition, if true, must be true for all who can think in accordance with the norms or principles of logic. By *mutual consistency* is meant that true propositions, whether they be about particular matters of fact, or about mathematical and scientific principles, cannot contradict one another. In so far as our beliefs and the theories of our sciences are inconsistent, thus far we have not reached the truth.

Thought has two chief stages—judgment and inference. A *judgment* is the most elemental act of logical thinking. It consists in the assertion, either in affirmative or negative form, that a predicate holds good of a subject. The predicate always involves a *universal, meaning,* or *"what"*; that is, the predicate is always a general term. For example, in—"Socrates was a Greek philosopher," "This room is warm," "Greek philosopher" and "warm" are universals, affirmed to hold good of subjects or "thats." Judgments are classified in various ways; with respect to their *quality,* as affirmative or negative; with respect to their *quantity,* as universal, individual, particular, or indefinite; with respect to the kind or mode of *assertion,* as categorical, hypothetical, problematical, disjunctive. There are other important ways of classifying judgments that are too complex to be entered into here. An important problem in regard to the nature of judgment is this—does the subject of judgment always refer, directly or indirectly, to reality, that is, to the world of real existence? If it does, then what is the logical status of judgments in regard to imaginary and contradictory objects of thought? How do judgments in regard to centaurs, hippigriffs, grins without cats, ropes of sand, perpetual motion, et cetera, refer to reality? I refer to these matters merely in order to indicate the scope of logic.

Inference is the passage of thought, *always by means of a universal,* from one judgment to another. Inference involves, either the transformation of a single judgment into a different one that follows from it (immediate inference) or the combination of two or more judgments, called the premises, from which a new judgment, the conclusion, is obtained.

The logical problem of inference is to state the laws or universal principles, to which the various types of inference must conform in order to be valid. There are many types of inference, from the precise and exact procedures of pure mathematics, through the less exact sciences, such as biology and psychology, to the various degrees of probability which judgments in historical inquiry and in practical life have. These types we cannot consider here. In inference one may start from a single particular fact of sense perception, memory, or historical record, or one may start from precise and universal principles as in mathematics or physics. *But all cases of inference have this in common—in no case can inference take place without the employment of universals.* Thus, the controversies which have been waged, from the days of Plato down to the present, as to the status of universals or general concepts, as to whether they are purely subjective formations of the individual human mind, or, at best, mere social conventions; or, on the other hand, have objective foundations in the nature of things; so far from being an amusement in the spinning of cobwebs by "highbrows" having no useful employment, are controversies which go down to the very foundations, and concern the very existence, of all science and all practical social order. If universals are but the subjective figments of human brains or, like bile or saliva, are but by-products of physiological processes, then all science, all ethical values, all social values, all æsthetic values, must go by the board. But such a proposition would, by the hypothesis, itself be a physiological by-product and not truer than any other. There would be no real distinction between truth and error. The only reasonable conclusion is that universals, relations, or meanings, inhere in, indeed constitute, the very texture or pattern of objective reality, and that there must be a *logic in the very substance and structure of reality, of which our human logic is the partial and growing apprehension. The validity of all human values and, indeed, the every, day utility of thought, as well as the ongoing of the social order, presuppose the reality of universals, that is, the logical structure of reality. Logic is just the most comprehensive formulation of the principles and procedure by which the human mind can apprehend and adjust itself to the logic of reality.*

It is evident that right judgment and inference, as exemplified in concrete cases, presuppose and imply certain most fundamental principles of knowledge. These are the laws or principles of all *sound thinking.* Such principles are: the principle of coherence or freedom from contradiction (two contradictory propositions cannot both be true); the principle of identity (a logical subject of thought must be identical with itself); the principle of sufficient ground or causation (there must be a sufficient ground for every event); the principle of uniformity (the same conditions or causes will have the same effects). Since this is but a brief indication of the province of logic, I shall not discuss whether the above named are the only ultimate fundamental principles of logic. It will be obvious to the thoughtful reader that the above principles are presupposed in all genuinely scientific or systematically thoughtful procedure of the mind and that, therefore, a sound logical theory is not only implied in every kind of scientific procedure, but as well that it is the primal condition of sound philosophy. Every true judgment and inference in practical affairs, as well as in science, is a bit of applied logic; and metaphysics is an applied logic of the whole universe of reality or experience.

Logic is frequently divided, in elementary textbooks, into two parts—deductive and inductive logic. Such a division, while it may have practical pedagogical justification, overlooks the fact that, in the actual work of science, deduction and induction are both involved and, while some sciences are more inductive or deductive than others, no science is purely either the one or the other.

III. Æsthetics

Æsthetics is the philosophy of æsthetic feeling and judgment. Since Kant's *Critique of Judgment* was written it has been recognized as a division of philosophy. We may investigate the psychological and physiological conditions of æsthetic feeling and, thus far, æsthetics is a branch of psychology and physiology. We may consider the history of æsthetic appreciation in relation to the history of art and, in this regard, æsthetics is a branch of the history of culture. But we may also ask, what is the significance of æsthetic feeling and judgment with reference to man's place in the universe? Does the fact that the sounding cataract haunts one like a passion, that one feels oneself to be a part of the mountains, seas, and sky; in short, does the whole human reaction in which we feel with Wordsworth

> "a presence far more deeply interfused, a motion and a spirit which impels all thinking things, all objects of all thought,"

does this æsthetic reaction to nature mean perhaps that nature is the expression of a life, of whose rich and harmonious meanings these sympathetic feelings of ours for nature are the echoes or adumbrations? Is beauty an avenue to the vision of reality? Does it unlock gates otherwise closed, by which, even though intermittently, we are permitted to enter into contact with reality in some of its glory? Or are all our feelings for nature, our sense of a divine mystery half revealed, half concealed in the sunset, the mountains, the forest brook, the quiet lake, and the majestic sea, merely subjective reverberations in our organisms of a world that in itself is but the stony and insensate realm of mass particles in motion or the dead and unfeeling completeness of some static absolute? These questions are hints as to the metaphysical problem suggested by man's æsthetic relation to nature; and similar questions arise from a consideration of the ceaseless striving of man to express and satisfy his emotion in art forms of beauty, sublimity, and terror, and from the consideration of the refining, purifying, healing, and refreshing influences which have come to men through converse with nature and art. It is beyond the scope of this introduction to discuss these questions. I must leave the matter with the suggestion that, perhaps, the painters, the sculptors, the musicians and the poets, apprehend an aspect of reality that is hidden from the eyes of the dry-as-dust scientist or arid dialectician. It is my own conviction, one that has grown upon me with the years, that the æsthetic experiences are more than subjective solaces or illusory refuges from the "fretful stir unprofitable and the fever of this world"; that the beauty and the grandeur as felt in nature, in human life and art, are forefelt apprehensions, though intermittent and fragmentary, of an order, a harmony, a concrete, and meaningful life that belongs somehow to the heart of things. The true greatness of poets such as Wordsworth, Shelley, and Whitman, and prose writers such as Ruskin and Thoreau, resides in the fact that they have been prophets of the æsthetic vision of a higher reality beyond and yet interwoven with the dumb shows of sense. The same fundamental notion of *living order or a harmonious organization of experience* is the basic motif of science and logic which aim, not at reducing individual centers of activity and experience to illusions, but at finding the world to be an ordered or organized realm of individuals. And the practical, moral, and social activities of man have the same aim—to construct a harmonious, well organized whole of living centers of experience and deed—the ideal society, in which the law of each member's being is fulfilled by expansion into harmonious action and feeling with the whole, as the fulfillment of the law of the whole through the individuality of each. Thus æsthetic experience interprets and fulfills, from the standpoint of feeling, the vocation of man which, more abstractly, or in more formal shape, urges on his theoretical and his practical life activities. At this point the transition to the consideration of the place of religion in philosophical system is readily suggested.

IV. The Philosophy of Religion

Religion in its most significant forms is the affirmation of the supremacy in the order of reality of all the organized and coherent values pertaining to the life of man in society. Religion idealizes man's values as a socialized individual, or as a society of individuals regenerated and redeemed through participation in the common life. Religion affirms that the system of ideal values not only must be the paramount goal of human life, but as well that these values, in their organic wholeness as fulfilled in the socialized individual, are securely seated at the heart of reality and control the process of things. God is the incarnation of the system of ideal values. Therefore God is essentially the perfect social self—the supreme self—who lives and fulfills himself in and through the regeneration or development of the spiritual man in and through the ideal society. God is the ideal embodiment of the values which are realized by the moral and rational self as a member of a social order which functions to serve these values. Religion affirms the ideal unity and ground of value to be the most real being.

The business of the philosophy of religion is to determine what religion means and aims at, in the successive and varied phases of its development in history and in its operations in the individual's experience and the social order. Religion is thus both social and individual, both historical and personal, and the philosophy of religion should evaluate the history of religion or interpret the movement of religious evolution, the religious experience of the individual, and the religious attitude of the social group. From this standpoint, too, it should determine the function and meaning of the God-idea, of salvation, regeneration, redemption, atonement, the freedom and vocation of man.

In short, the philosophy of religion is the metaphysics of selves, society, and values, applied to the constructive interpretation of the religious experience of the race in the light of the history of culture and psychology. So large and deep going an area of human social life and individual experience as religion represents must be taken account of by the philosopher; and, if he cannot find room for it in his rubrics, then it is more likely that his rubrics are too small and rigid than that the whole religious history of the race is an illusion.

References

Psychologies by Angell, Stout, Titchener, Calkins, Pillsbury, Kuelpe, James (*Principles*), Wundt (*Physiological Psychology*), Watson, Woodworth.

Logic

Introductory Logics by Aikins, Creighton, Joseph.

Bosanquet, B., *Essentials of Logic,* and *Logic of the Morphology of Knowledge.*

Mill, J. S., *Logic.*

Russell, Bertrand, *Principles of Mathematics.*

Windelband and Ruge, *Encyclopædia of the Philosophical Sciences,* Volume I, "Logic."

Æsthetics

Aristotle, *Poetics,* translated by Butcher.
Carritt, *The Theory of Beauty.*
Coleridge, *Biographia Literaria, et cetera.*
Croce, B., *Æsthetics.*
Hegel, *Philosophy of Fine Art,* "Introduction," translated by Bosanquet.
Kant, I., *Critique of Judgment.*
Langfeld, H. S., *The Æsthetic Attitude.*
Parker, D. H., *Æsthetics.*
Plato, *Republic,* Book X, and *Phædrus.*
Ruskin, J., *Modern Painters, et cetera.*
Santayana, G., *The Sense of Beauty.*
Schopenhauer, *The World as Will and Idea,* Book 3.

Philosophy of Religion

* Ames, E. S., *Psychology of Religious Experience.*
Balfour, A. J., *Theism and Humanism.*
Boutroux, *Science and Religion in Contemporary Philosophy.*
Bowne, B. P., *Theism.*
Caird, E., *The Evolution of Religion.*
* Coe, G. A., *Psychology of Religion.*
Dürkheim, E., *Elementary Forms of the Religious Life.*
Galloway, G., *Philosophy of Religion.*
Hocking, W. E., *The Meaning of God in Human Experience.*
* Hoffding, H., *Philosophy of Religion.*
* James, Wm., *Varieties of Religious Experience.*
Leuba, J. H., *A Psychological Study of Religion.*
* Pratt, J. B., *The Religious Consciousness.*
* Pringle-Pattison, A. Seth, *The Idea of God.*
Royce, Josiah, *The Problem of Christianity.*
Santayana, G., *Reason in Religion.*
Sorley, W. R., *Moral Values and the Idea of God.*
* Starbuck, E. D., *Psychology of Religion.*
Ward, J., *The Realm of Ends.*
Webb, C. C. J., *God and Personality,* and *Divine Personality and Human Life.*
* Wright, W. K., *A Student's Philosophy of Religion.*

CHAPTER XXXII

PROGRESS IN PHILOSOPHY

Some persons would deny that philosophy has made any substantial advances in modern times. They would assert that the history of philosophy reveals only a succession of systems, reflecting the respective individualities of their makers cross-fertilized by the cultural conditions of their times. No continuous advance is made. One system is not built upon the achievements of its predecessors. Philosophy is like poetry, only much more dry, cumbrous, and obscure in statement. It is primarily the expression of a temperament. "A man's philosophy depends on the kind of man he is" (Fichte). Science, on the other hand, moves forward with sure, if slow, steps, and by well-defined methods.

There is some truth in this view, but it is superficial and an exaggeration. Certainly philosophy shares in the vicissitudes of culture. It ripens only in a mature culture. There is no rectilinear or curvilinear nor, indeed, any other *regular form* of progress in the history of culture; therefore, none in philosophy. A culture develops in a specific historical situation, spreads and ripens, then perhaps undergoes either partial decadence or a critical transformation, owing to a complexity of causes, economic, political, moral, and intellectual (I do not mean, of course, that social causes can be sharply separated off from one another; they interlock). After an epoch of apparent dissolution a culture is again built up. While the movement of history cannot be strung out on the threads of the Hegelian dialectic, there is a dialectic in cultural history. There are ages of construction, of the upbuilding of cultural values and institutions, succeeded by stationary ages of conservatism. These, in turn, are succeeded by ages of criticism, radical inquiry, and revolution; followed by oscillatory struggles between the forces of reaction and of reconstruction. The Greek enlightenment was followed by the social disintegration of the Greek world. Upon this succeeded the conservative Roman Empire. The downfall of the latter was followed by a period of chaos, after which medieval culture was gradually built up to its apogee in the thirteenth century. An age of critical inquiry began again and, in the fifteenth and sixteenth centuries, there emerged a new type of culture which continued fairly stable until the French Revolution and the more important Industrial Revolution. No sooner had the latter seemingly reached a stabilized condition in the latter years of the nineteenth century than it began to issue in the social and political crises which culminated in the great war. The present age is one of transition and reconstruction, following upon the age in which the great scale, mechanized industrialism, struggling with the movement of democracy towards universal equalization of opportunity, ended in the terrific cataclysm which finishes the old epoch and begins the new. The task before the world to-day is the control of industrialism, to make it subservient to the principles of democratic humanism. Philosophy has its corresponding tasks. In order that we may see what these are it will be necessary to review briefly some of the salient advances in philosophy. Before doing so let us note that the claim that the special sciences advance continuously, with sure and orderly steps, cannot be allowed before the court of history. Science shares, too, in the vicissitudes of culture. And, during long stretches of time, for example, from the fourth to the thirteenth centuries of our era in European culture, there was no substantial advance made in either science or philosophy. The civilization of the Arab caliphates was relatively barren in both fields.

It is true that philosophy reflects the individualities of its authors more than does mathematics, or physics, or biology; although here, too, the history of science shows how the individuality of an investigator influences his work. Consider, for example, the differences in the contributions of Copernicus, Tycho, Brahe, Kepler, and Galileo to the new astronomy, and of Darwin, Huxley, and Spencer to the doctrine of evolution. But the individuality of a thinker enters more fully into his product in philosophy than in natural science, precisely because a philosophy is the concentration point at which the problems and interpretation of humanistic values and naturalistic facts and theories meet and must be synthesized into a global or total view. Since the personality of man is both source and center of reference for both naturalistic and humanistic interests, the results of their conflicts and concordats must reflect, as well as react upon, the medium in which they live and move and have their being—the spiritual individuality of man.

The course of Greek philosophy shows progress from the naïve hylozoism of Thales up to the formulation of two classical standpoints—the Platonic-Aristotelian idealism and the mechanistic philosophy of atomism. With the political decay of Greece and the spread and dilution of Greek culture in the Roman Empire there was progress in ethics, through the universalization, by the Stoics, of the ethical features of the classical idealism. In Plotinus, finally, we find a significant religious synthesis, in which a speculative and ascetic mysticism is based on the classical idealism. This is the last legacy of the dying Greek spirit to the future. Then ancient culture disintegrates. It is almost entirely submerged in the welter of social chaos and barbarism called the Dark Ages (end of fifth to beginning of ninth century). A new civilization must be built up—the Romano-Germanic-Christian. The heritage of classical culture is slowly recovered and utilized. But, not until the new civilization reaches maturity in the thirteenth century could there be a philosophical renaissance. Then appears a classical achievement—the christianized Aristotelianism of Thomas Aquinas, coincidental with the achievements of Gothic Art and of a new and high type of civic life. At the same time the stirring of the new spirit of scientific inquiry is marked by the movement of philosophy towards independence of ecclesiastical dogmas. The growth of the new mechanical system of the universe, in the science of the sixteenth and seventeenth centuries, a growth which involved the higher development both of mathematical and empirical methods of inquiry, is coincidental and interwoven with the development of the great systems of *rationalism* and *empiricism*. Rationalism is worked out with rigor and vigor, to a one-sided conclusion, in the school of Leibnitz-Wolff. At the same time, one-sided empiricism is worked out, with even greater clarity and thoroughness, in the impressionism or atomistic sensationalism of Hume. The very completeness and precision with which a one-sided standpoint, such as that of Hume, is carried out, is a necessary condition of further progress. By revealing the ultimate skeptical consequences of impressionism, Hume became the forerunner of a new and deeper speculative philosophy. Kant is the bridge, or halfway house, between the conflicting rationalism and skeptical empiricism of the eighteenth century and the new speculative, historical, and dynamic idealism of Fichte and Hegel. Kant did not achieve the synthesis himself; but, without him, there could have been no Fichte or Hegel. We may admit in turn that the soaring and imperialistic claims of Fichte and Hegel to compass the whole meaning of earth and heaven have not been made good, and are now discredited. But it cannot be gainsaid, by a competent and open-minded historian, that Fichte's dialectic gave the cue, first to Schelling and then, through him, to Hegel; *and that Hegel,* in turn, *by his analysis of the movement of mind as creator and bearer of, and as realizing itself in, the whole life of culture, made a permanent contribution to the race's heritage of philosophical insights.* Hegel's analysis of the development of selfhood, and of the meaning and function of social culture as an objectification of mind and the condition of the development of the individual mind, has carried on the work of Plato to a higher level and given us a lasting gain for the theory of mind and society.

Hegel's philosophy was an idealistic or spiritualistic evolutionism. Reality is a teleological process. It is the inevitable movement of the self-evolution of spirit. The final goal of this process is the coming to full self-consciousness of the Divine Spirit, through the historical progress of human culture in the life of the state and in art, science, and religion. Philosophy is the clear comprehension of the meaning of the whole process. Two defects Hegel's philosophy had—(1) Its arbitrary construction of empirical data in the field of history, and, still more, in the field of natural science: (2) It tended to merge the individual personality entirely in the institutional or social mind and thus, while proclaiming freedom to be the goal of progress, made it to consist in the complete identity of the personal spirit with the social and impersonal spirit (the Zeitgeist), culminating in the Teutonic state and the Hegelian philosophy. Consequently this philosophy fell into disrepute, both with those imbued with the temper of empirical and naturalistic science and with those enkindled with the spirit of the new democracy as the instrument for attaining universal freedom and individual self-realization.

The establishment of the doctrine of the *Conservation of Energy,* a succession of great discoveries in physics, especially in electricity and magnetism and radioactive transformations, the formulation of the *Periodic Law* in chemistry and the great developments in the latter science, more especially in organic chemistry, the rise of the *Darwinian theory of evolution,* the extension of the evolutionary standpoint in the fields of geology, cosmogony, psychology, sociology, ethics, and religion, and, finally, the successful application of experimental methods, as well as evolutionary modes of explanation, in physiology and psychology, have given new impetus to materialism, which, in the mechanistic theory of life and mind, society and culture, is a vigorous movement at the present time. The new materialism is different from the older form, in that it substitutes for the mass particles of the older theory punctual centers of energy. The course of things is determined by the blind alterations in the configurations in space of these energy centers.

At the same time the influence, on men's world views, of the historical and comparative methods employed in the humanistic or social sciences (to which Hegel gave a powerful impetus by his interpretation of the evolution of human culture) has tremendously increased. While workers in these fields have been impressed with the multiform and confusing array of facts and have, consequently, become shy of sweeping generalizations, the main inspiring motive of this work is the idea of an evolutionary order and meaning, to be unravelled by patient investigation. Fuller knowledge of the natural order will find practical application in the reconstruction of the social order, by supplying a philosophy of culture and progress. It will also satisfy man's appetite for an intellectual chart that will illumine the tangled facts of human experience and give a better clue to the meaning of human history and the significance of the human lot in the environing cosmos—a clue better grounded than the older systems, because based on the richer and wider insights into the naturalistic implications of human life and the nature of man and society which have been accumulating since the middle of the nineteenth century.

One man has attempted the task, no longer possible of achievement by one man, of a comprehensive synthesis of the results both of the natural and humanistic or social sciences. Since Hegel the most ambitious attempt at a philosophical synthesis is the synthetic philosophy of Herbert Spencer. His guiding thread is the concept of universal evolution. While Spencer covers the whole field of thought and action, including sociology, psychology and ethics, the categories of physical science have the best of it in his system. While his logic is often faulty and his synthesis too vague and viewy, the courage, persistence, and sweep of outlook with which Spencer planned and executed his herculean task are admirable. The system as a whole will not stand before critical examination; nevertheless he has contributed many valuable *aperçus* to philosophy. Examples of such are—the definition of evolution as the passage from a state of indefinite, incoherent homogeneity to a state of definite, coherent heterogeneity, by concomitant processes of differentiation and integration; and the working out of the conception of life and mind as continuous adaptation of internal relations to external relations.

The only other recent system that bears comparison with Spencer's or Hegel's is that of Wilhelm Wundt (+1921), who shows an enormous knowledge, not only of contemporary science and learning, but, as well, of the history of philosophical and scientific thought (in knowledge of the history of thought Spencer was notoriously deficient). Wundt's system is one of spiritualistic or psychical and indeed, *voluntaristic* evolutionism. *Will* is the reality manifested in all finite existence, and there is a *universal and absolute will* which includes all finite wills. Wundt's principle of *creative synthesis,* namely, that in psychical development and evolution, the results of a new synthesis are more than the sum of, or rise higher than the sum of, the qualities of the elements which enter into it, is perhaps his most significant contribution to general philosophy. Lester F. Ward, the American sociologist, makes much use of this principle.

Bergson's doctrine of evolution as a creative and psychical process, which eventuates in ever increasing differentiation and multiplication of individual psychical centers, as well as his attempt at a solution of the mind-body problem in dynamic terms will undoubtedly have to be reckoned with in the philosophy of the future.

The most important works in systematic philosophy by living English writers are those of Bernard Bosanquet and Samuel Alexander. A. N. Whitehead's contributions to the philosophy of nature are likewise very important.

The time is ripe for a new philosophical synthesis. The time is past when such a synthesis can be achieved by any one man. It must be the fruit of the coöperation of many minds. I will close, by indicating briefly the standpoints which seem to me to have been won and the directions in which we may look for further progress.

1. In *metaphysics:* With respect to the *mind-body* or *spirit-matter problem,* we have definitely left dualism and the identity-theory behind us. The issue lies clear-cut between materialism and the theory that man and the world are an organic unity or interdependent system of levels of actuality or energies, physical, vital, and mental. With respect to the problems of *space* and *time* the only tenable position is realistic. The spatial order is a true aspect of reality. The concept of eternity cannot be ad-

mitted in the sense of timelessness, if by that be meant that the temporal order is illusory. The actual world is a temporal order, but, since it is an *order,* there may be a permanent and continuously effective system or complex of meanings and laws. It follows too, I hold, that causal activity is a genuine reality. With regard to *teleology* and *values* (a teleological view is a doctrine of the conservation and augmentation of values in reality) the issue lies clearly defined between a metaphysics which would assert the final illusoriness of all human values and one which would find, in constructing its world picture, that there are valid grounds for a reasonable faith in the conservation of values, although it is impossible to say in what forms and how close in character to human estimation of values that conservation may take place.

With regard to the *relation of the individual to the world whole* the latter is to be interpreted, in so far as it is a unity, as, at its highest level, a dynamic and social unity.

With regard to the problem of the *self,* the study of the aberrations, the psychological development, and the social implications, of personality are shedding much new light on the nature of selfhood or personality. They seem to me to validate the view that the concept of socialized personality is the best key to the meaning of the world process; and, on the other hand, to show that personality is the resultant of the interaction of a complex of factors, physical, vital, mental, and social. Personality is the highest product of the world-order.

2. In *ethics and social philosophy:* Since, in these fields, we are concerned primarily with the doctrine of human values and of the social instruments for their realization, it is not to be expected that we should have made great progress beyond the deepest ethical and social insights of the past; that, for instance, with respect to the true values,

aims, and satisfactions of a rational human life, we should have far transcended those masters of humanism, Plato, Aristotle, and in special regards, the New Testament writers, and of such moderns as Kant and Butler. Nevertheless, we are gaining, as a result of more thorough psychological and sociological analysis, coupled with a larger historical outlook, a richer, better balanced, and more scientifically grounded, doctrine of human values and of the social conditions of their realization in the new economic order brought to pass by the Industrial Revolution. It is, indeed, a commonplace that, since the Greeks, we have gained considerably in depth of insight into the nature of, and the common right to the enjoyment of, the fundamental human values. The immediate problems now are, not so much the formulation of a new body of doctrine as to what are the true values of rational living, as they are the application of the insights we already possess to the reorganization of social institutions. The theory of education and of the whole organized activities of social culture must be seen in their right perspectives, with reference to the basic human values. *We need badly the extension and application of the idealistic philosophy of education, culture, and progress.* Our practitioners, in education and social administration are, to too great an extent, mere empirics and hand-to-mouth politicians. They are guided by no reasoned convictions; they have no philosophy of culture or progress, because they have no doctrines of social ends and values, no social philosophy. We must set about, straightway, to determine how the industrial order and the administration of educational and other social institutions must be reconstructed, in order to achieve *the democratization of man's opportunity to realize and enjoy all the basic human values, without cheapening these values or hindering the creation of new values. The humanization of industry and education and the civilization or cul-*

tural uplift of democracy are the central problems of social philosophy in the new day.

3. In *philosophy of religion* the assiduous cultivation of psychological methods of interpretation, interwoven with the results of the comparative and scientific historical study of religions, viewed as factors in the history of civilization causally influenced by the other factors, economic, legal, political, moral, and intellectual, as well as influencing these other factors, are bearing fruit in a synthetic conception of the place of religion in culture, of its evolution and its meaning for society and the individual. It is dawning upon cultivated men that no historical form of religion can be altogether false and none, in its past forms, the final and absolute truth. In fact the question of absolute and final truth or falsity becomes a juvenile irrelevancy. Since, in religion, man is ever seeking and finding for his own time, circumstances and individuality, a response to the postulate of the supremacy and conservation of the psychic and spiritual values of the social order and the individual soul, religion must evolve with the evolution of the consciousness of values, and that means with man's entire cultural history. For a religion is the idealization of the values sought and held by a social group or an individual. The new truth that is becoming clearer is that, while, on the one hand, there is no unchangeable form of *natural religion,* on the other hand, every important form of religion is natural to man in the given stage of human culture. The evolution of spiritual experience and apprehension cannot advance beyond the level of man's cultural development. Even the creative insights of seer and prophet are conditioned by their social media.

This attitude towards religion does not imply that, in times past, spiritual insights may not have been reached that will not be thrown away or transcended in the march of civilization. The spiritual evolution of man is a process in which, as, indeed, to a less striking degree, in natural evolution, *in critical moments of time,* permanent heights of achievement or insight have been reached. If Sophocles, Plato, the Apollo Belvedere, the Logic of Aristotle, Shakespeare, Newton, the elementary principles of mathematics and mechanics, stand for cultural goods that will never be transcended in their own order, or be cast away, it is quite as reasonable to suppose that the messages of Isaiah, the life of Jesus, the writings of St. John, will permanently minister to the spiritual needs of man. Surely this is all the finality required by man. For genuine progress, in all directions, takes place by incorporating, applying, and expanding that which is best in the past.

Thus, to the caviller at philosophy for its slow and circuitous progress we say—*Retrospice et Circumspice!* Look to what has been won in the whole history of culture! Raise your eyes above the din and confusion of the immediate present, in which you are immersed, and you will find that, in philosophy, as in other phases of human culture, there is a living and moving present which ever grows as it spans the generations, because it honors and includes the fruits of the travails of man's spirit in the past, and only thus is an effective ministrant to, and herald of, a better present in the future. Enlarge the bounds of your mental vision and spiritual comprehension, by a sympathetic appreciation of the growth of the spirit in history, and you will get encouragement and incitement to contribute, however humbly, to the intellectual comprehension and direction of the progress of the human spirit in time; will be guided to labor effectively for that enhancement and spread of intellectual, moral, and other spiritual values in which man finds his true immortality.

References

These are selected as fairly indicative of the present situation and next steps in philosophy.

1. In Metaphysics

Alexander, Samuel, *Space, Time and Deity.*

Bosanquet, B., *The Principle of Individuality and Value* and *The Value and Destiny of the Individual.*

Hoernlé, R. F. Alfred, *Studies in Contemporary Metaphysics.*

Leighton, J. A., *Man and the Cosmos.*

MacKenzie, J. S., *Elements of Constructive Philosophy.*

Marvin, W. T., *A First Book in Metaphysics.*

Russell, Bertrand, *Our Knowledge of the External World.*

Sheldon, W. H., *Strife of Systems.*

Spaulding, E. G., *The New Rationalism.*

Whitehead, A. N., *The Concept of Nature,* and *Principles of Natural Knowledge.*

2. In Ethics and Social Philosophy

Cole, G. D. H., *The World of Labor.*

Dewey, John, *Human Nature and Conduct.*

Dewey and Tufts, *Ethics.*

Hobhouse, L. T., *Justice.*

Hobson, J. A., *Work and Wealth.*

Russell, Bertrand, *Proposed Roads to Freedom.*

Wallas, G., *The Great Society,* and *Our Social Heritage.*

3. In the Philosophy of Education

Bagley, W. C., *Educational Values.*

Dewey, John, *Democracy and Education.*

EPILOGUE

William James said that the great thing about a philosopher is his vision. This statement we may accept subject to certain qualifications. Philosophy culminates in visions —in comprehensive and concentrated insights or intuitions. These intuitions must be built upon a wide range of fact, and penetrating keenness of insight, as well as power of synthesis.

We have traveled somewhat hastily through the field of philosophy and have examined critically its main problems and the chief theories offered on these problems. I venture to sum up what seem to me the main insights that we have won on this journey.

The universe is a dynamic and living whole, a superorganic system, which achieves its highest level in the perfecting of a society of spirits. It contains for us men, finite and fallible as we are, many unreconciled conflicts and not a few unsolved problems. The ways of life and the universe are sufficiently mysterious to keep men pondering for some time to come. But we have the right to believe that life will go on and increase in beauty and meaning and move towards perfection. When we sit down in a calm hour we know that in the quest for, and enjoyment of, responsible freedom, rational self-control, justice, love, companionship, and beauty, are the highest goods for man. Life and history are freighted with zest for those who can feel and with meaning for those who can see.

The world is the field for the fashioning of souls, and of civilizations, as instruments for the growth and free play of souls. Free and rational individuality, individuality made free through unremitting, clear-sighted and courageous *thinking,* lived out in friendly companionship with the great aspects of nature's life, suffused with intelligent sympathy for the beauty and grandeur of nature and sensible of its healing power, and with an equal sympathy for the tragedies, the pathos, the heroisms, joys and sorrows, defeats and victories of the common human lot—this is the life of highest good for man. So far, then, as human knowledge and insight can carry us and environed, as we must admit man is, by forces that seem blind and insensate, and indifferent alike to human weal and human woe, we may still believe that our universe is one of living and spiritual creativeness, the highest level of being that we can glimpse a society of selves moving on towards richer harmony and deeper satisfactions, through the joint power of reasoned insight and sympathetic feeling interfused.

INDEX

(1)